HARVEST OF A QUIET EYE:

The Novel of Compassion

"In common things that round us lie

Some random truths he can impart,—

The harvest of a quiet eye

That broods and sleeps on his own heart."

WILLIAM WORDSWORTH, *"A Poet's Epitaph"*

JAMES GINDIN

HARVEST OF A QUIET EYE:

The Novel of Compassion

INDIANA UNIVERSITY PRESS

Bloomington / London

Published in Canada by Fitzhenry & Whiteside Limited, Don Mills, Ontario

Library of Congress catalog card number: 75-135006

ISBN: 253-32705-9

Manufactured in the United States of America

To Joan, James Frederic, & Katharine

CONTENTS

P R E F A C E

WORDSWORTH'S "HARVEST OF A QUIET EYE" is an image for the artistic work created by one who responds to or assimilates experience, who, without preconceptions, and full of doubts about his world and himself, shapes his art from the earth and humanity he sees. In considering some English and American fiction of the past hundred years from this kind of loosely held and humanely limited perspective, one that does not seek to promulgate a truth or funnel experience through a dominant ethical or theological abstraction, I have tried to define a "tradition of compassion," a critical hypothesis based on an emotional attitude conveyed from author to reader. The critical hypothesis of "compassion" is not, however, simply emotional, for, like any hypothesis useful for illuminating fiction, it has formal, conceptual, and textural corollaries. Yet using a term like "compassion" and regarding art as a "harvest" permit relatively greater focus on the central qualities that fiction transmits to readers than do many more carefully formal or logical critical hypotheses. In recent years, literary criticism has become more hospitable to the less logical and self-contained formulation, more willing to venture into the varied, amorphous, often subjective and uncertain areas of emotional and intellectual response which most readers, sophisticated and unsophisticated alike, inhabit. Hopefully, this book suggests an entrance into that area.

I have chosen to discuss some novelists whose work can be centrally explained in terms of the "fiction of compassion," others for whose work this critical hypothesis is only partially or intermittently useful. Certainly, the "tradition of compassion" is not the exclusive or even necessarily the dominant "tradition" in fiction in the last hundred years. The choice of novels is, of course, somewhat arbitrary; the justification is in the insight and the particular understanding that these selections and this hypothesis provide.

Portions of this book have appeared as articles earlier. In a form only slightly altered, the chapter on D. H. Lawrence was published as "Society and Compassion in the Novels of D. H. Lawrence" in the Fall, 1968, issue of *The Centennial Review,* and the Fitzgerald chapter appeared in *Modern Language Quarterly,* March, 1969, as "Gods and Fathers in F. Scott Fitzgerald's Novels." In a vastly different form, some material in the opening chapter, the concluding chapter, and the chapter on Angus Wilson comprised the central argument of an essay in the Winter, 1967, issue of *Wisconsin Studies in Contemporary Literature* (now called *Contemporary Literature*), entitled "The Fable Begins to Break Down."

I am pleased to acknowledge my gratitude to the Horace H. Rackham School of Graduate Studies at the University of Michigan for two grants: one, at the initial stages of this study, from the Rackham Faculty Travel Fund; the other, to cover the cost of typing the final manuscript, from the Rackham Publication Fund. I am also pleased to thank my parents, Dr. and Mrs. J. P. Gindin, for the equivalent of a summer's grant during the writing.

Writings by various critics and conversations with students and friends over the years have helped to formulate my ideas about novels, although only in the rather vague way that would make specific acknowledgment sound inaccurate or condescending. My specific debt is also my deepest, that to my wife, Joan Gindin. Always a careful and committed reader, a stringent and efficient editor, and a willing disputant about literature and ideas, she is responsible for much of whatever insight and clarity can be found within. She is part of the process of putting the book together; more significantly, she is also part of its implicit attitudes toward both fiction and experience.

JAMES GINDIN

Ann Arbor, Michigan

HARVEST OF A QUIET EYE:

The Novel of Compassion

I

The Tradition of Compassion

MORE THAN ANY OTHER literary art form, the novel reflects the complexity of man living within a society he can seldom control or completely understand. Its spaciousness, range, and relative freedom from literary models and conventions allow the novel to mirror the author's version of human experience with a particular density and concrete force. Yet criticism of the novel has sometimes imposed disciplined systems that can narrow the novel's range or restrict the reader's understanding of the novel. Disciplined critical systems, like those dependent on uncovering symbolic consistency, thematic analysis, the patterning or structural arrangement of incident, and the development of ethical ideas, have helped to explain a great many novels; but these same disciplines also limit or oversimplify some novels, and are irrelevant to some others. Discussion of the "tradition of compassion" in the novel is an attempt to define and use a critical concept capacious enough to illuminate fiction, particularly that fiction least amenable to more systematic and precise critical formulation. A concept with implications for both the form and the content of the novel, the "tradition of compassion" is a synthesis of elements and attitudes that inhere within many distinguished works of fiction written in the last century.

Fiction within this tradition challenges the critical assumption—one that goes back at least as far as the works of Aristotle—that the artistic work dealing with the "universal" is superior to the work dealing with the "particular." Deriving from an attitude dubious about the possibility of asserting any universal qualities, the fiction of compassion frequently concentrates on the particulars of experience, reaches its audience through the relevance and intensity of its depiction of separate and thematically inconclusive aspects of experience. In Aristotelean terms, philosophy, which examines the implications of universal human experience, is a study superior to history, which records the separate facts of experience. But the fiction of compassion, likely to deviate from Aristotelean or paradigmatic models, implicitly rejects the judgment entailed in superiority, and exercises skepticism about the study of philosophy as a means of extracting universal truth for man. Consequently, the fiction of compassion is frequently itself a history, a detailing of the separate facts and implications, both personal and public, of an individual human existence; it is not a parable. Joseph Conrad, an author whose fiction relies too heavily on a version of the universal to be included within the tradition of compassion, once wrote:

> Fiction is history, human history, or it is nothing. But it is also more than that; it starts on firmer ground, being based on the reality of forms.

The second sentence of the quotation, the assurance that fiction is based on some higher abstract or universal reality, effectively excludes Conrad from the attitudes implicit within the tradition of compassion. But the equation between fiction and history is central to the fiction of compassion. Novelists like Thomas Hardy, despite all their consideration of theory and philosophy, are never able, as they feel no man is finally able, to go beyond the framework of "human history."

The dominating attitude or point of view in the fiction of compassion does not assume the sanction beyond the self necessary for a general truth or the objective assurance requisite for a universal lesson. No God exists in the fiction of compassion. Although the tone varies, for the absence of or skepticism about God can be viewed sadly, defiantly, nostalgically, bitterly, or nonchalantly as if no sane man ever expected anything else, almost all novels within this tradition fail to find a principle of God or establish a metaphysical truth relevant for man's experience. Abstract truth, abstract justice, is nonexistent in the world there assumed. Although some of the novelists, like Virginia Woolf, attempt with ferocious intensity to find some metaphysical essence valuable for man, almost invariably, as in *The Waves*, her "moments" of apprehension of a metaphysical something beyond the human are fictions that dissolve in the flux of separate and particular experience. More frequently, as in E. M. Forster's novels, the author emphasizes man's finiteness, his minuteness, his inability to capture or to verify the kind of extended experience or metaphysical entity he is capable of fabricating.

The lack of God or of universal truth in the fiction of compassion makes it difficult for the author to be prescriptive, to arrange his characters and events to shape a moral injunction to his readers. Although the difference between a prescriptive novel and a descriptive novel is not always easy to establish, for one can prescribe by describing or describe through apparent prescription, the novel of compassion generally tends to restrict itself to the descriptive, and not to shape the experience presented into an easily communicable lesson. Dickens and George Eliot, for example, despite the complexity of the characters and the worlds they present, are consistently prescriptive, underlining their ethical messages in novelistic terms, and their fiction is not within the tradition of compassion. Although both these novelists present specific characters in specific situations with compassion, in the ordinary sense of the term, their fictional worlds are consistently governed by a framework of ethical values and pietistic judgments. Their compassion is incorporated into a larger structure, a more universal umbrella, a system of value.

Trollope, on the other hand, most frequently restricts himself to description in his later fiction, rendering a presentation of human experience from which no guide or lesson can be extrapolated. Although Trollope recommends certain virtues, these recommendations are not consistently attached to an immutable framework of ethical value, are not sanctified as universally true. His stipulations come closer to moral preferences than to moral judgments. Compassion, then, becomes a much more pervasive authorial attitude, an attitude apart from any moral statement that infuses the depiction of all the characters. Both forms of compassion are undeniably genuine; only the second form, Trollope's, is appropriately part of the "tradition of compassion," as I define it, because only this characterizes fiction more centrally dependent on compassion than on the establishment of some universal framework of judgment. Like Trollope, other novelists sometimes move toward the tradition of compassion during their careers from a fairly stringent pattern of morality or judgment which they later widen, loosen, or abandon entirely. Writers like Trollope, Howells, James, and Fitzgerald all began with fiction close to the moral parable and moved toward a denser, more ambivalent, more descriptive fiction of compassion.

The fiction of compassion is also generally anti-Aristotelean in ignoring Aristotle's injunction that the plot or the action should embody all the issues in the work of art. E. M. Forster, in his criticism, has claimed directly that this criterion cannot reasonably apply to a form as loose and amorphous as the novel. And in many novels of compassion the central issues are not propelled by the plot or by patterns of symbolic action or character. Similarly, a general or thematic statement cannot always unify the direction or the effect of novels within this tradidition. For example, Arnold Bennett's *The Old Wives' Tale* could be compressed into its thematic statement that "All human beings grow old and die," but such compression takes no account of the richness, the vitality, and the tremendous force of the experience depicted in the novel.

Discussion of coherent elements like plot or theme is often less central to novels in the tradition of compassion than discussion of color or texture, vaguer terms usually avoided by the systematic critic because they are so difficult to talk about objectively and intelligently. Yet color and texture can be used to convey something of both the nature and the attraction of the fiction of compassion, and these terms have the authority of utility for some of the novelists themselves. Attacking the tendency in some writers to guide too severely toward abstraction the experience they depict, Henry James in his advice to young writers in "The Art of Fiction" wrote: "Do not think too much about optimism and pessimism; try and catch the color of life itself." Flaubert's statement, as recorded by the Goncourt brothers in their journal, sounds even vaguer and more impressionistic:

4]

When I write a novel I aim at rendering a color, a shade. For instance, in my Carthaginian novel, I want to do something purple. The rest, the characters and the plot, is a mere detail. In *Madame Bovary*, all I wanted to do was to render a grey color, the mouldy color of a woodlouse's existence. The story of the novel mattered so little to me that a few days before starting on it I still had in mind a very different Madame Bovary from the one I created: the setting and the overall tone were the same, but she was to have been a chaste and devout old maid. And then I realized that she would have been an impossible character.

Discussion of color or texture, which may seem excessively subjective or evasive applied to fiction that works in terms of a thematic or abstract consistency, can sometimes approach the center of the experience created in the fiction of compassion.

Densely textured and generally rendering a multiplicity of concrete experience, the fiction of compassion is always non-allegorical. Allegory arranges its counters precisely in a pattern and relies on the abstract pattern to make the connection with the reader's abstractions from experience. The form in allegory moves in a single direction, with a singular emphasis on the abstract qualities to be derived. The fiction of compassion, on the other hand, is never so carefully molded or directed toward a single set of abstractions, does not require the matching or equivalence of form and content necessary for allegory. Characters in the fiction of compassion are seldom abstract counters or tags representing certain qualities, as Trollope, especially in his later fiction, depends far less on grotesque caricature or humanized abstractions than does Dickens. What would be disastrous in allegory—a sense of contradiction between form and content, a novel in which the form suggests one direction and the content another—is fairly frequent and generally not damaging in the fiction of compassion. Some novelists, like Hardy, the later Fitzgerald, and Joyce Cary even draw a particular effectiveness from the contradictory suggestions of form and content.

Critics have often recognized that all the elements within a novel do not necessarily point in the same direction or coalesce into some massive unity. They have used a number of different terms to describe novelistic elements in conflict, as Arnold Kettle, throughout *An Introduction to the English Novel*, resorts to the

[5

opposed terms of "life" and "pattern" to illustrate the tension between different elements he finds in a great many novels. To talk of form and content (or "pattern" and "life") as inseparable seems appropriate only to allegory or fable in which the form carries and supports the content. In any novel, both form and content convey meaning and suggestion, and both need to be discussed in order to provide a full account of the novel. But discussing both and acknowledging that both convey meaning does not demand that the meanings conveyed be identical. Some of the more playfully formalistic novelists within the tradition of compassion, like Meredith and Iris Murdoch, mold some of their novels around forms which the content of the novel directly undercuts, gain fictional vitality by demolishing the assumptions of the structure they have created. Angus Wilson, too, with conscious irony, frequently plays his novels against their own carefully contrived structures to mock the human capacity to create myths. Sometimes, in the fiction of compassion, as in E. M. Forster's novels, the form is an introduction to human experience, a way of suggesting the various possibilities open to man, rather than a summary or encapsulation. Form and structure in the novel can be used in a variety of ways, for all novels are not dependent on formal elements resolving every issue presented. The fiction of compassion generally assumes varieties of the "open form," including even the openness achieved by centrally demolishing the novelist's own enclosure, in its attempt to approach human experience more directly.

"Open form," a term recently employed in literary criticism, refers to the form that does not completely enclose the work of art, does not resolve all the central issues suggested by the art. The open form is inconclusive, or only partially conclusive, transmitting the impression that the work of art, like experience itself, cannot resolve, define, or render controllable all the problems and dilemmas man confronts. Thus the reader's response to literature in the open form is more likely to be a more direct response to the particulars of fiction, a response less removed or abstracted by existing solely on the level of symbolic application. The open form aims at this direct response, at a sense of involvement that engages the reader more closely in the concrete details and the ambiguities presented in the art. The reader's response, of course, depends to some extent on which reader is responding. But the problem of subjective response has not been eliminated (rather, perhaps, only concealed) by more systematic and formalistic kinds of criticism. The concept of the open form can help to describe the kind of involvement possible between the reader and certain novels; at least this concept keeps the problems and possibilities of subjective response directly visible. At the same time, the open form has some kind of control over the terms of experience presented in the novel, can guard against completely uncritical subjectivity, against the undiscussable license simply to be pleased or moved by whatever one happens to be pleased or moved by.

Until the recent discussions of the open form, modern literary criticism tended to avoid areas—like the response to the particulars of a novel—which were difficult for critics to discuss coherently, objectively, and intelligibly. Although no good critic was ever arrogant or foolish enough to suppose that his criticism could completely explain or substitute for a novel, critics frequently did assume that the abstract critical terms they constructed were centrally relevant, that their symbolic or thematic or structural or linguistic analysis duplicated a centrally coherent focus within the novel. Such an assumption permits the extensive examination and thorough definition of analytic devices available in Wayne C. Booth's *The Rhetoric of Fiction* (1961) or the elaborate classification of types of novels in Northrop Frye's *The Anatomy of Criticism* (1957).

Few critics devised systems as elaborate and as self-contained as Frye's, but many critics made the same assumption that the novel was an enclosed artifice, resolving the issues it examined and coherently ending the experience it created. These critics did not necessarily assume that the novelist consciously used the principles on which the critic based his criticism; they did, however, assume a novelistic coherence and consistency, a structural completeness, in the examination of which the critical terms could be more or less central. They thought of the novel as rigidly restricted to what was given in the work, as complete and self-enclosed.

In the last few years, other critics have explicitly challenged the assumption that a great or a good novel is a closed form, have begun to speculate about some that do not resolve all the human problems and dilemmas they present. Although these newer critics value much of the textual, symbolic, and thematic analysis used to illuminate particular novels, they do not assume that the only effective means of analysis is connected to a centrally formal quality in the novel itself.

Some of the most seminal and provocative critical works dealing with the open form, like many of the seminal demonstrations of the use of symbolic criticism, have not been confined to the novel. In *Strains of Discord: Studies in Literary Openness* (1958), Robert M. Adams discusses the open form as the literary form that does not resolve or purge the audience's reaction to the art, and finds examples in Greek drama, the poems of Shakespeare, Donne, Keats, T. S. Eliot, and a number of novels. Pointing out that there are different degrees of openness in literary form, Adams uses D. H. Lawrence's novels to exemplify those in which the structural form is closed although the characters are open, incompletely formulated or defined by the patterns imposed. Faulkner's *The Sound and the Fury* is kept open, according to Adams, because the juxtaposed characters are never resolved into any pattern for the whole novel, and therefore produce a discordant effect. Adams includes, in his discussion of the open form, the art that turns round on itself, the work, like some of Ibsen's plays such as *A Doll's House,* in which the matter or the ethical statement contradicts the ostensible form of the closet domestic drama in which the trivial conflicts are reconciled. The form that fights itself is, for Adams, a kind of literary *trompe-l'oeil,* an example of the artistic framework disrupted within the work of art itself, producing discordance, an unresolved disunity.

At times, Adams suggests that the formal characteristics of art are related to different views of the world, for a society with a universal or fairly general belief in a philosophy or religion is more likely to create works in a closed form, a fully resolved art reflecting a society that believes its doubts and dilemmas can be resolved. Conversely, a world with no public patterns of belief is more likely to produce as well as to appreciate works with an open form. At the conclusion of his book, Adams suggests, with a rather disingenuous lack of dogmatism, that con-

8]

sideration of the open form may provide a way of talking about the "intensity and relevance" of literature not available to more consistent and formalistic critical systems.

More systematically and somewhat less speculatively than Adams, Frank Kermode, particularly in his brilliant *The Sense of an Ending* (1967), also discusses the open form. Ranging for examples throughout literary, theological, and scientific history, Kermode focuses on the human need for form, for coherent patterns that can explain or accommodate human experience. This form, which has an "end," a resolution, is the form of the "fiction." Yet, for Kermode, necessary as the "fiction" is, it loses power and relevance when it degenerates into "myth," for "myth" is believed in and offered as literal truth whereas the "fiction" is a formal, nonliteral coherence that conveys its own fictional quality. The "fiction" is the more open form, emphasizing that man has made rather than been granted his sense of order, avoiding the oppressive formal certainty of "myth." From Kermode's point of view, much of the most satisfying art exists in a conflict between form and freedom, a conflict apparent in Joyce's *Ulysses* which never hardens into "myth." Kermode approbatively quotes Iris Murdoch's statement (in an article entitled "Against Dryness" in *Encounter,* January 1961) : "Since reality is incomplete, art must not be too afraid of incompleteness." Despite the fact that Kermode recognizes that the work of art most completely amenable to formalistic or systematic treatment is not necessarily the best, and despite his awareness of the possible stultifying effects of the "myth" or fable, he still emphasizes the necessary nature of the human yearning for form, for an artistic "end" to substitute for the endless chaos of experience. In fact, he has been criticized in a recent article by John Bayley ("Against a New Formalism" in *Critical Quarterly,* Spring and Summer, 1968) as a spokesman for "a new generation of formalist," too addicted to discovering patterns in literature that are formal rather than experiential, "attaching far greater weight to the manipulation of the knowingly fictive, the explored illusion, than to the possibility that experience in the novel or poem represents, and joins up with, experience in life." Bayley goes on to call for criteria that will focus on the connection of art with both the personality of the creator and direct experience. Kermode's

[9

theory of the "end" also does not account for the fiction that terminates in loose ends, for the characters or issues incompletely resolved in terms of the work of art alone.

A few other critical works discussing the open form have been restricted to the novel. In *The Turn of the Novel* (1966), Alan Friedman attempts to demonstrate that the open form in the novel began near the beginning of the twentieth century. Friedman provides detailed treatment of some novels by Hardy, Conrad, Forster, and Lawrence, claiming that all earlier novels were examples of the closed form, in order to establish the beginnings of the open form and record a definitive historical change in the novel. For Friedman, the open form is a "stream of conscience" that engages the reader directly, terminating in "endlessness" and making connection with the reader through a shared sense of the "flux of experience."

Friedman's detailed criticism, particularly his reading of the final scenes or words in his examples and their connections to the rest of the novel, is often both ingenious and profound. But his historical point is too precise to be accurate, his localization of the open form's beginning too historically specific. At the same time, he avoids relevant historical discussion by generally restricting himself to discussion of particular novels and neglecting to suggest or examine possible causes of the "turn" to the open form. Occasionally, when a general statement escapes, such as the assurance that only in the "most extreme cases" does fiction of the open form become "anti-rational and anti-moral," the implications of the historical "turn" are particularly squelched and devalued. Friedman's treatment of the history of fiction, although never his reading of individual novels, lacks the wideranging and associative quality that would illustrate as well as defend his version of the theory of the open form.

Another recent critical book, Barbara Hardy's *The Appropriate Form: An Essay on the Novel* (1964), also challenges the assumptions of critical formalism, although it does not deal directly with the open form. Mrs. Hardy begins by proclaiming an interest in the "realistic" novel, not in the fable, and proceeds to establish the combination of a significant morality with "truthful realization" (the latter being the quality that most moves the reader) as criteria for the best fiction. Dickens, George

Eliot, Lawrence, and Tolstoy best exemplify the combination. The quality of "truthful realization," in Mrs. Hardy's terms, can be distorted by a form that is either excessively aesthetic or excessively dogmatic. Henry James and Virginia Woolf are those stigmatized as too aesthetic; Thomas Hardy and E. M. Forster, in whose work the critic finds a dominating metaphysical belief, are castigated as too dogmatic. Although I disagree with Mrs. Hardy's alignment of authors, as well as with some of her specific readings, I find her book another persuasive example of the argument that the criticism of fiction should be expanded in order to come to terms with a version of the relation between fiction and experience more direct than formalistic criticism generally permits.

"Open form" is not, however, an entirely satisfactory critical term. Although it possesses the neatness of paradox, for form can never be entirely open or free, a more fully satisfactory term for explaining the qualities in some fiction that involve the reader in direct response to particulars should include a designation of a kind of form, a kind of material, an attitude, and a point of view simultaneously. The "tradition of compassion" is a term sufficiently loose so that its connotations can be stipulated to include implications of content, of texture, of the author's attitude, of skepticism concerning any guiding truth in the universe, in addition to the implications of the incompletely resolved form. "Compassion," as a term, suggests a feeling or an emotion apart from or beyond "justice" or any strict measurement of merit against fortune. When one, in fiction or in experience, exercises compassion, he introduces into his attitude an emotion that systematic accounts of justice, of cause and effect, or of hierarchic lists of virtues cannot account for or include. Man is not measured against what he deserves—partly because no concept of justified expectation exists. Compassion is an extra element, a secular version of the extra infusion of grace or mercy which characterizes some theological doctrines. As such, the danger in any attitude of compassion is sentimentality, the possibility that the sympathy will become so disproportionate as to degenerate into the mindless bathos of endowing a trivial subject with a heavy investment of emotion. But the dangers need not prevent the writer or the person from recognizing that human systems and human justice cannot, by their very nature, include all the judgments and all the questions applicable to human possibility and fallibility.

As used here, "compassion" primarily inheres in the novel itself, in the author's attitude toward his characters, their situation, and their world. Most frequently, the compassion implies a world without moral or theological absolutes, for compassion often requires at least the suggestion of a chaotic cosmology if it is to avoid becoming insular special pleading or heavy sentimentality. Yet, to some extent, "compassion" is also part of the reader's response, part of the emotion elicited in the reader by the fiction itself, part of the responsive reader's comparison of fiction to experience, which, whether consciously or subliminally, frequently takes place beneath many of the most sophisticated readings of symbol or abstraction. In one sense, the reader who literally compares fiction to experience is naive, for fiction is neither a factual account of the family next door nor a decorative injunction to send a check for a worthy cause. Fiction is metaphor and needs to be read as such. Yet metaphors always contain two sets of terms, the literal terms of the novel and the vaguer, looser, often more arguable, terms of the novel's application to experience. The comparison of fiction to experience is far from naive so long as the reader does not deal with both sets of terms literally, recognizes the metaphorical nature of the novel, does not transfer a literal version of his own experience into a truncated version of the literal events of the novel. In this way, "compassion," a deliberately emotive term, one which conveys an attitude that is unsystematic and only vaguely formulatable, can perhaps best describe the kind of complicated mental and emotional experience which connects the terms of art and the terms of life without simplifying either. As long as the intelligence guards against sentimentality, and sophistication against a response to fiction on only the literal level, an emotive term like "compassion" can suggest something of the way in which the material of fiction is relevant to the reader's experience. Discussion of the reader's experience is, of course, made more difficult by the inevitable subjectivity of even the intelligent reader's response. But the problems of subjectivity need not demand that all such infected areas of fiction be surrounded by a quarantine of silence. Rather, it is just those areas of fiction most vulnerable to subjective response that have been most neglected by formalistic criticism and are most in need of critical discussion. "Compassion," as a critical term, is offered as one possible way of designating a quality in fiction which can radiate from the author's attitude toward his material to the intelligent and sensitive reader's response, a term that may facilitate discussion about the connection between art and experience.

Vague as "compassion" needs to be in order to accommodate its transference from fiction to the reader's experience, the term must also be more carefully distinguished in so far as it inheres in the fiction itself. The corollaries of the fiction of compassion, its denial of formal, moral, or theological absolutes, its dependence on a sense of history or social process rather than on a metaphysical truth, its opposition to the fable or the implied God who arranges events and destinies in some novels, and its tendency not to resolve plots and characters fully, are all necessary to distinguish the fiction within the tradition of compassion from that without. All these corollaries, negative in the form of their definition, although not so in effect, tend to keep the fiction unresolved, in tone, in theme, in attitude, tend to prevent the fiction from settling into a definable abstraction. By preserving an openness, a lack of moral or metaphysical direction, suggested in one way or another through all of the corollaries, the fiction of compassion preserves a connection to the experience of that reader whose own version of experience is flexible and uncommitted to a dominant abstraction, who has no explanation or truth to trumpet, who, in his puzzled and vulnerable openness, represents many contemporary readers.

"Compassion" is also a "tradition" because it exists within an historical context, even though it cannot be enclosed between the precise dates of a beginning and an end or exemplified by a specific "turn." In English and American fiction, novels of compassion have existed since about 1875, although elements of compassion were present in earlier novels, particularly in England, throughout most of the nineteenth century. In the twentieth century, in an age of increasing metaphysical skepticism and of increasing impatience with the confinements of established form, there have been many more examples of the fiction of compassion (with two particular clusters, one between 1900 and 1915, another since about 1945), although compassion has never been the only or even the overwhelmingly dominant tradition in English and, particularly, in American fiction.

Throughout the eighteenth and nineteenth centuries, novels frequently functioned as secular sermons. Although they were often decorated with copious action, farce, erudition, and wit, their central direction was instructive, providing guides to conduct or lessons on how or how not to behave. Novels assumed, as did Fielding's *Tom Jones,* a definition of what a man could and should be, even though, in the world of the novel, most men obviously did not measure up to the definition. These novels contained a thematic focus, a central assurance about what human virtue was, and the many examples of lack of virtue in a richly patterned novel like Fielding's only illuminated the central focus in a more forceful and interesting way. The "truth" was public and available, no matter how amusingly difficult to discover or how frequently preposterously misunderstood.

Different authors viewed "truth" in different terms. Richardson organized *Pamela* around the middle-class virtue of exacting the highest possible price for relinquishing chastity, viewing this concept of virtue as the human being's most important possession in a corrupt world. Fielding, on the other hand, realized the contradiction involved in marketable chastity and established a far more complicated ideal: the man who followed natural instincts but still maintained a modicum of civilized prudence and rationality. Yet neither Richardson nor Fielding doubted the possibility that a certain kind of person could both represent virtue and make his way in the world; both authors offered their readers instruction in surmounting the perplexing problems of human experience in an increasingly complicated environment.

This description of the novel as secular sermon cannot, however, explain all eighteenth century English fiction, for novels such as Sterne's *Tristram Shandy* and Smollett's *Roderick Random* and *Humphry Clinker* cannot be taken centrally as moral guides or object lessons. Both in the constant interjections that break apart the forms they establish and in the constant comedy that undercuts any kind of representation of the hero as ethical model, Sterne and Smollett veer away from the assumptions of the secular sermon.

The tradition of the novel as secular sermon continued into the nineteenth century, best represented by the vast gallery of object lessons and highly various yet cohesive formulations of ethical themes in the fiction of Thackeray and Dickens. At the same time, with the emergence of Romanticism and its emphasis on the unformulated self, a fiction began to develop in which the human being was depicted not as the illustration of ideal qualities or some usable virtue, but entirely in individual terms. A fiction with some connection to the comic iconoclasm of Sterne and Smollett began to challenge the possible universality of any equation between the novel and the secular sermon. The newer kind of fiction, the novel of education, of how the self develops, changes, discovers what it is, became, from the work of Goethe and Stendhal to that of Meredith or D. H. Lawrence, one of the principal forms of fiction. And what discovery the novel of education yielded for the hero might not be acknowledged or usable by anyone else within the framework of the novel, might force the discovered self to end in suicide as in Goethe's *The Sorrows of Werther* or in the lonely isolation of Stendhal's *The Charterhouse of Parma*. The romantic concentration on the self, on finding value in the individual emotions and in subjectivity, grants the possibility that nothing in the exterior world provides a satisfactory locus for the self, that there may be no public "truth." And, in such a world, the author generally emphasizes an attitude of compassion for his protagonist, a sympathy for the individual who can find no public "truth" or ideal to match what he has discovered about himself.

Although some later English romantic novels of education, such as Meredith's *The Ordeal of Richard Feverel* and Lawrence's *Sons and Lovers,* are also novels of compassion, the two classifications cannot always be equated. The interest in self and emotion which characterized the historical and literary Romantic movement were sometimes combined with the novel that dramatized the moral or ethical lesson. A number of romantic novelists, Dickens among them, framed elaborate structures in which their romantic values, the emphasis on human feeling, on kindness, on responsiveness, became themselves implicit guides to conduct. In this respect, Dickens' perspective is closer to Fielding's than it is to Meredith's. In *Bleak House,* for example, the humble and responsive virtues that Esther Summerson represents are not only valuable but ultimately victorious even against the corrupt and hostile world of legalistic chaos. And the process of education in *Great Expectations* or in *Martin Chuzzlewit* involves a kind of self-knowledge that both genuinely represents the author's version of "truth" and triumphs in the exterior world of the novel. Parables or allegories, Dickens' structures leave no loose ends, radiate no sense of compassion that the plots and structures of the novels cannot resolve. Even with all their vastness, their rich invention, their involved and complicated plots, Dickens' novels implicitly are guides to conduct, sermons on how the good man can make his way through the labyrinthine evil of industrial nineteenth century England. Similarly, George Eliot's novels are both romantic and instructive, both statements about the importance of recognizing the individual self and guides to worthy and moral conduct (Barbara Hardy's elevation of Dickens and George Eliot at the expense of other Victorian novelists is easily understandable on these terms). What compassion there is in the works of Dickens and George Eliot is abstracted as part of moral virtue, not left to dangle as an attitude toward issues never fully resolved or characters called worthy but never satisfactorily placed. Both these novelists, like Disraeli, another author of romantic guides to conduct, were able to systematize their perceptions about human experience, to convert them artistically into worlds with rules, order, and logic. The romantic doctrine of man can sometimes be funneled into the form of the novel as secular sermon.

Other characteristics of the romantic sensibility, however, cannot so easily be adapted to the novel as secular sermon. Sometimes, as in the romantic perspectives of Stendhal and Trollope, the focus on the individual leads to speculation about the radical disjunction between the private man and the public society essentially indifferent to the ethical concerns of the individual. Handled either comically or tragically, this disjunction does not allow public rewards for virtue or castigations for vice, does not permit the assumption that the nature of the individual is eventually revealed in public or explicit terms. This kind of disjunction, this realization that public judgment is flawed and that justice is accidental or nonexistent, detracts from the necessarily strong connection between cause and effect in the novel as secular sermon. In such instances, an attitude of compassion on the part of the author serves as a substitute for the justice that does not exist.

Still other romantic characteristics, which work against the novel as a cohesive moral guide, concern artistic form. Romantic theory is permeated by the Kantian idea that man creates his own forms. Form is not a higher "reality," as Conrad suggests, but rather a fiction man invents to express his own experience. If the form is viewed as man-made, temporary, and fictive, it cannot convey the same assurance and universal message that it can when regarded as a discovery of "truth." Romantic theory also frequently includes the idea that feeling overcomes or breaks apart form. As Wordsworth defined poetry as "the spontaneous overflow of powerful feelings," the romantic sensibility often depicted satisfactory art as that which broke from the confines of form to reach its audience all the more powerfully. Wordsworth's "overflow" indicates an unformulatable rush of emotion that cannot easily be systematized within the confinement of a parable or a structured guide to conduct. In fiction like Thomas Hardy's, this sense of "overflow," of emotions and sympathy breaking out of the formal shape of the novel, becomes one of the principal characteristics of the novel of compassion.

Gradually, through the nineteenth century, more novelists veered away from the secular sermon, away from providing ethical guides or lessons for their audience, toward the more descriptive and less implicitly dogmatic novel of compassion. Yet the fiction of compassion did not begin fully developed or all at once. A very early English example of fiction partially within the tradition of the secular sermon, yet pointing toward the tradition of compassion, is apparent in the rich ambiguity of the attitudes conveyed in some of Jane Austen's novels. The structure of all the novels follows the outline of the guide to conduct, as in *Pride and Prejudice*, Elizabeth Bennet's honesty, unpretentious good sense, and growing perception eventually win both public recognition and a suitable mate. But as to other of Jane Austen's young ladies in novels that superficially demonstrate the same tidy structural movement from perplexing mistakes to happy marriages, the comfortable equation between privately worthwhile self-knowledge and public or exterior recognition can be maintained only by oversimplifying and ignoring parts of the novel. In *Sense and Sensibility* both the young lady of sense and the young lady of sensibility settle at the end for tarnished versions of their former hopes, since neither sense nor sensibility, no matter how ardently and honestly pursued, can provide the perfect mate. This might imply that a combination of sense and sensibility is requisite, but there is no such combination in the novel: sense and sensibility are means of characterization, of defining two different and admirable women both of whom find no "truth" capable of holding all they feel and all they represent. The structure that apparently resolves the problems of the two girls, seems to provide a neatly summarized and capsulized lesson about choosing marriage partners. But the compassion, as an attitude directed toward two essentially guiltless young girls neither of whom gets what she really wants or deserves, is neither summarized nor expressed in the structure or the title of the novel.

Emma is a novel of education in which the matchmaking heroine learns the folly of manipulating others and the importance of discovering herself and her needs. This education is, in part, a guide to conduct, for Emma develops something of the Christian virtue of humility, but the resolution is neither as complete nor as convincing as a usable revelation of "truth" ought to be. Despite the fact that she has recognized the value of Knightly, Emma still tends to manipulate others. And, in a final scene with Mrs. Weston's child, Knightly reveals a spongy weakness beneath the firmly just and somewhat priggish sense of principle. The resolution is superficial, as if the author is indicating that from just underneath the surface all the old problems of men and women, of where to find a guide for conduct, will emerge again. The resolution of the secondary couple, Jane Fairfax and Frank Churchill, is even more superficial, for Jane, as intelligent and sensitive as Emma although a good deal less lucky, must settle for a man whose conscious cruelty, in terms of Miss Austen's society, will always be directed against her. In this novel, as in some of Jane Austen's others, the more the women learn of themselves, the less suitable are any of the men they can find. The men are irresponsible or stupid or priggish, limited in one way or another, although the inadequacies are not equivalent, for Knightly is obviously better than most. Ultimately, the women, who cannot be fully contained or satisfied by the men they marry, as the issues of the novels cannot be fully represented by the plots that simply arrange marriages, receive the author's compassion. The order in the novels is finally superficial, just as Highbury is, a tenuous capsule of settled society impinged upon by a far more chaotic outside world; and Mansfield Park, even more obviously, is an architectural and symbolic artifice from an earlier age, a conscious retreat from all the disorderly alliances and perceptions in the world of contemporary London. The fascination of Jane Austen's novels is in the "overflow," in all the sympathy and perception in the novels which cannot be packed into the careful structure of finite progression to a happy marriage.

Like the later fiction of Trollope and Hardy, Jane Austen's fiction shows a struggle between form and content, an interest divided between working out the formal patterns of the novel and the pressure of sympathies and attitudes that burst from confined form. We sometimes wonder how to take Jane Austen's work, as we wonder how to take Trollope's and Hardy's, wonder what to take seriously and what not, wonder whether the sympathy mocks the form or the form the sympathy. In contrast, we're never in doubt about how to take Dickens' fiction, about what his comedy laughs at or what he regards as important. The secular sermon emphasizes its lessons carefully; the fiction of compassion works within a more ambivalent point of view.

Like Jane Austen's heroines, the hero in many later romantic novels has individual emotions, ideals, aspirations that cannot be adequately satisfied within the society in which he must operate. The character, developed with complexity and sympathy, finds no locus or representation in the larger world he seeks. In fiction like that by Meredith, Lawrence, and Fitzgerald, the romantic hero receives the author's compassion, the romantic novel becomes the novel of compassion, one in which the author also cannot find a locus for the character's ideals and aspirations. In more recent fiction, like that of Bellow, reflecting a cultural attitude so accustomed to seeing unusual aspirations squelched and noble ideals corrupted or destroyed, the potentially romantic hero is reduced to the a-hero or the serio-comic bumbling dissident far more certain of his opposition to society than of his ideals. Yet the romantic hero and the a-hero share many characteristics: a refusal to be defined by the principal abstractions operating within their society, an insistence on allegiance to their own often unprogrammatic and accidental self-development, a defeat or destruction in terms of the world around them balanced by the sympathy they are accorded by the novelists who have created them. Bellow, in his constant use of and reference to the history of the romantic sensibility, recognizes the connection between the romantic hero and the a-hero, realizes one of the numerous ways in which the Romantic revolution in tastes and attitudes has not really been reversed among the authors and intellectuals of the West in the past century and a half. The lack of conjunction between the hero or the central representation of human interest and the larger world of society or nation in which he operates remains a fairly constant element in the tradition of compassion. And the author's sympathy, his point of view, generally favors the individual rather than the establishment, regards the identity of the self as preferable to adjustment.

The placement of the individual in a larger world he cannot master, as well as the avoidance of allegory or fable, might lead one to describe the fiction of compassion as realistic. But "realistic" and "realism" are confusing terms in the discussion of fiction. Almost every historical change in the novel can be introduced and defended as conveying a greater realism, as formulating some hitherto neglected aspect of what life is really like. Most readers would maintain that Arnold Bennett's fiction is more "realistic" than that of Virginia Woolf. Yet, in her famous essay, "Mr. Bennett and Mrs. Brown," Mrs. Woolf defended her then avant-garde methods of constructing fiction as enabling her to achieve a greater realism, a more acute sense of what Mrs. Brown, the subject, was really like, than Bennett had ever achieved. All her symbolic apparatus was fashioned in the cause of a deeper and more intense realism. In this sense, any novel is realistic. In another sense, since all novels are created, constructed, fabricated in one way or another, no novel is realistic. Every novel works on metaphorical terms that prevent comparison with a crude realism. Between these two extremes, the term "realism" does not provide any very valuable critical currency. Nevertheless, certain novels do adopt more of the conventions of verisimilitude than do others, use conversation approximately like conversations in which people do engage, detail actions probable or possible within our own experience, and depict characters who behave in ways we might imagine ourselves behaving. And the fiction of compassion, attempting a response from the reader more concrete and direct than that appropriate to some other kinds of fiction, generally works within a fairly flexible concept of the conventions of verisimilitude. Some writers, like Trollope and Bennett, hold to the convention of verisimilitude fairly stringently; others, like Hardy or Forster, practice a looser version. But almost all writers who can be designated as within the tradition of compassion rely, to some extent, on a similarity between the details of fiction and the details of experience, on the convention of verisimilitude.

Part of the texture in many novels of compassion is the density of social description. In a novel that has no universal message to convey, that need not focus and control its elements to direct them toward some reigning abstraction, extensive treatment of social issues and environments is likely to substitute for the truth or guiding interpretation the author does not have. A texture of copious social detail, describing carefully the sense of experience at a given time or in a given place, sometimes elaborating the changes in social experience through changes of time and place, is apparent in the work of novelists as varied as Trollope, Bennett, Lawrence, Joyce, and Saul Bellow. The social detail is not just the extensive description of time and place; rather, often, social experience is elaborated into historical experience, connecting the changes in a particular group to changes dependent on nations, public events, and the influence of historical change. History, a substitute for "philosophy," provides a public and coherent framework that does not commit the author to a version of universal truth or a dogmatic interpretation of human nature. The novel of compassion is not likely to be futuristic, incantatory, or apocalyptic; rather, in describing how man lives and what he faces, it is likely to extend its terms historically, to depict a greater quantity of experience instead of distilling experience to derive lessons from it. The changes, influences, and impositions of history, as well as the use of history to present the variety and extensiveness of human experience, are central to almost all the novelists connected with the tradition of compassion, to Bennett, Virginia Woolf, and Joyce, as well as to Joyce Cary, Angus Wilson, Bellow, and Norman Mailer. History provides documentation for all the versions of separate and individual experience depicted in the novel of compassion.

As the novel of compassion dwells on history, it also concentrates on character. The depiction of character is often an end in itself, and is different from the subordination of character to the demonstration of a general truth or theme for the novel. The depiction of character, in the novel of compassion, therefore, is more likely to be complex, finally unresolved, and unrelated or incompletely related to theme, more likely to reveal intractable human irresolution than the mark of an analyzable tag or "humour." E. M. Forster, in his criticism, discussed "the losing battle that the plot fights with the characters," a battle frequent in the novel of compassion, in which the sense of vitality and existential continuity in the characters often overwhelms the plot. This unequal impetus of character is particularly visible in Forster's own novels and in those of Hardy.

Character is also not isolated in the fiction of compassion, not examined for its single metaphysical essence, but, rather, most frequently seen in combination with other characters, reacting with and against each other. In the focus on human reaction and behavior, the novel of compassion examines the texture of human relationships, particularly sexual relationships as an indication of the closest and most revealing connection possible for the human being. Even Victorian writers within or close to the tradition of compassion, restricted by Victorian convention and their own reticence about what words could be used in detailing sexual relationship, writers like Trollope, Howells, and James, emphasize sexual relationships as the principal means of describing and defining their complicated characters.

Very young children who do not grow up during the course of the novel are often less interesting to the novelist in the tradition of compassion, for young children, in fiction at any rate, are likely to be useful only insofar as they convey the qualities transmitted by their parents and become a perpetuated judgment on the parents. Dickens, for example, often uses young children as a fictional representation of the dogma that the sins or virtues of the fathers are visited upon the children. The novelist in the tradition of compassion, on the other hand, like Trollope, rarely uses children, concentrates instead on characters who face more complicated and less deterministically predictable choices.

Twentieth century novelists within the tradition of compassion are also likely to concentrate on sexual relationships rather than on those that work out an abstract version of truth or error. The twentieth century novelist of compassion is generally less interested in the vertical relationship, the transmission of a truth or message from one generation to the next, than he is in the lateral relationship, the complex definition and redefinition of relationship in entirely human and equivalent terms. Fitzgerald, for example, developing the attitudes of the fiction of compassion late in his career, illustrates the change from an interest in the vertical relationship, in generations, to an interest in the lateral; and Saul Bellow, particularly in *The Adventures of Augie March,* fully examines the difference between the two sorts of relationship.

The complex character portrayal, the interest in the individual in all his relations with other individuals and with society, in the fiction of compassion has also entailed a focus on psychology. Interest in the character as a complex entity, in contrast to interest in character as an abstract counter in a universal message, presumes interest in the origin of character, in all the many influences and experiences that have made the character what he is. Often, in the work of twentieth century authors connected with the tradition of compassion, the childhood of an adult character is extensively described, not in the manner of Dickensian comment on the ethical formulation his parents represented, but, rather, as material for the origin of the conflicts and choices depicted. Particularly in a novelist like Angus Wilson, the psychological forces relevant in determining what the characters do are carefully, sometimes minutely, examined. Psychological examination in the novel, like the interest in the influences of history that often accompany it, is a form of determinism, of subtracting from the free choice available to a given character in a given situation. But psychological and historical forms of determinism are generally far less complete, less restricting, less inflexible, and more multiple than is that kind of determinism which relies on a concept of Original Sin or a metaphysical statement of the human creature's nature, the determinism conveyed through an attitude of certainty and universality in the author's judgment.

The focus on psychological and historical examination, in contrast to the focus on the revelation of universal truth through human agents, gives a texture of density and complexity, as well as an attitude of sympathy, to the novel of compassion. The detailed treatment of a variety of aspects of the individual character also helps to develop a sense of each significant character as a self, a personal unity, rather than as a convenience to be used by the novelist in totally different ways for different episodes or points in an argument. Throughout the fiction of compassion, characters are created fully and identifiably enough so that their reactions or behavior in one setting carries over into another. In addition, the fiction of compassion generally regards character existentially, treating the complex varieties of what is, instead of distilling and judging an essence of human nature. The existential attitude frequently implicit does not indicate that these authors have no preferences, no commitments to one character or choice over another, or that they regard all human beings and decisions as indiscriminately equal. Rather, in the fiction of compassion, preference or commitment is itself a human attribute, a quality of human response not bolstered with a simulacrum of the authority of ultimate judgment.

Frequently, the fiction of compassion is comic. Presenting a multiplicity of experience, often amorphous, it can acquire considerable force and vitality from juxtaposing one character or perspective against another in comic tandem. Man, bewildered by the multiplicity he faces, contradicting himself, choosing alternatives when neither he nor his author is sure which alternative is right, frequently seems a comic figure. Sometimes, as in Trollope, the comedy is genial and gently skeptical; sometimes, as in Angus Wilson, it is sharply ironic; seldom, however, is the

24]

comedy satirical, for satire generally requires a more inflexible standard of judgment than is common in the fiction of compassion. Resolutions, too, in so far as they exist at all, are often handled comically. The final symbolic connection between father and son in Joyce's *Ulysses,* a connection that is literally hazy, ineffectual, and momentary, is made through Molly Bloom, the unfaithful wife, the symbol of the earth that both the father and son sought to escape in each other. Although full of comic juxtapositions, the final position of the characters in *Ulysses* rests within the flawed symbol of compassion, the woman, the earth.

Saul Bellow, too, often resolves his novels through a serio-comic acceptance of all the multiple and unsortable juxtapositions of experience. As this acceptance of multiplicity indicates, the novelist within the tradition of compassion is likely to avoid judging his characters more often than are other kinds of novelist. On the matter of formulating judgments on characters, the novelists within the tradition, however, do differ. At one not very radical extreme, Meredith and Lawrence refuse to judge the unconventional and romantic hero, although they level severe judgment against the society or environment that holds the hero down. In attacking Puritanism so unremittingly, in attacking the theology of societal judgments, they themselves make judgments, although their judgments, their condemnations, are by no means the equivalent of those they oppose: their judgments always favor a wider acceptance of experience, oppose the restricted, the life-denying, and the codified legalistic interpretation of experience.

At the other extreme among the novelists of compassion, Bennett refuses to peg most of his characters on any scale of value at all. The difficulties of human experience itself and the lack of knowledge available to any human being about both others and himself, from Bennett's point of view, renders any human judgment tenuous and fallible. There are no real villains in Bennett's fiction, only a few shrivelled, pathetic deniers of life. This is not to suggest that Bennett sees no differences between people, has no preferences, but, rather, that, for Bennett, preference is insufficient basis for judgment. Somewhere in the middle, between the attitude of Lawrence and that of Bennett, is Trollope's attitude. Skeptical about judgment, often turning events in the novel to show the fallacy and inadequacy of most human judgments, Trollope, nevertheless, himself occasionally judges. With a mock humility, the author conveys the attitude of a personality judging because it is human and responsive in the midst of a world that offers no authority for judgment. Most of the novelists within the tradition of compassion demonstrate, in one way or another, their cognizance of this ambivalence in the problem of human judgment. They place the problems of judgment in an existential framework. As one who lives, observes, and responds, man inevitably makes judgments, uses reason and argument to convert his preferences into statements that sound certain and objective, entirely aware, at the same time, that his accuracy is questionable and his world affords him slight warrant for judging as he does.

This ambivalence about human judgment, common to a greater or lesser extent among all the novelists in the tradition of compassion, is one indication of the ambivalence that permeates the point of view in these novels. Another indication of ambivalence in the point of view is the author's sliding detachment, his ability to come close to his characters to demonstrate his sympathy and, at other times, pull far away to show a character's pretense or folly. In the novel of compassion, the author seldom defines a single stance for himself, a single point of view or single distance from which he views the characters he has created. Rather, the point of view shifts, alternates, circulates, encompasses different ranges and distances. Too close an identification with the characters in a world without God or truth would lead to sentimentality or the repetitious echoes of self-pity; too distant a stance from the characters and events would risk hardening into the presumptuous inflexibility of single-minded satire.

The novel of compassion, working with a density of characterization and social material without the assured direction of a guiding universal truth or parable, depends on the flexibility of its point of view, on its capacity to both express and involve the reader in the complexity of human experience. This flexibility is most characteristically conveyed through an ambivalent attitude, an insistence on the simultaneous recognition of man's powers, idiocies, presumptions, glories, unachieved desires and resilience. In this ambivalence, the novel of compassion reaches its reader through a shared density of concrete experience rather than through an abstracted statement about art or theology or the literary tradition, all themselves abstractions from experience.

Not every element attached to the tradition of compassion exists in the fiction of each of the novelists whose work is the subject of subsequent chapters. Novelists cannot easily be graded, nor their work measured against a check list of the qualities defined and classified by the critic, for each novelist has his particular color, his texture or his attitude which is likely to make his work uniquely interesting or valuable. The tradition of compassion is a critical fiction that attempts to explain the texture of novels which sometimes "overflow," which do not always contain unequivocal guidelines to keep the reader within the boundaries of the novel, and which sometimes treat human experience from a puzzling and ambivalent point of view. Some of these novels are also amenable to more consistent symbolic or textual critical fictions; some are not. But all of them may be read more sensitively and meaningfully if they are examined in terms of a critical fiction designed to confront more directly the immediate and concrete particularity of the novels. Such an examination is, at any rate, one degree less fictive.

II

TROLLOPE

ROLLOPE IS USUALLY THOUGHT OF as the purveyor of a settled green Englishness, an ultimately quiet and ordered
world disturbed by nothing more serious than clerical quarrels
that can be handled by a gently comic point of view. Frequently,
Trollope is talked about as if his works isolate a tiny and peaceful
community as a pleasant escape for his readers. Certainly his
depiction of Victorian society was limited, as any novelist's depiction of a society is confined to his perspective, his version of
significant human issues. But Trollope's vision did not simply
center on the creation of an island where all is ultimately ordered
and happy. He began his literary career with three novels dominated by melodramatic intrigue. And even the Barchester series,
from which the stereotype of Trollope's order is usually drawn,
develops an interest in the psychology of people, in the complexities of their actions and reactions to others, and in the difficulties
involved in judging them. Josiah Crawley, for example, the
parson whose thorny integrity defies the society trying to help
him, carries implications about human experience that go well
beyond easy generalizations about the balms of gentle Barsetshire. Trollope's later work, however, the work of his last fifteen
or twenty years, most clearly illustrates his far wider concerns and
sympathies. This width is particularly visible in the social, political and psychological issues that help to shape the series called
"The Palliser Novels," (*Can You Forgive Her?*, 1864–65; *Phineas Finn*, 1869; *The Eustace Diamonds*, 1873; *Phineas Redux*,

1874; *The Prime Minister,* 1876; *The Duke's Children,* 1880),
although almost all of Trollope's work from the mid-1860's
until his death in 1882 demonstrates this deeper version of individual and social concern.

The Palliser series deals with a political world in which
interest in policies and government is combined with interest
in the personal allegiances and divisions which manipulate the
policies. For Trollope, political life always combined ideas and
personalities. The principal character of the series is Plantagenet
Palliser, later the Duke of Omnium and Prime Minister. A man
of intelligence, principle, and monumental integrity, Palliser is
made an inadequate and unsuccessful Prime Minister when he
finally reaches the office toward which his whole scrupulous
career has pointed. In his autobiography, Trollope explained
the Duke's failure in office by underlining the fact that he, although endowed with a great many personal and public virtues,
was too "thin-skinned" for office, too sensitive to the criticisms
and maneuvers of others. Yet the novel itself, *The Prime Minister,* provides a much fuller and less completely personal explanation. Often Trollope's explanations in *An Autobiography,* like
many of his explanations for his characters' behavior inserted
in all the novels, is a vast over-simplification (Trollope generally
spoke slightingly and with a humility that we in the twentieth
century think false concerning his own work; too many twentieth
century readers, however, have taken the commentary for the
work). The Duke fails in office because he trusts some of the
wrong people, antagonizes others in his strictness about manners
and trivia, magnanimously pays the expenses of a dishonest man
whom the Duchess has encouraged to run for Parliament against
the Duke's wishes so that it looks as if the Duke privately sanctions the means of using influence that he publicly deplores, pays
little attention to political alliances, and seeks to award a vacant
Garter to an old humanitarian who deserves it rather than to
some political supporter. In addition to all these personal shortcomings as Prime Minister, the Duke embraces an unpopular
cause at the wrong time: chosen to form a moderate coalition
government to hold things together, he suddenly stakes his min-
istry on the radical issue of borough reform. The Duke of Omnium also has strong political ideas, although he is far less simply

a vehicle for the author's ideas than is a character like Disraeli's Coningsby.

In the early novels of the series, the Duke's program is based on the need for decimal coinage. Even here, in presenting the Duke's program, Trollope manages several things at once: he clearly satirizes the Duke's excessive concern for trivia as he makes him sit up night after night wondering what to do with the "quints" or "demi-tenths" that would be left over in converting from the twelve-pence scale of British currency to the ten-pence scale of a decimal system; he shows the Duke's dedication to work that initially alienates the Duchess, a spirited woman who prefers flashier and more ostentatiously romantic young men; he introduces, in the same presentation of dedicated work, the theme of the Duke's industry apart from anything he can gain for himself, his genuinely high-minded belief in constructing reforms and trying to follow them through. As the character of the Duke develops in later novels, more personal and political depth is added. He becomes an articulate aristocratic Liberal whose ducal instincts and personal stiffness sometimes contradict his intellectual sympathies and his Liberal ideas. In addition, he is prey to his mistakes, to the majority of lesser men, and to the manipulations of political hacks like Sir Timothy Beeswax who has no political principles at all. Trollope also contrasts the Duke with his eldest son, Lord Silverbridge, an amiable young man who is neither conscientious nor thoughtful about politics. The Duke, although universally accepted, never achieves wide popular appeal. Yet Silverbridge, in his first halting, inarticulate speech, given to help a less fortunate friend get a seat in Parliament, fascinates the crowd by his charm and his very inability to put two sentences together coherently. The son, with one of Trollope's characteristic comic switches, has all the adulation the father deserves.

Plantagenet Palliser is Trollope's model, his idea of what a perfect gentleman should be. Trollope felt that fiction should provide such models, and, in *An Autobiography*, he praised Thackeray for having established Colonel Newcombe as a model of honesty and probity. Trollope regarded Thackeray as the greatest English novelist, the most skillful practitioner of the art of molding characters to serve as models for appropriate or inappropriate behavior in a lively, intelligent, yet directly instructive manner. Trollope stated his own attempt to establish ideals of virtue explicitly in *An Autobiography*. Pleased by Nathaniel Hawthorne's claim that Trollope's work was "just as real as if some giant had hewn a great lump out of the earth and put it under a glass case, with all its inhabitants going about their daily business, and not suspecting they were being made a show of," Trollope commented:

> And the criticism, whether just or unjust, describes with wonderful accuracy the purport that I have ever had in view in my writing. I have always desired to "hew out some lump of the earth," and to make men and women walk upon it just as they do walk here among us,—with not more of excellence, not with exaggerated baseness,— so that my readers might recognize human beings like to themselves, and not feel themselves to be carried away among gods or demons. If I could do this, then I thought I might succeed in impregnating the mind of the novel-reader with a feeling that honesty is the best policy; that truth prevails while falsehood fails; that a girl will be loved as she is pure, and sweet, and unselfish; that a man will be honoured as he is true, and honest, and brave of heart; that things meanly done are ugly and odious, and things nobly done beautiful and gracious.

The possible contradictions implicit in the passage, the fidelity to men and women as they are, along with the use of their stories to teach a lesson, the attempt to avoid both "gods" and "demons," along with "impregnating" the mind of the reader with the most piously abstract of Victorian clichés, were not discussed or developed in *An Autobiography*. The fiction, especially the later work, is, however, another matter. Trollope's treatment was wider, fuller, far more sensitive to the complexities of moral judgment than were the maxims he apparently schooled himself to follow.

    An Autobiography, notable now chiefly for the accounts of his industrious schedules and lists of the payments received for his novels, reveals far less of the author's insight and sympathy than do many of his novels. His best work often modified the generalization or questioned the virtue it was trying to establish, but Trollope also sought in fiction the end he spoke of in *An Autobiography:* the arrangement of his characters and events around an ethical principle that could serve as a lesson. Always trying to describe the "good" man or the characteristics that made him "good," always concerned with matching his young lovers appropriately to people who deserved each other, Trollope attempted to demonstrate the importance of principles as simple and ancient as honesty, independence, concern for others. That his novels, at their best, seem to go beyond these principles, demonstrate a vitality, a sense of compassion, and an understanding far more searching than anything the principles demand, is not a statement designed to demonstrate that Trollope was a hasty or indifferent craftsman, nor a claim that he was unconscious of his sympathy and skill. Rather, the novels, more than instructive schemes, develop a comprehensiveness beyond their apparent boundaries.

Trollope's lessons were often involved with preserving order both in individual lives and in society, although he understood and charted both disruptive personal passion and disruptive public change. He was likely to satirize tenacious and inflexible allegiance to a past order, both personal and public, as in the character of Sir Roger Carbury in *The Way We Live Now* (1875), but a sense of order and control remain virtues even within a changing world or a personality exploring itself. As they introduce Trollope's world, the novels postulate a stratified and ordered society. For example, other characters in the Palliser series recognize and accept the superiority of the Duke of Omnium and know just what liberties proximity or friendship may allow them to take. The Duke himself, despite all his professional Liberalism and theoretical skepticism about the virtues of rank, retains both a strict sense of propriety and a fierce desire to protect the purity of rank for his own family line. Trollope, in fact, makes the Duke's complex social ideas intelligible, even if he disagrees in this instance, connecting the ideas and attitudes about rank with the Duke's combination of just, logical liberality and personal severity.

More important than the world Trollope initially assumes is the demonstration in the endings of his novels of a sense of society's order. Trollope's novels are not instances of the open form. Questions are always resolved; balances restored; society summarized as, if not always just, always yielding a kind of rational sense. And seldom, in the later novels, is the resolution superficial—merely a luckily inherited fortune or a just dispensation by a higher power. Phineas Finn gets the career and the wealthy woman he has worked so hard for; in *The Prime Minister*, Lopez commits suicide and liberates his wife, Emily, to judge men and issues more soundly, and to marry the man she should have married in the first place. Later novels other than those in the Palliser series also resolve their issues fully. *The Vicar of Bullhampton* (1870) ends with appropriate marriages and appropriate reconciliations, despite murder and meanness and snobbery. And, in *Ayala's Angel* (1881), Trollope does finally parcel off his large cast of young people pretty much as they deserve. Despite the order implicit in ending a novel with a series of marriages, Trollope avoids the euphoria of the assumption that everything ends happily. At the end of *Ayala's Angel*, he observes:

> If marriage be the proper ending for a novel,—the only ending, as this writer takes it to be, which is not discordant,—surely no tale was ever so properly ended, or with so full a concord, as this one. Infinite trouble has been taken not only in arranging these marriages but in joining like to like,—so that, if not happiness, at any rate sympathetic unhappiness, might be produced.

The sense of acceptance at the conclusion of Trollope's novels does not always involve perfect happiness or complete moral justice; acceptance is a recognition of the way things are in a world where individual and social considerations must be carefully balanced.

Another indication of Trollope's emphasis on the need for order in human affairs is his enormous fear of (and, not surprisingly, fascination with) emotional violence and excess. Just under the surface a number of Trollope's characters and scenes give a sense of possible excess that might, if unchecked, tear the society apart. The Othello theme, the dangers of thwarted and excessive feelings, obviously fascinated Trollope, a fact apparent both in *An Autobiography* and in frequent references in the novels. Particularly in *The Prime Minister*, Trollope often compares his characters at their weakest moments, their moments of least rationality or control, to characters in

Othello. The Duke, when deprived of office or, even in office, when at his weakest and most self-castigating, denied any power to act other than as mediator, is several times pointed to as an example of "Othello's occupation gone." Abel Wharton, in despair that his beloved daughter could have so unwisely chosen the alien Lopez, is extensively compared to Brabantio.

Trollope once tried to write a whole novel based on the tragedy of an Othello-like jealousy set in the Victorian social world, but this novel, *He Knew He Was Right* (1869), succumbs to its own excess, develops no rational counter to the obsessive jealousy, and, since searing tragedy does not demonstrate Trollope at his most skillful, is among the least effective of his novels. Artistically more convincing, his minor characters often love too well, and the consuming intensity of their passions is one of the indications that the young ladies have been wise in rejecting them. Tom Tringle, Jr., in *Ayala's Angel,* loves his cousin so extraordinarily that he must make a constant pest of himself and finally be shipped off on a tour around the world. Squire Gilmore, in *The Vicar of Bullhampton,* is unable to tend his estate and to follow any of his customary routines after Mary Lowther rejects him finally. Although these characters are treated with Trollope's usual sympathy, they are clearly, in the author's terms, less worthy men because they do not have sufficient control over their excessive emotions. And the very few characters who desire no control, who, like Quintus Slide, the opportunistic newspaperman who appears in many of the novels, fabricate a cause and push it to its very limits, whose excesses are not even the result of genuine passion, receive no sympathy at all.

More interesting, perhaps, than the men who succumb to emotional excess are some of Trollope's women who cannot easily mold their emotions into the rather narrow framework society establishes for them. Such a one is Lady Mabel Grex in *The Duke's Children,* an impoverished young noblewoman, beautiful, frank, and highly intelligent, who would marry Lord Silverbridge for his money and his amiability but who always loves Frank Tregear. Having, before the opening of the novel, encouraged Frank to find another love with more money (something he does with alacrity), Lady Mabel sets herself to capture Lord Silverbridge. Yet, at the crucial moment, she refuses to secure the capture, fritters away the possibility with flippant remarks, primarily because she is fundamentally too honest to pretend love where she feels only friendly fondness. And Silverbridge himself, although never very perceptive, gradually comes to sense that Lady Mabel is somehow too overpowering, too dominant, to be the perfect mate for him. As Lady Mabel realizes that she can follow neither her heart nor her designs, she becomes increasingly depressed. She begins to give way to self-pity, to upbraid Silverbridge for not following his clearly implied intentions toward her, and to become much less attractive. The more her emotions are paramount, the more despair she seems to exhibit, the less Trollope sympathizes. It is as if, for him, even people caught between the demand for money (and Trollope shows this demand had become, through expectations fostered in childhood, necessary for Lady Mabel) and the demand for fidelity to their own feelings, between the contradictory qualities of practicality and high romanticism, should not succumb to emotionalism or despair. Lady Mabel does not, however, remain engulfed in self-pity for long. At the end of the novel, her great intelligence and direct self-appraisal reassert themselves and she realizes clearly the different reasons she could not have either of the two men. And Trollope, himself exercising restraint and pathos, restores her to full sympathy.

Trollope's disapproval of excessive intensity is even more apparent in *The Way We Live Now,* his most sharply drawn novel and the one furthest from peaceful green Englishness. Two of the principal characters illustrate the flaws of consuming intensity: Sir Roger, the representative of the virtues of the landed past, judges with clarity and firmness, and refuses to forgive anyone who deviates from his narrow code, but Trollope shows that he misunderstands most of the issues raised in the novel and leaves him unhappy and alone with his land at the end; Sir Felix Carbury, the spoiled and irresponsible young man about town, who becomes extremely petulant and nasty when his opportunistic plans fail, is, at the end of the novel, exiled even from the greater flexibility of "the way we live now."

In contrast to the character of excessive intensity, his opposite, the man of flexibility or resilience, can survive, sometimes even master, all the changes and complexities of Trollope's world. The shady financier, Melmotte, has been found out before, but has always bounced back. This time, his crimes against society are too directly severe, but Trollope hesitates to punish him as he deserves, instead, has him both demonstrate his capacity for change and retain the reader's sympathy by a nobly sacrificial, if somewhat unconvincing, suicide. His daughter, deserted by Felix Carbury, is sufficiently resilient to love again, this time more suitably and wisely. The romantic hero of the novel, Paul Montague, is often accused of "softness," of lack of principle, partially because he is involved with two different women and can break with neither, partially because he senses that some of his business connections are dishonest but hesitates to do anything. Although Paul is hesitant, vulnerable, and sometimes mistaken, he is resilient, is able to acknowledge his mistakes and redeem himself.

A similar contrast between excessive intensity and resilience marks the major theme of *Phineas Finn:* Lady Laura, becoming more shrill and more intense as her role of powerful political hostess fails, is isolated and lonely at the end of the novel (or, rather, two novels since the characters and issues of *Phineas Finn* continue in *Phineas Redux*) ; Phineas, who makes many mistakes about love, money, politics, is able, by his good-hearted and temperate ability to bounce back, to emerge as the hero of the novels.

Excessive intensity is not, in Trollope's terms, always to be equated with violence, for, although many of the object lessons about what is to be avoided are both intense and violent, other violent characters, such as John Crumb, the stalwart farmer in *The Way We Live Now,* and Lord Chiltern, the honest huntsman in the Palliser series, are highly praiseworthy. Violence is acceptable if it is sporadic, hot-blooded, an honest reaction to understandable circumstances, as it is for both John Crumb and Lord Chiltern. The violence that damns, for Trollope, is the cold, the narcissistic, the calculated, the kind of intensity that rages inside, like that of Felix Carbury or Mr. Kennedy, and acknowledges no compromise or forgiveness. This unyielding intensity, this sense of excess, this kind of cold and intransigent self-assurance, destroys both the personal and social order so important in Trollope's fictional world.

Trollope's sense of order attempts to accommodate the complexity of human experience, but the sense of order and the awareness of complexity often work against each other. For example, Trollope's plots frequently pose the ancient question: should a young woman marry for love or for money? In one sense, marrying for money, along with all the social and parental approval that money implies, seems to support the idea of order, the idea of a stable basis for society's relationships. Yet, in another sense, for Trollope, marrying for love suggests a deeper order, a deeper sense of the importance of human relationships that should be established and conveyed to the next generation. In addition, some young ladies, brought up as impoverished gentry, under tremendous pressure to assure their fortunes and those of their families, are given special societal sanctions to marry for money or position. Other young ladies cannot sort out the issues so easily, are not always so sure whom or what they love. The question of marriage, particularly for the vulnerable Victorian woman whose single choice, at a young age, would establish the pattern for a lifetime, is highly complex, not easily reduced to following a simple guide for conduct, even though Trollope's ethical scheme grants approval only to those who marry for love.

An easy "right" or "wrong" cannot apply, for example, to Lady Mabel Grex, who remains a victim, who finds no genuine role within the rigid Victorian society. She has not even sinned. She has merely connived, entertained the possibility of sin, and recognized the complex questions an impoverished lady must face in choosing a husband. But, even so, she is in society's terms, tainted, and she cannot in Trollope's world cover past mistakes with the ease she could were she a man. A double standard always operates in Trollope. Men easily overcome the perplexities and indecisions of youth, regarded by society as normal aspects of growing up; women are often shelved for the very same perplexities and indecisions. And Trollope maintains a great deal of sympathy for these displaced women, who comprise some of his most memorable portraits. They are all highly intelligent, sensitive women who attempt to arrange their lives too consciously, who are slightly too aggressive and aware of themselves to be comfortable in the role of the conventional female that prevailed in Victorian society, the role of the passive and devoted servant.

Such a woman is Lady Laura Standish Kennedy who encourages Phineas Finn's political career, but, because she needs money to pay her improvident family's debts, marries the dour and puritanical Mr. Kennedy. After Kennedy's death, Lady Laura, still in love with Phineas but recognizing that a marriage between them might hurt his political future, is politely but thoroughly isolated in her comfortable salon. Another such example is Julia Brabazon, in *The Claverings* (1867). At the beginning of the novel, because they are both poor, she rejects the hero, Harry Clavering, and marries a degenerate lord simply for his money. Although the lord soon dies, and Julia genuinely loves Harry as she always has, and is regarded by society as far more sinned against than sinning, Trollope does not allow her a second chance and leaves her in isolation. All these women, incidentally, those who deliberately and frankly choose (or even almost choose) money over love, are the products of cold, unfeeling fathers and absentee mothers or dissipated fathers who squander their wealth, or relatives entirely indifferent to them. In other words, they have all, despite beauty and brains and birth, suffered from an inhumane environment. In contrast, most of Trollope's sweet, triumphant heroines have always been coddled in warmth and family affection.

A few of the forceful, intelligent, and unconventional women are more fortunate than the rest. Lady Glencora Palliser, lucky in birth, in fortune, and in an understanding husband, is one of the few vital and aggressive women who comes close to making a dreadful mistake yet because of her position avoids damaging conflict with the axioms of her society. Another who barely escapes the isolation usually meted out to those who even think of bargaining with marriage is Imogene Docimer in *Ayala's Angel*. In love with Frank Houston who is as poor as she, Imogene had originally suggested that they abandon their love and seek to marry fortunes. Despite her resolution, Imogene remains in love with Frank and is unable to accept anyone else, a fact which really saves her, in Trollope's terms. Frank, however, can for a time attach himself to Gertrude Tringle's fortune, for the male is always less maimed by the pursuit of the pound.

When Frank returns to her, Imogene eagerly accepts him, and they eventually marry. Even so, Trollope is skeptical, for, in his chronicle of all the marriages at the end of the novel, he explicitly wonders if Frank and Imogene's marriage will work, or if even the suggestion of their having been willing to sacrifice love to money might not have corrupted something vital. Imogene comes almost as close to the dividing line as possible. Very slightly more tainted heroines like Lady Laura and Lady Mabel are genuine victims of a society that operates on material principles at the same time that it values the romantic. One can only live as best he can within society's hypocrisy.

In matters outside the realm of marriage choices, Trollope is equally skeptical about the justice or fairness with which rewards or punishments are parcelled out. A murder in *The Vicar of Bullhampton* is never really solved; the most knowledgeable character, Sam Brattle, guesses that the wrong man was hanged, although the probably guilty one is in jail. Carry Brattle, his daughter, is stigmatized for what, given the circumstances, Trollope regards as a minor fault; Lady Tringle in *Ayala's Angel* retains her house and position despite ruining three children and treating her nieces with hypocrisy and inhumanity. Society often punishes with an intensity out of all proportion to the crime, and often fails to punish the most criminally inhumane.

Other mistakes women can make are, in Trollope's world, not so disastrous as choosing a man for money or position. Emily Wharton, for example, is allowed a happy and accepted second marriage to Arthur Fletcher after her disastrous first marriage to Lopez. But she had married Lopez because, no matter how completely mistaken, she had thought she was in love with him, and even total misjudgment is quite different from and more socially acceptable than a marriage bargain. This position on misjudgment in *The Prime Minister* (a novel in which almost everyone msjudges everything at one time or another) represents a change from some of Trollope's earlier novels. Victim of a kind of misjudgment similar to Emily's and also offered a happier, socially encouraged, and honorable second chance, Lily Dale, in the early *The Small House at Allington* (1864), feels so defined by her first mistake that she remains a spinster permanently. In Trollope's later novels, however, misjudgment can be redeemed, for it does not represent the kind of violation that marriage for money entails. Trollope's heroines, not always with justice or fairness even from his point of view, are placed in a highly difficult position: society presses them to marry for money and develops the myth that money means acceptance and happiness; yet, marriage for money is a kind of corruption of the human heart, a disavowal of the necessary warmth and tenderness of the woman's role, and, ironically, society often treats most harshly those who follow its material precepts instead of its unacknowledged and often unconscious emotional basis. No wonder that so many of the most sensitive and intelligent and directly forceful young women, like Lady Laura and Lady Mabel, are trapped by a combination of their own natures and the superficially realistic resolve to follow or to consider seriously the hard line that society seems to demand. As characters like Lady Glencora and Imogene Docimer demonstrate, survival in Trollope's difficult world requires the development of a talent for living honestly within a world dominated by hypocrisy.

Some of Trollope's more fortunate heroines insist on marrying for love, often despite the counsels of elders who constantly emphasize security and an income. And Trollope with characteristic irony shows that they earn the prizes and the security they never directly sought. Isabel Boncassen, although aware of Silverbridge's money and position, genuinely loves him. Her love makes her the right girl for the prize, although had she sought the prize directly she would have been dismissed as an American social climber by an outraged society. In *Ayala's Angel* neither Ayala nor Lucy Dormer ever consider marrying for anything other than love, and both are rewarded. Despite the fact that they are poor orphans, shuttled for much of the novel between genteelly poor Uncle Dosett and vulgarly rich Aunt Tringle, they remember keenly the warmth and affection of their dead father in his "bijou" of a house in South Kensington. And that memory helps to prevent them from considering anything other than love. Material success follows both of their decisions.

In rewarding these and similar heroines for their fidelity to love, society (in Trollope's terms) acts more wisely than it preaches or consciously understands. Society preserves its valid order, its humanity, despite the fact that it incessantly discusses its superficial forms of order, its money and its rank. The individual is in an incredibly difficult position.

Treatment of women and their choices in the marriage market is not the only way in which the complexities of Trollope's world qualify his announced intention of providing guides for ethical conduct. Trollope's kind of satire often begins as the label, tag, or stereotype, the quick designation appropriate to pointing the lesson. Yet, frequently, even in the early Barchester series and more often in the later work, Trollope's quick labelling satire is funny only when one first encounters it, for he soon switches to explore a deeper humanity behind the stereotype.

The change from simple exemplification of folly to complex and compassionate treatment of character is apparent in the portrait of the Marquis of Trowbridge in *The Vicar of Bullhampton*. The Marquis begins as an unintelligent snob who donates the land and money to build a huge and ugly dissenting chapel within a few feet of the vicarage gate, just to spite the Anglican vicar. Yet, when the Marquis discovers that the land the chapel was built on was not really his own, he has the chapel moved brick by brick, even though no one insists on the restoration. The old Marquis is honest about money and property, if not about himself and his own motives. Although he learns that the vicar is not a sinner and adulterer just because he won't defer to rank, the Marquis still thinks the vicar must be some kind of heretic. Trollope starts with simple satire in treating the Marquis, then develops him as a character who would like to be wiser than he is; thus sympathy begins to succeed simple satire; but finally the author concentrates on the satire again to prevent the sympathy in the delineation of the Marquis from overwhelming the original conception of the vapid man who insists on social distinction for its own sake. Whenever such characterizations become rigid, a quick switch sends them spinning around again.

Other of Trollope's snobs, however, receive much less sympathy, as, for example, the petty and vindictive Augusta Tringle in *Ayala's Angel*. She is inordinately proud of her marriage to the M.P., Mr. Septimus Traffick, the parasitic son of the exalted and remote Lord Boardotrade (Trollope never entirely abandoned the practice of using names as satirical tags). Much as the author satirizes the insistence on trivial distinctions of rank and station, he also satirizes the naiveté of the democrat who is completely oblivious to the existence of such distinctions. Mrs. Boncassen, the kind American lady in *The Duke's Children,* is laughed at for her innocence in not being able to understand what objections anyone might have to her daughter's marrying Lord Silverbridge so long as the two young people love each other.

Distinctions of rank and class are, however, often treated at a deeper level, become less useful as material for quick and gentle social satire. Although Trollope seldom depicts or discusses workers or members of the lower classes, seldom particularizes the miserable conditions of the English poor as Disraeli did in *Sybil* (1845), or zealously attacks Victorian institutions which reinforce the status quo as did Dickens (Trollope is always less interested in theories of history, and less romantically one-sided in dealing with human character, than is either Disraeli or Dickens), he still does demonstrate a good deal of sympathy for the less fortunate characters he introduces. Mrs. Parker, in *The Prime Minister,* whose husband is ruined by Lopez' financial machinations and schemes, is portrayed as a direct, hardworking woman bravely trying to keep her husband and children alive. Although the modern reader is likely to feel that the Whartons, the family Lopez has married into, don't really alleviate the situation by their bits of charity to Mrs. Parker, and that Trollope's insight has not sufficiently penetrated the economic problems involved (since the author so extravagantly praises the Whartons' generosity), Trollope's sympathy and humanity are genuine.

The working classes figure more prominently in *The Vicar of Bullhampton.* One of the plots in that novel centers around the Brattle family. The father, poor, proud, and self-reliant, operates a small mill, his independence restricted by the fact that the local squire owns the land and the buildings; one rebellious son becomes friendly with thieves and murderers, although he himself is defiantly honest; one beautiful daughter commits the sin for which no Victorian redemption was possible, the sin that even Trollope would not name directly. Throughout the portrayal of the family are suggestions that social and economic conditions alter attitudes toward experience, that these people are different from those at the manor house or the vicarage, but these differences are never really detailed or developed. Trollope's principal concerns are to show that his hero, the vicar, was right all along in forgiving the Brattles and regarding them as stalwart people even when others regarded them as rogues, harlots, murderers, and to demonstrate that the hard father, unlike two of his more materially successful children, has the grace and the humanity finally to forgive his erring daughter and let her live with him once more. In other words, Trollope uses the Brattles as a means of extending his sympathy, his humanity, and as a means of showing the constant human parade of differences between people and within families. He does not really examine the nature or the axioms of the poor, and his treatment of the Brattles seems somewhat condescending and sentimental as a result.

Trollope's poor are not always sentimentalized, for Ruby Ruggles in *The Way We Live Now* would gladly give up her rustic virtue for a few tinselled evenings with a well-born lover in London, and she is fierce in demanding the same rights that others have. Yet the characterization of Ruby is, in Trollope's work, the exception; the mill family in *The Vicar of Bullhampton*, which seems almost like gentry at a masquerade, is more typical. For Trollope, the social and economic differences between people were notable but not particularly important, not nearly as important as the issues of intelligence, humanity, concern for others—issues seldom dependent on class or income. If the poor are often victims in Trollope's world, they are victims for the very same reasons as are those with more money or social position: deceit, excessive intensity, the difference between what they were brought up to expect and what they find.

Although, in terms of historical verisimilitude, Trollope's depiction of poverty is both scant and unconvincing, he is considerably more successful with the genteel poor, the impoverished children of younger sons or the descendants of those who have squandered their money. The house of Reginald Dosett and his wife at Notting Hill in *Ayala's Angel* is done convincingly and fully. When, alternately, Reginald's nieces come to live at Notting Hill, the economies in buying butter and the mending of sheets demonstrated effectively the drabness of life at the Dosetts. Similarly, in *The Vicar of Bullhampton,* characters rigidly retain the emotions, the attitudes, and the pride of their far more affluent relatives, yet they care desperately, and must care, about money.

In fact, in all Trollope's novels, money is tremendously important. Characters love and hate, assume airs and puncture them, but they are always aware of living in a world in which financial security matters. Many of the men who go down into the City or to the Law Courts to make money are worthy gentlemen. Trollope always admires hard and purposeful work. Cautious old Abel Wharton in *The Prime Minister* may seem rather penurious at first, but, after we see him working hard to accumulate his money, painfully parting with it, piece by piece, to try to bribe happiness for his daughter in a disastrous marriage he opposed in the first place, we are made to feel a good deal of sympathy for him. Vulgar Sir Thomas Tringle, who is never happier than when counting the pounds coming into his City office, is, in his directness and lack of pretense, made the most admirable and farsighted member of his family in *Ayala's Angel.*

Money, a central issue in both *The Way We Live Now* (much of which takes place in the atmosphere of stocks and bonds in the City) and *Phineas Finn,* is not easily localized as either a part of or an opposing force to ethical virtue. Some of the older characters, like Sir Roger Carbury, equate money with sin and locate all value in an older landed society that had no need for complicated financial or industrial undertakings. But Sir Roger is living in a world that, for Trollope, no longer exists. In addition, many of the old landed families, the aristocrats, have become dependent on the new money, as the Longestaffs and Nidderdales cater to the Melmottes, an alliance in which neither side is more consistently or demonstrably honest than the other. And, if honesty is the criterion, what kind of honesty is important? Trollope allows Phineas Finn, like the young aristocrat he is trying to be, to run up debts to tradesmen; other young men are not heavily penalized for failing to pay gambling debts (although cheating at cards is quite another matter). Yet a lack of honesty about one's emotions can easily damn a young woman or withhold sympathy from a young man until he discovers what his emotions really are and is willing to act on them. Although the young man should make his own way through the world, Phineas is finally praised for being sufficiently liberated to accept Mme. Max Goesler's money as well as her offer of marriage, for scruples about money should not bar a worthy young man from fame and love. Trollope, approving of money for his characters in one situation, deploring its tendency to corrupt in another, avoids making any generalizations about money or materialism in the modern world. Rather, for Trollope, money is another counter in the various shifts and changes within society, another means, itself neither good nor bad, which gives form and shape to the human relationships depicted in the novels. Again, in the complicated question of money, Trollope multiplies the possibilities sufficiently to prevent his fiction standing for an instructive lesson.

Money is also significant in another of Trollope's principal themes: the rise of the energetic young man from middle-class beginnings to a career of distinction and fortune. Trollope's world is always flexible: rich men can squander money and poor men can make it; money cannot replace birth, but it can go a long way toward reproducing birth's social advantages. The prototype is Phineas Finn, son of a hard-working, not very wealthy Irish doctor, whose rise in Parliament forms the major issue of two novels. Able, resilient, and intelligent, Phineas carves his career in the patrician Parliamentary world despite the fact that he is constantly plagued by lack of money. At one point, he retires from Parliament because he feels he has not sufficient money to support his career properly; at other points, his choices of friends or women are based, at least in part, on the financial issues he constantly encounters. Finally, his second marriage assures financial independence, but before this point Phineas has had to walk a tightrope strung between moral and material considerations in order to make his way in the London worlds of fashion and politics. A similar character, less fully developed than Phineas, is Frank Greystock in *The Eustace Diamonds*. Having to make his way as a young lawyer, Frank Greystock (and his surname indicates the moral ambivalences that surround him) must choose between the money and slightly

[45

tainted excitement offered by a match with his cousin, Lizzie Eustace, and the rewards of an untarnished reputation with the poverty and fidelity of Lucy Morris.

Less fortunate and less worthy than either Phineas or Frank Greystock is Ferdinand Lopez in *The Prime Minister*. A dubious speculator, whose family and origins are unknown, Lopez marries Emily Wharton against her staid father's wishes. Trollope puts in a sufficient number of twists, early in the novel, to make us wonder about the character. At one point, even his father-in-law, Abel, almost comes to like Lopez and compares him favorably with his own rather indolent son, Everett. Abel understands enough of the City and the need for acquiring money to wonder whether or not the usual guides society establishes for judging people, the guides of family, background, discernible source of income, and manners, really are accurate. According to these guides, Lopez, a man of charm and intelligence but of no discernible family or fortune, perhaps even a Jew, is not to be admitted to society. Abel Wharton may wonder about the guides, but Trollope's stand is less hesitant: the guides are too easily exclusive, although, ironically, in this instance they have given the right answer for the wrong reasons. Lopez is really an adventurer, an exploiter of others, to be excluded from society on these grounds rather than on those of birth or lack of fortune. Early in the novel, only we and then Emily can see that Lopez exploits everyone with whom he comes in contact. We are made to realize that society must protect itself against him. But society itself only gradually recognizes why Lopez must be barred, for not until he suddenly proposes to run off to Guatemala with the now notorious Lizzie Eustace do most people recognize his dishonesty and complete lack of principle. And society then tends to make the obvious equation: unpedigreed alien equals unprincipled exploiter. Trollope, however, has shown us the situation in sufficient complexity to keep the equation unbalanced.

Often society's guides are even more clearly and directly fallacious in judging the worth of the aspiring young man. Frank Tregear in *The Duke's Children* is not an outright alien. His family is known and respectable, although neither wealthy nor prominent, when he appears as the friend of Lord Silverbridge and the suitor for the hand of Lady Mary Palliser, the Duke of Omnium's daughter. Society in general and the Duke in particular use the conventional guides. They are certain the suitor is an unprincipled adventurer bent on gaining money and useful connections through the relationship with the Duke's daughter, a conviction that the Duke, in his fierce opposition to the marriage, retains long after everyone else has relinquished it. Trollope emphasizes the fundamental irony in the fact that the Duke, publicly and politically a Liberal, frequently heard arguing about the evils of class discrimination in the abstract, is personally insistent on class distinctions in regard to his daughter's marriage; similarly, Tregear, who personally tries desperately to bridge the distance between classes, always defends the principles of class discrimination and enters Parliament as a militant Conservative (he even persuades the amiable Silverbridge to be a Conservative for awhile). Although Tregear appears, at first, rather cold and heartless in his effort to gain money and position, and although he has, in the past, been in love with another woman, we never doubt that he is a man of insight and principle, a worthy member of the reigning society and a suitable husband for Lady Mary. He is loyal to Lady Mary, even though forbidden to see her for months, and he intelligently examines his own motives for wanting to marry her. Society, Trollope points out, needs to allow room for the Frank Tregears. Yet the same guides that society follows, the matching of rank with rank and fortune with fortune, would, if rigidly followed, exclude a Tregear and a Lopez alike. Society's guides conventionally do not allow for comprehensive judgment and discrimination.

The principal problem in almost all Trollope's later work, from *The Last Chronicle of Barset* (1867) to *Ayala's Angel* is that of judgment, of learning to understand and evaluate the worth of all the varying issues and individuals one sees around him. Sometimes, as in *The Way We Live Now,* the questions of judgment are posed for the reader, leaving him skeptical and wondering if any clear guides for conduct can be extrapolated from the experience of the novel. At other times, Trollope (fairly early in the novels) gives the reader the standards on which the characters are to be judged, establishes a kind of ideal, but then depicts a world in which no one understands the issues

[47

as the author does, in which everyone, at least for a time, misjudges a central character or situation. This latter kind of novel,
less completely skeptical than the other, still underlines the tremendous difficulty involved in establishing any applicable guide
for ethical conduct. In *The Prime Minister,* for example, Trollope plants sufficient clues concerning Lopez' unprincipled exploitation of others early in the novel, but we gradually discover
how and when the rest of society will see through him. The interest is in the process of coming to know, rather than in the
suspense of what is to be known. Captain Marrable in *The Vicar
of Bullhampton* is also a shadowy figure for rather a long period
of time. Are his complaints about his father justified or is he
really a character dominated by indolent self-pity? Is he really
worth all the devotion Mary Lowther is willing to grant him?
In this instance, the reader has no guide, knows no more than
the several different characters through whose perspective he sees
Marrable, until Trollope finally focuses on the essential worth
of the man. Similarly, in the same novel, Trollope allows us to
wonder for a long time about young Carry Brattle, to ask whether
her "sin" was a single and understandable event or a symptom of
callous rebellion against family and society, before he finally
demonstrates his conviction that her flaw has been minute in
comparison with the kind of inhumanity man gets away with
every day. The whole texture of *The Way We Live Now* is one
of misjudgment, and emphasizes our inability to use any known
gauge to measure the worth of the characters in the novel. Financial and social reputations are governed by rumor and half-
apprehended hint; the origins and principles of Melmotte are
unknown; trusted people in responsible positions suddenly van-
ish with other people's money; Mrs. Hurtle has been violent and
scheming, but we wonder if she really did kill a man and, more
significantly, could kill another if provoked sufficiently. Even
the kind of character supposedly easy to peg, the spoiled and indolent young aristocrat, is hard to judge, for the two principal
examples in the novel, Adolphus Longestaff and young Lord
Nidderdale, turn out to be very different from each other and
Lord Nidderdale is far from the original cliché. In a novel in
which almost everyone changes character, shifts opinions and
convictions, only gradually discovers what he is and what his mo-

tives are, the dominant impression is that of the great difficulty and loneliness the sensible person undergoes in trying to find his way through contemporary experience.

Ayala's Angel, which depicts an apparently more ordered world than does *The Way We Live Now,* also deals primarily with the problems of judging character. Ayala is always looking for an "Angel of Light," rejecting mundane young men who do not fit her romantic preconceptions. For a long time, Trollope satirizes her, pointing out that a spirited horse she has been given to ride comes closer than any man to her idea of the "Angel of Light." Her preconception is also shallow, for she initially rejects Johnathan Stubbs because he is physically unattractive, even though she acknowledges that he has the wit and intelligence she associates with her romantic dream figure. Yet Ayala does learn, and eventually realizes that an "Angel of Light" can wear bristling red whiskers. In this instance Trollope lampoons exaggerated romanticism, although he defends the basic assumption of the romantic heroine that the young lady should wait for the truly superior young man who will stir her soul. Ayala waits and is rewarded. Yet, in other instances in the same novel, the whole attitude of the romantic heroine seems dubious. Ayala is frequently played off against her rather unattractive cousin, Gertrude Tringle. Gertrude suggests to her first lover, Frank Houston, that he overcome her family's objection by eloping with her to Ostend. When Frank refuses (as he also ignores her instructions to address all letters to her by unnecessarily mysterious means), Gertrude makes the elopement to Ostend the central issue of the relationship with her next suitor, Captain Batsby. She is more interested in the romantic fiction than in the man himself, and Trollope points out Gertrude's pathetic folly, that she simply isn't attractive enough or clever enough to afford the romantic role. The romantic attitude is a luxury in a world that grants graces and wisdom in unequal portions. Gertrude, like her brother, Tom, is the victim of both nature and an unwise mother, and must finally settle for a relationship in which her romantic assumptions are bound to be demolished repeatedly. Yet formulating the final judgment on Ayala and Gertrude takes time, consumes a major portion of the novel. In ways, *Ayala's Angel* is an elaborate and extensive treatment of a central question: under what conditions is fidelity to romantic attitudes possible and desirable? With his acute sense of the way the world operates, his recognition that justice seldom exists in society but that people do have a limited control over their own fortunes, and his genuine compassion for the people he describes, Trollope concentrates far more on the possible than on the desirable.

Trollope, in the later novels, places far more emphasis on man's accepting what he has to accept than on his establishing ethical principles that apply universally. And because man, half-ignorant and prone to mistakes, has to accept his world out of necessity, Trollope maintains a sense of compassion toward most human creatures. Especially toward the end of his career, the compassion dominates the novels, dominates them in direct proportion to the recognition that a meaningful code of virtue cannot be followed and applied within the unjust world. Compassion is a matter of emphasis, an attitude that fills the void left by all the codes, guides, and formulae that are inadequate for human experience. In the perspective of Trollope's later novels, only the very wise and the very fortunate could make their way successfully through a world that offered unequal possibilities. Man had no power to change his world, and, even if he had, he had no assurance that the changes would not involve inequities at least as great, or conditions that would destroy just as many individuals. He could only accept, follow whatever forms of order he could see and apply, remain resilient, and sympathize.

This kind of compassion was not entirely new with Trollope, for English poetry and drama have particularized it as far back as Chaucer's attitude toward those of his pilgrims whose characters did not fit their occupations in the highly stratified and schematized medieval society, or Shakespeare's feeling toward the historically doomed Trojans in *Troilus and Cressida,* or the humanity toward Shylock which leaks through and saturates the structure of *The Merchant of Venice.* Even in the early novel, generally molded more by the instructive lesson than was the drama, writers like Jane Austen had substituted compassion for what they could not justify as truth. Yet, in Trollope's world, the emphasis on compassion increased, accelerated, as the attempt to provide lessons or guides for conduct became increasingly difficult to sustain.

The novel of compassion frequently relies on a density of social characterization, a completeness in describing man and his environment, both to demonstrate the world's complexity and to fill the space left by the lack of a universal truth. In addition, Trollope, like other novelists of compassion, is often at his best in developing an extended relationship between people, another fictional richness appropriate to the novel that conveys no abstract message. If there is little discernible "truth" about man, little that can be labeled his fundamental nature, the novelist is likely to study his characters in combinations in order to demonstrate their variety and complexity. The self, since it expresses little essential truth, can be known only in its actions and combinations. Trollope writes most skillfully and profoundly when describing his characters interacting with one another, each helping to define and illuminate the other. The relationship between the Duke of Omnium and his Duchess, Lady Glencora, for example, is rich, complex, and humane. Lady Glencora had originally stayed with the Duke, in defiance of her love for Burgo Fitzgerald, because of the pressure of society and propriety. The pressure, in part, made the marriage work, and the constant memory of this makes the Duke, after Lady Glencora has died, apply so much pressure on his daughter to try to force her to follow his will. Yet Trollope deliberately avoids the generalization. The kind of pressure that is desirable and that works in one instance is both undesirable and ineffective in another; people and circumstances differ. This realization of complexity allows Trollope to trace the constant shuttling, the constant turns of position and attitude that go on within a marriage. He carefully develops the marriage of the Duke and the Duchess from its arranged beginnings in *Can You Forgive Her?*, through storms and the establishment of mutual although distant respect, to the genuine love and concern in *The Prime Minister*. By the time of *The Prime Minister,* the last novel in which the Duchess appears, each partner feels and acts as almost part of the other, absorbing the other's reactions to a given situation or person into his own. They incorporate each other's attitude toward the Duke's becoming Prime Minister, switching sides several times as the Duchess develops some of the Duke's reticence and desire for quiet while he adopts something of her zest (although in entirely different terms) for pursuing a job to its conclusion. The Fenwicks, the principal couple of *The Vicar of Bullhampton,* comprise another of Trollope's close marriages in which each partner adopts something of the other and learns, in part, to think through the other's perspective. Man, in Trollope's world, is both more visible and more humane in combination with others.

Human connections are, of course, not confined simply to those involved in marriage. *Ayala's Angel,* for example, also depicts along with numerous marriages, other familial relationships, such as that of two orphaned sisters. Lucy and Ayala Dormer are constantly defined through each other and against each other, and easy polarities of the differences between the sisters frequently change. The supposedly quiet sister (Lucy) is less happy in and less adjusted to the quiet life of the Dosetts; the more vivacious and social sister (Ayala) is really, at first, less sure of herself in society. Man's connections with institutions and conventions also change constantly, frequently in ironic and unexpected ways. Lord Silverbridge is originally provided with good reasons for deserting his father's Liberal allegiances and becoming a Conservative, even if the young lord does not fully understand the reasons he announces. When he later returns to the Liberal party, he is unable to offer any reasons, although, as a person, he has become far more forceful and independent. In an ironic way, he has become enough a man not to insist on having his own political opinion.

In *Ayala's Angel,* Lady Tringle, Lucy Dormer's aunt, objects to Lucy's connection with Isadore Hamel, the improvident young sculptor. And Isadore's father, also a sculptor, objects to the connection equally. Were the son willing to live a Bohemian life in Rome, the father would gladly support him, but the elder Hamel refuses to grant a penny to a son anxious to engage in a conventional and respectable marriage. Sir Thomas Tringle, superficially more vulgar and more interested in money than is his social-climbing wife, is at first willing to take a more generous view of young Hamel and his art, willing to try to help the young couple. A benevolent Philistine, Sir Thomas tries to work out ways in which Isadore's art might become commercially profitable. Yet, Isadore is intransigent, refusing to consider a change from vast allegorical figures to busts of people who will pay for them. Furthermore, he even refuses to defend his ideas or explain them to Sir Thomas. As Trollope brilliantly delineates the situation, the businessman's Philistine attitudes are exactly matched by the artist's priggishness. Each has, in his own terms, relevant motives for his own attitudes, yet no understanding or communication is possible. As the novel develops, Isadore's intransigence gradually lessens and he becomes more tolerant of conventional attitudes toward art. He does not become corrupt (again, Trollope always guards against the possibility of sweeping judgments) and he still under any circumstances would marry the girl he loves, but he does voluntarily turn from his allegorical Bacchus to more mundane and marketable forms of sculpture. Ideas, in Trollope never fixed or dominant, are always used to explain the motives or the attitudes of complex and changing characters.

Trollope's novels despite occasional prescriptive insertions are generally descriptive, emphasizing what man is and calling for compassion because man is not other than he is. Often Trollope and Dickens seem to be subscribing to the same values: love, humanity, genuine emotions, the importance of the individual in contrast to an indifferent or hostile society, values that can be connected with the Romantic movement. But they express these values in very different ways.

For Dickens, humanity or the importance of emotion is a truth, an essence, an idea, and the whole novel is bent to the structure of the reigning truth, molded to demonstrate the idea. In *Bleak House*, Esther represents the "truth"—Richard Carstone, Lady Dedlock, Horace Skimpole, various different errors. Appropriately, Esther gains a happy ending—relief from her suffering and the perfect mate—while the other three are shunted off to the death or disaster they have earned. We are left with a feeling of justice, no matter how difficult for man the terms may be.

In Trollope's fiction, on the other hand, the humanity or the importance of emotion is part of a point of view that may or may not work out in the world of the novel; the characters who represent the point of view may win or lose, may be justified or not, may be defeated and have to accept defeat for all the wrong reasons, like Marie Melmotte or Mrs. Hurtle. Dickens does, at times, portray victims of injustice with whom we sympathize; almost always, however, these are children crippled, twisted, or otherwise determined by the forces that surround them. Only children living out the destiny others' mistakes have established for them can be the victims in a world in which following the "truth" in the author's terms can enable grown men and women to survive. Trollope, unlike Dickens, has almost no interest in children as such, no fictional purpose for the creature who cannot possibly make meaningful choices. In Trollope's world, everyone can make ethical choices, can try to determine his own end, although the connection between the freely made choice and the result may well be far from anything the individual intended or anticipated. Trollope's world is more free and flexible than Dickens', but it is ultimately more mysterious, more chaotic, less amenable to human understanding or control.

Another way of stating the difference between the two authors is to point out that Dickens, despite all his objections to the church and other institutions, is a Christian writer. His perspective becomes a world view, a morality, a kind of guiding principle, although that principle is not necessarily in agreement with the hierarchical and organized principles of much conventional nineteenth century English Christianity. In addition, in Dickens' world, "the sins of the fathers are visited upon the children," actions have invariable consequences, and the world seems to operate on a fixed principle behind all the visible complexity. Trollope's world is far more accidental. He often prefers the very same virtues, the same emotion and human responsiveness, but these are seldom made into principles or guiding forces in the non-metaphysical universe he depicts. Despite all his piety, Trollope finally does not establish a world that operates on any principle beyond itself, does not develop a Christian universe. Compassion becomes an attitude in the fictional world that is unsystematized and unregulated, becomes a substitute for the metaphysical assurance man seeks without finding.

The prose techniques of the two authors also reflect the difference in their perspectives. Dickens frequently takes an image—the fog in *Bleak House* or the empty wind in *Martin Chuzzlewit*—and makes it dominant in the novel, repeating, developing, inventing, until the image comes to organize the life of the entire novel. For Trollope, imagery is momentary and never structural, used to explain an idea, or, at most, encapsulate a scene the point of which is likely to be reversed in a subsequent scene. Trollope's imagery is certainly less interesting than Dickens', is far closer to the cliché or the little moralistic proverb, and it never extends, never proliferates to explain anything further than itself. Dickens' language, like his thematic principle, coheres to provide an intricate but ordered cosmos which man can know. Trollope's language is bits and pieces, separate facts, conversations, points like tiny individual men in a cosmos never really knowable.

This is consistent with Trollope's concentration on men and women, on character, on depicting human beings the way he saw them, for he claimed in *An Autobiography* that drawing character was his greatest skill, although he attempted to provide models for behavior. *An Autobiography* recognized the contrast with Dickens, for Trollope, after complaining that Dickens' characters were not human beings (and Trollope's criticism was always sufficiently unsophisticated to make this his major reason for devaluing Dickens), went on to say, "It has been the peculiarity and the marvel of this man's power, that he has invested his puppets with a charm that has enabled him to dispense with human nature." Trollope did not see that the charm is partly that of having established a system, a coherent world in terms of which all experience can be explained and understood. Lacking such a system himself, Trollope concentrated on the individual, the particular, the man within a society that had no consistent guides for conduct, no justice, no God beyond itself.

In the later novels, Trollope's satire is seldom that of the elevated point of view looking down on all the follies and errors of the world, of the positive answer scoring off the negative examples. Rather, his comic point of view embodies frequent switches of character and perspective, developments of one side of human nature until that hardens and can then be turned to demonstrate the other side, and juxtapositions that indicate man is not the wise, purposeful creature he likes to think himself. Trollope, describing the human being within the hypocritical society he has himself created, concentrated on the difference between man's aspirations and his achievements, between his illusions and his nature. With all the comedy, all the development of the sometimes ludicrous differences in human behavior, the tone remained almost always gentle, sympathetic, aware that man would be much more than he is, never militant or strident, because Trollope recognized that saying "man would be more than he is" is different from saying "man should be more than he is." Comedy works on such differences, on inconsistency, on the juxtaposition between unlike people or events. Some comic writers, Swift for example, or Evelyn Waugh, fill the space between the differences with mockery, with a sharp and bitter sense of human inadequacy. Other comic writers, like Trollope, fill the spaces with a gentle version of the attitude of compassion.

Trollope's kind of compassion, particularly in the work of his last fifteen years, seldom degenerates into sentimentality, is seldom shallow or superficially comforting. Rather, the later work gives an extensive and profound description of man as he relates to and operates in his social setting. The acute problems of man himself and man in society are depicted, despite all the gentle comedy and some of the apparently smooth resolutions. If, at times, the acceptance of society seems shallow or the conviction that it is impossible to change man and society seems shoddily developed or sentimentally conservative, still Trollope's acceptances and resolutions never obscure the relevance of the questions as he poses, as well as the fact that the questions have no complete or fully satisfactory answer. As in a great deal of fiction, from Jane Austen's to that of numerous twentieth century contemporaries, the questions are far more memorable than the resolutions. And, in Trollope's fiction, the range of the questions, the skepticism, prevents sentimentality. The resolutions become the graceful and compassionate means of emphasizing that, for most people, for all save the accidentally fortunate, the difficult questions—the social and personal displacements, the injustices —really have no answer.

III

MEREDITH

Trollope used irony to explore his characters, to examine their actions and contradictions, to qualify rigid definitions of them and to puncture their pretenses. For Meredith, however, irony was more theoretical, less gentle and less personal, more a matter of general social commentary. Frequently in Meredith's novels a character is introduced only to provide the occasion for more generalized satire. For example, in *Rhoda Fleming* (1865), the satire in the following passage applies less to the character or to personal conflicts in the novel than to Victorian piety in general:

> Aunt Anne produced a bundle, and placed the hat on it, upon which she had neatly pinned a tract, "The Drunkard's Awakening!" Mrs. Boulby glanced her eye in wrath across this superscription, thinking to herself, "Oh, you *good* people! how you make us long in our hearts for trouble with you." She controlled the impulse, and mollified her spirit on her way home by distributing stray leaves of the tract to the outlying heaps of rubbish, and to one inquisitive pig, who was looking up from a badly-smelling sty for what the heavens might send him.

Often in introducing a character, as with Algernon Blancove in the same novel, Meredith inserts a short satirical essay. Algernon is called "the genius of the Champagne luncheon incarnate," and Meredith then goes on, marshalling the observations of his novelistic "philosophic eye," to discuss the phenomenon of elegant and worthless gentlemen who are parasites on their society.

He returns to his theme, the next time in the novel that Algernon appears, to add that by studying fools we can learn a great deal about human nature.

Meredith's satire requires this connection with a theoretical idea, however commonplace, or a general observation. It is characteristically more abstract than Trollope's, more directed against a type or representative of a fallacious idea. Whereas Trollope develops his fictional controls from the way people behave, constantly inserting appeals that his characters be regarded as true to life, only hesitantly and with qualification endorsing any theories of human behavior, Meredith frequently inserts appeals to philosophy and abstract theories about human nature to explain his fiction. The introductory chapter of *Diana of the Crossways* (1885) begins as a study of diaries, a statement of how we come to know what we know, and ends by appealing to a studied and worked-out philosophy:

> The forecast may be hazarded, that if we do not speedily embrace Philosophy in fiction, the Art is doomed to extinction, under the shining multitude of its professors. . . . Instead, therefore, of objurgating the timid intrusions of Philosophy, invoke her presence, I pray you. History without her is the skeleton map of events: Fiction a picture of figures modelled on no skeleton-anatomy. But each, with Philosophy in aid, blooms, and is humanly shapely.

The control of philosophy, of some reigning idea, is patterned most tightly in *The Egoist* (1879), the novel that delineates Sir Willoughby Patterne as an archetypal egoist, finding each of his qualities and his reactions to events in a mythical and universal "Book of Egoism." On the surface at least, the organization of the novel around the theme of egoism and the damage egoism does to human relationships provides a theoretical coherence and an implicit formula for human behavior.

That this kind of theoretical coherence and organization of the novel around a theme that could be applied directly to human experience was, at least for a time, one of Meredith's principal aims is apparent in his single extensive published essay, *The Essay on Comedy* (1877). In the essay, which directly precedes *The Egoist* in the chronology of Meredith's works, he argues for a comic spirit that would purge man of his snobberies and affectations, his pretenses and sentimentality, his egoism. Thus purged, man could become more truly civilized and rational, could create a wiser and better society. The aim of comedy, according to the essay, is socially prescriptive, reforming the individual vagary or egoism and assuming that a collection of individual reforms would beneficially alter the society as a whole. To a certain extent *The Egoist* illustrates the theory explained in the essay. Sir Willoughby Patterne embodies all the vanity of egoism, all the superficial self-glorification and irrational self-justification. His firm resolutions, like "I could not marry Laetitia Dale," easily fade from his consciousness as he hangs on to anything that momentarily supports his self-esteem; he defines egoism as a form of original sin, never realizing that he is defining himself; he is a parasite on others, as on his two devoted aunts, subsisting on their praises and flattery although he would willingly exile them from Patterne Hall. In addition, the novel contains paraphernalia appropriate to the demonstration of an abstract thematic statement: comic imps that puncture vanity, the "Book of Egoism," a cluster of minor characters whose incessant gossip and comic inconsistencies extend the range of the satire on human folly. In this sense, too, the recognition and revolt of Clara Middleton and Vernon Whitford are blows against egoism and, by implication, herald the formation of a new, more honest, and more civilized society.

Yet to explain the novel as only a demonstration of comedy and ridicule reforming human folly is to ignore much of the texture and vitality of *The Egoist*. Comedy aimed at reform, like the gossipy misperception and rivalry between Lady Busshe and Mrs. Mountstuart Jenkinson, frames the novel, beginning and end, but ignores the development of the heroine and hero, Clara and Vernon, that comprises the middle and substance of the novel. Clara, ticketed as "a rogue in porcelain," learns to change her roguishness, her iconoclasm, into a shrewd understanding of human values and to shatter the porcelain, the hard shell of conventional dependence which encases her. Similarly, Vernon, the quiet scholar, learns to feel and to act firmly on his feelings. The development of these two characters, an interior growth of sensitivity and struggle against the apparent rationale of society, illustrates the problems of a new force in Victorian society: the independent, educated young man or woman, unwilling to follow the trivial tribal customs and rites of the world in which he or she was brought up. Both Vernon and Clara are referred to as "a new kind of thing," as individuals not observable in English society previously. The comedy of the novel notwithstanding, the new man or woman has many difficulties in trying to assert independence and judgment within the world of the past. Vernon is economically dependent on Sir Willoughby, must risk comfort and security in attempting his literary career in the chaos of London. Clara, like any respectable young Victorian lady, is dependent on her father and her initial promise to marry Sir Willoughby: revolt against these is only too likely to render her an outcast. In addition, the plot gives Vernon and Clara the responsibility for young Crossjay, an indication that their decisions and actions have consequences beyond themselves. In one sense, the whole comic apparatus is a device to allow the new forces growing within society to triumph, a gesture consistent with imps and the "Book of Egoism" in favor of the revolt. But the substance of the novel, the long middle that recounts the struggles within both Vernon and Clara, acknowledges that the revolt is not nearly so easy or so surely triumphant. The problems linger after the bold gesture vanishes.

Meredith's other novels fit even less conveniently into the theme of *The Essay on Comedy,* although they often contain abstractions and examples of the reforming effect of ridicule. Sir Austin and his rigid system of education are clearly satirized in *The Ordeal of Richard Feverel* (1859), but the novel points to the formation of no new and more civilized society. Rather, Sir Austin's system helps destroy the son he loves, as Richard, in reacting against the system, helps destroy both himself and his wife. The novel, despite numerous satirical scenes, is almost an elaborate tragedy of relationships rather than a comedy from which the implication of a positive direction emerges.

Rhoda Fleming begins with comedy: the Fleming family on the farm where stalwart rustics are lampooned as slow and ignorant yokels; the uncle in London who brags about the fortunes he handles in a City bank but is only the guard at the door who carries the depositors' money once a day; both branches of the aristocratic Blancove family satirized as selfish, arrogant, indolent, indifferent to others. But most of the novel is not satirical. The central issue is the contrast between the two Fleming sisters. The elder, Dahlia, is warm and vulnerable, suggesting passion and the earth, connected through imagery with nature; she is seduced and abandoned by Edward Blancove and finally ruined when her stronger sister refuses to let her return to a now repentant Edward. The younger, Rhoda, is principled and unbending, destroying all possibilities for her sister while believing she is acting in Dahlia's best interest. The reader feels that the happy ending for Rhoda, gaining a worthy husband, is a manifest injustice that cannot be comically reconciled. As in *The Ordeal of Richard Feverel,* the central interests of this novel cluster around tragic relationships, around the cruelties people perpetrate on each other without intending to, around the destructive misunderstandings in human experience.

Yet, in *Rhoda Fleming,* Meredith often neglects to develop crucial chapters that deal with his characters' motives. Important issues are not worked out very clearly: Rhoda's understanding is still painfully limited, although she supposedly occupies the heroine's role at the end of the novel; Dahlia's attempted suicide seems gratuitous pain, for we do not know whether the attempt is the result of Rhoda's hardness or the strain of Dahlia's own social position or both. Rather than tragedy—for the novel does not develop fully the statement of man's position in the universe that classical tragedy implies—*Rhoda Fleming* communicates a pathos, a sense of defeat and diminished possibility for man, in which the comedy is only incidental and peripheral. Much of Meredith's early fiction is dominated by a pathos, a sympathy, about which he later expressed ambivalent feelings. In his preface to *The Egoist,* while mapping out the elements to be included in the novel, he followed his discussion of comedy with a few words on pathos:

Concerning pathos, no ship can now set sail without pathos; and we are not totally deficient of pathos; which is, I do not accurately know what, if not the ballast, reducible to moisture by patent process, on board our modern vessel; for it can hardly be the cargo, and the general water supply has other uses; and ships well charged with it seem to sail the stiffest; there is a touch of pathos.

Like the foregoing metaphor, Meredith's sense of pathos was often disguised, covered by elaborate terms, or buried under a series of philosophical abstractions, but the pathos almost always comes through the fiction, especially the fiction that sails "the stiffest."

Other of Meredith's novels are dominated neither by comedy nor, explicitly, by pathos. The early *Evan Harrington* (1860) is primarily the story of a young tailor's son, proud of his aristocratic ancestors, who attempts to climb into the narrow world where he feels he really belongs. Although the petty and grasping qualities of the aristocracy and those who climb so desperately are satirized, Evan's desire to achieve meaning and status through a rise in class is neither defeated in the novel nor questioned by the author. The novel is a narrative of triumph, of justice and reward, rather than either an example of pathos or a comic attempt to reform human folly. Much of Meredith's fiction is more comic and less triumphant.

Beauchamp's Career (1875), for example, satirizes both Nevil, the aristocratic and romantic hero who would reform society on the basis of his radical principles, and the complacent Tory world of Nevil's family and friends. But the comedy does not indicate a possible positive direction for men; rather it is a fabric of Nevil's missed opportunities and constant misunderstandings that finally render him useless. His death at the end of the novel in a romantic gesture, rescuing a boy from drowning, has been prepared for by a whole series of futile incidents and mistakes. Nevil first loses his chance to be elected as a radical member of Parliament by heeding the summons of a French girl, only to find that she is merely toying with him; he later loses Cecilia, whom he loves, because she misunderstands his response to the French girl's second and more genuine summons; much of the difficulty between Nevil and his relatives is caused by Rosamund's frightened initial reaction to the radical Dr. Shrapnel—her fright makes her lie, yet she only wants to help Nevil and advance his career. Many of the incidents that misfire throughout the novel are funny in themselves and are treated satirically, yet they do not cohere into a pattern that points toward any version of a more sane and rational society. As man, in *Beauchamp's Career*, only entangles himself more helplessly in the social and sexual traps he has constructed, so the comedy spins around and around without central direction.

In all these earlier novels, Meredith's irony is directed against the follies in the society around him as well as against some of the postures he himself advocated at other times (the longing for aristocracy, the value of the simple rural life, the eagerness to act and stake everything on the single romantic impulse). The irony is clever, satirical, sometimes protective and defensive in sheltering the author's own implicit point of view, as in the approbative attitude toward Nevil, but it seldom follows the role of the comic spirit described in *The Essay on Comedy.*

The problems of revolt against the triviality and convention of the past, central to *The Egoist,* also dominate *Diana of the Crossways.* This novel, in part a defense of the woman of unusual wit and intelligence, concentrates on the strains, partially self-caused, that Diana experiences in the midst of a mindless, chattering society. Separated from her husband, the dull, arrogant, and unjust Warwick, Diana attempts to earn her own living as a novelist. Despite her ambivalent position in society—alternately envied as an independent woman and scorned as sinful—and a number of serious mistakes, like her passion for Percy Dacier, she manages to hold her position until she marries the faithful Redworth after Warwick has died. Satire is levelled against Diana herself, also against the stupidities of the society by both Diana and the author, but the comedy purges nothing and points in no positive direction. The novel is organized around the battles of the unusual woman in a hostile society, not around the salutary effects of ridicule. Similarly, in *One of Our Conquerors* (1891) and *The Amazing Marriage* (1895), Meredith is more interested in characters working their way through difficult problems within society than in the reform of the whole basis of society. He concentrates on partial victories for the individual, despite the pain and the price involved, rather than on either the sweeping reform suggested by the comic spirit or the hopeless and ultimate dilemma conveyed by classical tragedy.

In the variety of Meredith's fictional concerns, the individual in revolt against his world gains the author's consistent sympathy. And women, limited most severely by Victorian convention, were the principal examples. Throughout all his fiction, one of the only consistent attitudes is the conviction that women were frequently the victims of the shams, hypocrisies, and double standards of nineteenth century society. Richard Feverel feels strongly that women merit as much freedom and consideration as do men. Part of his final failure originates in the fact that he feels so guilty about his affair with Mrs. Mount, which his father's test helped cause, that he does not return to his wife when she needs him most; infidelity is, to Richard, just as serious a crime for husband as it would be for wife.

Women are frequently articulate and perceptive in Meredith's fiction, far from being the pliant and sheltered shadows of their men that the Victorian stereotype encouraged. In *Beauchamp's Career,* for example, the aristocratic women can understand political issues and personal motives far more quickly and easily than can the men in the same society. Part of their understanding is based on their attraction to Nevil, their willingness to listen to such a handsome and energetic young man, but part, too, is based on their recognition of the social issues involved. Meredith comments on Cecilia, who loves and understands Nevil:

> She had merely been very angry on Nevil Beauchamp's behalf, and had dimly seen that a woman can feel insurgent, almost revolutionary, for a personal cause, Tory though her instinct of safety and love of smoothness make her.

In *The Egoist,* women are the first to see through Sir Willoughby's pomp and pretense; Clara is the first to defy Willoughby's wishes openly and even the ever-devoted Laetitia Dale finally perceives the hollowness of the egoist. For Meredith, women have a directness, an honesty, a sense of commitment, often absent in the posturing male who believes the fictions he has himself created. Women like Clara and Diana are wisely realistic about themselves and the worlds in which they operate, capable of responding to the constant shifts and nuances in human relationships. They do not, like Richard Feverel or Nevil Beauchamp, passionately endorse idealistic principles and stick to them no matter what happens. Nor do they, like Percy Dacier, become arrogant and petulant when arrangements don't work out, or, if betrayed in love, run off immediately to declare undying devotion to another. They have too much insight and feeling for such quick and easy consolations.

Meredith's intelligent and complex "new" women are seldom saints. Diana, bitter because Percy Dacier so coldly rejects her, does sell what he had told her in confidence to a newspaper editor. Mrs. Lovell, in *Rhoda Fleming,* is part of the cruel plot to get rid of Dahlia, and has been partially responsible for her husband's death. In both these instances, Meredith provides enough information to extenuate the moral flaw, to retain sympathy for the "new" woman even though she is surrounded with an aura of moral ambivalence. Moral judgment is not, however, the issue, for Meredith defends the "new" woman because of her perception, her honesty, her intelligence, and, as he describes it in the introduction to *Diana of the Crossways,* her "wit." And he defends these qualities against a society—no more swayed completely by moral issues than he   that would castigate these women for not remaining true to the Victorian cliché sweetly smiling at the domestic fireside. Although Meredith does not, in either his novels or his numerous explanatory prefaces, express the conviction that the woman of wit and insight can reform or transform society, can even help achieve the civilized and rational world through her wise mastery of the comic spirit, he does always defend her. His defense is an emotional preference, a demonstration of compassion for Diana and the others, precisely because society so constantly hounds them to be other than they are, so incessantly tries to relegate them to the conventionally passive and domestic role. Sometimes, like Clara and Diana, the "new" woman can win in Meredith's fiction, but, even in winning, she must endure suffering and accept limitations only because she is different.

Trollope recognized the woman of spirit, independence, and intelligence, and he sympathized strongly with her, but, in his world, her acceptance or banishment from society was never solely attributable to her unconventionality. Trollope's "new" heroines were also subjected to good or bad luck and to varying degrees of moral scrutiny, although unconventionality did generally make acceptance more difficult. Thomas Hardy also characterized the "new" woman, but, as in the portrait of Sue Bridehead in *Jude the Obscure,* he dramatically magnified her own neuroses in order to provide her with a role in his melodramatic conflict between the body and the soul. Only Meredith, in describing the "new" woman, consistently defended her newness, her wit, her iconoclasm, invariably contrasting her with the rigid, restricted, shallow woman promoted by the stereotype. Meredith's compassion, more aggressive than that of Trollope or Hardy, focused on the woman, whatever her fate, who had to waste so much of her time and energy defending her right to be what she was. This defense, most visible and articulate in *Diana of the Crossways*, was the nearest Meredith ever came in his fiction to espousing a cause.

Although the sympathy with revolt, particularly that of the spirited and intelligent woman, exists in all Meredith's fiction, this cause seldom provides a unifying theme for an individual novel. Meredith's fiction is crowded with ideas, but the novel seldom coheres around the ideas in the way Dickens' novels do. In the preface to *The Egoist*, Meredith has a passage skeptical about science, discussing the fact that man had placed his confidence in scientific methods and formulations but found them no more helpful than earlier systems or dogmas. The point is there, but is never used, never related to any of the issues demonstrated in the novel; it remains a dangling idea. One of the principal problems in discussing Meredith's fiction is the difficulty in establishing thematic consistency, a sense of where the author stands, for critics are always more comfortable confronting a precisely articulated point of view. In the variety of ideas and characterizations within any one novel Meredith's point of view is often difficult to discover. In *The Ordeal of Richard Feverel*, for example, the final chapter is written from the point of view of Sir Austin's friend, Lady Blandish. Although always close to Sir Austin and the important incidents in the novel, and sensible about the issues that arise from those incidents, Lady Blandish has constantly opposed Sir Austin's system, his science. Her narration of the final chapter, in the form of a letter, gives the whole novel an anti-science point of view, as if Richard is simply the victim of his father's mistaken theories. Yet such an account would leave out not only Richard's own failings and the consequences of accident, but also the gratuitous and unscientific cruelty with which Sir Austin applies his system. There is far more to the disaster of Richard Feverel than Lady Blandish's final statement indicates, yet Meredith articulates no counter to

Lady Blandish and applies no irony to the finality of her over-simplified explanation of the issues of the novel. The point of view is not worked adequately into the structure of the novel.

In *Diana of the Crossways*, the problem concerning point of view arises in another form. Many of the incidents of the novel are seen through Lady Dunstane, always sympathetic to Diana, whose attitudes seem to carry those of the author. Although Lady Dunstane always defends Diana and is right in feeling that Redworth is the only possible man for her, she is not developed fully enough to follow or articulate all the complexities concerning Diana's difficult relationships with society. She excuses but never understands Diana's betrayal of Percy Dacier. Lady Dunstane, as character, is insufficient for the structural role in which she is cast, and the reader is left, with occasionally inserted directions from the author himself, to extrapolate whatever he can of the complexities of Diana's nature and position. All of Meredith's work, even the tightly structured *The Egoist,* is marked by flashes, perceptions, ideas, that are insufficiently embodied within the structure of the novels themselves. The apparatus of thematic consistency, the imps and the book, have caused critics to praise *The Egoist* as the best of Meredith's novels, as that novel in which the material is most carefully controlled. But even *The Egoist,* divided between the framework of a reforming comedy and the substance of the gradual education and development of two heroic individuals, is not always in such clear focus.

Still, *The Egoist* is, as a matter of degree, more consistent and more tightly organized than are Meredith's other novels, although to praise this one novel at the expense of the rest of Meredith's work is to judge the writer on a standard that rather overvalues tidiness and thematic consistency, a standard about which Meredith himself was frequently skeptical and which ignores the vitality, the diversity, and the intellectual energy scattered among much of the rest of the fiction. The opposite hypothesis, the assumption that Meredith created a world in which no plans work, no experience can be systematized, also cannot be justified consistently in the fiction. *The Ordeal of Richard Feverel* may seem to focus on the folly of human planning or system, but that is only part of the novel, and other novels such as *The Egoist* and *Diana of the Crossways* present central characters whose careful and systematic effort can, in some measure, control what happens to them in the world. Meredith was interested in a series of observations, ideas, causes, and he incorporated these ideas into characters and scenes in fictional form. But the form itself seems dictated by momentary and intermittent convenience, and the use of the form is not centrally part of what the author is saying about human experience.

For the critic, patterns of theme and structure do not generally provide the most rewarding ways to approach Meredith's fiction. In fact, Sir Willoughby Patterne may be, in part, a satire directed against the logical and understandable attempt to schematize all experience, to understand through the formulation of logical and consistent patterns. As Willoughby is nothing beneath the pattern, so Meredith's fictional world is falsified by the critical imposition of too consistent a thematic pattern. Even examining the pattern of scenes or organization, the dramatic structure, of a particular Meredith novel is likely to distort the novel completely, for Meredith tended to omit crucial scenes, referring to the central actions only indirectly or at some later time, as Diana's disastrous original marriage to Warwick is discussed and portrayed solely through her sketchy letters to her friends. Meredith seems almost too anxious to avoid the possibilities of a melodramatic scene, almost evasive. Clarity is sometimes sacrificed for a defensive sophistication.

In addition to the variety of ideas and attitudes and the sometimes perplexing shifts in point of view, Meredith developed a tremendous variety of styles and tones. *The Ordeal of Richard Feverel* is alternately lyrical and crisply satirical; *Rhoda Fleming* combines comic rustic good humor with a thoroughly romantic, almost bathetic, presentation of the heroines; *Diana of the Crossways* develops essayistic examinations of the complexities of Diana's position and relieves the effect of these with sharply dramatic and satiric vignettes of the social scene around Diana as well as with lyrical passages dwelling on Diana's passions. Frequently, Meredith's prose is high-flown, almost bombastic. Sometimes, he uses this excessive quality effectively, as in the following passage from *The Ordeal of Richard Feverel* in which Sir Austin has just been brought a report of Richard's behavior:

"Exactly," said the baronet. "As I foresaw. At this period an in-satiate appetite is accompanied by a fastidious palate. Nothing but the quintessences of existence, and those in exhaustless supplies, will satisfy this craving, which is not to be satisfied! Hence his bitterness. Life can furnish no food fitting for him. The strength and purity of his energies have reached to an almost divine height, and roam through the Inane!"

Sir Austin's pompous and elaborate language represents the artificial nature of his system and demonstrates the cold arro-gance that allows him to toy with his son so disastrously. Mere-dith puffs up the language in order to satirize the character.

But the puffed up language is not always so relevant or so successful. As in the following passage from *Rhoda Fleming*, in which Rhoda discovers how inadvertently cruel she has been to her sister, Meredith's elaboration seems to drown and falsify the perceptions:

"You deceived me," she murmured; and again, "You deceived me." Rhoda did not answer. In trying to understand why her sister should imagine it, she began to know that she had in truth de-ceived Dahlia. The temptation to drive a frail human creature to do the thing which was right, had led her to speak falsely for a good purpose. Was it not righteously executed? Away from the tragic figure in the room, she might have thought so, but the horror in the eyes and voice of this awakened Sacrifice, struck away the support of theoretic justification. Great pity for the poor enmeshed life, help-less there, and in a woman's worst peril,—looking either to madness, or to death, for an escape—drowned her reason in a heavy cloud of tears.

Meredith's phrases frequently follow the allusions and sugges-tions they establish, as one image leads to another whether or not the succession or association is controlled by the issue under dis-cussion. When Clara Middleton is first introduced in *The Egoist*, Meredith writes: "She had money and health and beauty, the triune of perfect starriness, which makes all men astronomers." The reference to all men as astronomers is suggested by the fore-going image, but it is never used or made relevant in the subse-quent development of the passage or the character. Rather, it is an associated elaboration. When Meredith does use symbols, like the red-stained handkerchief that Mrs. Lovell in *Rhoda Fleming* carries hidden in the cameo brooch she wears over her bosom, the emblem of her secret guilt, the symbol is frequently over-dramatized and reverberates heavily throughout the novel. Far more often, however, metaphors and images are temporary, dec-orative, a richness that spins off, fascinates momentarily, and evaporates. As Laetitia Dale shrewdly comments, in reference to Mrs. Mountstuart Jenkinson who superficially pins people with her imagistic phrases, "Similes have the merit of satisfying the finder of them, and cheating the hearer." Meredith's rich prose seems sometimes similarly self-indulgent. Full of digressions, the style of all the novels is copious, diffuse, allusive, crowding in relevant or irrelevant connections, embroidering a subject comi-cally or seriously. These additions give the prose a quality of crowded energy, of spinning insights and ideas, even though they do not always provide a sense of precision or direction.

Meredith's dramatic scenes, however, are individually of-ten crisp and brilliant: the scenes in Venice in the beginning of *Beauchamp's Career* in which Nevil first falls in love with the French girl, Reneé; the witty exchanges at the dinner parties in *Diana of the Crossways;* the arrival of his father's representative, Adrian, at Richard's love-nest on the Isle of Wight; much of the conversation in *The Egoist* through which Clara learns how ludicrous both her father and Sir Willoughby are. Meredith could write sharply, brilliantly, lightly; he could also write heavily, didactically, portentously; he seldom, for the space of a whole novel, wrote consistently. In addition to the deft comic touches, the witty exchanges, and the effective descriptive scenes, Meredith also wrote skillfully satiric passages in a more compli-cated manner. In *Diana of the Crossways,* for example, the epi-sode in which Diana, riding to Lady Dunstane's, is overturned by a drunken coachman, allows Meredith to satirize the coachman's rustic self-assurance and folly and, simultaneously, to demon-strate how Diana's merciless wit only aggravates the situation. From this, Meredith moves to his general point and quickly de-velops a short essay about wit being alien and antagonistic to the English. Characteristically, he commands more sympathy for his abrasive heroine through the inserted essay than he does in the presentation of the incident itself.

Meredith's novels are highly literary in the sense that

many of the techniques seem adaptations from other literary sources rather than devices shaped by the demands of the fictional material. The stylized group, divided into good and bad, anatomized into particular virtues and vices, that surrounds Sir Austin Feverel on his country estate is reminiscent of Squire Allworthy's dependents in *Tom Jones*. In each instance, the whole morality play focuses on watching the development of a young man. *Diana of the Crossways* uses the device of the novel within the novel; *The Egoist* uses the aristocratic prattle of the local gentry as an imperceptive and mistaken chorus, a counterpoint to the development of the hero and heroine. All these devices have literary origins; none of them is central to the structure of the novel in which it appears.

Meredith's use of coincidence also seems more literary than essential. Richard Feverel finds a house for Lucy in London, a respectable place from which they can marry, and discovers that the friendly landlady is his loving old nurse. In *Rhoda Fleming*, the young man who works on the Fleming farm is an aristocrat in disguise and his father has an estate conveniently close to the one on which the Blancoves are plotting against Dahlia; the young man's most helpful friend turns out to have known and loved Mrs. Lovell, the Blancove's instigator, when both were in India. This use of coincidence is far from that in Dickens' novels in which the fabric of coincidence suggests a world where human actions have inevitable physical and moral consequences. Rather, in Meredith's work, coincidence is a trick to resolve the plot, a literary convention.

The distinction of Meredith's fiction often resides in bits and pieces, in comic scenes and sharply evocative descriptions, in comments about man or society that flash into the novels. Society is observed and depicted with intelligent commentary, but Meredith's social attitudes are no more consistent than his fictional themes. Often Meredith displays an attitude or develops an idea, only to reverse it in subsequent chapters or a subsequent novel. In a number of the novels, the aristocracy or the leaders of London social and commercial life are the principal targets for Meredith's satire. In *The Ordeal of Richard Feverel*, he frequently lampoons Sir Austin's narrow world and the indolent selfishness of the sychophants who surround him, each ticketed with his own brand of narcissism. In *Diana of the Crossways*, the most scathing satire is applied to the wealthy London gossips, the malicious and self-seeking people who gather at Lady Wathin's assemblies. Yet, members of other classes are satirized as well. The snobbery and the complete acceptance of the most vacuous of the aristocracy's values characterizes the commercial lower middle classes in *Evan Harrington*. In *Rhoda Fleming*, Meredith presents numerous conversations among farmers and workers which demonstrate that no one listens to or answers anyone else, that all human interchange among these people is a kind of comic, self-locked noncommunication. This novel, more markedly perhaps than any of Meredith's others, upholds the values of the aristocracy. Although all the wealthy and well-born Blancoves are concerned only for themselves and deceive the innocent heroines, they all confess and repent at the end. The only unrepentant villain in the novel is Sedgett, a lower class hireling who has not the grace or the honesty to acknowledge the harm he has done.

Beauchamp's Career, the novel that deals most explicitly with politics, yields no clear and unambiguous political position, just as the other novels yield few unequivocal generalized statements about social classes. Nevil Beauchamp, an aristocrat by birth, seeks election to Parliament as a radical under the influence of his mentor, Dr. Shrapnel. The Tories in the novel, most of Nevil's relatives and friends, look ridiculous as they talk of Nevil betraying his class and abandoning his roots, as if all political principles should be genetically conveyed. At the same time, in conversations in the novel, some of the Tory arguments are given a good deal of force and coherence. When the Tories complain of the insidious influence of Manchester, of what industry has done to the lives of great sections of the working class, of the national moral decline wrought by an all-consuming interest in commerce and trade, Meredith seems to be on their side, to support a rejection of industry and Manchester that Nevil would strongly oppose.

Dr. Shrapnel's letter enunciating his principles attacks the "ego" implicit in an hereditary crown and peerage, in the whole notion of an aristocracy and social stratification. But Meredith also demonstrates the "ego" implicit in Dr. Shrapnel's position:

the pride of intransigent self-righteousness. To a certain extent, Meredith sympathizes with Nevil's radical political position, as he sympathizes with the radical struggles for Italian freedom in *Sandra Belloni* (1864) and *Vittoria* (1866). At the same time, he sees the radical position in politics as forcing out some of the virtues, the concern for others less fortunate, the freedom, the expansiveness, of the aristocracy at its infrequent best. In addition, despite frequent discussions of the subject, *Beauchamp's Career* is not centrally a novel about politics. Nevil is defeated not because of the truth or falsity of his political ideas, nor because of the wisdom or stupidity of an all-powerful society. Rather, it is Nevil himself, his vulnerability, his sudden changes, his willingness to stake all on single romantic gestures, who insures his own political impotence. The novel analyzes the romantic in an unromantic environment, the man who would break away from society's conventional mold if only he could decide for more than two consecutive scenes which mold he wanted to break. Nevil in his intense and varying loves is at least as important to the novel as Nevil engaged in politics, and the novel is far from a demonstration of consistent political or social principles.

Meredith is even more ambivalent about certain changes in nineteenth century society. He clearly saw both sides of the industrial changes symbolized by Manchester, and he presents both sides of the controversy over the extensive building of the railroads. Redworth, the man who wins the heroine in *Diana of the Crossways,* is a progressive capitalist who makes a fortune from the new railroads and believes that easier transportation will greatly benefit society. Yet most of the other characters, including Diana, regard the railroads as dirty, enslaving commercialism carving up the country. Even a kind old farmer, who tries to show Redworth the way to Crossways one dark night, regrets the noise, dirt, and intrusion of the railroads. And Meredith himself regards Redworth as someone not quite heroic, someone slightly tainted by dirty industrial money. Yet the latter is always loyal and understanding in regard to Diana, and he clearly occupies the hero's role in the story. The novel ends on a note of second-best, as if Diana, because of all the problems with her first husband and with society, has had to settle herself in the comfortable but very slightly graceless and uncouth world provided by the railroad magnate. This is only a small price for the survival of her wit and independence, qualities so fiercely threatened by the rest of society, but it is a price. Even in Meredith's fiction, social attitudes change very slowly.

Social and political references are common in Meredith's fictional world, but these references are different from the density and completeness of social depiction in Trollope's novels. Trollope drew a vast social map, created a metaphorical county, and worked out his version of the conditions under which man and society operated. Meredith's creations are both less complete and less mutually coherent; they are points, references, an example leading to a generalization, a striking idea, a type satirized, a stereotyped opinion overthrown. No density of social depiction or characterization gives coherence to Meredith's fiction, just as no ethical program or consistently reforming principle gives shape to his treatment of human experience.

Meredith's sense of compassion is also less a constant attitude, less a permanently visible suffusion than that of Trollope. Always more sophisticated and defensive, always connecting his perceptions with more general ideas, Meredith's sense of compassion toward his characters is cloaked, protected, by his wit, his ideas, and his general astringency. Occasionally, Meredith's heroes and heroines manage to win through, like Clara and Vernon in their gesture against the past and the society of egoism, or, in the limited sense of survival, like Diana Warwick; more frequently, especially in the earlier fiction, the hero or heroine is hounded to dramatic disaster like Richard Feverel, Dahlia Fleming, or Nevil Beauchamp. Yet, the victories are either gestures or severe reductions of the individual's possibilities. Meredith's world, like Trollope's, yields no justice, no divine principle, no idea that can serve as a comprehensive guide to conduct, despite the many ideas played with throughout the novels. And underneath all the wit, astringency, and philosophizing, Meredith maintains a sense of compassion, a recognition that no "truth," no justice, can be applied meaningfully and consistently to all human experience.

Meredith's compassion is connected with his romanticism, his frequent sympathy for the witty and talented woman opposed by the conventions of her society or the young man rebelling against his restrictive social moorings. He often venerated the effort to get beyond the ordinary or the usual, glorified the impulse to rebel against the solid, dull, respectable, self-satisfied. In addition, Meredith's images are often romantic. Frequently, when his characters do understand and feel close to one another, like Redworth and Diana at the end of the novel, or Nevil and Cecilia, Meredith describes the communication in terms of a blazing fire or a sense of electricity that momentarily transforms the character. Yet the romanticism like the compassion is often turned around, made ludicrous, as Meredith always retained the capacity to play with his own attitudes and convictions, to protect his own vulnerability. He never stands for very long in Trollope's kind of open sympathy; for Meredith, compassion becomes aggressive as in the gesture of Vernon and Clara's victory and the essays defending Diana's wit, or melodramatic in the totally undeserved defeats of Richard Feverel and Dahlia Fleming. Compassion is a weapon he uses to defend the romantic hero or heroine, the person who insists on being himself, from the assaults of conventional society. Yet this kind of compassion, so much more militant and potentially melodramatic than Trollope's, could seem banal, one-sided, itself vulnerable in a world of growing sophistication. To protect his compassion for his Claras, Dianas, and Richards—and Meredith's compassion is generally confined to the hero at odds with the world, not extended to all of society —he also satirizes his principal romantic characters and ideas. In all the novels, Meredith makes fun of the destructive fire of continuous romantic blazes or the incessant crackle of constant electrical flashes. The romantic heroes are sometimes ludicrous: Richard is occasionally pompously and ridiculously idealistic; Clara is sometimes arch and Vernon dense; Diana, especially when distraught, can be gratuitously vicious. Meredith even satirizes his favorite romantic hero, the man, like Nevil Beauchamp, who would give all for love or stake everything upon a principle in defiance of society.

A more interesting and complex comic creation than Sir Willoughby Patterne, Nevil illustrates the extremes of veneration and satire that Meredith uses to both illustrate and defend his sense of compassion. Although Nevil's dynamism stirs many women, he is apt to desert one for a quixotic leap to another lady in distress. Finally, he marries the quietly sane and practical Jenny, Dr. Shrapnel's ward and the only woman who does not especially love Nevil, a hard blow for the romantic hero to accept. The scene in which Nevil successfully proposes, where Jenny's concern for Dr. Shrapnel and her efforts to prevent Nevil from going out into the cold trick her into a promise, is a masterfully handled comic treatment of romance reduced to domesticity. And Nevil, the rebellious opponent of all conventional forms of worship, soon agrees to both a church wedding and baptism for his child. Not only have his romantic and radical politics come to nothing, but his personal romanticism is absorbed into the conventional framework of Victorian society. His death is less a martyrdom than the final spoof, the final reduction, of the romantic hero. Similarly, Diana Warwick, for all her romantic gestures against the society around her, is brought to earth, with the author's approval, by her need for money. She finally marries Redworth partially because his money can free her from the anxiety and ambivalence of the "new woman" in society. Her marriage is presented as a welcome relief.

Meredith's kind of self-mockery is evident in his switch in the use of the term "romantic" in *Diana of the Crossways*. For most of the novel, Diana is referred to as the romantic heroine and her relationship with Percy Dacier is described as the overwhelmingly passionate and romantic attachment. Yet, after Diana betrays Dacier and Dacier quickly dashes across London to propose to Miss Asper, Meredith plays with the term: in a chapter entitled, "Reveals how the True Heroine of Romance comes finally to her Time of Triumph," Dacier thinks of the heretofore dull Miss Asper as genuinely romantic and dismisses Diana as the flawed and "flecked heroine of Reality." At this point, Meredith advocates the idea of the heroine of reality, however flawed, rather than the postures and self-deception of romance.

Such instances of the rational destruction of romantic postures do not, however, indicate a consistent point of view. Nor can Meredith's fiction be explained as shuttling between the critical polarities of "reason" and "romanticism," for, as *The Egoist* illustrates, the puncturing of pretense associated with "reason" is both positively connected with and subordinate to the development of rebellion associated with "romanticism." The "reason," protecting the romantic vulnerability, combines with the honesty, the independence, the acknowledgment of human emotion, and the rebellious individuality implicit in "romanticism." That Meredith's "romanticism" and his sense of compassion were sheltered, often disguised, defended against their own possible excesses by rational satire does not diminish the romantic sympathy or the compassion for the human being in conflict with a sterile society that has allowed its mechanistic perpetuation to become "truth." The comic spirit of reform explained in the essay does not guide or control Meredith's fiction. Rather, the comic reform, like the interspersed general ideas, like the "Philosophy" that the author in several of his prefaces wanted to incorporate into his fiction, is a kind of persiflage. This persiflage, often exciting and effective in itself, never coheres into an attitude or a system, remains a defensive decoration. Meredith was far from a philosophical novelist in the sense that a philosophy can control, organize, the writer's material; but the philosophy, the persiflage, does prevent the compassion from standing as an undigested suffusion, and does give the novels an urbane and complicated tone. In addition, the persiflage represents the human being, his questions, his attempts to systematize, his inconsistency, his flashes of insight and idea that never cohere. Behind the persiflage in Meredith's fiction is another version of the romantic hero challenging a world he can never defeat, another instance of a description that renders compassion the only ultimate reaction possible. The wit, the astringent comments, and the ideas sparkle and fascinate; they also defend the compassion that lingers in this incoherent and unsystematized fictional world.

I V

THOMAS HARDY

Like Trollope's Barsetshire, Hardy's Wessex (the fictional name for the large area of southwestern England in which all of his novels take place) is a comprehensive and carefully particular analogue of nineteenth-century English experience. Hardy even provides maps and geographical information, for each of the major novels is concerned with a different section of Wessex: seacoast, dairy farm, market town, heath, pasture land on the downs, country estate, cathedral town with a growing industrial proletariat. Each of the major novels also treats of Wessex at a different time, spanning the nineteenth century from the period of fear of Napoleon's invasion in the first decade, central to *The Trumpet-Major* (1880), to the era of bleak rootlessness in the changing society of the nineties, integral to *Jude the Obscure* (1896).

Hardy's fictional territory is not organized by a message, a "truth" that might explain human experience; his reconstruction is phenomenological and symbolic of the diversity of nineteenth-century England, not pointedly fabulistic. Wessex, far more varied and more comprehensive than Trollope's Barsetshire, retains its fascination because so much of life is so skillfully reconstructed, and because the subject is always imperfect man in his confusing and unsatisfactory world. Hardy's novels create, at many different levels of experience, nineteenth-century man; Wessex, in copious detail and complexity, is where and how he lives. The very density of Wessex, the detailed proliferation of the imaginary world, elicits the compassion, the human sympathy, so evident in almost every one of Hardy's novels.

Yet, in creating Wessex, Hardy clearly did not intend merely to duplicate the confusions, uncertainties, and multiplicities of the world he experienced. He meant Wessex to illustrate laws about human behavior. Hardy wrote no autobiography and few essays, but the two-volume biography his wife published after he died contains so many quotations from his notebooks, and relies so strictly on what he said and thought that critics have unanimously and justifiably regarded it as an autobiography. In it Hardy sometimes talked of art, always treating art as a means of giving direction, shape, and meaning to human experience. He disdained fiction that merely records or duplicates, invariably thought of worthwhile art as providing meanings and messages for man. He compared fiction to a carpet with a pattern, a pattern that could both unify a particular novel and formulate an ethical or moral direction for the puzzled human being. Something of the conscious assurance of Hardy's theories about fiction is apparent in the following passage quoted from his notebooks:

> A story must be exceptional enough to justify its telling. We tale-tellers are all Ancient Mariners, and none of us is warranted in stopping Wedding Guests (in other words, the hurrying public) unless he has something more unusual to relate than the ordinary experience of every average man and woman.
>
> The whole secret of fiction and the drama—in the constructional part—lies in the adjustment of things unusual to things eternal and universal. The writer who knows exactly how exceptional, and how non-exceptional, his events should be made, possesses the key to the art.

Fortunately, neither the easy distinction between the "exceptional" and the "non-exceptional" nor the assurance that any writer can work out what is "eternal and universal" can be derived from the fiction itself. Hardy's fiction is too full, too humane, and too richly inconsistent to be unlocked by any single "key."

One of Hardy's novels conforms more closely to an aesthetic pattern than does any of the others. *The Mayor of Casterbridge* (1886) is, in both theme and structure, a kind of classical tragedy. The hero, Michael Henchard, illustrates excessive reliance on his own changing emotions from the drunken moment when he sells his wife and daughter at the county fair, through his disastrous attempts to predict the season's weather, to his final attempt to restore himself to his position in Casterbridge by welcoming royalty. A large, zealous, aggressive, often generous man, Henchard is destroyed by his own temper, his need for drink, his hot excessive humanity which is a kind of pride, a reliance on his emotional self. Balanced against Henchard is the cool, calculating, rational Scotsman, Farfrae, whose judiciousness enables him to survive and to supplant Henchard as the mayor of Casterbridge. The contrast between the sympathetic although doomed Henchard and the calmly successful Farfrae is reflected and underlined in a parallel contrast between the two principal women in the novel: the tempestuous and rebellious Lucetta who is destroyed, the docile and devoted Elizabeth-Jane who, although given sufficient motive for rebellion, remains calmly rational and becomes the suitable wife for Farfrae. Throughout the tragedy of Henchard, and the subsidiary tragedy of Lucetta, Hardy's message remains consistent. Man needs order, control, a rational balance between the claims of his individual feelings and the exterior universe; no matter how difficult, to curb his energy and his pride is imperative for man.

The novel, with a tightness of structure not always characteristic of Hardy's work, reinforces the classical theme of the necessity to restrain excessive emotion and to subsume individual judgment to the community's rationality, provides a form like that of Greek drama. At the end of the novel Elizabeth-Jane and Farfrae dance, much as they danced when they first met, a ritual that is a public and consistent frame for the action. As in classical tragedy, public events mark all the significant stages. The first scene, Henchard selling his wife at the county fair, reveals in public his destructive hot temper; his final disclosure is similarly open. Lucetta is destroyed by the effect of the skimmity-ride, the grotesque popular parade and ceremony that reveal to the world that she and Henchard have secretly lived together. The townspeople, like a vulgar and brutal chorus, comment on all significant action, are frequently given the final words of the scene or chapter. Some of the plot concentrates on origins, the question of who is whose child, as the fact that Elizabeth-Jane is Newson's daughter, not Henchard's, is gradually revealed. To emphasize the theme that focuses on the disaster of personal pride and the importance of submitting the individual will to the wider claims of the social and exterior world, Hardy adopted a consistent structure that made all things in the novel publicly known, that, like the structure of Greek tragedy, revealed the darkness of man and exposed it to public light and judgment.

Classical tragedy requires both a flaw in the otherwise heroic individual and a universe which judges the flaw mercilessly but justly. *The Mayor of Casterbridge* assumes a permanently just universe, one in which a proper balance of reason and emotion, an ability to temper the energy of the strong individual by submission to the exterior concerns of the public society, can insure success and survival. Man can know the principles by which his world is governed; and his defeat, although sympathetically understood and made inevitable by his flaw, is consequently his own responsibility. In his other best-known novels, *The Return of the Native* (1878), *Tess of the D'Urbervilles* (1891), and *Jude the Obscure,* however, Hardy postulates no such just and knowable universe. The principal characters possess heroic flaws, but the novels provide no consistent framework in terms of which the flaws can be judged and responsibility assigned. As a result, despite the quasi-tragic atmosphere, structure, plot, and theme seldom cohere neatly.

The relationship between the principal characters and a dominant unifying theme is far less clear. In *The Return of the Native,* Clym Yeobright is caught in a combination of rebellion from and dependence on his mother, and this renders him an inadequate husband for Eustacia. At the same time, the force of his psychological incapacity is never made sufficiently clear or important to precipitate all the dire consequences of action and judgment attributable to Clym in the novel. Similarly, Eustacia is caught between the passion and force of her feelings and the narrow darkness of her environment, between her sexuality and her addiction to shabby finery, between her dignified pride and her petty lies. Yet all of these conflicts are, in the novel, never shaped in such a way that they explain her fate. Society, even the crude society of the heath, is not made rigidly exclusive in a way that would necessarily demolish Eustacia for her sexuality and her rebellion.

Rather, in *The Return of the Native,* part of the disaster seems gratuitous, pasted on, although part of it is also explainable in terms of the characters involved. *Tess of the D'Urbervilles* illustrates a similar imbalance between the development of character and the extent of destruction into which that character is pushed. Tess is too trusting, too innocent, for the changing world in which she lives, yet Hardy makes her mistakes too trifling for a convincing demonstration that character is the principal determinant of fate. Jude Fawley, the hero of *Jude the Obscure,* is also hounded by circumstance, pushed down every time he tries to rise, although only a small proportion of his fate can be explained in terms of his character. For all the disasters in these novels, for all the defeated aspirations and the destroyed possibilities, some additional explanation is necessary, something beyond the tragic equation that man's failings and mistakes cause his defeats within the context of an impartial exterior world.

In terms of plot, Hardy tried to fill the void, alter the imbalance between natural cause and disastrous effect, with a series of coincidences, a series of accidents for which the characters could not be held responsible. Yet, in Hardy's novels, coincidence is sometimes so massive, so central, that it seems to dominate the plot completely. In *The Return of the Native,* for example, Mrs. Yeobright's visit to reconcile herself with her son and daughter-in-law just as Eustacia is talking with Wildeve is a plausible coincidence, accident made possible and convincing. But, for the function of the plot, Hardy must add that Clym has only just entered the house yet is so soundly asleep that he cannot hear his mother knock, that Eustacia, after dismissing Wildeve, rushes to answer the door but cannot see the departing Mrs. Yeobright even though characters usually spot others miles away across the heath in daylight, that Clym is dreaming of his mother and utters the word aloud which causes Eustacia to think he has answered the door.

Other improbable accidents inundate Hardy's plots. Documents that might have explained and patched up breaches between husband and wife invariably misfire: Hardy toys for pages with Eustacia's just missing Clym's conciliatory letter; Angel

Clare never finds the confession that Tess slides under his door. *Tess of the D'Urbervilles* is full of massive coincidence, of the incredibly constant mistiming that leads the reader to say, "If only she had known a moment sooner or if only he had waited to finish breakfast." In both these novels, coincidence so dominates the plot that it works against the characterizations. The characters of Eustacia and Tess are never developed fully enough to account for the disasters that overtake them; at the same time, the accidents designed to fill the void are granted such overwhelming prominence that the characters are swamped. No balance between character and accident is ever achieved, no consistent point of view permits either Eustacia or Tess to represent a coherent statement about either the nature of woman or the nature of the universe.

Coincidence also figures significantly in the plot of *The Mayor of Casterbridge*. Here, the old woman who sells furmity at county fairs just happens along and reveals Henchard's past at the crucial moment in the novel. Yet, this coincidence is justifiable, for the furmity woman's revelation, like the coincidental revelations in many of Dickens' novels, is part of the structure and point of view of the novel, part of a statement that human actions have invariable and inescapable consequences, that all will be made known. In contrast, the vast accidents in *The Return of the Native, Tess of the D'Urbervilles,* and many of the other novels just happen at the most inopportune moments possible and hover over the novels as instances of gratuitous mischance.

The overwhelming reliance on coincidence in the plots can be attributed to Hardy's clumsiness, for he clearly was not a minutely neat and carefully controlled writer either in describing a particular dramatic scene or in working out a complicated and intricate plot. An early scene in *The Trumpet-Major* contains both stage directions in the middle of a conversation and one character calling "in a slanting voice towards the staircase" downstairs to another. The description of Tess's seduction by Alec D'Urberville, accomplished while Tess is asleep in the woods, is incredible both in terms of physical probability and of Tess's character; the scene is a clumsy device to accommodate Tess's "purity" to the literal-minded strictness of ethical codes in

Victorian fiction. *The Return of the Native* is full of ominous hints and forebodings, heavy and abstract prefigurations of the doom prepared for the following chapter. *Far from the Madding Crowd* (1874), in which the heroine chooses from among three men, ends with an essay explaining why the heroine has finally chosen correctly, although the whole novel has already demonstrated the wisdom of her choice in far more convincing detail. Seldom a meticulous or subtle craftsman, Hardy frequently spoils some of his best effects with heaviness, moralizing, and underscoring the unpredictability of human concerns.

Thirty or forty years ago, critical custom explained Hardy's excessive use of accident and coincidence as part of a philosophy, a worked-out position that malevolent accident governed the universe. Yet Hardy called himself a "meliorist," a man who believed that human effort could ameliorate the harshness of an indifferent universe, that conditions could become better for man. The idea is inconsistent on two different levels with that of a universe governed by a principle of malevolent accident: meliorism is an ethical position relevant to the question of what man can do about his position, not a statement about the nature of the universe; in addition, if the principle of malevolence really were universal, none of man's efforts, melioristic or otherwise, could alter his fate. Various phrases throughout Hardy's work, like the statement "the president of the Immortals, in Aeschylean phrase, had ended his sport with Tess," seem, on first inspection, to substantiate the theory that Hardy had some concept of a malign power dominating the universe. Yet the novel itself does not substantiate the phrase. Tess's disaster is caused partially by her own innocence and foolishness, by the cruelty and indifference of a society interested only in class and money, and by a shadowy doom never articulated into consistency or philosophy. Hardy also, in the same novel, makes fun of those who would philosophize about a principle of benevolence in the universe, about "Nature's holy plan," indicating the shallowness of such wide theorizing. Certainly he could recognize that a rigid theory of universal malevolence is just as shallow.

In *The Return of the Native,* Hardy's view of the idea that his characters have been doomed by a malevolent universal force changes back and forth. Eustacia blames forces beyond her control—the "Prince of Darkness"—yet Hardy's attitude toward her shifts: at times, he seems to accept and endorse her explanations; at other times, he depicts her as full of grandiose self-pity; again, he advances plausible environmental explanations for her actions, her past in Budmouth and her expectations of Paris. Clym also sometimes attributes his failures to the operation of universal principles, but Hardy carefully shows that Clym, through his own psychological inadequacies, rejects sex and Eustacia and retreats into the cold shadow of his mother's influence. He even, after his mother's death, becomes his mother's voice in dealing with Thomasin. Yet toward the end of the novel, in summing up Clym's fate and the changes in his character, Hardy seems to subscribe to exactly the sort of universal theory that his characterizations often, in fact, deny:

> He did sometimes think he had been ill-used by fortune, so far as to say that to be born is a palpable dilemma, and that instead of men aiming to advance in life with glory they should calculate how to retreat out of it with shame. But that he and his had been sarcastically and pitilessly handled in having such irons thrust into their souls he did not maintain long. It is usually so, except with the sternest of men. Human beings, in their generous endeavour to construct a hypothesis that shall not degrade a First Cause, have always hesitated to conceive a dominant power of lower moral quality than their own; and even while they sit down and weep by the waters of Babylon, invent excuses for the oppression which prompts their tears.

Here, Hardy shows Clym unperceptive for only momentarily realizing that his failures have a universal cause. Such instances that imply some general philosophy behind Hardy's treatment of individuals are seldom illustrated by the vastly more complex characterizations in the novels.

The Woodlanders (1887) also contains many references to universal principles and first causes. At one point, Hardy derives the great principle of the "Unfulfilled Intention, which makes life what it is," as if he is trying to establish a universal formula even out of the fact that one does not exist. At another point, he talks of an "intangible Cause which has shaped the situation no less for the offenders than the offended." But, in context, the capitalized "Cause" is a linguistic exaggeration rather than an explanation. Similarly, Hardy talks of the "divinity" who shaped the attitudes of the villagers toward a particular character, but that "divinity" is just ordinary social snobbery. In this as in the other novels, Hardy's language expands to cosmic proportions, even though this language does not necessarily indicate the presence of a cosmic theory or a consistent universal explanation for man's fate. The cosmic language seems automatic, expanding, explosive, sometimes heavy, a human concern that radiates outward rather than the documentation of a coherent philosophy or theory about man.

Like his language, Hardy's imagery automatically reaches toward the cosmic and universal. *Two on a Tower* (1882) tells the story of a love affair between a poor young man and a wealthy aristocratic woman eight years older than he, a story which begins as a rather light romance and ends in melodrama. The young man is an astronomer, and images from his work permeate the novel. But the slightness of the novel jars against the constant references to stars and heavens, the microcosmic images, the scanning of human horizons. All the astronomical parallels give the work a dimension that has no parallel in the development of the plot or the characters, as if Hardy is adding a message he never makes coherent in more conventional novelistic terms. A simple description of the terrain around the mill in *The Trumpet-Major* has "footpaths crossed in different directions, like meridians at the pole." In *The Woodlanders,* two characters go for a walk in the woods at night and are immediately "part of the pattern in the great web of human doings then weaving in both hemispheres from the White Sea to Cape Horn"; small villages may be narrow and provincial, but are capable of "dramas of a grandeur and unity truly Sophoclean." In the same novel, in describing the way the unfaithful husband, Fitzpiers, loves, Hardy compares him to the lower organisms, like paramecia, in which partition causes a multiplied existence rather than death. All these cosmic and organic images do not function structurally, are not part of patterns consistently manifest and meaningful. Rather, they are exaggerations, fictional exuberances, that add an unsystematic weight and dimension to the novels. From one point of view, many of these images are pretentious, too elaborate for the frameworks in which they occur; from another point

of view, these images are rich and full, giving the novels an atmosphere of greater meaning than can be contained in plot and
character, an intimation of man dimly conscious of more than he
can explain and assimilate, of a fullness and interconnectedness
within human experience.

Many of Hardy's descriptions concentrate on nature, relate man to the natural world around him. Often the use of nature conveys an extension or elaboration of human emotions. In
Far from the Madding Crowd, when the heroine, the passionate
and troubled Bathsheba Everdene, is bothered by the hostility of
her suitors toward each other and wonders what to do, she goes
out at night and gazes at the "indecisive and palpitating stars."
When her shepherd, Gabriel Oak, in love with Bathsheba but regarding himself as socially and financially beneath her, works
furiously to shield her harvested grain from an impending storm
because her husband has drunkenly abandoned his responsibilities, Hardy projects Gabriel's emotions into the exterior world
by writing of "an infuriated universe." Whole chapters of this
novel are dominated by the weather or images of the forces of
nature: Sergeant Troy demonstrates his indifference to the farm
and responsibility in a chapter permeated with dry, sultry, brood-
ing weather, the too thickly ominous calm before the storm; an
earlier chapter, which initially presented the attraction between
Bathsheba and Sergeant Troy, works entirely in imagery of soft,
luxuriant movement, riding through hollows and foliage, playing with swords and cutting off a lock of hair, all entirely sexual
imagery even though the chapter ends with a single chaste kiss.
In these instances, the use of nature and natural imagery is not
merely decorative; rather, the sense of nature magnifies the human emotion, provides a richness and depth for the description
of human activities, a sense of human importance. This sense is
particularly relevant to a novel like *Far from the Madding
Crowd,* in which the characters, like Bathsheba, slowly come to
recognize their own passions, feelings, earthiness. The man-
centered use of nature emphasizes Hardy's tremendous sense of
compassion for his characters, for all human beings.

The use of the heath in *The Return of the Native* is a
similarly humanistic extension of nature. Frequently, the characters are described in terms of the heath, related to the ants,

moths, parasites, and flowers that crowd the thick foliage; at the same time, the trees and foliage are given human characteristics, weep and sing and suffer pain. The heath becomes a vaster, more complicated, and more profound chart of human nature than Hardy might otherwise have been able to describe. The extension of man is not only in terms of feelings and emotions, but also in terms of time and space, for the heath has a history and an imagistic cosmology. The major portion of the novel takes a year, goes through each season on the heath; but the single year is made to stand for all years, the seasonal changes for all the moods, complexities, and changes of human emotion. The imagery provides the opportunity for extension, for enrichment, adds an important dimension to the atmosphere of the novel, gives the characterization a greater sense of depth and meaning. But "enrichment," "atmosphere," and "depth" are not words that connote a coherent and rational philosophical position. At the same time, the fact that Hardy's novels cannot be explained in terms of a coherent theory of the nature of man does not necessarily indicate that his images are just pretentious decoration. Suggestion of meaning is not always amenable to rational formulation.

The suggestive quality of Hardy's imagery demonstrates that his sensibility was consistently that of a poet. All his analogies and correspondences, all his verbal extensions, throughout his works, have the kind of immediate connotative force that infuses his language in a poem rather than the consistent pattern of metaphor common to many novels. Understandably, modern poets and critics, operating on the standard that language and image create their own form, value Hardy's poetry highly, more highly than did his contemporaries who often held more formally rigid criteria for poetry. But, apart from changes in literary fashion, Hardy's work is full of the strikingly suggestive image or idea that is not always made manifest in the pattern of the novel. Even many of the melodramatic and improbable events, like the guilt over killing the mother in *The Return of the Native* or selling the wife and child in *The Mayor of Casterbridge,* have a powerful impact as dramatic psychological fantasies, but the realm of psychological fantasy is not sustained or developed in the novel as a whole. Hardy's novels are full of connotations, enriching suggestions, but framed by more conventional structures that restrict or confuse what the imagery suggests.

In describing rural Wessex of the nineteenth century, Hardy often deals with primitive superstitions and omens. Characters, particularly the rustics, frequently interpret experience in terms of traditional and fatalistic superstitions: the position of the moon at a man's birth affecting his nature, the assumption that by his profession the reddleman bears the mark of Cain, the belief in witchcraft. Although Hardy uses the omens and superstitions to give vitality and character to his rustics, he does not subscribe to them or allow them to mold the events of the novels. In *The Return of the Native,* Susan Nunsuch regards Eustacia as a witch and feels Eustacia responsible for her son's illness. Susan makes a wax image of Eustacia, sticking it with pins and burning it on the stormy night on which Eustacia, trying to escape, drowns in the weir beside the heath. Yet Susan's image does not cause Eustacia's death (Hardy develops both Eustacia's character and the circumstances that surround her, fully enough to prevent the reader's assuming that Susan's methods really work) ; the use of superstition, rather, extends the story of Eustacia's doom into another aspect of the heath, a more primitive and superstitious context. The superstition exists along with the account in terms of character and circumstance, adding to the atmosphere and the sense of rustic environment, providing just enough ambivalence to prevent any other easy attribution of cause for Eustacia's death.

Elsewhere, Hardy renders witchcraft as even more mundane. In one of his earliest novels, *Under the Greenwood Tree* (1872) , the young heroine tries to persuade her father to permit her to marry a poor young rustic she loves. She consults a witch and asks that a spell be cast. The witch whispers a long list of directions which is really just advice not to eat. The heroine follows the advice, becomes thin and pale, languishes so convincingly that her fond father can no longer deny her anything. Witchcraft, from Hardy's point of view, often represents wise tradition and common sense rather than the demonic supernatural. Omens and ghosts abound in *Two on a Tower,* but a more rationally plausible explanation always removes the suggestion of the supernatural. One ghost is really the hero, Swithin, dressed in the clothes of Lady Constantine's dead first husband; the other ghost, seen by Lady Constantine, is really her own hallucination, her symbolic realization that she is pregnant. Throughout the novel, omens, in the form of the weather or the unlucky lateness of the clergyman, prefigure the disaster of the marriage between young Swithin and Lady Constantine. She believes them and mourns; Swithin, the scientist with his "philosophy," regards them as ridiculous and inconsequential. Yet the marriage is a disaster, not because of the omens, but because Lady Constantine is hasty, excessively importunate, desperate, and ultimately dishonest, and because Swithin, in his youth, is callow, uncompromising, and far too literal. Hardy does not advocate the truth of omens and mysterious signs. The omens are part of Lady Constantine's inadequacy as the smug and assured "philosophy" is part of Swithin's. Belief in omens and the belief that man can live by some consciously worked out and consistent "philosophy" are, for Hardy, both vulnerable, both myths that deny the deep and uncontrollable nature of the human being.

Hardy's point of view toward his characters can no more be equated with that of the primitive rustics he describes than it can be enlisted in support of a consistent theory about man as the victim of universal malevolent accident. Although their customs and attitudes are often extensively described in Hardy's earlier novels, the rustics most frequently function as a kind of semi-comic relief, represent a cloddish and insensitive counterpoint to the major characters and issues of the novel. With his somewhat Shakespearean use of rustics, Hardy never makes them the central focus for his point of view. In each of the early novels, they are fixed in a chorus-like routine built around a theme: Christian Cantle's lack of manliness in *The Return of the Native,* and Grandfer Cantle's pride in his virility and his military service forty years earlier; the cheerfully irresponsible drunkenness that impedes all the action, from harvests to burials, in *Far from the Madding Crowd.* Sometimes, the comedy is less a repeated routine than an extended scene, like the dice game on the heath, played by the light of glowworms in *The Return of the Native* or the comic drilling of the rustic militia (a scene closely reminiscent of Dogberry drilling his constables in Shakespeare's *Much Ado about Nothing*), the guarding of the royal summer visitors, and the frightened midnight troop and civilian evacuations around the countryside during the threatened invasion by Napoleon's forces in *The Trumpet-Major.*

Occasionally, Hardy uses his rustics to articulate a satirical point of view that seems to be his own and that has little connection with either the major focus of the novel or the life of the rustics. This occurs, however, only in the very earliest novels, as in *Under the Greenwood Tree,* in which the tranter, Reuben Dewy, makes a few jibes at religion, at politics, and at conventional morality which seem to come directly from Thomas Hardy. In the later novels, beginning with the sordid chorus of vicious gossips in Mixen Lane in *The Mayor of Casterbridge,* the rustics become far less comic and their failings more sinister. Tim Tangs in *The Woodlanders,* understandably jealous because his wife had, before he married her, once spent a night with Fitzpiers, uses his last night before leaving for Australia to set a mantrap to mangle Fitzpiers. Most of the dairymaids, farmers, and workers in both *Tess of the D'Urbervilles* and *Jude the Obscure* are crude, self-seeking, and disloyal. Even admirable rustics, like the Widow Edlin in *Jude the Obscure,* can only chatter that things were different when they were young. Hardy's pastoral heroes, characters like Gabriel Oak in *Far from the Madding Crowd* or Giles Winterborne in *The Woodlanders,* are always placed several degrees in intelligence, sensitivity, and honesty above the rustics with whom circumstances have forced them to associate. Hardy's principal interest was not in the rustics, despite all their color and comedy; rather, he devoted his central attention to those characters exceptional enough to clash with society, those intellectually and emotionally able to feel a conflict between aspiration and achievement, between themselves and their world. Even Tess has a vision of her noble ancestors and a desire not to be like the other dairymaids around her. Hardy, like Shakespeare, concentrated on the character at least potentially heroic.

Although Hardy's characters can seldom be explained in terms of a formula that illuminates human heroism or that makes a general statement about man's nature, the force of the characters themselves is both Hardy's principal interest and his major achievement. *The Return of the Native,* for example, often melodramatic in plot and wobbly and inconsistent in theme, achieves vitality in its characterizations: Clym's weakness and indecision, his rebellions from and connections with his mother, his excessive blame of himself—the easiest evasion—, his symbolic half-sight; Mrs. Yeobright's jealousy and rigidity, all the more harsh because it cloaks her own lack of assurance and decision; Thomasin's gentle sense of vitality and resilience; Wildeve's selfishness and moral incapacity combined with his occasional sharp insight; all Eustacia's conflicting emotions, her desperate attempt to live out the romantic dreams she knows are false. Similarly, *Tess of the D'Urbervilles* most brilliantly demonstrates Tess's befuddled and inconsistent attempts to accommodate her feelings honestly to the world she sees around her; and *Jude the Obscure* describes, with great effectiveness, all Jude's puzzled and plodding efforts to be both moral and successful, all Sue's neurotic impulses and false intellectualizations manufactured with true intensity, all Arabella's crude soundness and rightness for all the wrong reasons. This account of Hardy's greatest strength is necessarily adjectival, for his principal novels cannot be explained by noun-like abstractions and equations or verb-like accounts of plots that fascinate by continuous and convincing action. Hardy's people for the most part *are,* and their phenomenological quality, intensified by all the natural and cosmic imagery, elicits a powerful sense of sympathy.

Hardy's characters are also presented within a social setting, and are affected by the world around them. In many of his novels, social distinctions and the barriers they form between people create the incidents that comprise the plot. The action of *Under the Greenwood Tree* is propelled by Fancy Day's hesitancy about marrying Dick Dewy, the son of tranter Dewy, because he is less educated and less prosperous than she. Her feelings of class and snobbery even lead her, in a weak moment after she has already promised to marry Dick, to promise to marry a foppish and calculating minister. Hardy never develops Fancy's inconsistency and what it might lead to in marriage with Dick; he merely uses the inconsistency to propel the plot and to suggest the social origins of the obstacles to true love. Similarly, in *Far from the Madding Crowd,* Bathsheba is more educated and of a higher class than Gabriel Oak. She must certainly refuse him when he even loses his farm and comes to work for her. Although the issues in *Far from the Madding Crowd* become far more complex and are developed far more adequately than those in *Under the Greenwood Tree,* the novel begins with a simple and similar recognition of class distinction. *Two on a Tower* and *The Woodlanders,* although essentially concerned with more intrinsic questions within the marriage relationship, both begin with discussion of marriages that may or may not take place between people on different social levels. The suggested conclusions differ, for the socially mismatched couple in *Two on a Tower* would have been better off apart, whereas Grace Melbury's marriage into the class for which she was trained and educated in *The Woodlanders* violates both her security and her emotions. She would, by implication, have been better off descending socially. But the conclusions need not be consistent, for Hardy was not making a generalization about crossing class lines in marriage; rather, he used the issues of class to initiate his characters' actions, actions that often revealed a greater depth and intensity than class or education or money could explain.

The *Trumpet-Major,* chronicling a seaside town at the beginning of the nineteenth century, charts all the distinctions within the army and the navy, the status of trumpeters, the work of naval press gangs, the highhanded arrogance of the aristocracy, and the excessively skittish primness of young ladies brought up in the respectable middle classes. The young heroine, Anne Garland, is aware of all these distinctions as she chooses from among three possible suitors, frequently although not consistently counseled by her mother to opt for the money and position of the one she likes least. Again, however, class is not finally the central issue, for Anne easily rejects the arrogant aristocrat. Her difficult choice is between the two sons of the simple miller, one steadfast and faithful, the other charming and irresponsible. She chooses the latter because "gratitude is not love," but, unfortunately for the modern reader, the novel ends with the marriage.

Issues of class become more serious in Hardy's later novels, particularly *Tess of the D'Urbervilles* and *Jude the Obscure.* In these, class judgments and designations help stifle the protagonists, as the smug insularity of the Christminster colleges is one of the forces that prevents Jude from achieving his ambition.

The question is not simply that of the earlier novels, one of marriage and relationship, but rather of impingement, of destruction, of the whole fabric of society weighing down on the man who refuses to accept mutely a pre-established social designation. Yet, even in the later novels, class and society are far from the only issues. They still function as ways to understand people, approaches to the problems of human experience. Class and society, extensions of the human being, become, for Hardy, a way of working from man's institutions and creations into the complicated nature of man himself. As such, Hardy's interest in social and class description is further evidence of his consuming interest in and skill at presenting human character.

Hardy's attempt to formulate, his effort to structure artistic meaning, would not allow him to rest content with merely presenting character. Often in the novels, he tried to order his observations about human character, to give them the kind of shape and direction that would permit general statement. For example in *Far from the Madding Crowd* Hardy uses different arrangements of similar terms in introducing each of the three principal male characters among whom Bathsheba must choose. Gabriel Oak is presented as a perfect man, responsible, stalwart, and sensitive, praised because "his intellect and his emotions were clearly separated" and he is therefore capable of sound and dispassionate judgment. The prosperous farmer Boldwood is a cold and rational man on the surface, but he has no equilibrium; if, Hardy tells us, an "emotion possessed him at all, it ruled him." The third man, the irresponsible Sergeant Troy, has both reason and emotions, but the reason seldom exerts any influence whatever, particularly when women are concerned. Hardy ties this scheme to a mechanistic notion of human force, as if a man has only a finite number of ergs of capacity and what is spent in one activity must be taken from another:

We discern a grand force in the lover which he lacks whilst a free man; but there is a breadth of vision in the free man which in the lover we vainly seek. Where there is much bias there must be some narrowness, and love, though added emotion, is subtracted capacity.

In one sense, the equation of the three men works, for Bathsheba, attracted at first to Sergeant Troy's charm, marries him, and then, after Troy's irrational bigamy has been exposed (and Troy killed by the passionately mad Boldwood, thus melodramatically eliminating them both), recognizes that Gabriel's solid virtue has paralleled her own growth, and wisely marries him.

But to read the novel in this way is to ignore the fact that Bathsheba is the principal character, not merely a rational cipher who finally chooses the man who most deserves the prize. Bathsheba is a forceful and passionate woman who helps to create Boldwood's single-minded madness, Troy's attraction to her and eventual willingness to desert her, and Gabriel's steadfast loyalty. In part, she makes each of the men what he is, and her need for different kinds of relationship, her capacity both to ennoble and to destroy the men around her, is at the center of the novel. In addition, the quantitative idea of human force is demonstrated only in the rigidly neurotic character of Boldwood; Gabriel is resilient enough to expand to fit the demands of any situation in the novel, and Sergeant Troy, whether in love or not, is the same genial, easily moved, and thoughtless fellow. Hardy's equation, his paradigm of valuable masculine qualities, does not order or explain very much of the human character in the novel.

In introducing Clym in *The Return of the Native*, Hardy establishes a polarity similar to the equation of intellect and emotion in *Far from the Madding Crowd*:

The beauty here visible would in no long time be ruthlessly overrun by its parasite, thought, which might just as well have fed upon a plainer exterior where there was nothing it could harm.

But the conflict between beauty and thought cannot begin to explain all the ambiguities of Clym's relationship with both his mother and Eustacia, all the inadequacies which lead to his disaster. In later novels, Hardy developed this kind of polarity more fully, tending in *Tess of the D'Urbervilles* and *Jude the Obscure* to try to explain his protagonists as caught between the problems of the flesh and the problems of the spirit. Tess's two lovers, Alec D'Urberville and Angel Clare, are introduced as representatives of the flesh and the spirit respectively; appropriately, Alec is handsome, forceful, and passionate, and Angel is philosophical, principled, and religious. Although Tess is attracted to both of them, the polarity does not really explain the characters. Alec, the supposed representative of the flesh, is also a kind of diabolic spiritual force, and, at one point, himself becomes an itinerant fundamentalist preacher. Angel, presumably spiritual, is also a farmer, a social snob, a terrible prig, and, in some ways, a materialistic opportunist. In addition, the conflicts within Tess are ones of honesty, of security, of finding some kind of place for herself in society, not only those of the contradictory claims of the flesh and the spirit. The abstract terms cannot begin to account sufficiently for all the human problems that make up the novel.

Similarly, in *Jude the Obscure*, the hero is involved with two women, Arabella connected with the flesh, and Sue with the spirit. In this novel, the representations are abstracted, almost grotesque, for Arabella is constantly described in terms of pigs and drink and vulgar squalor, whereas Sue is always connected with the church, purity, and sexlessness. Yet, despite the abstraction, the characters are both far more diffuse and more complex than the roles given them by the flesh/spirit equation. Arabella has an incisive mind and a kind of principled honesty, despite her crudeness. And Sue, a tease, a coquette who uses her sex to keep both Jude and Phillotson panting after her, a woman whose principal motive is always jealousy, intellectualizes her own neuroses into an aura of spirituality. Jude, like Tess, in his geographic and occupational wanderings around Wessex (these two protagonists are Hardy's homeless, his alienated), faces a great many problems of society and history other than those represented by his woman of the flesh and his woman of the spirit. For Hardy, the polar alternatives, the equation, can only work in the lighter novels, those like *The Trumpet-Major* in which the heroine's final decision can be explained by her choice of emotional attraction rather than security. But the lighter novels are lighter because they consistently simplify experience, reduce it to understandable conflicts and polarities. In Hardy's fuller and more profound novels, the attempt to formulate the equation, to order the perceptions about human character, often works against the force and profundity of the novel itself.

The conflict between the flesh and the spirit, between body and soul, was one of nineteenth-century religion's principal explanations for the human dilemma. Hardy, as his allusions and references so consistently demonstrate, absorbed much of the Church's climate and custom. He also apparently tried to apply the Church's conventional means for explaining the human being to the experience described in his novels. At the same time, the final novels are essentially agnostic. Both Alec's preaching and Angel's principles are entirely hypocritical; Tess preserves her dignity by her immunity to the hypocrisy of all the religious teaching around her, although, as an innocent, she retains an allegiance to exterior religious forms. The point of view in *Jude the Obscure* is even more strongly anti-religious. Jude, in his early reverence for Christminster and his awe at the "fine" spirituality Sue represents when he first meets her in a church, is always made to seem a fool when he is taken in by the institutions or the teachings of religion. Through the events of the novel, as he reaches greater wisdom about himself and his world, he comes to regard creeds and churches as producing dangerous intoxication, as lethal as gin. Both Arabella and Sue turn to religion only when everything else has failed, and Arabella—wisely from the novel's point of view—is willing to abandon religion again as soon as another man appears. For Hardy, in these last novels, the attempt to derive an explanation for human character from the religious culture grinds jarringly against the persistent attitude that belief in God or churches is a naive delusion. Not only is the flesh/spirit polarity an inadequate explanation of the characters, but it also works against appreciating the full and complex humanity that Hardy so powerfully describes. The formulation both restricts and distorts. Yet Hardy's massive sense of humanity comes through these novels despite the obtrusion of the simplified and irrelevant categories he establishes.

Religion was not the only Victorian institution that Hardy examined, for he was very much involved in his time, in the changes of history. The novels span the nineteenth century, generally deepening and saddening as the century ends. Jude, in his wanderings, in the folly of his naive faith in education, in his disillusion with Christminster, his realization that what he took for the symbol and spirit of glorious and ennobling scholarship is really only the cloister of snobbish and desiccated medievalism, becomes Hardy's symbol for the age—one of the forms of "the modern vice of unrest." Jude's aspiration might have been successful in an earlier, simpler world, or he might never have had the consuming desire to be other than a stone cutter; but the growing insecurity and complexity of the end of the nineteenth century holds out the promise and denies the fulfillment. The plight of the next generation is suggested in the symbolic figure of Jude's son, little "Father Time." He has no aspirations, kills the other children and himself, representing the extreme and melodramatic form of "the coming universal wish not to live." The same historical pattern is apparent in *Tess of the D'Urbervilles*. The responsible old aristocracy, the D'Urbervilles, have degenerated into the selfish and demonic Alec and the shiftless ignorance of John Durbeyfield. Within the clergy, the old Reverend Clare, Angel's father, had at least more compassion and understanding than do his sons. Tess's mother, who represents a kind of traditional soundness and humanity, is defeated by events. The one idyllic farm in the novel, Talbothays, belongs to the past and no longer functions. References throughout the book chronicle both the severe depression in agricultural England in the 1880's and the restless movement of agricultural laborers, who had stayed on one spot for generations, into the rootless and amorphous towns and cities.

Hardy also symbolizes his version of the changes in history in his characterizations of the "new woman" in some of the later novels. The neurotic Sue in *Jude* is his principal example. Willing to be unconventional and share a house with a man to whom she's not married, highly intellectual and competitive, often blasphemous about churches and universities, Sue is unable to live any of the positions she holds to their logical conclusions. She is frightened and uneasy, acts out of impulsive jealousy, and regards the sex act only as a punishment diabolically thrust upon unwilling women by male lust. In Hardy's terms, the "new woman" is inevitably doomed by her education and her sensitivity, for she spends most of her life denying the warmth and responsiveness of her female nature. A less melodramatically treated example of the "new woman" is Grace Melbury in *The Woodlanders*. Educated beyond the level of her rural family of woodsmen and possessing the social style appropriate to her education, Grace is torn between the social and intellectual world of Dr. Fitzpiers and the homely rural world of the faithful Giles Winterborne. Her intelligence as well as social snobbery draws her to Fitzpiers, but she sees, in his casual infidelity, that she has made a social as well as a personal mistake. She cannot always respond to events in terms of her intelligence and education, and, distraught, she temporarily becomes very much like Sue:

> but from a corner a quick breathing was audible from this impressionable creature, who combined modern nerves with primitive feelings, and was doomed by such co-existence to be numbered among the distressed, and to take her scroungings to their exquisite extremity.

She, too, does her best to deny sexual feeling, for she can only acknowledge her physical love for Giles when he is too ill to do anything about it, and can only defy her world, in a useless romantic rebellion, by falsely claiming after he is safely dead to have spent a night with him. The novel ends unconvincingly, hastily patching up the marriage between Grace and Fitzpiers and ignoring all the implications of complicated character that have given it strength; but, until then, the depiction of the "new woman" is done with greater insight, restraint, and effectiveness than is that in *Jude the Obscure*.

Hardy's "new" women—like his earlier complicated women who combined passion and defiance, dignity and foolish illusions, women like Eustacia and Bathsheba—cannot be explained or understood by any of the formulae about human character that Hardy used. In fact, Hardy's interest in history and its changes works against the attempt to impose a consistent abstract explanation on the nature of the human being. History moves, whereas the formula about human character presumes to hold a static truth. As Hardy involved himself more completely in history—for *Jude the Obscure* is his most historical novel, his work most dependent on the changes in time and circumstance throughout Wessex—the strain between his characters and the formulae imposed to explain them became greater. In *Jude* the conflict between the flesh and the spirit becomes more completely irrelevant to what Hardy has to say about people and their world than it ever has been before. He tried to be

[99

faithful to both his conviction that art required an explanatory formula and to his observation of experience. Yet the two
increasingly pulled in different directions. Small wonder he
stopped writing novels. At least, this seems a more plausible
explanation than chagrin at the bigoted, narrow-minded, and
unappreciative reviews *Jude* received. The contemporary reviews of *The Return of the Native,* eighteen years earlier, had
been just as bigoted and stupidly misunderstanding, but he had
not stopped writing novels then. In addition, Hardy's view of
the course of current history became more despondent. In *The
Return of the Native,* the educated young Clym, apparently
successful in Paris, returns to his native heath and is unable to
reconcile the conflicting claims of his life there. His education
and sophistication are only a small part of his problem, for most
of it resides in his personal and psychological inadequacies. He
is reduced to the role of an itinerant Sunday preacher, removed
both from his own ambitions and from the life of the heath. In
Jude the Obscure, the problem is far more intensely general.
Despite his personal mistakes and naiveté, Jude's defeat comes
primarily from his world, its snobbishness, its cruelty, its indifference. He is reduced and reduced and reduced, hounded
until death is a welcome relief. *Jude* is permeated with Hardy's
growing belief in the horror of late nineteenth-century civilization for the honest and simple man. In the portrayal of the
village in which Jude grew up, Hardy's doomed conservatism
is clearly manifest:

> Above all, the original church, hump-backed, wood-turreted, and
> quaintly hipped, had been taken down, and either cracked up into
> heaps of road-metal in the lane, or utilized as pig-sty walls, garden
> seats, guardstones to fences, and rockeries in the flower-beds of the
> neighbourhood. In place of it a tall new building of modern Gothic
> design, unfamiliar to English eyes, had been erected on a new piece
> of ground by a certain obliterator of historic records who had run
> down from London and back in a day. The site whereon so long
> had stood the ancient temple to the Christian divinities was not even
> recorded on the green and level grass-plot that had immemorially
> been the churchyard, the obliterated graves being commemorated
> by eighteen-penny castiron crosses warranted to last five years.

Hardy would have liked to believe in the creeds and institution
of the nineteenth-century church he knew, but these contradicted

his observations of human experience. Similarly, he would have liked to follow the rules and formulae he established for his art, but the contradictory, profound, and unstructured observations kept breaking down the rules. His art is all the richer for the fact that the rules couldn't hold.

The one constant element of Hardy's point of view toward his characters is his compassion for their struggles and their defeated aspirations. Although he does include villains, snobs, the arrogant, the irresponsible, each novel contains several principal figures with whom the reader is sympathetically involved. For the reader, a sense of compassion for failed humanity lingers long after the structural inconsistencies, only partially applicable abstractions, and bits of cosmological pain have been forgotten. As Hardy's artistic formulations and theories about character increasingly broke down, more of the novel's energy turned into compassion. Sometimes, when he tried to force the formula to fit the novel, or felt his characters' doom more strongly than his events could express, his plots are melodramatic; at other times, such as the conclusion of *The Woodlanders,* when Marty South, having always carried a futile torch for Giles Winterborne, dedicates herself to humanity, Hardy's point of view is sentimental. But, despite these flaws, Hardy's fiction is often powerful and deep, propelled by his compassion and his imagery that so forcefully extends human consciousness and human concerns. At his best, whatever his conscious intentions were, he is a comprehensive and profound historian, an historian in the sense that he gives so rich an account of Wessex, his time and place. The historian is, despite Aristotle's judgment, not necessarily inferior to the philosopher or the universal theorist about the nature of man. In giving us Wessex so fully, deeply, and compassionately, Hardy has also allowed us to exercise our own perception, emotion, and intelligence in order to sense what of Wessex still applies.

V

HOWELLS & JAMES

THROUGHOUT MOST of the nineteenth century, American fiction revealed little evidence of the tradition of compassion, showed far less unresolved and unstructured experience than did English fiction. Tending toward the abstract and allegorical, as in much of the work of Hawthorne and Melville, or shaped by the metaphor of discovery, as in the work of Cooper and Twain, American fiction frequently diminished the importance of social environment and regarded the human being as free to seek his own destiny, able to stand or fall on terms that neither required nor left room for an attitude of compassion toward man. Hawthorne's judgments about human behavior may have been ambivalent, but his terms were those of allegory: sin, good and evil, pride. And the allegory, constantly directing attention to the theological and universal, prevented the kind of particular focus which discovers compassion.

As Richard Chase, in *The American Novel and its Tradition* (1957), has pointed out, the American tradition, throughout the nineteenth century, was primarily that of the romance rather than the novel. Defining the romance as a form that uses mystery and that frequently ignores issues of class and society as well as "realistic" plausibility, Chase adds that "The very abstractness and profundity of romance allow it to formulate moral truths of universal validity, although it perforce ignores home truths that may be equally or more important." Chase quotes William Gilmore Simms, the nineteenth-century southern writer of romances, who regarded the historical romance as the modern form of the epic, following classical definitions of unity and achieving classical order, a form vastly superior to the novel, in order to indicate the American critical consciousness of the romance's abstract and allegorical qualities. Romance could be vast, profound, and ponderous like *Moby Dick,* or comic, iconoclastic, and closer to folk legend, like the works of Mark Twain, but, in both instances, romance sacrificed a central interest in how man operated within a particular time and place for a universal truth about human experience.

Only with the fiction of William Dean Howells and Henry James, toward the end of the nineteenth century, did American writers assume with any degree of consistency that more of human experience could be apprehended, could, in James's terms, be "felt" by the reader, if allegorical forms and interest in universal truth were abandoned for a presentation of experience more dependent on verisimilitude. American fiction, although still dominated by a concern with morality, began to move toward the novel, toward interest in human relationships and the careful depiction of social environment. Of the two novelists, James was, of course, the more comprehensive, profound, and consciously artistic. James also, particularly in his early fiction, combined the romance with the novel, developed symbolic, sometimes almost allegorical, patterns from his very deliberate concentration on man within the framework of his society. Howells, simpler, less artistically self-conscious and less consistent, wrote essays setting himself deliberately against the romance. His novels also, like *The Rise of Silas Lapham* (1888), are full of satirical jibes against the abstractions and the implausibilities of contemporary romances, implying Howells' conscious attempt to use the novel to approximate actual human behavior in actual situations.

The term "realistic," however, although Howells himself approved of it, is inadequate even for beginning a description of his fiction. His best known novel, *The Rise of Silas Lapham,* for example, depends on both a strong moral framework and a description of the density and complexity of human relationships. Silas Lapham, son of a poor Vermont farmer, markets the paint from the ore on his farm and amasses a fortune in the world of quickly growing industry after the Civil War. Believing in money and hard work, Silas also aspires to gentility, wants to crash Boston society for his daughters and build a pretentious mansion on Back Bay. But his commercial rise is his fall; as he succumbs to the hollow values of the fashionable society he apes and neglects the solid moral ore of his farm background; similarly, as the novel turns, his moral rise coincides with his commercial fall, for he honors a moral obligation to a dissolute former partner and loses all his money, returning to the Vermont farm.

In the pattern of the novel's inversely paired commercial and moral elevators, Silas' wife, Persis, functions as his conscience, always reminding him of the wrong he once committed in business, goading him to full repentance, and standing for the homespun religious virtue that finally allows his moral rise. Yet, at the same time, the relationship between Silas and Persis achieves a fullness and complexity that has no connection with the moral fabric of the novel, a relationship which, for the twentieth-century reader, is probably much more vital and interesting than is the moral pattern or the social commentary. Silas and Persis argue fiercely, adopt each others' points of view as the arguments turn around, are intensely loyal, and project their own befuddlement at the social rules of Boston society onto imagined failings in each other. Silas grumpily takes the perplexing world out on his wife; Persis, even at sixty, is capable of an irrationally jealous rage.

The subplot of the novel, concerning the Lapham's two daughters and the misunderstandings that involve them with the eligible Tom Corey, also mixes concern with relationships and concern with morality. Tom prefers the intellectual, abrasive, and witty Penelope, the woman capable of formulating a relationship of tension, individuality and worth, to the vapid beauty, Irene. But everyone in Boston society, even including the Laphams, has thought Tom favored Irene, and Penelope's acceptance of Tom might make it seem as if the Laphams would do anything, even sacrifice daughters, just to capture a Corey. Here, however, the moral perspective is more pragmatic and less stringent than that concerning Silas' business ethics. The Laphams consult the Reverend Mr. Sewell, the voice of sane common sense, who ridicules the "false ideal of self-sacrifice" and suggests that Penelope accept Tom so that "one suffer instead of three." Had this precept been applied to Silas' business, he would have remained a wealthy manufacturer at the end of the novel. The Old Testament stringency of Howells' business or public morality is both dramatically and intellectually at odds with the moderate and compassionate recommendations about the morality of personal relationships. Howells' condemnation of post-Civil War commercial society throws the moral perspective into divided and contradictory categories.

An earlier novel, *A Modern Instance* (1882), illustrates another conflict between Howells' moral judgments and his attempts to describe a changing American world. For almost four-fifths of its length, it chronicles the unhappy marriage of Bartley Hubbard and Marcia Gaylord. Bartley's spoiled irresponsibility is played against Marcia's unremitting puritanical judgment, her insistence on bringing up all of Bartley's previous failings in the midst of each quarrel. Howells carefully provides a causal background for the incompatibility: Marcia's silent and harsh father who never forgives the first minor instance of Bartley's looser concept of fidelity; Marcia's own fiercely repressed passion, the overwhelming and explosive emotion that made her chase Bartley to the railway station and get him to marry her; Bartley's struggles as the Midwestern orphan attempting to capture Boston society by his talent and amiable charm, struggles which leave him insensitive to moral issues. The incompatibility is that of two different strands of American experience as much as that of two individuals. Although the causes of the bad marriage are fully detailed, Howells does exercise a moral preference for Marcia, does value her warmhearted and genuine emotion, no matter how inappropriately explosive, in contrast with Bartley's weak and immoral irresponsibility. Marcia, at least, in Howells' terms, has the capacity to love someone other than self. This moral preference, however, is balanced by the fact that, after Bartley leaves, Marcia is enveloped and propped up by the support of her narrow world, full of righteous outrage and self-pity, while Bartley is banished to lonely and unsuccessful wanderings in the hinterlands. This far, the moral framework of the story is, given Howells' point of view, provided with sufficient and convincing reference in terms of detailed description of both the marriage and the society.

The last portion of the novel, however, is overwhelmed by a moral theme that, although present earlier, has little intrinsic connection with the marriage or the social conflict. Ben Halleck, once a college friend of Bartley's, has always befriended Marcia. Now that Marcia is divorced (and to make the possibility of remarriage even more plausible Howells has Bartley killed in Arizona sometime after the divorce), Ben wonders whether or not he can morally offer marriage to Marcia, especially since he had silently loved her when she was still married. He feels that to propose would be immoral; his friend Atherton, a lawyer and a practical man, argues that Ben had in fact done nothing immoral or even questionable and is therefore free to propose. Much of the last part of the novel is occupied with this debate concerning moral motive and moral action. The "ideal of self-sacrifice," sanely disposed of by Mr. Sewell in the later novel, *The Rise of Silas Lapham,* is part of Ben's self-denial, part of his guilt for having loved Marcia earlier, but the psychological connection between guilt and moral self-sacrifice is never explored. The moral debate, a kind of arid dithering unresolved and unconnected with the chronicle of relationships within the novel, is left dangling. Atherton, explaining the debate to his own wife, ends the novel by saying, "Ah, I don't know! I don't know!" Howells might have made the debate relevant by characterizing the argument as part of the high-minded triviality and irrelevance of Marcia's puritan world. But no such perspective is provided and the debate remains a moral quibble.

The moral element is more convincingly assimilated into the description in Howells' most comprehensive work, *A Hazard of New Fortunes* (1890). This novel depicts the changing America after the Civil War, as all the characters, torn from their provincial ante-bellum roots, are poured into the melting pot of guideless and cosmopolitan New York. The organization of a magazine, which provides the unifying issue of the book, is a microcosm for the organization of the new America, drawing talent and characters from the Middle West, Boston, New Hampshire farms, Syracuse, the unreconstructed South, and Central Europe. The characters cannot transport their old ideals or their traditional moralities with them, for this, the new world of money and strikes and contradictory opinions, is "a hazard of new fortunes," and the simple honesty of the farm, the aloof puritanical virtue of Boston, the violent equalitarianism of the Europeans who, crushed in 1848, migrated to the land of democracy—all equally cannot apply to the new moment of history. Some of the characters, like Alma Leighton and Angus Beaton, approach "new fortunes" with an attempt to wrest whatever they can from them, to consolidate their own careers in the jungle of the new world by a primary allegiance to the self. But these characters, as well as the jingoistic capitalist and believer in the "survival of the fittest," Jacob Dryfoos, are themselves finally isolated, damned, granted the paper currency of the "new fortunes" but none of the warmth or satisfaction of achievement. At the other extreme, characters like Lindau, the German radical, Conrad Dryfoos, capitalist's son turned minister, and Margaret Vance, society girl turned religious votary, attempt to apply some religious or political principle to "new fortunes," to guide the amorphous mass by an ideal. Although Howells sympathizes with these characters far more strongly than he does with the selfishly isolated, for they are all shown as noble and genuinely principled, he depicts them as doomed by allegiance to impossible ideals in the modern world. Conrad and Lindau are killed; Margaret Vance is shunted away from the new world into a convent.

In contrast with both those who grasp for themselves and the visionary idealists, the principal couple in the novel, Basil and Isabel March, are both connected with and separated from other characters. The Marches are strongly dependent on each other in a marriage relationship in which each partner is capable of assuming the other's role and adopting the other's point of view. Because each represents a different geographical region and attitude, this relationship is more complex than that of the Laphams and, in addition, March modifies his wife's stringent Puritanism instead of succumbing to it. The Marches, alternately elated and frightened by the possibilities of "new fortunes," hesitate to move to New York at all. Yet the move is inevitable—to stay in Boston is to remain in a pre-Civil War America—and, once in New York, they slowly discover when to insist on self, when to insist on principle, when not to insist at all. March finally takes his stand, a defiance of capitalism that might cost him his job with the magazine, a stand that incorporates both self and principle, in defense of Lindau when the latter is unfairly fired by Jacob Dryfoos. The stand is not visionary or diffuse, not even particularly heroic or attached to a general economic or social cause; rather, it is personal, specific, and backed into cautiously. Ironically, Lindau's adamant refusal to be reinstated saves March from the possible consequences of his stand, an accident that allows material survival without the abrogation of principle. March is capable and lucky enough to weather "new fortunes," is sensitive to others yet able to include morality within his sensitivity, represents finally as much of principle as can survive in the strident industrialism and economic conflicts of the new society. Although successful in terms of both the magazine and the novel, March is wise enough to temper his sense of victory with a strong feeling for the dead visionary, Conrad, who always stood for his principles entirely, and with admiration for and trust in Margaret Vance who denies the world.

Howells does not endorse the mediator as such, for March is distinguished from another commercially successful mediator within the novel, Fulkerson, the organizer and managing editor of the magazine. Fulkerson is too mediate, too much the go-between, too insensitive to issues and personalities, for it is his excessively amiable mistake that brings Lindau and Dryfoos into position for the unforgiveable rupture. Only March and his wife are able to maintain the combination of sensitivity and principle, of self and not-self, of flexibility and rigidity, that an honest approach to "new fortunes" demands. Their public success, and the author's qualified approval of this success, is parallel to their capacity to understand and to relate to one another fully. Their relationship insures the fact that March cannot isolate himself in either the selfishness of an Angus Beaton or the morally pure martyrdom of Conrad Dryfoos. Personal relationships and public attitudes are brought together.

Much of *A Hazard of New Fortunes* concerns the process of March's coming to understand the new world of the magazine and his role within it. The novel, like many of Henry James's, is in part a novel of process, of how the man of understanding manages to become what he is. The observer—and March is very much the cautious observer of "new fortunes" at the beginning—becomes the subject; the point of view from which the new America is seen becomes as important to the novel as America itself. In this way, the novel is also a defense of the intellectual, a statement that the man who carefully thinks and works his way into perception, who consciously solves the balance between sensitivity and principle or between self and not-self, finally manages best in terms of the world around him. March's morality is pragmatic, muted, carefully achieved and hesitantly approached, far more complicated and ambivalent than the simple fall or rise on a single issue that characterized Howells' treatment of public morality in *The Rise of Silas Lapham*. Similarly, relationships, in the novel of process, are depicted with far greater density than simple matters of attraction, companionship, and conviviality. The intellectual, the man of both thought and feeling, is able to formulate and experience a wider version of humanity, able, despite all the difficulties and hesitations and impure moral considerations, to live more truly and more capaciously among the "hazards" of the new industrial and commercial society.

Basil March, imperfect and unheroic as he is, understands and can assimilate the possibilities of "new fortunes" better than the idealists like Conrad and Lindau, better than the loyally unreconstructed Southerner, Colonel Woodburn; at the same time, his humanity and sensitivity have not been, like that of Angus Beaton, completely blunted by the new world. Howells, in his interest in the process of coming to be and his defense of the man who consciously comes to be, develops a structure and a focus that provides room for both his morality and his interest in the ways in which people connect with one another and with society.

None of Howells' later novels is as Jamesian in its focus on point of view or as complete as *A Hazard of New Fortunes*. But the muting of moral questions, the partial subservience of a rigorous morality to the considerations demanded by a given time and place, evident in the perspective of this novel, left a residue that, in other ways, was carried over into some of the later books. The capitalist himself is treated less as the grasping and selfish sinner in *The Landlord at Lion's Head* (1897), a novel that traces the origin of the incipient capitalist, Jeff Durgin, from poor rural beginnings through Harvard to the successful management of a summer resort on his family's New England farm. Jeff, even from childhood, ignores the New England code around him and makes his way, successfully fending off his mother's grandiose plans for his future, his brother's spiritualistic religion, the narrow virtue of Cynthia to whom he is engaged for a time, and the constant disapproval of the artist, Westover. In showing how the capitalist develops, showing both what is innate meanness and what is formed by environment, Howells avoids the kind of moral framework, the system of timeless sin and repentance, apparent in his treatment of the capitalist in *The Rise of Silas Lapham*. Howells emphasizes causation in describing Jeff's career: his mother's strength, ambition, and protectiveness; his social ineptitude at Harvard until he finds a mode that suits him as the modern and enterprising young man; the decadent representative of the Boston aristocracy he must defeat. Howells never defends Jeff's morality, never even develops an apology for the limited or pragmatic morality as he does for Basil March, and seems willing to let Westover's moral castigation of Jeff stand as his own. Yet Howells' statement in the preface to the 1909 edition of the novel indicates the kind of ambivalence from which Jeff's career is viewed:

I myself liked the hero of the tale more than I have liked worthier men, perhaps because I thought I had achieved in him a true rustic New England type in contact with urban life under entirely modern conditions. What seemed to me my aesthetic success in him possibly softened me to his ethical shortcomings; but I do not expect others to share my weakness for Jeff Durgin, whose strong, rough surname had been waiting for his personality ever since I had got it off the side of an ice cart many years before. . . . . What I most prize in him, if I may go to the bottom of the inkhorn, is the realization of that anti-Puritan quality which was always vexing the heart of Puritanism, and which I had constantly felt one of the most interesting facts in my observation of New England.

Other ambivalent judgments occur in the novel, like the attitude toward Genevieve Vostrand, the girl Jeff finally marries,

after the failure of her marriage to the dissolute Italian nobleman her family had bought for her. Yet, despite all the ambivalence, the novel is not just a descriptive account of the problems
and relationships of modern life. Westover, the artist, often
speaks for Howells. Westover has the first words and the last;
throughout the novel he paints pictures of Lion's Head, the
mountain that borders the Durgin family farm, just as he observes and interprets all the actions of the Durgin family. The
artist is both recorder and judge, and, clearly, from Westover's
point of view, Jeff has deserted the morality of his origins, and
the family's success in drawing resort visitors suggests the destruction of sturdy New England independence. Westover, originally only the morally sound observer, also develops from commentator to character. As he becomes capable of relationship, his
virtue is rewarded with the girl, the pure noble Cynthia who
would not forgive Jeff's doubts and ambivalences. The reliance
on Westover and his art makes the novel part moral tract, although the illustration, the career of Jeff Durgin, is treated with
so much ambivalence and complexity that it does not reinforce
the moral.

Another late novel, *The Vacation of the Kelwyns* (first
published in 1920, the year Howells died, but written about ten
years earlier), demonstrates in another way the breakdown of
Howells' moral judgments. Subtitled "An Idyl of the Middle
Eighteen-Seventies," the book, lighter than any of the others discussed, introduces the Kelwyns, a middle-class family from Cambridge where Mr. Kelwyn lectures at the University, looking for
an inexpensive summer vacation more comfortable than their
customary boarding at a farmhouse. A dying Shaker community
provides a large house on easy terms as well as a lower-class family, the Kites, who are to farm the land and care for the Kelwyns.
But the families clash: the Kites are slovenly and incompetent,
failing to do what they have promised to do and incapable of
learning; the Kelwyns, principled and high-minded, have every
legal and moral justification for kicking out the Kites and dissolving the agreement. Yet the Kelwyns, a close married couple
who understand one another, although the fiercely practical
woman is more dominant in this instance, are tortured with guilt,
question their own principles and values simply because the
Kites are obdurately unable or unwilling to understand them.

Although the Kelwyns finally leave for another farmhouse, their assurance in their class-bred morality has been dissolved and they are, in Howells' terms, wiser for recognizing the narrowness of their principles.

The Kelwyns' young cousin, Parthenope Brook, a fiercely idealistic and artistic young lady falls in love with Elihu Emerance, a pragmatic and wandering opportunist, sometime schoolteacher, animal trainer, and cook, who becomes a playwright. Emerance's victory is also that of American circumstance, of life as it is, over principle and idealism. In addition, throughout the summer of the novel, Howells frequently mentions an economic depression and has tramps, sordid itinerant peddlers, a man with a dancing bear, foreign wanderers, and sullen Negroes out of work all prowling the countryside. The fact that the novel is set in the American centennial summer of 1876 provides an ironic counterpoint for the decline in the specifically American virtues, principles, and traditions. Kelwyn even buys a gun he would never use in reaction to the general sense of menace around the countryside. But the Kelwyns, like Parthenope, accept the dissolution of their standards, accept the realization that their principled, high-minded, homogeneous world does not exist beyond their own cloister. And Howells is calmly willing to close on this note, on the willingness to suspend the justice of a once fiercely guarded and morally defended tradition in favor of the acceptance of a wider, less easily structured and judged version of experience.

Despite the compassion and acceptance advocated in *The Vacation of the Kelwyns,* Howells' fiction does not generally or consistently illustrate the tradition of compassion as does that of Trollope or Hardy. Howells' sense of morality is generally too firm and too obtrusive. Often, as in *A Modern Instance* or *The Landlord at Lion's Head,* the morality fights against an interest in the descriptive presentation of individuals, relationships, and changes in society. Howells' loose ends, too, are less likely to be statements that all the issues of the novel cannot be reconciled, less likely to be admissions that the intellectual framework of the novel is not adequate to express all the issues of the novel, than are those of Trollope or Hardy. Rather, in Howells' a loose end is just that, failure to work the elements of

the novel deeply enough. His form is less "open" than unfinished. As a result the fiction conveys a lack of tension, a kind of
ease, an ultimate superficiality that is overcome only in *A Hazard of New Fortunes*—in its cohesive brilliance, its articulate
point of view, its extensive characterization of a new America.
Howells' fiction contains some of the prerequisites for the fiction
of compassion: a willingness to abandon fable or allegory, a
questioning of morality, a deep interest in presenting man in
combination with others and with his social environment. But
the fiction is too much a collection of elements, too often fixed
on the very moralities it questions, to belong entirely within
the tradition of compassion. At the same time, the direction of
Howells' fictional career, the gradual movement away from the
firm system of moral judgment in *The Rise of Silas Lapham* to
the suspension of judgment in *The Vacation of the Kelwyns*,
along with the consistent avoidance of the romance and the consistent interest in human relationships, do point toward the
tradition of compassion.

Henry James's career in fiction, more consciously controlled and developed than Howells', points in the same direction, although James's concern with consistent form, with the
novel as a closed and completed entity, is frequently unlike the
more open or more ironically undercut structures in the novels
of most writers within the tradition of compassion. At the beginning of his career, the attitude James conveyed in fiction was
almost the reverse of compassionate. Establishing an authorial
point of view rather like God's, arranging, disposing, and pointing out lessons through his characters and themes, James's work
is full of the elements of mystery and concern with sin and symbol which are common to both the Gothic tradition and the
American tradition of the romance. But the quality that most
completely characterizes James's early fiction as alien to that
within the tradition of compassion is its emphasis on simplistic
and, for him, conventional moral judgment.

In James's first novel, *Roderick Hudson* (1876), the
young American sculptor falls in love with a mysterious and
elusive woman in Rome and both his art and his character dis-

integrate. His patron, an older moralistic mentor from New England, much like Howells' Westover in *The Landlord at Lion's Head,* constantly warns Roderick of passion's dangers but the young sinner necessarily falls and is judged by the author as melodramatically as he is presented. Very quickly in subsequent novels, James's morality became less the Puritan stereotype, but the framework of moral judgment remained. In *Daisy Miller* (1879), the American narrator who has lived in Europe "too long" judges the spirited and unconventional Daisy from the stuffy standards of the superficial manners he has worked so hard to acquire. Only when, in another melodramatic conclusion, Daisy suddenly dies from Roman fever, the semi-symbolic malady fatal to uninhibited American girls, does the narrator realize his callow misperception. The judgment turns around and James focuses his moral disapproval on the hollowness of the European reflected in the mannered and spiritless narrator.

The central moralism of James's perspective in his early fiction is most coherently and effectively developed in *The Portrait of a Lady* (1881). In learning to perceive and understand how art and history have helped to dictate European consciousness, Isabel Archer also develops an adequate moral sense. Free to choose her own destiny, as the post-Civil War American was economically and traditionally free from the inherited customs and restraints of Europe, Isabel can reject eligible suitors. Yet, in James's still puritanical framework, free choice involves an equivalent responsibility, and, once having made the mistake of choosing the cruel and desiccated Osmond, Isabel must remain with him and do what little she can in the midst of his restricted world. The end of the novel is not, as some critics have charged, Isabel's inexplicable and life-denying renunciation, for neither Isabel nor James at this point in his fictional career is fully aware of the sexual implications of her decision to abandon Goodwood's "white lightning" to return to Osmond; rather, Isabel's final decision is a statement of her morality, her willingness to accept, in all its difficulty, her own responsibility and self-punishment for the mistake she freely made.

The novel also provides the first extended example of James's use of fiction as itself duplicating the process of discovery. The morality of the novel is never pasted on from the outside. As Isabel is shown coming to understand both the people she encounters and the social and historical forces that have influenced them, she develops the moral sense necessary to make her final decision. The novel is the account of her development of a perception that is simultaneously both realistic and moral, simultaneously because, in terms of the author's assumption throughout the novel, full understanding necessarily involves acting on the basis of that understanding, and such action, in terms of the novel's Protestant ethic, is necessarily moral. This equation between perception and morality remains unchallenged even in some of James's later fiction like *What Maisie Knew* (1897), another novel in which the moral framework is the nineteenth-century Protestant ethos of responsibility and self-denial rather than the Roman Catholic framework of compassionate redemption. Young Maisie, initially a pawn used by divorced parents and surrogate parents to battle or attract each other, develops a knowledge that is both an accurate appraisal of others' motives and a clear "moral sense." Maturing, becoming less passive, more forceful and decisive, Maisie is able to reject an offer to live with her mother's second husband, Sir Claude, and her father's second wife, Mrs. Beale, who have fallen in love with each other through Maisie. She is able, instead, freely to abandon the attractions of the fashionably sophisticated, amoral world and choose the simple and moral loyalty of living with her dowdy governess, Mrs. Wix. Among James's novels, *What Maisie Knew,* in its equation of knowledge with morality and its assurance that the "moral sense" is really what it pretends, often sounds as if it had been written twenty years before it was.

All James's novels discussed thus far assume that man has free will, that he inhabits a world in which moral choice is fully possible. But, in his fiction of the mid-1880's, James began to question these assumptions, to depict wider and more complex social and political worlds which did not always leave the characters so free to choose. *The Bostonians* (1886) presents the struggle between Olive Chancellor, the intellectual Bostonian spinster and suffragette, and Basil Ransom, the casual and sophisticated Southerner, for the allegiance of the beautiful and eloquent innocent, Verena Tarrant. Olive and Basil are both individuals and products of their cultures: Olive part of the dry, cold New England Puritanism; Basil, although far from the stereotype of the indolent gentleman among the magnolias, a strongly masculine representative of provincial and unintellectual virtues. The representative quality of the major characters gives the novel a social and political dimension that had frequently been absent in James's earlier fiction, and the fact that the characters have historical and personal pasts, pasts which impinge upon and help to determine their actions and attitudes, removes the emphasis from a free choice between moral right and wrong. Basil has sometimes been characterized, like some of D. H. Lawrence's creations, as a sexually liberating hero who rescues Verena from the aridity of Olive's intellectual and latent homosexuality. But even if this reading strains James's dry reticence and slightly falsifies the end of the novel, in which Verena's choice of Basil is significantly tearful, joyless, and untriumphant, James's awareness of sexuality and his refusal to dismiss or demolish it merely because it is sexuality provides another complexity that does not permit the free moral choice of the earlier novels. Human experience cannot be summarized or directed as surely as seemed possible in *The Portrait of a Lady*.

Placed in the setting of the anarchistic movements of the 1880's in Europe and dealing significantly with class warfare, as well as opening with extended scenes in the North London slums and Millbank Prison, *The Princess Casamassima* (1886) makes relevant an even wider social and political world than does *The Bostonians*. The young hero, Hyacinth Robinson, is even more the victim of predetermination than are any of James's other characters. Illegitimate son of a French seamstress and an English duke, whom the seamstress later murdered in a quarrel, Hyacinth is torn by the national and class conflicts his origins represent. In a mechanical manner reminiscent of Zola, James never allows us to forget the influence of the genetic polarity that determined Hyacinth. In addition, as he grows up the ward of a poor London dressmaker and becomes a skillful bookbinder, Hyacinth acquires numerous surrogate parents who intensify the conflict by pushing him to the alternate extremes of defying society in a violent anarchist plot, and climbing steadily to power and social position through his charm and ability.

Tragically torn, unable to be either the anarchist or the aristocrat without incorporating something of its polar opposite, Hyacinth commits suicide with the gun he was given to fulfill his
part in the anarchist plot to kill a duke.

Throughout the novel, James connects the political idea
with personal psychology, a connection that is sometimes complex, not necessarily mechanical or completely predetermined.
The representative of English aristocracy, Lady Aurora, who is
selflessly sympathetic to the anarchists and spends all her time
visiting the ill and the downtrodden, is the plainest of eight
daughters who, despite their noble lineage and social position,
have very little money; the Princess Casamassima, an American
girl who felt herself betrayed by a mercenary marriage to a cruel
Italian prince, combines her expiation and her desire for power
in devotion to the anarchist cause, a devotion too single-minded
to recognize Hyacinth's complicated ambivalence as anything
other than back-sliding.

Although he depicts the social and political problems
sympathetically, James never sentimentalizes the poor, frequently shows their self-righteousness or self-pity or desire for
a wealth and power they can never obtain without overturning
society; at the same time, he presents as rewarding and civilizing
the art and grace that leisured aristocracy permits. The character
of Hyacinth reflects all these divisive conflicts, which are too violent to permit survival in the world of the 1880's and which are
not amenable to moral judgment. Despite the suspension of
James's earlier morality, some attitudes from the earlier fiction
remain. The scene in which Hyacinth pledges himself to kill for
the anarchist cause is never presented directly, yet it, with attendant melodrama, reverberates throughout the novel, producing an air of sinister mystery not unlike that of some romances.
The vital and aggressive young girl from the slums, Millicent,
really is, at a moment crucial for Hyacinth, as casually amoral as
society would expect her to be, and Hyacinth, who has often before judged more astutely, accepts the symbolic evidence without
question, James's easy gesture that adds to the melodrama of the
conclusion. These are, however, minor flaws in a full and moving
novel, a novel in which James transcends the simplicities of
moral judgment to render a man caught in a complicated di-

lemma of self and society he cannot solve. James wisely resists his frequent temptation to make his theme more universally applicable and judgmental than that.

After the interlude of interest in the social and political concerns of *The Bostonians* and *The Princess Casamassima,* and a longer interlude spent in his generally unsuccessful attempts to write for the stage, James returned to some of the themes and moral concerns of his early fiction. The situations depicted, for example, in *The American* (1877) and *The Ambassadors* (1903), the sentient American absorbing and reacting to Europe with the moral issues these reactions involve, have a great deal in common. But the treatments of the situations and the kinds of morality are vastly different. In *The American,* Christopher Newman, having made his fortune, goes to Europe to learn, to appraise, and to marry. He falls in love with the sheltered, elegant Madame Claire de Cintré, but her family, dishonest, snobbish, and aristocratic, breaks their earlier promise and forbids the marriage. Claire, always too fearful to act against her family, retires to a convent, and Newman, although bitter, chooses to burn information that could cause a scandal for the family. In James's terms, the American, who can both accept defeat and forgo revenge, who always remains strong and self-possessed, is morally superior to the various types of decadent Europeans depicted in the novel: the passive and submissive Claire; her arrogant and dishonest mother and elder brother; her weak, sensitive younger brother killed in a duel over a woman he knows he should not care for; Mlle. Nioche, depraved and designing because these are the only ways she can survive in society. Newman is treated, however, with considerable wit and irony. He is crude, sometimes clumsy, and openly claims that he has come to Paris to marry the best article "on the market." Yet the irony is only superficial and never qualifies the judgment that Newman, the new American of the post-Civil War era, is the moral superior to everyone else in the novel. *The American* also contains a number of melodramatic elements: the death in a duel, the ominous hints that prefigure the disclosure that Claire's mother and elder brother have murdered their ailing father, the loyal servant lurking behind curtains to reveal dark family truths. These Gothic trappings reinforce James's simplified moral elevation of Newman and his equally simplified condemnation of the arrogant and sinister Bellegardes. Although James intends to parody the excessively moral in the character of Babcock, the Unitarian minister with whom Newman travels for a short time, and who is so scrupulously moral that he cannot enjoy or appreciate Europe at all, the novel itself remains almost its own unintentional parody, the depiction, in puritanical terms, of the New World's superiority to the debased and corrupted Old World. But the focus differs in *The Ambassadors*.

Unlike Newman, Lambert Strether is fifty-five before he makes his journey to Europe. And the journey is propelled not by adventure or the search for a wife, but by the mission from his friend, the matriarch Mrs. Newsome, to reclaim her wayward son, Chad, from Paris where he has lingered too long with a woman. On his mission, however, Strether learns, perceives, appreciates, comes to understand that the kind of American judgment that initiated his trip is limited and inhumane, may be right about simple facts but is wrong about feelings, attitudes, and people. Strether discovers that Puritanism, far from a righteous alternative to the depravity of Europe, is itself an evil, a "joyless," dogmatic attitude that cripples any human experience. The equivalent of Babcock in this novel, Waymarsh, is not gently satirized but is depicted as insensitive, dishonest, and inhumane as he righteously clenches his teeth to "sit through the ordeal of Europe." As Strether becomes less innocent, he learns that Chad's affair with Madame de Vionnet has made Chad more sensitive, responsive, human, than he had ever been before. Strether is finally willing to betray his original charge from Mrs. Newsome and advocate that Chad remain in a relationship that has done him so much good. Although the advice may not be entirely relevant for Chad, as all advice is predicated to some extent on the self who offers it, Strether has come to achieve, through the novel that illustrates this process, a far wider morality and more completely humane judgment than would have been possible among the black and white standards of Woollett, Massachusetts.

Strether's decision to return to America, despite the fact that he has alienated Mrs. Newsome who had supported his magazine, proceeds neither from motives of simple renunciation nor from a recognition of America's essential rightness. Rather, he refuses to stay in Europe and marry his attractive instructor, Maria Gostrey, because he recognizes that his own fifty-five years of humanity have not allowed him to take the chance, that his past has created enough vestigial scrupulosity to prevent him, finally, from having "got anything" for himself. For James, Strether is more pitiably determined by his own past than morally right or wrong. This is not the responsible self-punishment of Isabel Archer's final decision, approved by the author; it is just Strether, with regret, learning what he is able to do. And he has "got" a great deal from his experience, a realization that the mistress, like Madame de Vionnet, can be both more serious and more perceptive, can both understand and care more for others, than the conventionally righteous woman.

Although both novels are moral lessons, the morality in *The Ambassadors* is far wider and more profound than that in *The American,* for, in James's terms, Strether has learned to keep his balance within another culture, to understand other attitudes and perspectives while seeing clearly what he can and cannot, given the influence of his past, assimilate, to recognize values in which he cannot entirely share. Morality, for James in *The Ambassadors,* is personal, humane, contingent on the self and its past, not a matter for rigid dogma or clearly articulated and easily applied universal judgments.

The contrast between *The American* and *The Ambassadors* is also apparent in the different uses of painting and sculpture in the novels. Christopher Newman at first eagerly visits galleries, but he has atrocious taste and remains insensitive, rather like the dense Sir Claude in *What Maisie Knew,* to the humane values art represents. Newman is made a man of superiority to art in a novel that seems to suggest that excessive concern with art is an indication of distance, trivial arrogance, or cultural depravity. The only artist in the novel, Mlle. Nioche, copies Old Masters who have no connection with her experience. In contrast to Newman, Strether gains much of his understanding of European life through art, acquires perception into human situations through the humanity crystallized in works of art. *The Ambassadors,* in this sense, is a defense of the intellectual, a presentation of the valuable life as the fullest possible aesthetic and intellectual apprehension of experience. For James, in his later novels, morality required the highest possible use of all human capacities, the fullest possible development of sensitivity, intelligence, and aesthetic response. Through Strether's discovery on his visit to Notre Dame, we see that even religion, for James, is a symbolic faith in human and artistic perceptions, emphasizing, in Roman Catholic terms, compassion and humility, rather than the puritanical mode of righteous and inflexible judgment. Morality, in *The Ambassadors,* severs its connection with primitive judgment and becomes an attitude praising a greater stretch of man's artistic and intellectual capacities.

Another element in James's fiction that shows his changing attitudes and his growing compassionate concern with humanity is his use of the symbol of money. Early novels frequently dismiss the problem of money, of surviving within society, in order to isolate the character to his moral choices. The moral choice can be free, and the judgment on it therefore absolute, in a world not complicated by the human necessity to survive. Christopher Newman has made his fortune before the story concerning him begins; Isabel Archer is conveniently left a fortune at the beginning of her novel so that her choices may not be debased; Maisie Farange, in *What Maisie Knew,* is assured sufficient income by her parents although they may neglect her in every other conceivable way. In most of James's later fiction, however, the characters are not granted such convenient isolation within which to work out the purity of a moral position. Human misery imposed by society, the need for money in order to maintain grace and position in the world, greed, and the class distinctions money creates all represent complexities concerning money that dilute the purity of moral disdain in all the later novels. Hyacinth Robinson needs to work as a bookbinder in order to eat, a fact that necessarily enters the conflict between his anarchism and his aristocracy. And one of James's three great last novels, *The Wings of the Dove* (1902), uses money to depict and symbolize its central human conflict. The spirited Kate Croy, socially acceptable but poor, having seen her father shabbily try to keep up appearances and her sister bitter in genteel poverty, loves Densher, a journalist as poor as she. Were money Kate's only motive she could easily marry Lord Mark, but she refuses. Discovering that a visiting wealthy and innocent American cousin, Milly Theale, is sure to die within months, Kate proposes that Densher marry Milly to secure her money. Milly, a Jamesian heroine from his earlier fiction—beautiful, exciting, evanescent, removed from the sordid world of European need for money and social position—does die, and though she has discovered the plot between Densher and Kate nevertheless leaves her money to Densher. But when the latter, influenced by Milly as the world is influenced by the myth of that which transcends it, returns to Kate, he says that she may have either the money or Densher but not both. He hopes for marriage "as we were," for a return to their innocence before corruption by the dream and influence of money. Kate's final line in the novel, "We shall never be again as we were!", indicates the impossibility of disassociating oneself from money or survival within society, of retreating to the pure vacuum within which moral decision is clear and significant. Milly Theale, about to die, with no concern for money, can afford the pure idealism of what is apparently a perfectly moral action but can also be taken as a means for revenge; Kate Croy, alive, without money, finds moral decision more complicated and purity attenuated. In terms of the novel, since Milly and Kate are almost identical apart from their necessary circumstances, life demands incessant attenuations and the material interchange money represents is inevitably connected with moral decision. In contrast, the earlier novels, removing money from the realm of morality, protecting the characters from concern with circumstances, sanction an easier morality that is both more trivial and more absolute. Kate Croy has the harder and more widely representative choices.

Kate's purity is also attenuated in another sense, for she consents to Densher's demand that she sleep with him before they are married, her part of the bargain if he is to marry Milly. James does not, however, judge the premarital sexual act as just "evil" in itself; rather, the sexual act is part of the relationship, an act to be judged, moderated, considered, in terms of all the other actions and relationships in the novel. James hardly endorses the act as healthy sexual liberation, but he also does not take the standard puritanical point of view. Milly's innocence is also flawed, for her will is a document designed to corrupt and manipulate others. Closest to "evil" in the novel is the character of Lord Mark, the man without love, without spirit or emotional development, the hollow show of form who reveals the plot to Milly out of his own frustration and bitterness. James's qualified and ambivalent judgments about sex in his later novels represent a sharp contrast to the attitudes implicit in his earlier work.

Earlier, he had venerated the innocent, like Daisy Miller or Christopher Newman, and tended to regard sexual experience as invariably corrupting, linking it to the depraved European in contrast to the innocent American. The American in Europe was likely to be cast in terms of the innocent from Eden tasting the sinful apple of worldly experience. But, from the time of *The Bostonians* and *The Princess Casamassima* to the end of his fictional career, sexual experience is no longer invariably corrupting, and the American in his innocence is likely to be even less morally acute than is the depraved European. Paul Muniment, a cooler and more dedicated revolutionary than Hyacinth, is able to sleep with the Princess Casamassima, whereas Hyacinth himself would never dare suggest such a consummation of their relationship. This, for James, becomes primarily a distinction between the self-assured calculating anarchist and the more frightened and ambivalent one, a descriptive distinction of character rather than a moral judgment. Although James still recoils from any public expression of sexual activity (some of his characters, on a walk in the park, "watched the young of both sexes, hilarious and red in the face, roll in promiscuous accouplement over the slopes"), the private sexual relationship is always seen in a wider, more fully human context. Even Maisie Farange's decision to follow the "moral sense" and live with Mrs. Wix is, to a slight extent, undercut by her own recognition that she would run off with Sir Claude alone if he would abandon Mrs. Beale. Something of morality is a posture that covers sexual frustration. When, in *The Ambassadors*, Strether first hears the relationship between Chad and Madame de Vionnet described as a "virtuous attachment," he assumes, naively, that the phrase must mean that the two are not sleeping together. But it is the measure of Strether's expanding moral capacity that, when he discovers that the two have spent numerous discreet weekends together in the country, he can still on completely different grounds describe the relationship as a "virtuous attachment." The definition of virtue has grown far beyond the simple puritanical fact of technical carnal innocence.

James's final more complicated attitude toward sexual relationship is most clearly apparent in his last great novel, *The Golden Bowl* (1904). Maggie Verver, an American living in Europe with her widowed father, marries the impoverished Italian nobleman, Prince Amerigo. Fearing that her marriage and her child might leave her father bored and isolated, Maggie arranges that he marry Charlotte Stant, her old friend, who had, although unknown to Maggie, been in love with the Prince. After both marriages take place, the two couples live in close proximity, a fact that allows Charlotte and the Prince to resume their affair. Maggie's eventual discovery of her husband's infidelity with her best friend is not, however, simply a justification for moral disapproval. Rather the discovery impels introspection in each of the principal characters, sets in motion speculations, examinations of motives, and resolutions that permit the possibility of a more conscious and a more moral life. Maggie, for example, recognizes that her closeness to her father and her dominating treatment of others—as if they were precious art objects she had discovered in out-of-the-way shops—has helped push her husband into an affair. Only after recognizing something of her own motives and her own behavior can Maggie realize that her marriage must take precedence over her concern for her father and her desire to surround herself with a comfortably inviolate foursome. The idea of the foursome is like the golden bowl itself, an art object with an almost imperceptible crack that Charlotte and the Prince reject in a shop, but which Maggie later buys, an appealing amalgam that cannot sustain the strains of a vital relationship. Maggie learns what the crack in the golden bowl means, is able to accept the smashing of the bowl, and can develop the allegiance necessary for a marriage to the primary emotionality and sexuality of her husband. Moral issues in the novel are subsumed under the necessity for each individual to develop healthy, complete, private, and honest relationships of his own. In this, James's most thoroughly anti-Puritan novel, the extramarital affair, examined and assimilated consciously, is the event that allows the central character to create a fuller version of experience for herself.

The relative unimportance of a simple version of moral issues in James's later novels brings him closer to the writers in the tradition of compassion than is any other nineteenth-century American novelist. He moved gradually toward an attitude of compassion, but the attitude is also visible, if atypical, in some of his earlier work—for a change in direction in such a career is not as clearly marked as the turning off of one faucet and the turning on of another. In *Washington Square* (1881), for example, the heroine, Catherine Sloper, is able finally to achieve independence from the influences of her cruel father, her designing suitor, and her silly aunt. Although her independence is lonely, her survival, depicted in terms that do not involve moral judgment or any kind of lesson, illustrates James's compassion. Catherine, far less free than Christopher Newman or Isabel Archer, is able to understand something of the circumstances that threatened to define her life completely and manages to survive independently in spite of them. Although Catherine is less interesting than Strether or Maggie Verver because less intelligent and less conscious of herself, the treatment of her character nevertheless signifies a compassionate attitude in James's early fiction.

In addition, James's prose, in its developing prolixity, moved toward the incompleteness characteristic of the tradition of compassion. In his critical work, he explicitly rejected allegory, maintaining that allegory worked against the presentation of both life and meaning, even though some of his earlier work can clearly be read in allegorical terms. Neither the frequent superficial irony nor James's apparent intentions prevent *The American* from being read as the innocent American's confrontation with the mysterious and sophisticated depravity of the Old World. Yet James, with increasing consciousness, moved away from any similarity to allegory in his later fiction. The balance of his critical work, such as his famous essay "The Art of Fiction" (1884), argued for the novel as a loose form that would recreate reality rather than the moralistic and heavily-pointed fantasy so popular in his day. Increasingly, in the later novels, James's prose became fuller, more complicated, more heavily proliferating with qualifications and dilemmas, an accurate although not always easily comprehensible vehicle for all the complexities of experience he attempted to render. The prose, like the characters and attitudes apparent in the later novels, inhibits the formulation of easy or simplified judgments.

James's later novels as structures also point toward the tradition of compassion. Despite the massive consistency involved in working out the developing consciousness of his characters, James leaves loose ends in his last novels, for even the shaped development of comprehensive consciousness cannot hold all the psychological reverberations the author suggests. At the end of *The Golden Bowl*, Adam Verver, Maggie's father, takes his wife Charlotte back to America, the two couples separating from each other so that each marriage may work on its own terms. All four characters recognize that such a separation is necessary and desirable. But, the reader wonders, what of the demanding and importunate Charlotte back in America? Will Adam try to relegate her to the status of the grandest art object in his collection and will she be satisfied to play a quietly regal role in a calmer and more innocent society? And Maggie, too, has a moment of sheer terror when her father leaves, despite her realization that she needs and wants to love her husband. The characters live, and may yet change again, beyond their resolutions in the novel.

Similarly, in *The Ambassadors,* although the major emphasis of the novel is consistently worked out in terms of Strether's developing recognition of himself and the world, not all the issues are fully resolved. Strether has persuaded Chad to reject the bribe to return to America, and Chad will remain in Paris with Madame de Vionnet. But both Strether and Maria Gostrey, like the reader, wonder how long Chad's devotion to the salutary influence that formed him will last. The commerce and the new industry of advertising in America fascinate Chad, Madame de Vionnet is beginning to show signs of age, and Chad, after all, is only twenty-eight. As the novel has so clearly demonstrated, Strether himself was fifty-five before he could surely recognize what was vital and valuable in human experience. Despite Strether's triumph of understanding, he is unlikely to return to Europe and he cannot transmit that understanding to another generation, no matter how close he is to it. Chad, only half-conscious of his own motives, may well become more callow, more simply "amenable," than Strether ever was. As Maria Gostrey says, in one of her last conversations with Strether, "I'm sorry for us all!" Her statement is a generally applicable suffusion of sympathy that goes beyond the structures of Strether's developing consciousness.

This strain of compassion in the novels cannot, however, finally designate James's fiction, for such a designation would falsify both James's carefully placed emphasis and the controlling stance generally behind the characters and incidents of the novels. Pre-eminently, James's novels praise the efforts of the intellectual, the value of human consciousness and sensitivity in working one's way through experience. Isabel Archer, Strether, Maggie Verver—all are better off through the exercise of their intellectual and aesthetic perceptions than they would have been without them. And "better off," for James, means more morally admirable as well. This faith in the ultimate moral and practical, although incomplete, triumph of intellectual and aesthetic capacity distinguishes James from many of the writers within the tradition of compassion, writers such as Hardy whose stance is less certain and whose faith is invariably undercut by doubt and questioning.

James's faith itself becomes an abstraction, a means for the author to play God, to arrange and dispose his characters and events in terms of ultimately knowable and definable principles. Only in *The Golden Bowl* do the characters suggest their capacity for an existence not completely accounted for in terms of the novel, not completely resolved and finished. For the most part, James explains, rewards, and judges his people. At the same time that this disposition to control every aspect of the novel, to be God, characterizes James's fiction generally, the increasing complexity and the vast widening of the humanity involved in his definition of morality move the fiction gradually toward an attitude of compassion.

The fiction of compassion was not indigenous to nineteenth-century America, for much of the writing was influenced by the fable of the new Eden or propensity of the New World to deliver a universal message with energy and imagination. But

Howells and, more consciously and more brilliantly, James grew into a less simply moralistic, if less certain, understanding of the actual and particular humanity they tried to portray, and, in so doing, came closer to the tradition of compassion already apparent in English fiction. Howells and James had their followers in the direction of an attitude of compassion, novelists like Edith Wharton in *The House of Mirth* and *The Age of Innocence*. Mrs. Wharton was less likely to assume a God-like point of view than James, more likely to dissolve her characters in questions and irresolution, although her characters and situations most frequently lack James's range and profundity. For the most part, American fiction in the early twentieth century retained the focus on good and evil, on salvation and damnation, on judgment and morality rather than on compassion. Not until a third of the way through the twentieth century, in the work of Faulkner and the later work of Fitzgerald, did compassion, as a fully articulated and developed attitude, become a term useful in designating a significant quality in the best of American fiction.

VI

ARNOLD BENNETT

I N 1896, before he had published a novel, Arnold Bennett wrote in his *Journal:* "Essential characteristic of the really great novelist: a Christ-like, all-embracing compassion." Bennett's *Journal,* like Trollope's *An Autobiography,* is a reticent document, swamped with numbers of words written and prices paid, using mundane fact to cover the writer's fear of pretense in his own artistic ambition. The posthumous publication of the *Journal* (1933), again like that of Trollope, did little to enhance Bennett's reputation as a serious novelist, and frequently the observations in the *Journal* seem superficial when measured against the range, diversity, and depth of the fiction itself.

In the novels, his compassion was "all-embracing," but it had none of the divine origin nor the tone of instant injection that the quotation suggests. Rather, Bennett's sense of compassion was part of his perspective, part of his automatic response to the experience he both observed and created, an attitude that contained little of the deliberate or programmatic mercy, the forgiveness, or the justice that the comparison to Christ implies.

Bennett's world is conveyed through a density of material objects. Man lives in a rich, crowded, tangible world, one always impinging upon him. A large part of the novelistic force of the Clayhanger trilogy, *Clayhanger* (1910) *Hilda Lessways* (1911), and *These Twain* (1915), is in the description of the environments against which the major characters struggle: the

[129

misery of child labor in the potteries, and the stockade from which Darius, as a child, is rescued; the careful accretion of small pieces of property and stone houses from which Hilda breaks away; the musical ease of the Orgreaves which either coddles or cripples their children; the shabby boarding houses in the back streets of Brighton, which provide Hilda with a second prison; above all, the smoke, provincialism, and narrow religion of the Five Towns, the environmental confinements that Edwin Clayhanger both absorbs and revolts against. The sense of the Five Towns, its bluntness, its taboos, its darkness, its strength, infuses the novels so thoroughly that when, in *These Twain,* Edwin and Hilda spend a weekend at the Devonshire manor belonging to Alicia Orgreave's husband, the reader feels as if he has suddenly been transported from the conditions of human experience into a country-house fantasy. With characteristic irony, Bennett places his most literally described prison and the one most central to the plot of the novel in the middle of Devonshire.

In *The Old Wives' Tale* (1908), Bennett also constructs the material environment with an accuracy and specificity that indicates its importance. The novel is full of minute descriptions of the Bursley square and houses, of Paris dresses and Paris maps, of all the material, like the Baines's draper's shop itself, of human existence. The human body is also material, and at least half the chapters of the novel begin with an account of how a particular character has aged or grown stouter since last encountered; physical descriptions are invariably both precise and revealing. Despite all the insistence on environment and physical description, the characters are not merely ciphers that reflect their world or their physiognomy. In *The Old Wives' Tale,* as in the Clayhanger trilogy, the principal characters both reflect and struggle against the material constrictions around them. *The Old Wives' Tale* describes the long and complex relationship between each of the two sisters and the provincial square that helped to form them. The Five Towns has produced Constance's stolidity and self-righteousness as well as her stiff and rather unexpected kindness and shrewdness concerning her husband. Sophia, superficially more rebellious, deserted by her husband in Paris, saves herself by running a boarding house with Five Towns' stringency and thrift, an attitude that insures both economic survival and personal and sexual isolation.

In addition to these best known of Bennett's novels, others also rely heavily on the background and influence of the industrial Five Towns in the grim north. *Anna of the Five Towns* (1902) carefully catalogues the stringent economics and the equally stringent religion of the Five Towns in a novel in which the heroine, only gradually aware of her impulse to revolt, marries the respectable product of the area just as she realizes that a weak, insolvent, religious hypocrite was the only man she could have loved. In somewhat melodramatic terms, this novel contains much of the ambivalence, the simultaneous revolt against and absorption of background, that characterizes *The Old Wives' Tale* and the Clayhanger trilogy.

After 1915, Bennett's novels were no longer set in the Five Towns, the area he had personally left almost twenty years earlier. Yet his characters never escaped the formative environment easily, for numerous novels, from *A Man from the North* (1898) to *The Roll-Call* (1918) (the latter could be added to the Clayhanger trilogy to form a tetralogy, for it deals with the early career of George Cannon, Hilda's son and Edwin's stepson), present many of the issues of taste and behavior facing the young man from the Five Towns in the more open and cosmopolitan world of London. Some of Bennett's lighter novels give less lethal force to the environment and allow the individual trying to change his social role unmitigated triumph. In *The Card* (1911), Denry Machin, a brash, enterprising, and unselfconscious young man, rises from the very bottom to the very top of Five Towns' society. The heroine of *Helen with the High Hand* (1910) deftly insinuates herself into her wealthy, settled, elderly uncle's house and manipulates him into buying a mansion and occupying a principal social position in the town. With a further ironic turn, Bennett has the hero of *A Great Man* (1904), a stodgy young clerk with none of Denry's or Helen's charm or brash assertiveness, rise through society because of the accidental composition of a novel that captures popular taste. Not only, in many of the light novels, is society's hierarchy amenable to as-

saults from the talented and energetic, but society sometimes encourages flexibility and changes in class for entirely superficial
and accidental reasons.

The lighter novels set in the north deal extensively with
class, those barriers of birth or money that man establishes in
order to divide himself from his fellows, and Bennett never takes
the divisions seriously as indicative of permanent human worth.
The heroes enjoy an easy journey through the divisions and
finally achieve the freedom of unquestioned financial and social
position. Doubts, moral issues, and concern for others never dilute their pleasure in the good life they have acquired. In the
more serious novels, the characters' rise is more difficult and complicated. The character is likely not to get all he wants; his rise
is circumscribed both by environment and by the moral doubts
or consideration of others he sees along the way. He does not, at
the end of the serious novel, rest comfortably in the complete
achievement of the good life, although he is not completely defeated or betrayed. His rise is an achievement within a social
environment that also reacts against him, not, as in the lighter
novels, the rosy path to success. In Bennett's world, where people
are basically very much alike, where the author seldom makes
distinctions in the ultimate value of a particular person, where
he in fact objects to pegging human beings on a scale of value,
the interest in society, in manners, in social differences, often becomes a principal subject for the fiction. The difference between
Bennett's light and serious novels is a difference of tone, of depth,
of perspective, not a difference of subject matter or of environments.

The Old Wives' Tale treats issues of class on at least two
levels. More lightly, Bennett shows the changes in the Baines's
servants through the more than forty years of the novel, from the
loyal Maggie ensconced in the cellar, who surprisingly has a
love life for half-an-hour every third Thursday afternoon, to the
impudent young Maud who tyrannizes her aged mistresses. More
seriously, Bennett shows the rise of Samuel Povey from tight-
lipped work, paper collars, and rigorous Methodism to the genial and respectable draper who, finally, can even afford the luxury
of dying in his allegiance to an unpopular cause. Samuel Povey,
always treated with respect even though his early rigidities are

satirized, reflects all the questions of taste and principle faced by the man patiently rising through late nineteenth-century northern industrial society, and Bennett at Samuel's death even breaks the structure of the novel to underline his admiration and respect for the man.

The Clayhanger trilogy, similarly, often treats class issues. Edwin's rise from proprietor of the printing business to the progressive and respected industrialist who holds musical evenings and is the closest friend of the cultured Orgreave family covers as much social distance as does his father's rise from the pot-banks to his own printing shop, although Edwin neither has nor needs his father's single-minded dedication to rising. How far Edwin has moved from Darius is apparent in *These Twain* in the contrast between Edwin and the Benbows, his sister Clara and her husband who have remained fixed in an earlier and less sophisticated materialism. The Benbows come to Edwin's house, intent on patching a children's quarrel between their son and Edwin's stepson, revealing all the tyranny, the strict Methodism and misunderstanding control in the way they bring up their children. Edwin has moved into a class willing to treat children with a more genial humanity, to leave them room for their own quarrels and reconciliations. Although Bennett finds Edwin's method more humane and more attractive, the judgment is far from ultimate or underscored as a theme in the novel; the mixed results in the second generation of Orgreaves works against making too binding or inflexible any generalization about bringing up children. Rather, the incident emphasizes a social difference, a category, a contrast that establishes the author's preference without allowing conversion into an absolute judgment.

In a world without absolute judgments, without a final "truth," Bennett's concern centers on life, on existence. There are preferences and gradations in life, people are more or less honest, classes are different and some are more comfortable and more humane settings for human experience than are others, but the basic material of life is common to all. Bennett's materialism is pervasive and thoroughgoing, finally dependent on the basic material of existence, the human body. Bennett's universe has no abstract truth or justice, has no God. *The Old Wives' Tale* ends with both sisters dead, Constance having died in loyalty to the anti-Federation cause that is bound to lose, as Sophia's old dog hobbles to her plate to eat. The physical image, the necessary creatureness, overwhelms the novel. In Bennett's last novel, *Imperial Palace* (1930), a man of unusual skill, Evelyn Orcham, attempts to manage a vast and complicated hotel, a microcosmic image of a highly organized and interdependent human society. Evelyn's aim is not based on an abstract principle or belief, for, as Bennett comments at the end of the novel, the human attempt to create order is self-generated, an artificial construction within a multiple world where man has no God or principle to guide him. Insofar as Hilda and Edwin represent Bennett's point of view toward issues in the Clayhanger trilogy, Bennett's agnosticism is carefully and consistently presented. Hilda shocks the fundamentalist Five Towns with her skepticism about church-going and the efficacy of prayer; Edwin, less overtly blasphemous, spends long passages in *Clayhanger* considering the evidence and working out his atheism. The attraction between Hilda and Edwin, the relationship central to the entire trilogy, is sparked by Edwin's early statement:

"You can't help what you believe. You can't make yourself believe anything. And I don't see why you should, either. There's no virtue in believing."

This statement reverberates through Hilda's mind, creating there a vision of Edwin as unusually wise and perceptive. It also reverberates throughout the novels. The centrality of the Hilda/Edwin relationship to Bennett's scheme is the centrality of their agnosticism, their refusal to delude themselves into thinking man has any permanent or absolute truth. In Bennett's terms, Hilda and Edwin can serve as the central focus because, even in the midst of the pious and fundamentalist Five Towns and in spite of all their subsidiary pettiness and fallibility, they never succumb to the human need for abstract assurance. They can, consequently, in Bennett's terms, consider human issues and problems, houses and industries, marriages and children, hate and love, for what they are.

In a world without God or an acceptable substitute, man finally faces only time, change, and death. Physical death, the decay of the body, ends everything because neither physically nor metaphorically can man surmount death. And, consistently in Bennett's serious fiction, all the secondary issues of class and occupation, of masters and servants, of domination and weakness, evaporate when confronted with decay and death. The classic statement of Bennett's constant position is in *The Old Wives' Tale* when Sophia is called to Manchester to identify the dead body of Gerald, the husband who had deserted her almost forty years earlier:

> Sophia then experienced a pure and primitive emotion, uncoloured by any moral or religious quality. She was not sorry that Gerald had wasted his life, nor that he was a shame to his years and to her. The manner of his life was of no importance. What affected her was that he had once been young, and that he had grown old, and was now dead. That was all. Youth and vigour had come to that. . . . Everything came to that. . . . The whole of her huge and bitter grievance against him fell to pieces and crumbled. She saw him young, and proud, and strong, as for instance when he had kissed her lying on the bed in that London hotel—she forgot the name—in 1866; and now he was old, and worn, and horrible, and dead.

The staccato sentences and the repetition in the passage hammer the finality of death relentlessly. Even the use of the date, "in 1866," is characteristic, for Bennett always charts the trivia, all that fades in the face of death, with accuracy and care to underline the unappeasable power and irony of death. One whole book of the four in *Clayhanger* concerns the slow decay and death of Darius from a gradual softening of the brain and paralysis. Although the power struggle between father and son, the decline of Darius parallel to the rise of Edwin, is part of the book, Bennett dwells relentlessly on the sheer misery of Darius' physical decay, the growing mental and physical feebleness of the once determined man. Similarly, in the other novels of the trilogy, Sarah Gailey ages slowly as her joints stiffen in pain and her skin becomes like parchment; and Auntie Hamps, still trying to impose her parsimony and her religion on others, dries gradually to a harsh whisper before she expires. Repeatedly, Bennett creates, in his long descriptions of illnesses and deaths, the sense that this is the inevitable end of man's struggles and that time and change necessarily extinguish all of the human being.

[135

In his *Aspects of the Novel*, E. M. Forster made the famous statement that "time is the real hero" of *The Old Wives' Tale*. In one sense this is true, for nothing can arrest or overcome time. But, in another sense, the statement reduces Bennett's multiplicity to a single theme, judges the life he presents only from the point of view of what permanent message can be extrapolated from it. Time and only time does win, but Constance's time, stodgy, traditional, and satisfying, is different from Sophia's time, prodigal and unhappy. Within Bennett's insistence on material existence, on physical decay, many other concerns are prominent. The changes in the novel are historical as well as personal: the decline of mid-Victorian certitude and morality; the rise of Samuel Povey and the extinction of his libertine cousin, a relic from an earlier age; the career of Constance's son, an engaging but aimless "fin de siecle" dilettante. Even the concern with the characters of the sisters does not confine itself to the inexorable workings of time. Although the differences between the sisters may always have been the same, as the early scenes which contrast Constance's righteous goodness to Sophia's spirited rebellion indicate, the novel is more than the working out, through time, of a germinal comparison. The novel, more than theme, is the recording of *how* the contrast works out, of Samuel Povey against Gerald Scales, of Bursley against Paris, of a drapery against a boarding house, of a constant series of similarities and differences that gives vitality to the contrast between the two sisters. If man is formed by his social and psychological environment, that statement, for Bennett, is often less interesting than a copious and careful account of just what that environment is and just how it works on man. The message of Bennett is that man dies and times change, but the life of *The Old Wives' Tale,* like that of much of Bennett's other work, inheres more in the minute particulars of description than in the message.

Similarly, the compromises involved in Edwin Clayhanger's revolt against his father are determined and predictable, established in the first book of the first novel in the trilogy. But the forms these compromises take, the relationships they lead to and the positions and contradictions they cause Edwin to establish, sustain a sense of life through three novels. The particulars in themselves, without connection to possible generalizations, always fascinated Bennett:

(11 January 1897) . . . And then, in King's Road, the figures of tradesmen at shop doors, of children romping or stealing along mournfully, of men and women each totally different from every other, and all serious, wrapt up in their own thoughts and ends— these seemed curiously strange and novel and wonderful. Every scene, even the commonest, is wonderful, if only one can detach oneself, casting off all memory of use and custom, and behold it (as it were) for the first time; in its right, authentic colours; without making comparisons.

The changes in personality and history must, for Bennett, be looked at freshly, as they are, without judgment, without pre-conception, without "making comparisons." The only warrant-able generalization is the fact of change itself.

Bennett's treatment of the human personality follows this interest in particular and separate facts. In his attempt to portray as much of the human being as possible rather than to select or organize his portrayal around a doctrinal or metaphysical per-spective, Bennett often did not distinguish between different stages in the revelation of human personality. To resort to the conventional onion: most of us think that we peel away periph-eral layers of personality in order to reach or approach the kernel of "truth," the guiding or determining force of personality, at the center of the onion. But Bennett often found the peripheral layers as important as the center, the outer man as revealing as the inner, and he seldom, in his novels, distinguished between them, seldom labeled a particular fact the core or center of the onion. Centrality is more a matter of time and process than of depth or finality. In one of the more helpful passages in his *Journal,* Bennett himself said this:

(24 January 1909) . . . In becoming acquainted with people you uncover layer after layer. Using the word in my sense, one person may be most *distinguished* of a crowd on the first layer, another on the second, and so on. Until after uncovering several layers, you may ultimately come to a person who, down below, is the most dis-tinguished of all—on *that layer*. The final result may be quite un-expected. I suppose that the inmost layer is the most important, but each has its importance.

Critics have sometimes claimed that, because he so often failed to distinguish between inner and outer manifestations of personality, Bennett was superficial and not interested in psychology. Quite the contrary: his careful multiplicity and his refusal to assert that the most deeply hidden characteristic is necessarily the most significant one demonstrates a profound interest in the complexity of human psychology and a skepticism about the theology of first causes or causal hierarchy.

Bennett describes the interplay of inner and outer forces of human personality most fully in the Clayhanger trilogy. At the beginning of *Clayhanger,* when Edwin is just leaving school, he wants to become an architect. Architecture for Edwin combines his talents, his revolt, the "flame" that makes him an aspiring and unusual person in the Five Towns, and his admiration for the genial culture of the Orgreaves (Osmond Orgreave, the father of the family, is an architect who encourages him) . Edwin, however, loses, for his father keeps him financially and emotionally dependent, and Edwin eventually takes over the printing shop. Yet Edwin is not really defeated: he becomes a successful and progressive printer, retains his "flame" and his friendship with the Orgreaves. As the novels go on, architecture no longer has the representative meaning it once did for Edwin, no longer provides the central clue to his personality. By *These Twain,* Edwin's interest in architecture has dwindled to a talent for arranging the interiors of houses, primarily exercised in keeping the arrangements as they always have been, and a mildly nostalgic pleasure in discovering that his stepson intends to become an architect. What seemed a statement about the inner man is really less important to Edwin than is his Five Towns' punctuality or concern for the organization of his business.

Similarly, Edwin's marriage to Hilda unites his "flame" with her "intensity," combines two characters with a capacity for passion and understanding beyond that of most of the people in the Five Towns. The "flame" and the "intensity," along with the strong sexual attraction they suggest, remain throughout the novels, but the marriage is also compounded of Hilda's bitchy scheming and Edwin's lovingly cherished resentment, of Edwin's prissiness and Hilda's unpredictability, of each being unjust to the other. After a climactic argument, near the end of *These Twain,* Edwin takes a long walk to consider ending his marriage to Hilda:

And then there flashed into his mind, complete, the great discovery of all his career. It was banal; it was commonplace; it was what every one knew. Yet it was the great discovery of all his career. If Hilda had not been unjust in the assertion of her own individuality, there could be no merit in yielding to her. To yield to a just claim was not meritorious, though to withstand it would be wicked. He was objecting to injustice as a child objects to rain on a holiday. Injustice was a tremendous actuality! It had to be faced and accepted.

Yet Edwin's reconciliation to injustice is no more the clue to his marriage than the defeated desire to become an architect was the clue to his career. Rather, Edwin's reconciliation is a particular point in his marriage, no more or less significant than a number of other points and understandings. Bennett's characters seldom achieve a permanent kernel of self-awareness. They focus on a particular incident or perspective, often magnifying its meaning at the moment, only to see that particular dissolve in the continuum of time.

Bennett's later novels frequently exhibit the same refusal to distinguish between the significance of inner and outer aspects of the human personality. In *Imperial Palace,* the masterful entrepreneur, Evelyn Orcham, never knows whether his facade or his inner dependence attracts the woman he wants. In another late novel, *Lord Raingo* (1926), in which the successful hero from the North has become a member of the Prime Minister's war-time cabinet (versions of Lloyd George and Winston Churchill are easily recognizable), Bennett has his hero spend the last third of the novel dying from pneumonia. While indulging in reveries at various stages of consciousness, Lord Raingo learns that his mistress has committed suicide and he tries to unravel the cause. In a series of wide leaps in his own consciousness, he thinks of her tenderness toward him, of her clothes, of her relationship with a younger man, of her "melancholia," of her dependent sister, of his offer to marry her, a mixture that completely confuses the conventional distinction between the superficial and the profound. All the possibilities are equal to Lord Raingo, and Bennett never solves the problem: Lord Raingo dies and human experience remains a series of separate facts with the causal patterns unknown.

Bennett's characters frequently try to leave some mark on the universe, to achieve something to ameliorate the necessary inexorability of time and death. Sometimes, this attempt is made through sheer industry, through fidelity to their work. One of the later light novels, *Mr. Prohack* (1922), is designed almost entirely around a more modern version of the Victorian gospel of work. The principal character, Mr. Prohack, having amassed wealth and position, retires in order to find out what contemporary life is like. Quickly bored with sedentary clubs, he comes to understand more of the changes in London since World War I, more of his children and their generation; he even learns to dance. But the uncertainties and confusion of his new knowledge make him unhappy, make him constantly wonder about himself and his roles. At the end of the novel, he starts another business, recognizing that, no matter what the general virtues of the uncommitted man about town, he needs the restricted function of a steady occupation. Edwin Clayhanger, too, works assiduously at his printing factory, even when neither his interest nor his need for money compels him. And his stepson, George, as a young architect in London in *The Roll-Call,* leaves one of his first theatre parties in order to go home to finish some drawings. The drawings are not immediately required; the compulsion is within George rather than in the nature of his job or his success. These examples, however, indicate that Bennett's use of work is different from the standard version of the Victorian gospel, for, in Bennett, work does not insure salvation or generate any positive moral virtue. Rather, work is a means of staving off disaster, a kind of control the individual uses to cloak the abyss of his uncertainty and lack of commitment. Bennett, a compulsive worker himself, recognized something of this early in his career:

(20 May 1896) . . . I regard it as a serious and disquieting symptom that, now that my novel is finished, I have a positive *wish* to work. No man healthy in mind and body ever *wants* to work.

Work is never a cure, rather a distraction from dwelling on the inevitability of disease.

More frequently than work, power is important in Bennett's fiction. Social, political, or commercial power represents control, indicates the individual's ability to organize the forces of the world around him, to prevent him from being carried along only as time's puppet and victim. The later novels particularly, novels such as *The Pretty Lady* (1918), *Lord Raingo,* and *Imperial Palace,* all contain a principal figure who exercises considerable power over the fortunes and destinies of his fellows, and all debate the issues that power involves. Power, like work, never leads to salvation, never, in fact, even allows the individual the degree of control he had thought possible. Lord Raingo may be able to influence the Prime Minister and the Cabinet, but he cannot control his wife, his mistress, or his war-shocked son, an example of a new and indifferent generation, even before he becomes the victim of his heart and lungs. G. J. Hoape, the hero of *The Pretty Lady,* cannot isolate himself or his emotions from the war no matter how decorously and carefully he constructs his shelter with the French prostitute. Evelyn Orcham may control the intricate network of the luxury hotel, but he cannot control Gracie, the example of the contemporary emancipated young woman. Gracie first seduces Evelyn and then dissolves the affair, initiating every change in her relationship with the supposedly dominant master of princes and commercial pirates. For Bennett, the hotel or the department store is frequently the image of the highly complicated organization of modern society, all the human requirements of food, shelter, love, and amusement managed and organized under a calm and efficient facade. It was not, as critics have often claimed, merely the opulence of the luxury hotel that fascinated Bennett; more significantly, it was the organization of the hotel, as in all the passages concerning the kitchens and the cellars and the linen rooms in *Imperial Palace,* a mirror for all forms of human organization and control, that led him to use hotels as subject matter. Even in the Clayhanger trilogy the first George Cannon, Hilda's first husband, is intrigued by the possibility of owning and managing a group of hotels. George, like the other hotel managers whom Bennett treats seriously, extends himself too far; he is arrested for bigamy before his plans for owning hotels are complete.

In addition to light novels, Bennett wrote a large number of fantasies or, as he referred to them, "fantasias." The earliest were often detective novels, another form that emphasizes what man can control, for carefully examining the clues and solving the crime is a limited artifice within which rational and intelligent man can exercise his control over a bewildering universe. The detective fantasy, the puzzles of the universe momentarily solved, is evident in such novels as *The Grand Babylon Hotel* (1902), *Teresa of Watling Street* (1904), and *Hugo* (1906), the last of which combines the mystery solved with the controllable microcosm of the large London department store. These three novels, heavily and ungracefully written, full of stereotyped characters, are among Bennett's worst. Later fantasies, like *The Vanguard* (1927), in which a wealthy newspaper proprietor controls a small society on his elegant yacht, are more urbane, more complicated, more obviously comic, and written with greater skill. The yachtsman can easily make whole wardrobes, sumptuous dinners, and charming prisoners almost magically appear from all the luxurious resources of the modern world, but he cannot control his own wife. Throughout the fantasies, early and late, Bennett's sharp sense of improbability and his mocking tone demonstrate that he never takes them seriously, never feels that his solution of the artificial mystery or his surrounding his characters with efficiency and luxury can do anything more than provide diversion from all the problems of self and society that man cannot solve. The fantasies, clearly labeled as such by tone and treatment as well as title, imagine a control that does not exist, and, within themselves, in the later examples, undercut even the imagining.

Although Bennett described the social issues and social system of his time meticulously, he never defended the system. On the other hand, his fiction contains no pleas for violent reform, no bitter condemnations of the system. His consistent interest remained in individuals and how they reacted within and against the social system as it existed and changed. The Clayhanger trilogy offers Bennett's most complete treatment on this point. Although part of the attraction between Edwin and Hilda is based on their mutual skepticism about religion and God, another part of their attraction develops through their shared realization that society is frequently unjust. They both, in the first novel, sympathize with strikers, realizing that they too would march in the streets if they were hungry or overworked. As they age, Hilda, more harshly treated by life and more selfish, changes somewhat, although she still loves Edwin partly because he always sympathizes with strikers and treats his workmen as fairly as he can. Darius' difficult scrounging for success had made him harsh and indifferent to others; Edwin's easier path left him room for more sympathy and equivocation:

> Something wrong! Under the influence of strikes and anarchist meetings he felt with foreboding and even with a little personal alarm that something was wrong. Those greasy, slatternly girls, for instance, with their coarse charm and their sexuality,— they were underpaid. . . . Not those girls, not his works, not this industry and that, was wrong. All was wrong. And it was impossible to imagine any future period when all would not be wrong. Perfection was a desolating thought. Nevertheless the struggle towards it was instinctive and had to go on.

His recognition that the system is entirely wrong does not prevent Edwin from living within it, nor does it lead him to look back with nostalgia on a simpler world before the system developed. Edwin knows his grandfather had lived and died in miserable slave labor, and Edwin is also pleased with the new radiator that heats his front hall easily and efficiently. When, in *The Roll-Call*, years later, George Cannon comes from London to visit the Five Towns, he is not surprised to find Edwin richer, heavier, but still with doubts about the system and still concerned for his workers, while Hilda, with Edwin's admiration, has become one of the first women in the Five Towns to drive an automobile.

Bennett rarely, in his novels, discussed questions of social justice as such. Almost always his opinions were filtered through individuals, his concerns expressed through a fictional creation. His *Journal* is generally even less revealing, but one passage shows some of his own concern and ambivalence:

> (23 May 1908) . . . I honestly think I care quite as much for other people's happiness as for my own; and that is not saying much for my love of my own happiness. Love of justice, more than outraged sensibility at the spectacle of suffering and cruelty, prompts me to support social reforms. I can and do look at suffering with scientific (artistic) coldness. I do not care. I am above it. But I want to hasten justice, for its own sake. I think this is fairly sincere; perhaps not quite. I don't think I scorn people; I have none of that scorn of inferior people (i.e., of the vast majority of people) which is seen in

many great men. I think my view is greater than theirs. Clumsiness in living is what I scorn: systems, not people.

Unlike some other novelists, D. H. Lawrence for example, Bennett does not, in his fiction, reserve his compassion for the special people, the elite or the sensitive. Bennett's compassion is as wide and diffuse as are his creations; only the system, the generalization, the theology, is beyond its reach. In one novel, *The Lion's Share* (1916), Bennett deals extensively with militant reformers, a group of forceful, heroic, and appealing campaigners for women's suffrage. Yet the intense campaigners suffer in their futile struggle, sometimes become more narrow and inhumane themselves as their cause consumes their lives. In contrast, the young heroine, Audrey Moze, is never bound or defined by her cause, is able to care for art, for people, for wisdom, and for experience as well as for women's suffrage.

In Bennett's fiction, the allegiance to a cause invariably restricts the human being, cuts off dimensions of experience that will, in any event, eventually be consumed by time and change. Within time, however, experience is multiple and diverse, often beyond the individual's control, a matter of environment and circumstance and luck. Although Bennett sympathizes with all people, for no one can overcome time and few people can control very much within it, he does have preferences, does express an additional veneration for those, like Edwin or Samuel Povey, whose points of view encompass a breadth and intensity of appreciation one would not have expected from a simple account of their backgrounds and circumstances. On one level, Samuel Povey is the stereotype of the young clerk rising into the Five Towns' middle classes through perseverance, cheek, and devotion to his religion; yet he can also grow, learn, appreciate the humanity in those very different from himself. Similarly, Edwin could be regarded as just the successful Five Towns' businessman at the end of the nineteenth century, genial, smug, and prissy, but Bennett also shows his sense of excitement, his doubts, his understanding of others. Bennett characteristically switched stereotypes, showed discoveries in unlikely places or unexpected qualities in expected characters, in order to demonstrate the multiplicity of experience and the difficulties with ordinary judgments.

In one novel, *Lillian* (1922), Bennett characterizes the young heroine, a middle-class girl whose parents have died and left her penniless, as an opportunist who schemes to marry her boss. Just as everyone thinks she has no scruples or conscience and has gone off with him to the Riviera, she upsets the judgments with scrupulous self-sacrifice when he becomes ill. In this instance, Bennett's switch is melodramatic and unconvincing, but, in other novels, his devices destroying easy judgment are far more illuminating and effective. In the Clayhanger trilogy, the first two novels are balanced against each other, for many of the events seen from Edwin's point of view in *Clayhanger* are repeated from Hilda's point of view in *Hilda Lessways*. At the scene of the Sunday School celebration in *Clayhanger,* Edwin increases his self-esteem and thinks he has impressed Hilda with his handling of the feeble old Mr. Shushions and his witty superiority about Sunday Schools; he easily covers his fright at Hilda's strangely passionate silence. From the same situation in *Hilda Lessways,* however, we see Hilda's impatient scorn for Edwin's calm patience, as well as the fact that she can be moved, in spite of her agnosticism, by the chorus of Sunday School hymns. Edwin's judgments, like ours, are fallible. Bennett comments more directly on the inadequacy of human judgment in *The Old Wives' Tale*. At a crucial moment, after Sophia has run away with Gerald to London, she recognizes that she has cut herself off completely from the Five Towns, that she is now entirely dependent on her lover:

"I've got no one but you now," she murmured in a melting voice.

She fancied in her ignorance that the expression of this sentiment would please him. She was not aware that a man is usually rather chilled by it, because it proves to him that the other is thinking about his responsibilities and not about his privileges.

The device in the Clayhanger trilogy is more sophisticated, but both create the same skepticism about human knowledge and judgment. Sometimes, as in *The Vanguard,* where the yachtsman casually masters everyone until his wife arrives, Bennett's switches are playful; at other times, as in the trilogy, they are serious and carefully developed. But, at whatever level, Bennett seldom allows his reader to repose in an easy judgment or an un-contested stereotype.

Bennett's switches and devices constantly underline the complexity of the human personality. Evelyn Orcham revolves from his hotel to Gracie, to his business interests, to the tidy and efficient housekeeper he finally marries in a series of turns so rapid that he does not know where he is, all the exact opposite of his facade which exudes a calm mastery of his environment. In *Whom God Hath Joined* (1906), a novel about two divorces in the Five Towns, one of the principals, Lawrence Ridware, a clerk in a law office, shuttles between dullness and perception, be-tween reserved and conventional shock at his own position and a sense of emotional freedom entirely alien to the Five Towns. As he scratches the surface of his own complexity, Ridware hardly knows what he wants to do or be. Edwin Clayhanger, too, never really discovers or resolves himself. Despite all his speculation and all Hilda's attention, as both adversary and mate, no clear definition of Edwin emerges from the novels. Edwin is not just as he sees himself, not just as Hilda sees him, but something in addition to this picture drawn by switches and negatives. No character in Bennett's fiction really understands himself, achieves anything close to total self-awareness. The partial perceptions, the understanding only in retrospect, and the inability to sum-mon conscious control at the necessary moment are made quali-ties of all human nature demanding tremendous compassion. Yet Bennett is also distant in spite of all his compassion. He dem-onstrates the complexities, the mysteries, and destroys the pos-sible stereotypes and easy generalizations. The reader is left with a series of facts, multiple and often apparently contradictory, about the individual, an accumulation of perspectives that can-not be guided by an interpretative pattern or judgment. If the reader pushes for pattern relentlessly enough, he finds Bennett saying, "This is what humanity is like," yet that statement is less important and less interesting than is the particular and multi-ple nature of the humanity described.

One of the reasons that man in Bennett's fiction resists definition is that he is almost always seen in combination: within his environment, absorbing and reacting; within a marriage, presenting the multiple sides of himself to the multiple sides of another person. Much of the Clayhanger trilogy and *The Old Wives' Tale* deals with marriages, the complicated abrasions and adjustments of two different individuals living in constant proximity. Because of his interest in relationships, in marriages, Bennett often scrutinizes women carefully and extensively. In nineteenth and early twentieth century fiction generally, a "truth" could best be represented by a man, striking out, carrying a message or symbolizing a point of view relevant for the whole society. But the woman, so often circumscribed by the home and by close relationships, embodies no exterior "truth," represents an interest in the facts and feelings of human relationships. Bennett, in this sense, followed the conventional fictional attitude and used his women to demonstrate the multiplicity and inconsistency of the facts and connections within human experience, the impossibility of drawing a usable "truth" from life. His women, from the early heroines of *Anna of the Five Towns* and *Leonora* (1903), to Gracie in *Imperial Palace,* are often his best creations, vital, sexual, trying to find a place for themselves and their impulses within the world. Leonora, an attractive woman of forty, unhappy with her dishonest husband, falls in love with an exciting man who has made his fortune in America and returned to the Five Towns. After presenting the issues sharply and convincingly, Bennett resolves them melodramatically with a convenient suicide, and the novel falls apart. But the issues, the mistake in marriage, the attempt to preserve loyalty to a dishonest mate (both Hilda and Leonora lose respect for dishonest husbands not because of the dishonesty but because the husband, in his own guilt, rejects his wife's willingness to share everything), the need to find a focus for passion and intensity, the need to be loved completely by a man more respectable than they, are all brought up again and treated far more completely in the character of Hilda Lessways.

Bennett often used one novel as raw material for another, developing and expanding his original concept. The relationship of the prominent man and his mistress, begun in *The Pretty Lady* and *Lord Raingo,* is given sharper and more extensive treatment in *Imperial Palace*. Bennett also demonstrates some interest in the varieties of sexual relationship, although this is hinted at delicately rather than described exhaustively. In *The Pretty*

Lady, the prostitute becomes a symbol for the willfully destructive sexual debasement manifest in London during the war. In addition, both *The Pretty Lady* and *The Roll-Call* present glimpses of Lesbians and possible sexual flagellants, glimpses that are tame from the point of view of 1970 but relatively daring in terms of 1918. Despite the charge, in Virginia Woolf's essay entitled "Mr. Bennett and Mrs. Brown" (1924), that Bennett was so interested in houses and furnishings and the map of the towns that he never got the essential character of the human being, the basic nature of Mrs. Brown, Bennett demonstrated the variety of Mrs. Brown, at least insofar as she is a sexual creature, with as much depth, completeness, and frankness as did Mrs. Woolf in her novels. And the complex combination of sexuality and intelligence, of passionate intensity and a shrewdly focused appraisal of the world about her, has seldom been rendered more thoroughly and effectively than in the character of Hilda Lessways.

Bennett's prose reveals the same multiplicity of detail, the same complexity that is evident in his treatment of characters and relationships. At one point, in *The Pretty Lady,* G. J. Hoape is attending a Gallery's showing of paintings and drawings for a war-time charity. Bennett describes the elegant and social gathering, but he also includes a sharp and detailed reminder about the brutality of war:

Thus all the very well-dressed and very expensively-dressed women, and all the men who admired and desired them as they moved, in voluptuous perfection, amid dazzling pictures with the soft illumination of screened skylights above and the reflections in polished parquet below—all of both sexes were comfortably conscious of virtue in the undoubted fact that they were helping to support two renowned hospitals where at that very moment dissevered legs and arms were being thrown in buckets.

Later in the novel, G. J. Hoape and his mistress are caught in an air-raid on a London street. Bennett describes the bomb and G. J.'s feelings, his automatic calm, his memory that he has a flashlight in his pocket, his solicitude for Christine, his mistress; but Bennett also describes the architecture, the plan of the streets through which G. J. runs, and the debris the bomb leaves, like "a child's severed arm, with a fragment of brown frock on it and a tinsel ring on one of the fingers of the dirty little hand." Many aspects, both ordinary and horrifying, of London at war are crowded into the very short scene. Similarly, in *The Roll-Call,* when George Cannon visits the northern town for which he has designed a new Town Hall, Bennett uses George's short walk, taken because he has been neglected by the town's dignitaries, to describe all levels of northern society: the showy vulgarity of the music hall and its newly rich patrons, the stodgy desolation of a provincial hotel dinner, the huge new trams carrying men in caps and women who swear in public. Bennett's prose, clear and direct, is also crowded with detail, with revealing and separate facts that give vitality to the fiction.

Bennett's view of the complexity of human character is matched by his view of the complexity of history. History, like the human personality, is a composite of separate facts not easily amenable to comparison or judgment. In the first book of *The Old Wives' Tale,* Bennett spends many pages establishing the time and place of his story, describing Bursley and the Five Towns with meticulous care, establishing the social atmosphere of the 1860's in order to reveal all the influences that shaped his characters. Describing the 1860's in 1908, Bennett is extremely careful to avoid historical stereotypes, to characterize the past without adopting a simplified and condescending attitude toward it. In a series of ironic passages, and the beginning of *The Old Wives' Tale* has a consistently ironic tone, Bennett describes the past from a number of different perspectives. At times, within a complicated irony, he directs his description against those who would think of the past as a primitive era, who would look down on the poor creatures who suffered through the difficult existence in the Baines's shop on the square:

> For Constance and Sophia had the disadvantage of living in the middle ages. The crinoline had not quite reached its full circumference, and the dress-improver had not even been thought of. In all the Five Towns there was not a public bath, nor a free library, nor a municipal park, nor a telephone, nor yet a board-school. People had not understood the vital necessity of going away to the seaside every year. Bishop Colenso had just staggered Christianity by his shameless notions on the Pentateuch. Half Lancashire was

starving on account of the American war. Garroting was the chief
amusement of the homicidal classes. Incredible as it may appear,
there was nothing but a horse-tram running between Bursley and
Hanbridge—and that only twice an hour; and between the other
towns no stage of any kind! One went to Longshaw as one now
goes to Pekin. It was an era so dark and backward that one might
wonder how people could sleep in their beds at night for thinking
about their sad state.

The passage, its irony alternating with details of the genuine
shocks and difficulties of the 1860's, conveys a good deal of Bennett's ambivalence toward the past. His satire is even more
sharply pointed against those who would romanticize the past,
would nostalgically lament the end of the good, old, spirited
days:

> It was the morning of the third day of Bursley Wakes; not
the modern finicking and respectable, but an orgiastic carnival,
gross in all its manifestations of joy. . . . You could see the atroci-
ties of the French Revolution, and of the Fiji Islands, and the rav-
ages of unspeakable diseases, and the living flesh of a nearly nude
human female guaranteed to turn the scale at twenty-two stone,
and the skeletons of the mysterious phantoscope, and the bloody
contests of champions naked to the waist (with the chance of pick-
ing up a red tooth as a relic). You could try your strength by hitting
an image of a fellow-creature in the stomach, and test your aim by
knocking off the heads of other images with a wooden ball.

More characteristically, Bennett is more objective, his emotions
further from his material. Family and friend take a last look at
the dead John Baines:

> They knew not that they were gazing at a vanished era. John Baines
had belonged to the past, to the age when men really did think of
their souls, when orators by phrases could move crowds to fury or
to pity, when no one had learnt to hurry, when Demos was only
turning in his sleep, when the sole beauty of life resided in its inflexible and slow dignity, when hell really had no bottom, and a
gilt-clasped Bible really was the secret of England's greatness. Mid-
Victorian England lay on that mahogany bed. Ideals had passed
away with John Baines. It is thus that ideals die; not in the con-

ventional pageantry of honoured death, but sorrily, ignobly, while one's head is turned.

History, like the individual, is subject to constant change and cannot be interpreted by a consistent pattern. History remains a series of separate, multiple, and fascinating facts, and all Bennett's irony is employed to keep it so.

Later in his career, some of Bennett's serious work moved toward greater abstraction. No longer could the statement "This is what life is like" be the sole generalization suggested in the fiction, for a few of Bennett's later novels are organized around theme, do point toward a kind of message. The first of these novels is *The Pretty Lady*. G. J. Hoape tries to insulate his concerns with his attractive mistress in her comfortable little flat, but the war keeps breaking in. Even his token work for a committee that runs hospitals in France is not enough to assuage the obtrusive omnipresence of the war. As a parallel to G. J. Hoape, Christine tries to isolate herself to a decorously practiced version of her trade and G. J., but the economics of war, being caught in a zeppelin raid, and her own mystic impulse for the battered soldier (an impulse, which, ironically, at the very end of the novel, G. J. mistakes for crude soliciting and consequently abandons her) all prevent her from shutting off the outside world. Both characters wanted physical and emotional privacy, the shelter of uncomplicated sex, but the world and the characters themselves keep creating complications. Other characters, like Concepcion, widowed in the first days of the war, almost driven mad by witnessing a horrible industrial accident and the death of her best friend in the zeppelin raid, always know that life, during the war, cannot be controlled or isolated, that the insulated security of the upper classes before 1914 has permanently vanished. And Concepcion is, finally, with all her high-strung responses to experience, the right woman for G. J., the one who forces an awareness of the horrors and irrationalities of experience into G. J.'s calm traditionalism. The whole novel, with its direct treatment of sexuality and war-time violence, is organized around the theme that physical and emotional insulation are no longer possible or desirable, that the world has changed enough to make the inherited attitude of a class, the assurance of security and the value of the calm facade, both ludicrous and impossible. As returning soldiers, destruction, and frank sexuality crowd the pages of *The Pretty Lady*, the attitudes and axioms of the prewar upper classes are doomed.

Riceyman Steps (1923) is even more dependent on and tightly controlled by theme. In the midst of changing London and decaying old buildings, balanced against the well-lighted shop with a telephone across the road, Henry Earlforward, bookseller and miser, tries to retain what he has, to lock away all his money in his safe. Although he marries Violet, a woman initially almost as miserly as he, Earlforward wants only to preserve himself against the changes of time. Within a year he literally starves himself and his wife to death. Against the shrivelled miser, Bennett places the healthy servant Elsie who steals food, lights fires, and nurses her war-shocked lover, Joe, back to health and sanity. Throughout the novel, the narrow, dark, crabbed, miserly quality of Earlforward and his shop is constantly contrasted with Elsie's warm animality and the lighted shop across the street. Some of the characterization, dictated by the thematic contrast, becomes grotesque: Henry trades his wife's first wedding ring (she had been married and widowed before) for a new and less expensive one, proudly giving her the money saved to keep as her own; when Violet surprises Henry by having the shop vacuum-cleaned as a wedding present, he asks the workmen "What do you do with the dirt? . . . Do you sell it? Do you get anything for it?"; Elsie's hunger, repeated so often, begins to sound like the result of a tapeworm. Appropriately for the heavily thematic novel, Bennett uses imagery more carefully and consistently than he usually does. The Earlforwards are always dark, shrivelling, moving inward on themselves, faces pinched, seen in rooms and shadows; Elsie, in contrast, is always warm, glowing, moving, embracing, reaching outward. A scene in the Chamber of Horrors at Madame Tussaud's waxworks serves as a miniature analogue for the whole novel, as Henry, dissembling assurance and confidence, leads a slightly frightened Violet down the long steps to see monstrous examples of historical crimes in the same way that, in the novel, he leads her down into the horrors of his own life-denying nature. The whole novel is a statement on the importance of psychic and physical health, on the body, on reaching outward toward life, as against the narrow preservation and anal narcisscism of the miser. Bennett includes such statements in other novels, as in one of the reveries of the dying hero in *Lord Raingo,* but only in *Riceyman Steps* can the whole novel with all its details be interpreted in terms of the theme.

Despite its carefully controlled theme and consistently imagistic prose, *Riceyman Steps* is not completely different from Bennett's other novels. The fact that it has so consistent a theme does make a difference, for it implicitly assumes that man has some power to control his future, that he can consciously reach outward toward health and light, whereas many of the other novels leave the possibility of conscious and meaningful human action shrouded in luck, accident, and environmental destiny. But the theme itself, the importance of the physical, the necessity for man's accommodation to inevitable change (in these terms very much like the theme of *The Pretty Lady*), is a message extrapolated from the detailed text of novels like *The Old Wives' Tale* and the Clayhanger trilogy. In the latter, change is simply recorded and characters grow old and die; in the more thematic novels, Bennett reverses the emphasis and warns us that we had better recognize our dependence on the physical and acquire the ability to respond to change. *Riceyman Steps* also cannot be taken as an indication that Bennett's change in fictional method was permanent or the final result of a long evolution. In his very next work, the long short story, "Elsie and the Child" (1924), often read as a sequel to *Riceyman Steps,* Bennett continues with several of the principal characters. Elsie has married Joe, now fully recovered, and they both work for Dr. Raste, the human apostle of health who had tried to save the Earlforwards in *Riceyman Steps.* But this time, Elsie, despite her glowing health, almost poisons the situation by letting her own vanity lead the affections of Dr. Raste's daughter away from the child's mother. Joe is able to save the situation, to show Elsie what she has done. The animal creature, Elsie, may represent perfect health in some situations, but, at other times, a more uniquely human consciousness and wisdom is necessary. In this switch, Elsie loses her role as the representative of Bennett's message. In addition, later novels like *Lord Raingo* and *Imperial Palace* return to the form not completely explainable by theme, return to presenting a multiple perspective on life from which no usable message can be extracted. *Imperial Palace,* establishing the vast hotel that mirrors the vastness of human society, emphasizes, again, the dilemmas, the inconsistencies, and the superficiality of conscious control within the human creature.

The heavily thematic novel, the demonstration of the "truth" or validity of a particular perspective toward experience is less compassionate than is most of Bennett's work. Yet, even in *Riceyman Steps,* the ever-present sense of time and death, the strain of the Earlforwards' effort to preserve what little they have had from life, calls forth some compassion. Bennett's sense of compassion extended to all people, was not reserved for the particularly sensitive or the estranged. His fiction has no villains, except for a very few characters in the early and superficial detective stories. Frequently, the compassionate treatment of humanity emphasizes someone particularly victimized, hounded or betrayed by the world beyond the point where most people are hounded or betrayed, like old Mr. Shushions in the Clayhanger trilogy, one of the founders of the Sunday Schools, who had rescued Darius from the stockade, but who lives long enough to become feeble, befuddled, impoverished, ignored, and finally dies within the stockade himself.

Since time is the disease, the very old, those who have excessively survived their age, have become most useless, sometimes receive a particularly intense compassion. But, for the most part, Bennett's compassion is applied equally to all people, to all the victims of time and change, to all who would represent something enduring and are necessarily dissolved by time. And that compassion, insisting that judgments are less important than sympathy, that the comparisons between people are superficial, and only the death they share ultimate, becomes Bennett's principal point of view toward the humanity he describes so carefully and minutely. The compassion is part of the novels, a logically necessary corollary to the perspective that gives man no finally valid definition, that proposes no "truth" about human nature, that postulates no God. Compassion is, in Bennett, part of the very understanding of the indefinable multiplicity of human nature. At the same time, Bennett's changing distance from his characters, his sense of irony, prevents his sense of compassion from sinking to the sentimental or the merely pathetic. The thorough treatment of Edwin's vanities, hesitations, and inconsistencies, like the comic demonstration of the ludicrous sides of the Baines sisters, in Bennett's best work, keeps the compassion hard and profound, an attitude that recognizes necessary human fallibility and impermanence, rather than spongily sentimental with the emphasis sinking on the victim or the martyr. Bennett's distance, his ironic switches, the texture of his multiple and inconsistent details, gives his best fiction a depth of compassion that could not be matched by simple thematic statements like "Life is difficult" or "Man is mortal."

VII

E. M. FORSTER

E. M. FORSTER's five novels have a highly controlled and patterned texture. Like the famous echoes in the Marabar
Caves in *A Passage to India* (1924), echoes which frighten Mrs.
Moore into a strangely remote silence and which cause the spinster, Adela Quested, to accuse Dr. Aziz of assaulting her, thematic echoes repeat themselves and reverberate through each of
Forster's novels. Themes are always announced in miniature
before they are expanded and developed. At the beginning of
A Passage to India, a group of Indians casually discuss the fact
that, given the circumstances of Anglo-India, the individual
Englishman and the individual Indian never can become close
friends, a fact that, in a much more intense and complicated
way, the whole novel demonstrates. Physically, identical caves
repeat throughout the dry landscape of Marabar, the scene of
the expedition central to the novel; similarly, the hollow and
sinister echo within each cave develops into the sound of colonial
India, the sinister emptiness of one civilization imposing on another. People, even the well-intentioned like Dr. Aziz, Mrs.
Moore, Adela, and Fielding, are trapped, frightened, and isolated by the echo, by the radiating repetition of the social and
historical landscape.

A *Room with a View* (1908), a simpler novel than *A
Passage to India,* also begins with an announcement of its theme.
Lucy Honeychurch, the prim young English girl traveling in
Italy for the first time, is advised, both by the clergyman, Mr.

Beebe, and the sage, Mr. Emerson, to let her perceptions and her personality expand, to express in personal interchange the same emotion and understanding she can express when she plays Beethoven on the piano. And the novel, as a whole, traces Lucy's growth, the development of her capacity to understand, express, and finally live by this same capacity for emotion. Her growth begins with her defense of the unconventional Emersons, father and son, against the nasty innuendoes circulating within the cloistered society of the English pension in Florence, but the major growth is charted by the difference between the two incidents in which George Emerson, the son, kisses Lucy. The first kiss, in Italy, is almost accidental, a product of the warm day and the flowers and the view of Florence, and Lucy understands nothing from it; the second kiss, the reprise back in England, is equally unexpected, but, this time, although she is immediately angered by the kiss, it does instigate a chain of events and perceptions that cause her to break her engagement to the socially eligible but desiccated aesthete, Cecil Vyse.

Forster uses patterns of detail similar to these kisses more frequently and more tightly in his next novel, *Howards End* (1910). Early in this book, two glass photograph frames are accidentally broken. Leonard Bast, the poor insurance clerk who is excited and befuddled after meeting the intellectual Schlegel sisters at a concert, breaks the frame around the picture of Jacky, the sensual and soddenly stupid woman he has promised to marry; Margaret Schlegel, fascinated and puzzled by the graciously aristocratic Mrs. Wilcox, nervously drops the photograph of Mrs. Wilcox's daughter-in-law. Both characters, in their clumsiness, are uneasy about encounters that lead them out of the worlds they have known. In deliberately extending her range of experience, Margaret realizes that one must have a sense of proportion, but must not cultivate this balance too soon, must be willing to immerse herself in experience, to love all sorts of people, before settling into proportion. Yet Forster gives her this realization twice: once before her encounters with the Wilcoxes begin, once after Mrs. Wilcox is dead and Margaret has begun to see through her preconceptions about Mr. Wilcox, the successful business man. The less abstract and more romantic sister, Helen, repeats her own mistake, her use of the nearest man to resolve the dilemma of trying to extend her consciousness to all people and all classes. The first time, with Paul Wilcox, the result is only a kiss and an engagement quickly broken; the second time, with Leonard Bast, the result is a baby. And Helen herself recognizes the connection. The patterns demonstrate both the repetitive predictability of so much of human experience and the careful control Forster keeps over his characters in order to illustrate his themes.

Other instances of contrivance crowd the novels. Forster often kills off characters suddenly and inexplicably as soon as they serve no further thematic purpose. The famous example is the chapter in *The Longest Journey* (1907) that begins "Gerald died that afternoon," although Gerald has just been described as the healthy, insensitive, animalistic athlete. But Forster needed this stupid and brutal character only to show his appeal for Agnes Pembroke, the woman whom Rickie Elliot eventually marries. Gerald, lingering in Agnes's mind, is as useful dead as alive, and his one-dimensionality would render longer direct presentation boring. Rickie's mother is also killed quickly: apparently in good health and liberated by the death of a cruel husband, she survives him by only eleven days. Yet her death is necessary for the suspense of the plot, for delaying the revelation about Rickie's illegitimate half-brother in order to focus on the impact of the revelations on the developing Rickie. In other novels, too, death is often sudden and convenient. Mrs. Wilcox in *Howards End* and Mrs. Moore in *A Passage to India* die shortly after they have established a thematic role in the novels, functioning as symbols of a lost humanity and understanding more completely in death than they convincingly could in life. Other characters, like Lilia in Forster's first novel, *Where Angels Fear to Tread* (1905), die as soon as they have performed their function in the plot, Lilia having given birth to the baby whom the conflicting worlds of England and Italy can struggle to possess.

Forster's novels sometimes contain intrusions established at the appropriate time but disrupting the course of narrative and probability. This is particularly apparent in *The Longest Journey,* in which the accounts of both Rickie's past and that of his half-brother, Stephen, are given in set pieces interrupting the narrative, Forster, at each point, revealing just enough to draw an emotional reaction from Rickie. The thematic focus on Rickie's emotional development, the destruction of his "inner life" by the world and his wife and his background, is kept consistent even at the price of a somewhat clumsy structure and uneven novelistic pace. Occasionally, too, Forster relies on extravagant coincidence in order to advance the plot, as in the revelation in *Howards End,* that the lumpish Jacky, brought to the Wilcoxes along with the suffering Leonard by Helen Schlegel, was once the very proper Mr. Wilcox's mistress. Forster is often willing to violate probability in order to connect a thematic strand or establish a forceful irony. Characters from one novel sometimes appear in another, carrying their thematic roles with them: Cecil Vyse from *A Room with a View* makes a momentary appearance as an example of the isolated and sterile Oxford don he has become in *Howards End;* Miss Herriton, the malicious and principled Puritan spinster who is responsible for the baby's death in *Where Angels Fear to Tread,* reappears quickly in *A Room with a View,* ironically cited as an authority on suburban respectability.

All the pattern, the repetition, and the violation of probability focus on Forster's emphasis on theme, on the general truth that gives each of the novels coherence. In one instance, *A Room with a View,* an account of the theme can summarize almost all the issues. Early in the novel, Lucy has an image of herself, reinforced by her spinster chaperon, as a medieval lady, chaste, removed, and dignified, sensitive to art but allowing nothing to touch her. The perfect mate for the medieval lady is Cecil Vyse, chivalrous, ascetic, removed from emotion. Yet, in the course of the novel, Lucy comes to realize that the medieval image is false for her, that, as Forster explains, "A Gothic statue implies celibacy, just as a Greek statue implies fruition," that George Emerson, depicted at one point as a Greek hero naked in the sun, is a more suitable mate than is Cecil. George's father, in a conversation with Lucy, articulates the issues the novel has developed, pleading for love of the body, "not the body, but of the body," as more important, more the "truth" of human experience than all the conventional visions and gentilities. The final chapter, with George and Lucy happily married, is called

"The End of the Middle Ages." One can either recognize the "truth" of the body and openness and human concern, represented by the Greek, or remain swaddled in medieval dignity and remoteness. Although some characters, like Charlotte, the spinster chaperon, remain ambivalent, the theme itself is unequivocal and infuses the entire novel.

Forster's other novels, although organized around themes, cannot be so easily encompassed by them. *The Longest Journey*, for example, openly presents a theme much like that of *A Room with a View*. *The Longest Journey* presents the conflict between the life of the earth, of passions, directness, and fellow feeling against the conventions, the life of money and respectability. Yet Rickie Elliot, hounded, sensitive, and born with an hereditary club foot, is unable to live the life of the earth, is too weak to follow his feelings in defiance of the conventional commercial and domestic world around him. Forster traces the development of Rickie's sensitivity and fellow-feeling, praising his "imagination" as a quality far too rare in the world; yet most of the novel demonstrates Rickie's slow disintegration, under pressure from his greedy and conventional wife, Agnes, from her priggish brother, from the brutal public school, and from Rickie's cynical and malicious aunt. Rickie succumbs, refusing to acknowledge his half-brother Stephen until too late, until the acknowledgment has to be a cathartic gesture of sacrifice and self-destruction.

For Forster, the character of Rickie is not just a negative example of the positive theme, not just an instance of the man who did not follow the direct life of the earth and was so destroyed, for Forster gives Rickie a hero's amount of space and a highly worthy man's measure of compassion. Nor is Forster implying that no man is able to follow the prescriptions of the theme, for both Ansell, Rickie's intelligent friend from Cambridge, and Stephen, the sketchily educated and rudely honest half-brother, are satisfactory men of the earth. Rather, the novel coheres in two different ways: the theme of the earth against the conventions, in which many of the characters are symbolic counters, like Ansell and Stephen on the positive side of the earth and Agnes and her brother on the negative side of inhumane convention; the development and defeat of Rickie, an imaginative man but a weak one whose "inner life" and honest insight are destroyed by the world around him. Forster's attitude is similarly divided between praise for the "truth" of the life of the earth and compassion for the man too weak to live in the way he sees is true.

In Forster's fiction, the interest in particular characters often works against the dominance of theme, leaves loose ends that cannot be resolved by applying the thematic abstraction. Like Rickie Elliot, other of Forster's characters learn too late or go down to defeat with the wrong side just as all their instincts and imagination recognize the right. Both Caroline Abbott and Philip Herriton, in *Where Angels Fear to Tread,* recognize, in different degrees, that their English coldness and propriety is a less satisfactory environment for the baby than his father's slovenly and unscheduled warmth. Yet Caroline and Philip, by their background and their mission, are involved in the militant Harriet Herriton's disastrous stealing of the baby. They can only return to England, Caroline hopelessly in love with the Italian father of the baby, Philip hopelessly in love with Caroline but knowing he had never been sufficiently committed to life to inspire love in return, both having achieved a sensitivity that the events of the novel leave them no room to express. The development of the characters lingers beyond and in contradiction to the relentless theme that has pushed them to its conclusion.

Similarly, in *A Passage to India,* Adela Quested understands her own neurosis, her combination of sexual fear and desire that leads to hallucination, after she has falsely accused Aziz of assaulting her in the cave. Despite Adela's honesty at the trial (which, given the environment of Anglo-India, requires tremendous courage and self-awareness) and the fact that Aziz is acquitted, the damage has already been made irreparable in the accusation itself. One more event, no matter how unintentional, has divided Indian and Englishman; one more injustice has been pushed on the conquered. And Adela is responsible. Yet the development of her character persists, although her function in the theme of the novel is finished. Forster sends her back to England, allowing her only the minor action of introducing Fielding to Mrs. Moore's children, suspending Adela in spinsterhood in the useless atmosphere of her painful understanding. Compassion pulls our feelings one way, justice in terms of the theme pulls the other. Forster resolves this combination in a suspension that is both complex and inevitable.

Despite the tightness and emphasis of Forster's themes, they are seldom made universal. Not only do the characters often develop beyond the boundaries of the theme, but Forster himself injects qualifications into the very themes that organize the novels. In *The Longest Journey,* having insisted on the importance of allegiance to fellow-feeling and sensitivity, he turns aside to speculate about whether or not Rickie is wise, at the end of the novel, to throw off his comfortable evasions and follow Stephen and the "incorruptible" way of "God." Rickie, after all, has much to lose and may no longer be able to survive his own dedication. *A Passage to India* develops the necessary conflict, necessary alienation, between Englishman and Indian, each believing at bottom in the rightness of his own culture, his own God. But many of the Englishmen, all the educated and sensitive, Forster points out, no longer believe in their God, no longer know what they believe. And the Indians, Moslem and Hindu, believe in different Gods, for there are different Indias. All the varieties of belief and skepticism, of religious experience and indifference, qualify the theme.

The conclusion of *Howards End* provides Forster's most apparent example of thematic qualification. Margaret Schlegel, the apostle of the "inner life" and the desire to "connect" with different ranges of human experience, has both married and modified the successful Henry Wilcox. She also shelters Helen and the illegitimate baby at Howards End, the house which represents the best of English ease and graciousness and which Margaret has rightfully inherited. Thematically, Margaret is triumphant; the truths and understanding she worked so hard for throughout the novel have been reaffirmed. Yet, as she and Helen watch the sky over Howards End, the smoke and gloom of London are approaching, a new and more hostile environment threatens the peace achieved with such difficulty. And Charles Wilcox, the most callous and implacable materialist, has killed Leonard Bast, the muddled representative of the aspiring lower middle classes. Margaret's domain, although thematically triumphant in the novel, becomes small and temporary through

Forster's final qualifications, becomes almost a valuable gesture rather than an achieved conclusion.

In addition to these qualifications attached to the themes themselves, Forster also qualifies through his style, through his way of treating issues and personalities. Lionel Trilling has made this point:

> Across each of his novels runs a barricade; the opposed forces on each side are Good and Evil in the forms of Life and Death, Light and Darkness, Fertility and Sterility, Courage and Respectability, Intelligence and Stupidity—all the great absolutes that are so dull when discussed in themselves. The comic manner, however, will not tolerate absolutes. It stands on the barricade and casts doubt on both sides. The fierce plots move forward to grand simplicities but the comic manner confuses the issues, forcing upon us the difficulties and complications of the moral fact. . . . "Wash ye, make yourselves clean," says the plot, and the manner murmurs, "If you can find the soap."

True as this statement is, Forster's qualifications are not only apparent in his "comic manner." Through character, through symbol, through direct intrusions, as well as through the "comic manner," he covers with ambiguity the straight lines of his plots and themes.

Forster is apparently, himself, conscious of the inner conflict between various elements in his fiction. Although he has not provided specific notes on the composition of his novels, his general remarks, in the casually acute lectures called *Aspects of the Novel,* contain many references to all the discordant elements in the amorphous form of the novel. At the beginning of the famous chapter "The Plot," Forster quotes the Aristotelean dictum that the plot, or action, embodies all the issues of a literary work, and comments that although Aristotle's point may well be important for the more rigid form of the drama it is not very useful in considering the looser form of the novel. After giving specific examples of novelists whose greatest skill was not in plotting events, whose plots sometimes stifled other elements, novelists such as Thomas Hardy, Forster continues:

> Still the moral from the point of these lectures is again unfavorable to Aristotle. In the novel, all human happiness and misery does not

take the form of action, it seeks means of expression other than through the plot, it must not be rigidly canalized.

In the losing battle that the plot fights with the characters, it often takes a cowardly revenge. Nearly all novels are feeble at the end. This is because the plot requires to be wound up. Why is this necessary? Why is there not a convention which allows a novelist to stop as soon as he feels muddled or bored?

Whether the plot or character wins in a given instance is immaterial. Forster's point is the conflict between different elements in the novel, between those, like plot or theme, that are fixed and conclusive and those, like character or symbol, that, when successful, radiate and suggest beyond careful boundaries.

In the next chapter, Forster restates the idea in somewhat different terms:

> The idea running through these lectures is by now plain enough: that there are in the novel two forces: human beings and a bundle of various things not human beings, and that it is the novelist's business to adjust these two forces and conciliate their claims.

Conciliation often involves ambiguity. Forster's use of the novel form seems deliberate and purposeful, a demonstration of the ambiguity in human experience. In Hardy's fiction, the conflict between the characters and plot or theme seems accidental, an instance of the author's imaginative skill and power at creating characters bursting the containers of his melodramatic plots and over-simplified themes. Hardy believes in his containers, and they burst erratically and clumsily because of the tremendous and largely unconscious pressure of his humanity and his genius. Unlike Hardy, Forster breaks his containers deliberately. And because the method is deliberate, the containers never violently explode or burst; rather, they are modified, qualified, gently shrouded in ambiguity. The containers of plot and theme become means, seldom wholly or literally believed in, to organize the fictional exploration of the human condition.

Forster's characteristic fictional method is illustrated in his treatment of social issues. Each of the novels begins with social satire. *Where Angels Fear to Tread* opens with a scene in which the Herritons, mother, son Philip, and daughter Harriet, see Lilia off on a trip to Italy. Lilia had been married to another Herriton son, now dead, and has left her daughter with the Herritons. Forster mocks them as snobbish, interested only in the forms and proprieties of social behavior, self-righteous in trying to educate Lilia to be one of them. They are soon shocked to learn that Lilia has married an Italian, bitterly outraged to discover that he is a dentist's son. *The Longest Journey* begins with an undergraduate discussion of philosophy, quickly interrupted by Agnes whose major concern, despite all her protestations, is to discover who is or is not a gentleman. The collection of the English at the pension in Florence at the beginning of *A Room with a View* provides Forster with an opportunity for satirizing the national characteristic of hypocrisy: the hypocrisy of Lucy's radical opinions so long as they do not include Irish Home Rule; the hypocrisy of Charlotte's self-effacing gestures; the hypocrisy that covers the Reverend Mr. Eager's interest in blood and gore; the general hypocrisy of all the people who cloak malicious gossip in genteel formulae. *Howards End* starts with mockery of both the Wilcox's world of money and motorcars and Leonard Bast's shabby concern with his umbrella and the impression he is making when he meets the Schlegels at a concert. Yet Forster's condescension toward Bast throws the satire off balance. Described as at "the extreme verge of gentility," Bast is made so pathetic in his desperate need to keep his job and his promise to Jacky, his desperate self-inflicted courses in fine reading and self-improvement, and his frightened alternations of self-effacement and self-assertion that he becomes more a grotesque caricature than a vehicle for Forster's satire on different elements in the English class structure. Forster can sometimes characterize quickly those socially below the middle classes, like the bedmaker at Cambridge in *The Longest Journey* or the young louts in the park in *Howards End* who interrupt and mock a conversation between Henry and Margaret, but extensive characterization of the lower fringes of the middle class, as in the instance of Bast, degenerates into condescension and caricature just to avoid sentimentality.

Forster's initial satire, however, generally moves fairly quickly into theme. The social satire proliferates into a generalization that expresses one of the major thematic conflicts in the

[165

novel. In *The Longest Journey,* for example, the satire of Agnes'
materialism and gentility quickly becomes thematically important when Rickie must teach her, almost force her, to feel
some semblance of emotion when her fiancée, Gerald, suddenly
dies. Agnes is incapable of feeling, of love, and Rickie, mocked
as an innocent despite all his sensitivity, is capable of loving only
in his imagination, only through vision and ideal. This leads
Forster to generalize that many of the best of the English can
love only through imagination or intellect, unlike Southern
Europeans who love physically, through the "desires." At times,
as in this instance, Forster's cultural generalizations enhance
the thematic pattern of the novel; at others, as in the complaint
in the same novel that Salisbury is being ruined by modern civilization, by "ugly cataracts of brick" spilling over its slopes as
evidence of the "modern spirit," the generalization is a less
relevant intrusion. *Where Angels Fear to Tread,* more tightly
organized, illustrates the progression from satire to thematic
generalization even more closely. As soon as Lilia, the English
girl in revolt against the narrowness of the Herritons' life,
marries her warm, charming, callous, sometimes cruel Italian,
Gino, the clash of cultures is visible in the unhappy marriage.
Forster generalizes the conflict:

> No one realized that more than personalities were engaged; that the
> struggle was national; that generations of ancestors, good, bad, or
> indifferent, forbade the Latin man to be chivalrous to the northern
> woman, the northern woman to forgive the Latin man.

This conflict is, however, only a rehearsal for the major conflict
in the novel, another instance of Forster's early minor prefigura-
tion of a theme that is to become major. After the baby is born
and Lilia dies, the Herritons determine to claim the baby, buy
him from his father and bring him up with all the advantages
of the cold, material, just, English way of life. When they get to
Italy, they find Gino less corruptible than they thought: for all
his cruelty and amorality and dirtiness, he loves his son fiercely
and will not sell him. Here, English morality and self-righteousness directly confront Italian warmth and emotional responsiveness, principled death confronts unjust life. Although two of the
English, Caroline and Philip, are convinced that Gino should

keep his baby, the third and most militant, Harriet, steals the baby and, in doing so, accidentally kills him in a carriage accident. In Forster's terms, the cold and self-righteous north, incapable of love, destroys the more responsive and disorderly south. The satire on the Herritons has developed into a demonstration of the cold destructiveness they represent.

A Passage to India moves in a similar manner. The opening conversation that announces the theme also gently satirizes the Indians as aimless, evasive, and inconsistent. Other early scenes depict the British colonials as foolish, convinced of their divine mission to civilize India and stick together, full of pretense and touchy insularity. As the two cultures conflict, Forster changes from satire to generalizations that demonstrate the differences between the cultures, orating about the importance of hospitality to and the greater sense of "heart" in the Indian, or the crudeness of the Indian from the Western point of view. Although Forster conveys more sympathy for the Indian than for the British colonial—for, after all, the Indian is the victim rather than the instigator of a cultural imposition—his generalizations are far from one-sided. They are sufficiently complex to render the struggle between the cultures a matter for compassion rather than a weapon useful in forwarding a cause:

> Suspicion in the Oriental is a sort of malignant tumour, a mental malady, that makes him self-conscious and unfriendly suddenly; he trusts and mistrusts at the same time in a way the Westerner cannot comprehend. It is his demon, as the Westerner's is hypocrisy.

Such generalizations, along with the satire and the plot, both explain and advance the theme.

In *Howards End*, Forster focuses on a kind of thematic generalization different from those in the other novels. The other novels all contrast the Englishman to the Indian or the Italian, establish a kind of median English middle-class point of view as the focus for the observations about England and the contrast to elements in another culture. *Howards End*, however, is confined to England itself, as the house Howards End represents a continuity of English experience, and the generalizations explore the range of class experience within England. The opening satire of the affluent Wilcoxes and the struggling Bast is quickly developed to show that these representations are more complicated: the Wilcoxes, in particular, are also shown as the stalwart defenders of England in commerce and war. Many of the individual characters, like Charles Wilcox, Tibby, Helen, Leonard Bast, represent particular points of view about England, but Margaret Schlegel, never oversimplifying, the conscious inheritor of the tradition of Howards End, works to bring them all together, to synthesize them in a reconciliation of all the Englands. To demonstrate what Margaret tries to reconcile, Forster uses a great many generalizations. He talks of town life and country life, agriculture and industry, the cosmopolitan and intellectual middle classes contrasted with the proper and commercial middle classes. Yet the generalized accounts of English life in this novel have a vague and petulant sound, a lack of intrinsic connection and reference to the terms and characters of the novel, and an absence of fictional energy:

> The feudal ownership of land did bring dignity, whereas the modern ownership of movables is reducing us again to a nomadic horde. We are reverting to the civilization of luggage, and historians of the future will note how the middle classes accreted possessions without taking root in the earth, and may find in this the secret of their imaginative poverty.

Like the portrait of Leonard Bast, the generalizations concerning the social and historical range of England seem condescending, arch, more a perverse grumble against modern civilization than any coherent social perspective. Forster seems to understand and present national barriers far more clearly and cogently than he does those of class or history. *Howards End,* as a result, crowded with a number of irrelevant essays, is Forster's least convincing novel.

In the other novels Forster's generalizations rest on a coherent notion of English national character. He consistently demonstrates its insularity and self-righteousness. But the idea of the national character gives focus and sharpness to Forster's generalizations and comparisons, gives a starting point for his wider humanity. This version of it can be seen most clearly in Forster's 1920 essay entitled "Notes on the English Character." Here he traces the origin of the middle class English character to the public school:

Many men look back on their school days as the happiest of their lives. They remember with regret that golden time when life, though hard, was not yet complex; when they all worked together and played together and thought together, so far as they thought at all; when they were taught that school is the world in miniature, and believed that no one can love his country who does not love his school. . . . And they go forth into a world that is not entirely composed of public-school men or even of Anglo-Saxons, but of men who are as various as the sands of the sea; into a world of whose richness and subtlety they have no conception. They go forth into it with well-developed bodies, fairly developed minds, and undeveloped hearts. And it is this undeveloped heart that is largely responsible for the difficulties of Englishmen abroad. An undeveloped heart—not a cold one. . . .

For it is not that the Englishman can't feel—it is that he is afraid to feel. He has been taught at his public school that feeling is bad form. He must not express great joy or sorrow, or even open his mouth too wide when he talks—his pipe might fall out if he did.

It is the "undeveloped heart" that causes the failure of the Herritons in Italy and the inability of the British colonials to understand either the Indians or what the British themselves have done in India; the mass pressure of the "undeveloped heart" destroys the weak Rickie Elliot and impedes Margaret Schlegel's attempt to synthesize another, perhaps older, England. Only in *A Room with a View,* the simplest and most triumphant of Forster's novels, does the heart successfully develop.

Because this idea of a national character so strongly infuses Forster's attitude, the concept of place is strongly emphasized in his novels. Place frequently determines the ordinary character; place, not time (for Forster's idea of history is less strong and less specific than his idea of locality), helps to mold the perspective and becomes symbolic of that perspective. In *A Room with a View,* Cecil Vyse is his fashionable segment of London, at ease only there, Lucy's mother is her house at Windy Corner in Surrey, poor Charlotte is the house with the broken boiler. Only Lucy and the Emersons are not bound by the place they inhabit, can be part of Florence, Greece, or the Home Counties. The Herritons in *Where Angels Fear to Tread* are connected with Sawston, their suburban home, and their attitudes are Sawston. When Caroline and Philip must return home, having understood something of Gino and Italy, they talk about the difficulty of living in Sawston without believing in it any longer. Still, they have both been formed by Sawston and their projected inability to break away physically indicates that they have not entirely overcome their background. In *The Longest Journey*, Forster comments that "places have a genius," a spirit that affects the people who live there. This novel is divided into three sections, each the name of a place: "Cambridge" in which Rickie develops his sensitivity and inner life; "Sawston," the home of Herritons and the site of a public school—here Rickie's inner life is destroyed; "Wiltshire," the rural county in which Rickie's acknowledgment of his half-brother, the earth, comes too late. The influence of place is even more strongly marked in *Howards End*. In addition to the calm suspension of Howards End itself, the novel describes the creeping, importunate grubbiness of modern industrial London, the stately town houses, the wild and mystical quality of the country home in Shropshire, and the dull overcrowding of Charles Wilcox's suburban home in Wilton.

Forster's insertions about the decline of England, the crippling effect of modern life, are most frequently conveyed by images of place: crowded smoky cottages contrasted with homes surrounded by trees and sunlit hills, stacked service flats with spacious Georgian houses. The sense of India, its separateness and its influence, hovers over *A Passage to India*. In a long section describing Fielding's return to England, Forster shows how he gradually loses India through the greenness and sumptuousness of Alexandria, Crete, and Venice, supplanting the dry intensity of India with the lush harmony of the Mediterranean. Place is for Forster always more than an accidental setting; it becomes an influence on, almost a determinant of both character and action.

His more spirited and worthy characters, like Lucy Honeychurch or Fielding, try to overcome the accidental influence of place, to achieve understanding in spite of atmosphere, or, like Margaret Schlegel, to create an atmosphere, a setting, conducive to understanding. The question of how the influence of place can be avoided, of what the human being can do, thus becomes important in much of Forster's fiction. On the title page of *Howards End* he has printed the phrase "Only connect

. . . ," a phrase which becomes symbolic for Margaret's attempt to reconcile her own sense of the inner life with the energetic Wilcox world of "telegrams and anger."

The means for connection is the personal relationship, personal warmth and responsiveness. But, in this novel, the personal has its public, social, or political corollary, connected through Forster's imagery and the events of the novel. At one point, he explains that a lie, repeated often enough, may become true, a statement whose soundness can be exemplified equally in the process of women falling in love and the justification for nations going to war. Similarly, Margaret's attempt to understand and reconcile all the various people she encounters is also her attempt to preserve and reconcile England, the public manifestation of what these individuals represent. Her synthesis at Howards End, although neither permanent nor perfect, demonstrates that the private and the public are analagous, that private connection achieves public unity. In *A Room with a View*, the private and public are also made analagous, for Cecil's ascetic remoteness and incapacity for love are equated with his social and political snobbishness. Lucy and the Emersons, on the other hand, are both emotionally open and politically "democratic."

In Forster's later work, the analogy between public and private is more questionable, more riddled with the problems of scale that qualify the connection between the two. In *A Passage to India*, the public political attitudes and the personal relationships obviously influence each other a great deal, but they are not analagous. At the end of the novel, when the crucial trial of Aziz is several years in the past, Aziz and Fielding meet again and clarify all the slight but edgy misunderstandings within their personal relationship. Yet the public difference, the fact that one is Indian and the other English, the fact that they belong to two different cultures and two different histories, cannot be similarly reconciled. And, despite the full and genuine personal connection, they cannot really, in Forster's terms, be friends, "not yet" at any rate, "not there."

The later essays also present the idea that the public and the private, although connected, are not always analagous. In a 1941 essay called "Tolerance," Forster develops the idea that "love" is the aim of personal relationships, but extending this aim publicly to nations and worlds is impossible, for we cannot, no matter how strong our intentions, "love" so many different people. Therefore, to Forster, "tolerance" among nations is imperative, although, among individual people, "tolerance" is inadequate and condescending. Another essay, the famous "What I Believe" (1939), labels as "tragedy" the fact that "no device has been found by which these private decencies can be transmitted to public affairs." As the terms of the comparison indicate, Forster would choose the "private" rather than the "public," but the imminent imposition of the "public" on all private concerns, the fact that the two can never be kept entirely separate, demands both attention to and choice within the realm of the public form. In this way, Forster reaches his conclusion of "two cheers for democracy," for only "love" and achievements as intense as those of personal relationship ever warrant three. Although the conclusions concerning the relationship of "public" and "private" vary, although the analogy sometimes works and sometimes does not, this kind of analogy, like Forster's cultural generalizations, is both wide and clear enough to furnish him with a starting point, a basis for all the qualifications about human experiences he wishes to make. The analogy does not codify solutions; rather, it asks questions.

The analogy in Forster is, like his nations—Italy, for example, itself a symbol—a cluster of ideas capable of modification and amenable to further development. All Forster's novels contain symbols, details or images which are made large and loose enough to represent some of the questions in the novel and, then, developed sufficiently to suggest the range and complexity of the experience the novel creates. In *Where Angels Fear to Tread,* the church in Monteriano, the Italian village, is that of Santa Deodata. At first, this is a detail, a fact in tourist guides, but the statue and the story of Santa Deodata are developed into a symbol of Italy, its warmth and its lack of respect for the famous or the remarkable. As the story of Santa Deodata is related —she was not an "important" saint and did not, according to Forster, accomplish anything other than suffering in bed for her fifteen or so years—the church becomes a symbol for presence, for being, for the human situation contrasted to the English world of activity, morality, and human rules. Talking underneath the statue, Caroline and Philip first come to understand each other and what they have learned in Italy.

Early in *The Longest Journey*, when Rickie brings his bride to visit his aunt in Wiltshire, their train runs over a child at the level-crossing near the local station. At first, this is only an incident, but its terms reverberate through the novel. The dead child is also Rickie and Agnes's child, deformed hereditarily, who cannot live, and indicates the disastrous mismating of their marriage; the train represents the journey carrying Rickie back to his past, a journey punctuated by the unexpected, for he is not aware of the accident until Stephen tells him about it later; the level-crossing of the road and track is the junction of different attitudes toward life, the crossing of Agnes and Stephen, which "wants a bridge," and it is this crossing, this conjunction, that poor Rickie can never master. The incident is recalled throughout the novel, and, at the end, Rickie is killed, in his sacrificial rescue of the drunken Stephen, at the same level-crossing.

Symbols of shape and color appear throughout *A Room with a View*. The scene of the first kiss, in Italy, is a sheltered hollow in the woods, a bank of violets down which Lucy, wearing a white dress, tumbles to the waiting George. But the blue and white within the hollow, the emotion and the kiss, are interrupted by the shrieking figure of Charlotte, "brown against the view." Later, in England, Lucy first sees George again in a wooded hollow with a pool. George is a flash of color, "barefoot, bare-chested, radiant," within the "shadowy woods." And George kisses Lucy for the second time surrounded by the shrubbery on the narrow path leading to her house. The circular hollow and enclosed space is not always, however, equated with warmth and emotion; it can also be the constricted circle of suburban privilege by which Lucy is surrounded until she recognizes what the Emersons represent. As the novel develops, enclosures—themselves a symbol of human perspectives—are seen to be different: some are entirely interior, overstuffed and constricting drawing rooms; others, although inside, like Lucy's bedroom at Windy Corner, have windows and views, permit perception of the exterior world; still others, like the hollows in the wood, are outside, points of view from which the characters can see human experience openly and comprehensively. Forster's symbols are expanded and qualified, used to establish the terms through which fuller and sometimes contradictory experience can be presented. Even Charlotte's "brown" is equivocal at the end. In the beginning of the novel, Forster twice depicts Mrs. Wilcox "trailing noiselessly over the lawn" at Howards End, quietly soothing the feelings of others and bringing conflict and divergent character together within the atmosphere of her spacious grounds. Although Mrs. Wilcox dies early in the story, this image of her as the gentle custodian of England persists, and Margaret is her spiritual descendant. Appropriately, the final scene takes place in a reassertion of peaceful quiet, after all the storms of failure and murder and destructive emotion, on the lawn at Howards End. The final scene is the completion, after all the concrete facts of division and conflict, of the synthesis suggested by the image of Mrs. Wilcox at the very beginning.

Each of Forster's titles is itself a symbol. Howards End, the house, is England, the representation of the traditional value of reconciliation, and appropriately it is vacant during all the conflicts that take place in the center of the novel. When Margaret, alone, visits the house, she hears a noise and suspects it is the heart of the house beating. The noise is, in fact, the sound of old Miss Avery, a servant who arranged all the furniture and kept the house occupied while its owners were absent. Margaret was quite right, for Miss Avery was the heart of the house, did maintain the continuity of Howards End, did keep the house from becoming dead and useless. Howards End is not only a house, but a tree as well, a large elm that dominates the view of the house from the meadow: both man and nature have been necessary to create Howards End. Where angels fear to tread is where fools rush in, but, in Forster's novel, some of the fools, like Caroline and Philip, become less foolish through their unangelic intrusion. As Forster has stated, a passage to India refers to Walt Whitman's poem, stands for a route to new knowledge, to discovery, to exotic and unfamiliar insights. But as Forster's title it also suggests an ironic passage, the route the conquering English take to the ancient world, the route of colonizing imposition which inhibits full understanding. The novel is divided into three sections, three aspects of India the alien must try to comprehend: "Mosque," the Moslem temple in which the best of the English, like Mrs. Moore, can establish understanding with Aziz; "Caves," multiple caverns, subterranean, and dominated by the fearful echo, which defeat even Mrs. Moore, and the darkness of which leads to Adela's hallucination and the conflict in the novel; "Temple," the Hindu shrine and ceremony, still another religion and another culture which magnify the impossibility of full reconciliation between Englishman and Indian. The action of each of the three sections also takes place in a different one of the three Indian seasons: "Mosque" in the cool, dry winter, the most hospitable climate; "Caves" in the heat, the baking intensity that almost no northerner can stand; "Temple" during the monsoon rains, the cleansing yet muddling torrent that asserts the final difference.

A Room with a View opens with a discussion in the pension about whether or not Lucy and Charlotte, disappointed because their reservation of rooms on the side with a view has not been honored, can accept the Emersons' offer to trade rooms. They finally accept, and throughout the novel the Emersons continue offering Lucy wider views, not just of Florence but of all Italy, nature, emotions, life. Not until the end does Lucy choose the full view, choose to see all she can of human experience. Other people in the novel are compared with rooms—Cecil for example is like a kind of stuffed drawing room. But the hero, George, cannot be confined to a room or even, finally, to a particular view; he claims that all that matters about views is "distance and air."

The title *The Longest Journey* is taken from Shelley's *Epipsychidion* and Forster quotes the relevant stanza in the novel, a stanza in which Shelley claims that he never was one of those who chose just one mistress or friend as a companion for "the longest journey," for life. Rickie, despite his reverence for Shelley, fails to follow the poet's advice and chooses Agnes. Agnes, in turn, cuts Rickie off from Stephen and the earth, insists on confining Rickie to the greedy triviality of Sawston and its school. At the end, Rickie revolts, breaks away from the insulation of his single companion, but he has been so completely defeated that he cannot sustain independence and his journey ends abruptly. The "longest journey" is also Rickie's attempt to un-

[175

cover his past, his origins. Agnes might have been a suitable wife for other, more conventional, journeys, but, for this attempt toward the center of the earth, she is evasive and useless. The symbolic nature of each title is suggestive, allowing Forster room for all his themes and qualifications. The title symbols explore rather than summarize.

The symbols, like the cultural generalizations, the sense of place, and the repetitious patterns and echoes throughout the novel, are part of Forster's form, his novelistic control. He never pretends that the form represents "truth," that the symbols or the cultural generalizations encapsulate human experience. Rather, the elements of form are an introduction to the vastness of human experience, a partial statement of the ranges of human possibility. Beyond the limits of form, symbol, and generalization, in Forster's terms, is a mystery we can never fully explain, a sense of passion and power like Beethoven's that is not translatable into words.

Since, for Forster, the novel is, as he said in *Aspects of the Novel,* "one of the moister areas of literature," there is no reason why his forms should be complete, no necessity for his symbols or his patterns to express all of human experience. The form is part of the conscious search, the attempt. But this leads to a paradox at the very center of Forster's fiction. At the same time that his patterned forms are a search or an approach, the paraphernalia of pattern, symbol, and cultural generalization is so heavy that it severely restricts almost all human beings. Forster's use of form, in practice, is so contrived and predictable that it leaves his characters very little room, seems to mold them into puppets illustrating an idea, or into victims of historical and cultural forces.

Theoretically, Rickie Elliot or Fielding or Margaret Schlegel, all devoted to the "inner life," have almost limitless possibilities; in fact, as Forster presents them, they are so conditioned by his themes and patterns that they seem small and limited. Forster's ideas, his refusal to accept absolutes, and his constant qualifications both in matter and manner suggest the mystery, the inexplicability, and the vastness of the cosmos possible for man; but his technique, his reliance on patterns and places, the predictability of environment's effect on his characters, all reduce the size and scale of the human being. With the exception of *A Room with a View,* the least equivocal novel, the one in which the possibility of color, music, and feeling exists if only man is perceptive and courageous enough, all the novels leave, to some extent, the impression that man is held in by echoes and environment, reduced by contrived and cultural forces. Forster's attitude of enormous compassion for man, the attitude toward Rickie, Fielding, and Margaret, toward many of the less dedicated characters as well, comes through this sense of man's smallness, the realization that man can be so limited by patterns, generalizations, and symbols. And the force of the patterns impinging on and reducing man is particularly poignant because none of the patterns ultimately represents truth.

Man's smallness is not, in Forster's work, always lamentable. He once wrote that, during World War I, he appreciated T. S. Eliot's early poetry because, in contrast to the grandiose generalizations of the war, it "sang of private disgust and diffidence, and of people who seemed genuine because they were unattractive or weak." The defense of smallness or weakness is apparent in the novels as well. Some of Forster's best writing is devoted to minor, particular images, like the "white" air on a cold day in *Howards End* that "tasted like cold pennies,"—a small perception, a particular fact unrelated to anything else. And at one point, in *A Room with a View,* George Emerson appears clumsy and weak, suffering from "unexplained desires" and an inability to conceal his emotions. Lucy notices, and realizes that this is weakness, but neither she nor Forster thinks less of George as a result. On the contrary, to Forster, this weakness is a sign of George's vulnerability to genuine emotion, of his value. Similarly, the compassion toward Rickie Elliot is not diminished by the fact that he is weak both physically and spiritually. Forster's attitude toward strength and dignity is not Hemingway's, and Forster frequently regards the strong and certain, like Gerald in *The Longest Journey* or Charles Wilcox in *Howards End* or some of the British colonials in *A Passage to India,* as vicious bullies who impose themselves on others. The weak man, vulnerable and human, is regarded with respect for retaining his vulnerability and compassion despite frequent defeats by stronger and more malicious forces.

[177

Man's weakness and reduced size in Forster's fiction do not, as some critics have charged, make the fiction trivial. To call Forster's work trivial requires a point of view from which one sees the individual as necessarily great and important, able to impose himself significantly on both human history and the cosmos. Much of Forster's fiction implicitly denies this viewpoint, considers the particulars of history and shows how they reduce and enfeeble man, requiring him to operate within severe limitations. The charge of triviality is also insensitive to Forster's negative method, his practice of establishing a generalization only to see through it, constructing a pattern only to speculate and qualify. Forster refuses to let generalizations stand, to allow principles of organization to be thought of as truths, to believe in either a conventional God or a new God who will alter convention. Forster's fiction plays, contrives, qualifies, constructs a framework in order to examine it or explores an issue that cannot, in any terms he or we understand, be resolved. And Forster does this with intelligence and feeling, wit and compassion, which, although different from truth, are from his point of view, as close to insight or meaning as the human being can get.

VIII

VIRGINIA WOOLF

BETWEEN 1910 AND 1930, many writers explicitly attacked
the idea of compassion in literature. In revolting against
what they thought of as the excessive piety, sentimentality, and
complacency that characterized Victorian and Edwardian literature, writers often included compassion among the qualities that
would distort the search for truth or muddy the clarity of the
essential concept of human nature they tried to present. Poets
like Ezra Pound and T. S. Eliot, as well as novelists like Virginia
Woolf, D. H. Lawrence, and James Joyce, attempted, on the
surface of their works at least, to veer away from an attitude of
compassion, to penetrate the thickness of Edwardian literary fog
and emotional dampness in order to reach a centrally significant
truth about human experience, to approach what was, in one of
Amy Lowell's poems, represented as "clear, reticent, superbly
final." Like the poet and essayist T. E. Hulme, these writers
often regarded the compassionate as sentimental and slushy,
thought of "romanticism" as banal self-deception and flagrantly
wordy self-pity. In reaction, they sought what was harder, firmer,
what was humanly or metaphysically true no matter how bleak
or difficult that truth might be. They were not, at least in their
initial attempts, skeptical about the possibility of finding some
metaphysical truth, some central essence of man; in fact they
were, in this sense, less skeptical than Trollope, Meredith,
Hardy, or Arnold Bennett. But they were skeptical, militantly
so, about Victorian pieties and assurances, about the kind of ulti-

mate acceptance of man and his imperfect world that characterizes Trollope's fiction.

Virginia Woolf illustrates this consciously new and anti-
romantic point of view in *Orlando* (1928). More parable or essay than novel, *Orlando* is a comic survey course, complete with
stylistic parodies, in English social and literary history from the
Elizabethan age to the present. The central figure, Orlando, first
as man and then as woman, lives through the more than three
hundred years observing and experiencing the customs, attitudes, and atmospheres of the changing eras. Yet it is highly
slanted social history. Mrs. Woolf seems to appreciate the adventurous energy of the Elizabethans, the macabre gloom of the
Jacobeans, the gilded elegance of the restoration, and the witty
eloquence of the eighteenth century. But nothing is attractive
about her portrait of the nineteenth century. She sharply satirizes the trancendant slush of Romanticism and expresses her
greatest scorn for Victorian pretense and domesticity:

Love, birth, and death were all swaddled in a variety of fine phrases.
The sexes drew further and further apart. No open conversation
was tolerated. Evasions and concealments were sedulously practiced
on both sides. And just as the ivy and the evergreen rioted in the
damp earth outside, so did the same fertility show itself within. The
life of the average woman was a succession of childbirths. She married at nineteen and had fifteen or eighteen children by the time
she was thirty; for twins abounded. Thus the British Empire came
into existence; and thus—for there is no stopping damp; it gets
into the inkpot as it gets into the woodwork—sentences swelled,
adjectives multiplied, lyrics became epics, and little trifles that had
been essays a column long were now encyclopaedias in ten or twenty
volumes.

Changes in era are frequently characterized in terms of
weather and the whole nineteenth century is a murky mist. The
atmosphere begins to clear after World War I, although the
clearing is lonely and taut with the impact of recent disasters. In
1928:

How narrow women had grown lately! They looked like
stalks of corn, straight, shining, identical. And men's faces were as
bare as the palm of one's hand. The dryness of the atmosphere
brought out the color in everything and seemed to stiffen the mus-

cles of the cheeks. It was harder to cry now. Water was hot in two
seconds. Ivy had perished or been scraped off houses. Vegetables
were less fertile; families were much smaller. . . . There was something definite and distinct about the age, which reminded her of
the eighteenth century, except that there was a distraction . . . her
thoughts became mysteriously tightened and strung up as if a piano
tuner had put his key in her back and stretched the nerves very
taut; at the same time her hearing quickened; she could hear every
whisper and crackle in the room so that the clock ticking on the
mantlepiece beat like a hammer.

The new clarity has neither the violent extremes of heat and
frost of the Elizabethan age nor the calm peace of the eighteenth
century, but it does provide some meaning for the survivor with
sufficient strength and control.

A more explicit defense of her own age, of herself and
her contemporaries appears in Mrs. Woolf's famous essay, "Mr.
Bennett and Mrs. Brown," written in 1924. The essay, attacking
the fiction of the Edwardians, Wells, Galsworthy, and Bennett,
also consciously forwards the cause of the new fiction, the avant-
garde which would substitute new conventions and concerns for
the old. Mrs. Woolf agrees with Bennett that depicting human
character and human life should be the novelists' primary concern, but she maintains that Bennett, like Galsworthy and Wells,
never caught the central character of the human being, never
really captured Mrs. Brown. Concerned with social details or
political programs, the great Edwardians, according to Mrs.
Woolf, missed the fundamental character of Mrs. Brown, the
shabby woman in the railway carriage:

With all his powers of observation, which are marvelous, with all
his sympathy and humanity, which are great, Mr. Bennett has
never once looked at Mrs. Brown in her corner. There she sits in
the corner of the carriage—that carriage which is travelling, not
from Richmond to Waterloo, but from one age of literature to the
next, for Mrs. Brown is eternal, Mrs. Brown is human nature, Mrs.
Brown changes only on the surface, it is the novelists who get in
and out—there she sits and not one of the Edwardian writers has
so much as looked at her. They have looked very powerfully, search-
ingly, and sympathetically out of the window; at factories, at Uto-
pias, even at the decoration and upholstery of the carriage; but
never at her, never at life, never at human nature.

The substance of the estimate of Bennett and the other Edwardians is questionable and the separation between the character and her environment, between Mrs. Brown and her past or the railway carriage itself, not nearly so complete nor so easily identifiable in fiction as Mrs. Woolf makes it seem; but the major point of the passage is Mrs. Woolf's assurance that there is something eternal about Mrs. Brown, a metaphysical essence of the human personality not dependent on circumstance or environment. It is this quality, this metaphysical truth, that Mrs. Woolf, in her novels, tried so often to distill, to extract from the varying impressions and sensations of experience. To capture the character of Mrs. Brown becomes a metaphor for the attempt to formulate the essence of human nature, to see through the complexities of ordinary experience to the centrally meaningful, metaphysically symbolic, question of what man is.

Mrs. Woolf's most famous novel, *To the Lighthouse* (1927), comes closest to formulating a metaphysical truth, to dealing with that aspect of the human being which represents his eternal nature. The lighthouse itself, distant and ambiguous across the water, stands as the central symbol of meaning and achievement in the novel. Seeking the lighthouse, seeking the metaphysical truth about human nature, if successful, can provide focus for all human energy, and render subsidiary values, like compassion, trivial and irrelevant. As in many other versions of the searcher for the holy grail, for the object that would give meaning and direction to all human activity, Mrs. Woolf's symbolic searcher must suffer, must pass through the tumult of destruction and war, before he can reach the lighthouse. From the author's point of view in this novel, World War I, despite all its horrors and devastation, seemed to create new and meaningful possibilities for man, to provide a necessary albeit bleak demolition of sheltered and sentimental nineteenth-century impediments. The twenties decade, although tinged with nostalgia and regret, was also, for Mrs. Woolf, a time of hope, a period that could revive the clear conditions in which man could understand and achieve what had been permanently latent in human nature. Even the search for metaphysical truth, the attempt to reach the lighthouse, which unifies the novel, is to some extent, dependent on historical change, for the two major sections, each the depiction of a day during which the inter-locking characters and relationships are brilliantly analyzed, are divided by ten years in the brief "Time Passes" section.

The novel begins with a day at the Ramsays' summer house in the Hebrides before World War I. "Time Passes" opens with a description that is simultaneously of the rain ending the particular day and the ten years of war and death that will pass before the house is visible again. In the midst of the general dis-solution, Mrs. Woolf places the insertions that announce changes, deaths, and disasters. The theme of dissolution is re-peated, more condescendingly perhaps, through Mrs. McNab, the old cleaning woman who comes to put the house in order before the remaining Ramsays return. As she works, she sings:

> . . . something that had been gay twenty years before on the stage perhaps, had been hummed and danced to, but now, coming from the toothless, bonneted, care-taking woman, was robbed of meaning, was like the voice of witlessness, humour, persistency itself, trodden down but springing up again, so that as she lurched, dusting, wip-ing, she seemed to say how it was one long sorrow and trouble, how it was getting up and going to bed again, and bringing things out and putting them away again.

General decay is combined with the specific ten years to make the prospect of reaching the lighthouse, of achieving some di-rection, seem nearly impossible.

The two major sections, both full of moments of percep-tion attributed to the characters and shifts in perspective by the author, are less directly dependent on history. The first section, "The Window," is Mrs. Ramsay's. It opens with her statement and ends with her triumph. Mrs. Ramsay is warm, humane, a charming mother hen who protects her husband and children and enchants a constant series of guests. She is able to draw a genuine response from Charles Tansley, her husband's self-conscious student who is alternately ashamed of and egotistically defiant about his lower class origins; she can persuade Bankes, a priggish and fastidious bachelor, to eat one of her dinners; she can take care of the greenhouse roof and the other practical af-fairs that her husband neglects. Much as she loves her children, she does not want them to grow up, to lose what she feels is the happiest time. And, much as she loves her husband, she cannot tell him so, for she cannot abstract or articulate her feelings, cannot get beyond the active and immediate. Her thoughts end the section:

She knew that he was thinking. You are more beautiful than ever. And she felt herself very beautiful. Will you not tell me just for once that you love me? . . . And as she looked at him she began to smile, for though she had not said a word, he knew that she loved him. He could not deny it. And smiling she looked out of the window and said (thinking to herself, Nothing on earth can equal this happiness) —
"Yes, you were right. It's going to be wet tomorrow. You won't be able to go." And she looked at him smiling. For she had triumphed again. She had not said it: yet he knew.

Her triumph is not only in her refusal to say that she loves him, but also, ironically enough, in the fact that they will not go to the lighthouse the next day. Although she had overtly hoped they would go, encouraged her son James to hope, and been furious at her husband's pessimistic weather prediction, she represents the kind of warm domestic encirclement that keeps man from ever achieving the lighthouse. Mrs. Ramsay is fascinated by the sea, but she will never step into it; she sits on the shore, near-sightedly watching the others, ready to protect and comfort, but she does not strike out. She becomes, in the novel, the humane domesticity that inhibits the forceful direction and independence that reaching the lighthouse demands. She cannot, symbolically, survive the war, nor can the comfortable domesticity she arranged. Even the marriage she engineered between Paul and Minta obviously crumbles after she is dead.

At the beginning of the novel, Mr. Ramsay seems rude and distant. He glowers or barks at his children, insists that it will rain the next day, and is impatient with his guests. He is a philosopher, an intellectual, always trying to reach beyond his limitations yet always blunt and honest in appraising his ability. He knows that his mind, like very few others in England, can reach Q. But he is also easily distracted by domesticity. He might have written better books, achieved more, had he not had eight children, yet he is always attracted to the image of his wife as a mother hen, to a charming fool like Minta, to his children and their games. His marriage and his children, despite the fact that they have worked against his scholarship, have been the central emotional facts of his experience:

> He wanted sympathy. He was a failure, he said. Mrs. Ramsay flashed her needles. Mr. Ramsay repeated, never taking his eyes from her face, that he was a failure. . . . It was sympathy he wanted, to be assured of his genius, first of all, and then to be taken within the circle of life, warmed and soothed, to have his senses restored to him, his barrenness made fertile, and all the rooms of the house made full of life—

The balance of Mr. Ramsay's linear force with Mrs. Ramsay's circular warmth makes a marriage, but, in Mrs. Woolf's terms, the balance prevents the kind of achievement possible for the linear force alone. Mr. Ramsay must wait until her death, until after the war, to reach the lighthouse.

In the final section, Mr. Ramsay's, the lonely old man is ready. He can still be distracted by trivialities—he is enormously vain about his boots; he still looks for female sympathy, but Lily Briscoe, the spinster artist, is unable to give it to him. Left alone, he must proceed with a kind of craggy, determined, linear force. The poem he continually quotes has changed from the impotent fury and meaningless bravery of Tennyson's "Charge of the Light Brigade" of the first section, to the deeper and lonelier sense of human meaning in Cowper's "The Castaway." And he now reaches the lighthouse:

> He rose and stood in the bow of the boat, very straight and tall, for all the world, James thought, as if he were saying "There is no God," and Cam thought, as if he were leaping into space, and they both rose to follow him as he sprang, lightly like a young man, holding his parcel, on to the rock.

His achievement has even liberated his ego sufficiently to allow him to praise James, which he had never done before. For Mr. Ramsay reaching the lighthouse represents a metaphysical meaning and achievement, a triumph over circumstance and domesticity, a step beyond the human Q.

A secondary, although parallel, line throughout the novel involves Lily Briscoe. She is linked to Mr. Ramsay early in the first section, for her blank canvas is like his philosopher's plain white kitchen table. But, before the war, she can never finish her picture, for she idolizes and would like to emulate Mrs. Ramsay, and she is half in love with the glittering Paul who sees only the charming fool Minta. After the war, knowing that she cannot give Mr. Ramsay the sympathy he needs, she has only her art. As she sees Mr. Ramsay, in the distance, reach the lighthouse, Lily Briscoe draws her final line completing the picture. Getting to the lighthouse is also a specifically artistic achievement, creating form out of man's disparate and difficult experience.

The novel has as well a historical theme: the modern Englishman needed to break out of the comfortable security of Victorian assurance in order to reach something significant outside himself. But history is here only a small part of Mrs. Woolf's concern. In this instance, she has moved her whole novel toward the significant moment, the symbolic achievement. For once—and there is no similar example among Mrs. Woolf's novels—man has symbolically created an artistic and intellectual truth beyond humanity, has in a way supplanted God. The novelist's frequently reiterated attempt to localize the essence of humanity, to be able to say, "There it is," in *To the Lighthouse* succeeds. Having found truth, in novelistic terms, *To the Lighthouse* has no need to express sympathy, compassion, the humane qualities that died with Mrs. Ramsay during the war.

The sense of personal victory in *To the Lighthouse* was, however, only momentary in Mrs. Woolf's fiction. Even the essay, "Mr. Bennett and Mrs. Brown" recognizes that truth or essence are, despite all human attempts, not permanent, that they are contingent upon the changes and relativities of history. After discussing the importance of character and asserting that everyone can judge character, Mrs. Woolf switches away from the expected universality of her theme:

And now I will hazard a second assertion, which is more disputable perhaps, to the effect that on or about December 1910 human character changed.

The very use of the date, the specific historical statement, seems surprising, particularly coming from an author long associated with a subjective and nonhistorical world, and with an interest in the modes of human perception. Yet Mrs. Woolf qualifies and expands her statement. She realizes, of course, that the specific date is arbitrary, that such changes are not sudden transformations, and she acknowledges that writers such as Samuel Butler and G. B. Shaw have earlier recorded the same change in human character. The changes are evident in one's dealing with one's cook and in considering the partial emancipation of women from Victorian paternalism, in relationships both between classes and between the sexes, in religion, politics, and literature. Human character is inextricably connected with the social environment that surrounds it.

Mrs. Woolf's earliest fiction demonstrates this awareness of historical change. Her first novel, *The Voyage Out* (1915), follows young Rachel Vinrace, a naive and sheltered member of the upper classes, classes compared in the novel to "a small golden tassel on the edge of a vast black cloak," on a voyage to South America, a voyage into the experience of the twentieth century. Shortly after reaching South America, Rachel suddenly sickens and dies, ending the theme and the novel. Although her death is, in part, an historical statement about the irrelevance and incompetence of her class in terms of contemporary experience, the emphasis of the novel is on the simpler statement of the uncertainty and unpredictability of human experience. Mrs. Woolf's second novel, *Night and Day* (1919), also subordinates a sense of social and historical change to a novelistic commonplace. In this instance, the changing social structure that finally allows the aristocratic young lady to marry the intellectual from the lower middle classes is buried within a love story that sounds like those in women's magazines of the time, complete with fairy-godmother ready to reconcile the true lovers whenever difficulties intrude. Not until Mrs. Woolf's third novel, *Jacob's Room* (1922), do the historical and social issues become central forces in shaping the events and concerns of the novel; not until then are the changes in human character that occurred around December, 1910, made intrinsically part of the novel.

Jacob's Room is also distinguished as the first of Mrs. Woolf's novels to develop some of her characteristic fictional techniques. Following the experimental prose in certain short stories (those collected under the title *Monday or Tuesday* in 1921), this novel exhibits frequent changes in point of view, a network of subjective impressions of experience, and many of the devices that use key words and symbols to provide transitions and telescope time. The novel relates the career of Jacob Flanders from childhood through Cambridge to his premature death in World War I. Jacob is seldom seen directly. He is observed by friends, acquaintances, and relatives in a series of shifting perspectives, as if no one person or point of view can discern the essence of a human being. Mrs. Woolf mixes the thoughts and feelings of her characters with the remarks they make in conversation, fabricating a world in which essential communication is difficult if not impossible, producing a kind of Chekhovian disjointment. The human mind, too, is presented as reflecting different ideas and emotions simultaneously, as an incongruous instrument that combines the significant with the trivial or the domestic. The irony of the domestic detail undercutting the 'significant concern is a frequent device in all Mrs. Woolf's work. Jacob's mother, Betty Flanders, illustrates this incongruity when she is awakened one night during the war:

"The guns?" said Betty Flanders, half asleep, getting out of bed and going to the window, which was decorated with a fringe of dark leaves. . . .

Again, far away, she heard the dull sound, as if nocturnal women were beating great carpets. There was Morty lost, and Seabrook dead; her sons were fighting for their country. But were the chickens safe? Was that someone moving downstairs? Rebecca with the toothache? No. The nocturnal women were beating great carpets. Her hens shifted slightly on their perches.

The next thing the reader learns is that Jacob has been killed. And the novel ends with Betty Flanders wondering what to do with Jacob's old shoes.

Although the sudden and incongruous shifts from guns to hens to Jacob's death to old shoes are melodramatically ironic, the incongruities essential to Jacob are more subtle. As a student, Jacob venerates the ancient Greeks, reads Aeschylus, Sophocles, and Plato. In turn, Jacob is regarded by others as a kind of Greek god, handsome, remote, and vaguely meaningful. For all his sensitivity and attractiveness, Jacob is isolated within himself. Sought by young and well-bred girls, he is remote from them; chased by the less well-bred Florinda, he is difficult to seduce:

Then Florinda got upon his knee and hid her face in his waistcoat. With one hand he held her; with the other, his pipe.

Within his general remoteness, Jacob seems to focus only on his desire to go to Greece, as if the journey will provide a direction he cannot articulate. But, once there, just before World War I, he spends his time falling in love with the languid Mrs. Wentworth Williams. Mrs. Williams, a shallow and egotistical beauty, willing to accept Jacob's puppyish devotion, feels herself an image of the high-souled tragedy of Greece, a tragedy that continuously inspires her as she looks at herself in the mirror or poses against historic ruins. Although Jacob never sees through Mrs. Wentworth Williams, he does see through the myth of Greece, the illusion begun by governesses and encouraged by reading Xenophon, Euripedes, and Aeschylus. Jacob never finds the message he thought Greece would provide. Disillusioned, he returns to fight in World War I and never has the chance to go beyond disillusion.

Jacob's Greek quality is also made Edwardian in the novel, part of the national character that vanished about 1910. He resembles the myth of perfect Edwardian upper-class manhood, that narcissistic yet sensitive product of generations of peace and security. Throughout the novel Jacob represents the well-bred young man of his time: intelligent, stalwart, dutiful, and ultimately unreachable. Mrs. Woolf hints, at several points in the novel, that the day of the Greek-Edwardian hero was passing even before the cataclysm of World War I. As Jacob is disillusioned before he leaves Greece, so Mrs. Woolf imagistically clouds Edwardian sunshine before the beginning of the war. Early in the novel, Jacob sails to the Scilly Isles with one of his Cambridge friends:

It wore an extraordinary look of piety and peace, as if old men smoked by the door, and girls stood, hands on hips, at the well, and horses stood; as if the end of the world had come, and cabbage fields and stone walls, and coast-guard stations, and, above all, the white sand bays with the waves breaking unseen by any one, rose to heaven in a kind of ecstasy.

But imperceptibly the cottage smoke droops, has the look of a mourning emblem, a flag floating its caress over a grave. The gulls, making their broad flight and then riding at peace, seem to mark the grave.

   . . . We start transparent, and then the cloud thickens. All history backs our pane of glass. To escape is vain.

Reference to class also fills the novel. In shifting points of view, Mrs. Woolf often moves from master to servant or from aristocrat to worker, showing how social status shapes perception. Part of Jacob's remoteness, part of the reason that the Greek-Edwardian hero is only a myth, is his inability to understand people outside his own class. His breeding insulates him from understanding Florinda or the devoted Fanny Elmer or the ridiculous Bohemians he encounters in London. When Jacob feels slightly uneasy because Florinda has seemed to want some kind of contact he did not provide, he little realizes how much an evasion his sexual reticence is:

All night men and women seethed up and down the well-known beats. Late home-comers could see shadows against the blinds even in the most respectable suburbs. Not a square in snow or fog lacked its amorous couple. . . . Bullets went through heads in hotel bedrooms almost nightly on that account. . . . Little else was talked of in theatres and popular novels. Yet we say it is a matter of no importance at all.

The distant Greek hero is out of contact with both his city and his time. Jacob never has the chance to learn. Like Rachel Vinrace's, his education is cut off by something he cannot control. But, unlike the principal character in *The Voyage Out,* Jacob stands as historical statement, fictionally represents something of human character, the dominant English male, before the 1910 change. His death is both a pitiable individual disaster and the representation of an era's end.

The emphasis on historical statement itself introduces compassion into the novel. Insofar as man is determined by history, conditioned by his time and place, he is unable to achieve or become all that he would wish, perhaps unable to realize the essential truths of human nature and experience. The author's statement that history limits the individual is also the author's statement that the individual may well not receive justice, may not find his truth no matter how dedicated his search or how wisely persistent his efforts. And the human creature who would be a self-consciously metaphysical entity but is necessarily compromised by social, psychological and historical accident receives compassion for conditions he cannot alter.

Mrs. Woolf's last two novels, *The Years* (1937) and *Between the Acts* (1941), demonstrate the concern with social history more explicitly and directly than do any of the earlier works. *The Years* is a conventional novel of generations (perhaps the most conventional novel Virginia Woolf wrote), tracing the Pargiter family, with its numerous cousins and connections, from 1880 to the mid-1930's. The members of the family reflect rather than represent the changes in style, modes of transportation, and occupation that occur throughout the years. Each successive generation seems more taut, more sensitive, as communication among the various members of the family becomes more difficult and more fragmentary.

The wholeness of Colonel Abel Pargiter, who died in 1911, is missing in his children and grandchildren. Long passages throughout the novel connect the characters to public events: the death of Parnell in 1891, the death of Edward VII in 1910, the hope for a better world and the end of class barriers after World War I. In addition, the novel is full of echoes of London at various periods: old carriages, the fashionable and unfashionable shops, speakers at Hyde Park corner, mud and noseless beggars in the streets, quiet and insulated clubs. Through three generations, the characters speculate about "life," while life itself is continually altered by changing environment and institutions. Any initial interest in the metaphysical speculation is overwhelmed by the panorama of social history.

Between the Acts, a far better novel, is closest to *Orlando* among Mrs. Woolf's earlier works. Most of *Between the Acts* depicts a comic pageant, given in a small village in 1939, which traces the history of England. The pageant, acted by local citizens like the butcher and the village idiot, recounts the glory of Britain since Elizabethan days. Against the local pageant Mrs. Woolf places the family which inhabits Pointz Hall, the area's historic home. Old Bartholomew Oliver, the owner, is interested only in genealogy and isolated facts contained in the encyclopedia; his sister, Mrs. Swithin, constantly re-reads H. G. Wells's *Outline of History,* never getting beyond a fascination with the prehistoric era when the mastodon roamed through what is now London; the heir, Giles Oliver, is drawn from farming to a job as a stockbroker by the pressures of his time, his class, his society; his wife, Isa, writes bad poetry and feels herself in love with a local gentleman farmer. The history of England is mocked in two ways: by the conventional slogans and speeches somewhat garbled in the pageant and by the fragmented triviality of its representative prominent family. As the Oliver family, guests, and local citizens watch the pageant, echoes from the frightening actual world of 1939 obtrude and are muffled by the mass of village triviality.

During the last interval (the interminable pageant has taken most of a long June afternoon and evening), the audience becomes impatient waiting for the final scene, announced as "The Present Time. Ourselves." They had been expecting Union Jacks and a grand ensemble or pious prayers for the continuity of the English Way of Life in these difficult times, but they suddenly realize that they themselves are the last act of the pageant. The false drama and the trivial reality have come together to give a picture of contemporary English life. The pageant and the procession of grand English country houses are both playing their last act.

Interesting and deftly done as such social and historical commentary is, *Between the Acts* does not represent Mrs. Woolf's best or most significant fiction. The tension between the metaphysical and the historical, between man searching for a truth beyond himself and man bound to himself by time and history, lacking in this book, dominates only three of the novels, but they are Mrs. Woolf's three greatest: *To the Lighthouse, Mrs. Dalloway* (1925), and *The Waves* (1931). In *To the Lighthouse,* the metaphysical search is completed, the truth, in symbolic terms, is achieved as Mr. Ramsay reaches the lighthouse and Lily Briscoe paints her picture. In the other two novels, truth is hidden, changed, or necessarily compromised, as man finds his essential truth, if at all, only at the price of his own destruction. In *Mrs. Dalloway* and *The Waves,* the tension between the metaphysical and the historical turns from a decision to a question of human survival, from a choice between two attitudes toward experience to a realization of the only terms on which experience is possible. With this realization comes the author's compassion for all her characters who wish to stand for something more permanent and more essential than they do.

Mrs. Dalloway, in which Virginia Woolf for the first time carries her characters and her theme beyond the change of 1910 and the barrier of World War I, follows Clarissa Dalloway through a single day in London in June, 1923. Working entirely through the perspectives of the various characters (a tighter and more consistent development of the techniques first visible in *Jacob's Room*), Mrs. Woolf also provides distinctive imagery that creates a thematic statement for the novel as a whole. Clarissa, socialite and wife of a conscientious M.P., is often depicted as a bird. She holds herself erect, concentrated, flits quickly, and "perches"; sometimes her emotions flutter, but more often she resembles a bird in gathering her tiny forces into a concrete and concentrated presence. She has been ill during the war, known unhappiness and disappointment, but she is determined to survive. Peter Walsh, returning from five years in India on the day on which the novel takes place, acknowledges her force:

> But it was Clarissa one remembered. Not that she was striking; not beautiful at all; there was nothing picturesque about her; she never said anything specially clever; there she was, however; there she was.

Peter, because he often misunderstands her, even feels that her birdlike concentration is more like iron or flint "rigid up the backbone."

Yet Clarissa's force has been developed at the expense of a fundamental quality within herself. She recognizes what she has lost in order to gain concentration and independence:

> For the house sat so long that Richard insisted, after her illness, that she must sleep undisturbed. And really she preferred to read of the retreat from Moscow. He knew it. So the room was an attic; the bed narrow; and lying there reading, for she slept badly, she could not dispel a virginity preserved through childbirth which clung to her like a sheet. Lovely in girlhood, suddenly there came a moment—for example on the river beneath the woods at Clieveden—when, through some contraction of this cold spirit, she had failed him. And then at Constantinople, and again and again. She could

see what she lacked. It was not beauty; it was not mind. It was something central which permeated; something warm which broke up surfaces and rippled the cold contact of man and woman, or of women together.

A kind of virginity is part of Clarissa's force and independence, part of what always kept her from Peter Walsh, part of what makes it easier for her to talk with other women than with men, part of the price for her survival in the chaotic post-war world. She is able to understand the importance of physical contact, but, toward the end of the novel, she realizes its implications for her:

> Death was defiance. Death was an attempt to communicate; people feeling the impossibility of reaching the centre which, mystically, evaded them; closeness drew apart; rapture faded, one was alone. There was an embrace in death.

Survival for Clarissa requires careful self-preservation and deliberate illusion. Her illusions, her parties (and the whole novel builds to one of her parties), create a semblance of life, whereas immersion in the central emotion of experience would, for Clarissa, lead to dissolution and death. The parties are not entirely selfish, for others, like Peter Walsh and Sally Seton, derive vitality from Clarissa's created illusion. The parties are Clarissa's chirps, her perches, the minute creations that preserve her from dissolving in the truth of human emotion and relationship.

Parallel to the theme of Clarissa Dalloway is that of Septimus Warren Smith, the young war veteran who lost the ability to feel anything when his friend and officer was killed during the war. Without a perch, Septimus has frequent paranoid hallucinations and is increasingly unable to recognize the real world. He sometimes feels he's a tree. Unlike Clarissa, who can, with great difficulty, control her experience by concrete restrictions, Septimus is subsumed by everything his emotions register. He feels that he's a part of the whole world, animate and inanimate, thinks he understands the universe and receives messages from God. His Italian war bride, Lucrezia, a skillful milliner, tries to give him sanity through chatty gossip and making amusing little hats: the sewing-scissors, for Lucrezia and Clarissa alike, is an instrument to snip and fashion, to control and create. But the war and life have been too much for Septimus. Hounded by the blundering "human nature" of Dr. Holmes and Sir William Bradshaw, who keep insisting that Septimus be a man and face up to things, he finally commits suicide.

When Clarissa, at her party, learns that the war veteran whom she never knew personally has committed suicide, she feels closely linked with him. She, sharing his horror of Sir William's mindlessly athletic gusto, sees herself in Septimus:

Somehow it was her disaster—her disgrace. . . . She felt somehow very like him—the young man who had killed himself. She felt glad that he had done it; thrown it away. The clock was striking.

The clock, the measured beat of focus and sanity, brings Clarissa back to her party. That she has survived and Septimus has died is a statement of the force she has so consciously developed to keep her precarious hold on experience. Yet she has also been luckier than Septimus has been, and social and sexual differences have made it easier for her to realize and acquire the necessary concentration. Clarissa has always been rich and sheltered, married to the estimable Richard and allowed the independence of her narrow bed. Septimus, a poor boy, had worked as an auctioneer's clerk and had thought he was learning about the beauty of life at Miss Pole's lectures on Shakespeare given to evening classes in the Waterloo Road. The value of both Miss Pole's arid culture and of assiduous work in the auctioneer's office has been, for Septimus, demolished by the horror and death of war. And Lucrezia understandably wants a husband and a baby, demanding more of Septimus emotionally than anyone now demands of Clarissa. Age, class, and sex, all make sanity and survival that much more difficult for the man in no position to divert himself by creating tiny illusions.

Historical and social issues and distinctions occur frequently in *Mrs. Dalloway*. Hugh Whitbread, a friend of the Dalloways, is the example of the aristocratic toady, always seeking to ingratiate himself with those in power. Servants and tradesmen are given perspectives solely dependent on their class and occupation. But, more important, throughout the novel Mrs. Woolf provides the sense that society since the war has changed, that the perspectives of 1923 are significantly not those of the days in which the Dalloways and Peter Walsh grew up.

[195

Peter, after his five year absence, is particularly aware of the changes as he walks through the park. How people look, what they talk about, what the newspapers print, what people are concerned with—all seem different. And Peter himself is the image of an historical change. Regarded by all as a most intelligent and talented man Peter had envisaged an imposing career in India administering justice and improving conditions as his family had for generations. Yet, despite all his ability and his level-headed respect for the great imperialists, Peter has never quite been successful. His "susceptibility" (he is always in love with one woman or another, usually a woman married to someone else) is an indication of his sensitivity, his willingness to experience and understand as much as he possibly can, his refusal to be guided by the narrow rules of a stuffy Hugh Whitbread. But this very vulnerability and responsiveness, this capacity to question and criticize and understand, has made him less successful than he might have been, than his ancestors were. In public terms, Mrs. Woolf seems to be saying that the days of imaginative possibility in the colonies have passed, that administration has become the province of the dull and unsusceptible.

Similarly, Lady Bruton, a representation of a robust and militant Britannia, is now almost silent and impotent. She must even ask Hugh Whitbread and Richard Dalloway to draft her letters to *The Times*. Despite their impotence seen in historical terms, both Lady Bruton and Peter are able to survive personally, to hang on: Lady Bruton as an obselete spider, holding the obsequious Hugh and the affable Richard to her by threads of forceful and magnetic personality; Peter with his pocket knife. Throughout the novel, Peter continually opens and closes his pocket knife, using it as an instrument to gather and focus his control over himself, much as Clarissa uses her scissors or thinks of herself as a bird, much as Lucrezia snips at her hats to try to give Septimus some shape or control. During this visit, both Peter and Clarissa recognize why they could never have married, realize that he would have demanded too much, violated her independence and his own control, and that they would have destroyed each other. Although Peter's bed is less narrow and he has been married, he, too, has snipped off an area of emotional experience in order to survive, for he has never taken the responsibilities love demands, never involved all of himself with one woman, never had children. Bird-like concentration and pocket knives work only as a restricted ordering of individual sensibilities; they can control or shape illusions, but they can neither relate nor combine.

The sensitive, those who are responsive to the feelings and changes of the world around them, those who try to find the essence of human personality, the meaning of human experience, like Clarissa, Peter, and Septimus, must struggle merely to endure. In their struggles, they all abandon sexual relationship: Clarissa sticks to her narrow bed and is grateful to her kind, undemanding husband; Peter's promiscuity masks his incapacity for a consistent relationship and his constant playing with the knife is a symbolic masturbatory release; Septimus can never acknowledge his latently homosexual relationship with the dead officer, a statement about class as well as about sex, and his wife's desire for a baby drives him further from sanity. For all of these characters, the emotional intimacy that sexual relationship demands works against survival, the "embrace" leads to death. As in *To the Lighthouse,* the warm circle of sexuality dissolves the search for truth, the achievement beyond humanity. Yet this is true only for the characters Septimus, Clarissa, and Peter, already directed toward the attempt to discover some essence of human personality within themselves. Others, more fortunate, can recognize and accept relationship and procreation, circular continuity, as all the human being ever can achieve. Sally Seton is happy with her balding husband in Manchester and her five huge sons. Incidental characters, like the wise Mrs. Dempster in the park or the old crone that Peter and Septimus pass near the tube station, never search beyond the circle of sexuality and are content within it. Only those with exposed nerve endings, those attempting to extend human consciousness, need to deny relationship, to focus on insular independence or to create illusions, in order to survive.

Survival is difficult for the responsive because other forces in society, completely self-contained and insensitive, belligerently impose. Dr. Holmes advocates a rousing round of golf to cure any depression; Sir William Bradshaw talks of a "sense of proportion" and the spirit of the English public schools; Miss

Doris Kilman, who for a time influences Clarissa's daughter, Elizabeth, tries to convert others to the stern, ascetic religion she has developed out of her own social hostility, thwarted love, and self-pity. These forces—athleticism, proportion, and conversion—are all magnifications of old shibboleths that destroy the sensitive or independently searching personality. All these forces have been carried, with renewed intensity, from the past into the post-war world to batter the questioner into submission, to impose the formula. More than anyone else in the novel, Clarissa stands for the individual personality, against the intense experience or the imposition of one personality on another (and the intense relationship necessarily involves imposition) :

Love and religion! thought Clarissa, going back into the drawing-room, tingling all over. How detestable, how detestable they are! For now that the body of Miss Kilman was not before her, it overwhelmed her—the idea. The cruelest things in the world, she thought, seeing them clumsy, hot, domineering, hypocritical, eavesdropping, jealous, infinitely cruel and unscrupulous, dressed in a mackintosh coat, on the landing; love and religion. Had she ever tried to convert anyone herself? Did she not wish everybody merely to be themselves?

The world of 1923 offers little promise for the independent person searching for meaning beyond himself. He is lucky if he can even hold his independence, hold himself together by precarious control, by the fabrication of sheer illusion, by the effort of trivia.

Mrs. Dalloway presents only one day, one moment in time. That the resolution of the day, the suicide and the illusion of the party, may not be permanent is apparent in the characterization of Elizabeth, Clarissa's only child. With her dark beauty and "oriental eyes," completely unlike either parent, Elizabeth questions and searches. She has escaped from Miss Kilman's narrow possession and she is able to see London clearly, to examine a part of the city no one in the family has examined before. Her search has also not yet inhibited the rich possibilities of humanity and sexuality, latent qualities apparent during the party scene. But Elizabeth is the unknown future, mysterious, not yet defined or defeated. In the moment of the novel itself, time and history have reduced the wholeness of the metaphysical search to a severely limited concentration on the concrete and individual survival, to the denial of the fullest humanity in order to salvage any humanity at all. From Mrs. Woolf's perspective of sympathy with a dying class, not only is the human bird unable to fly beyond the tree, unable to search for an essential truth beyond humanity, but the tree itself is a barren substitute. The bird can only cling to the branch, tenaciously, precariously, independently virginal, for its tiny and restricted life. This is far from the dense foliage, dimly seen but richly imagined, that Clarissa and Peter felt in her family's parkland at Bourton before 1910.

Less concentrated upon a moment, upon a distillation of a particular point in space, time, and psychology, *The Waves*, Mrs. Woolf's greatest fictional achievement, deals with many of the issues apparent in *Mrs. Dalloway. The Waves* depicts six characters, all of whom had known each other at school, through most of their lives as they keep meeting and parting. The novel, rich, suggestive, and interior, probes each character and relationship thoroughly and deeply. Yet the characters are not all equivalent entities, and the end of the novel is not simply a discovery of six separate points of view. One of the characters, Bernard, the story-teller, the poseur, is more able to survive against the waves of experience than are the others. Yet Bernard, unlike both Mrs. Dalloway and Mr. Ramsay, does not compose and concentrate himself toward a single aim or identity:

For myself, I have no aim. I have no ambition. I will let myself be carried on by the general impulse. The surface of my mind slips along like a pale-grey stream reflecting what passes.

Diffuse, far from heroic, Bernard is able to survive most fully because he has absorbed the life around him most completely, tried to live less entirely in terms of the definitions (husband, novelist, philologist) that he has made up. Unlike Mrs. Dalloway, Bernard is not afraid of love. He is the first of the six to marry and, although the marriage does not work out, he realizes that man must keep defining and redefining himself and his relationships, must remain flexible and open to experience.

At the other end of the scale from Bernard is Rhoda. Whereas Bernard has no identity because he is constantly changing identities and absorbing himself in different experiences, Rhoda is unable to find any identity at all. Even as a child, at school, she is the outsider, withdrawn, diffident. Even at the moment when, meeting the others for dinner, she feels most comfortable, she is alone:

> I walked straight up to you instead of circling round to avoid the shock of sensation as I used. But it is only that I have taught my body to do a certain trick. Inwardly, I am not taught; I fear, I hate, I love, I envy and despise you, but I never join you happily. Coming up from the station refusing to accept the shadow of the trees and the pillarboxes, I perceived, from your coats and umbrellas, even at a distance, how you stand embedded in a substance made of repeated moments run together; are committed, have an attitude, with children, authority, fame, love, society; where I have nothing. I have no face.

An affair with Louis is unable to give Rhoda any significant identity or relationship with anyone else. More neurasthenically perceptive than the others, more sensitive and more frightened, she remains completely isolated and finally commits suicide. She is another Septimus, although the forces that have hounded her to death are less specific and more universally relevant than Sir William Bradshaw and the horror of World War I. Yet, in this novel, the alternative to suicide is not a precarious control; rather it is an immersion in experience, a willingness to become involved even though conquest or victory is impossible.

The four characters of control, of definition, are more limited than either Bernard or Rhoda. Louis, from Brisbane, culturally an outsider, is defined early as the opportunist, the young man who needs to prove himself in material terms in order to live down his background and his accent. Although he becomes a successful businessman, Louis cannot give or receive love. His definition is too rigid, too circumscribed. As in the depiction of Charles Tansley in *To the Lighthouse,* Virginia Woolf's account of the man from another background or another class is excessively intense. It is as if in Mrs. Woolf's world a different class or background so marks a man, so conditions his responses and reactions, that little room is left for the complexity that distinguishes many of her characters who have in common, at least, an upper-class English background. The depictions of Charles Tansley and Louis, so exclusively reliant on background and class, are among Mrs. Woolf's least convincing.

The other three central characters in *The Waves* are equally but more convincingly circumscribed. Neville is the pedant, neat, prissy, entirely self-absorbed, the extreme version of Clarissa Dalloway's concentration; in the novel, his order and rigor become increasingly isolated and meaningless. Jinny is a lively girl, interested only in parties and dances, but she becomes too old to dance all night and the memory of youthful vitality is only a sentimental inadequacy. Susan, always longing for a farm and a husband and children, defines herself as an earthmother; yet achieving these longings, she becomes suffused with the boredom and emptiness of sacrificing herself to process, she is "glutted with natural happiness." These three characters, like Louis, are victims of the definition too rigid, the concentration too inflexible, the circumscribed artifice supposedly necessary for survival that, in fact, cuts off dimensions of experience. As victims they receive the author's sympathy, the compassion they deserve as creatures caught in the machinery they designed for their own survival. The rigid definition, like the inability to define at all, leads to a kind of death, to succumbing to the waves of time and experience. Only the mutable definition allows man to float.

The Waves has an historical dimension as well. All six characters, while at school, venerate a slightly older boy named Percival. Percival, the seventh character, is never presented directly, and his thoughts and actions are seen only through the perspectives of the other six. Yet his stalwart composure and assurance haunt the novel: all the characters recall his wise words and heroic deeds; Rhoda, silently, and Neville, far less silently, are in love with him. While still fairly young, Percival is killed serving in India—before 1910. He represents a past glory, the wholeness of an assumed historical and moral tradition, no longer possible in the world of *The Waves*. Without his historical assurance and security, the characters need to search for themselves in order to discover any metaphysical assurance, any sense of meaning for man. The more they concentrate or define themselves, the less likely they are to find any significant possibility for the human being, the more likely they are to be fixed and to stagnate within a circumscribed limitation. Only the fluid, the role player, the poseur, like Bernard, who can change definitions as easily as others change clothes, can achieve significant survival. Bernard discovers no essence of human nature; he merely remains alive with the metaphysical possibilities still open. In this sense, *The Waves* is different from any of Mrs. Woolf's other novels: the character who can best survive, by historical and psychological accident, is the one who remains most responsive, most amorphous, who never finds a metaphysical truth and is content never to settle for a quasi-metaphysical assurance as a substitute. Bernard is closer to the amorphous a-hero so frequent in fiction since 1945 than to the defining, questing hero of his own generation. Mrs. Woolf's frequent skepticism about the possibility of man's getting beyond himself, reaching metaphysical truth, is extended, in *The Waves*, to a skepticism about the value of even making the attempt.

Another way of illustrating the differences between *The Waves* and Mrs. Woolf's other novels is apparent in her treatment of sex. In theory, Mrs. Woolf frequently made the point that domesticity dampens achievement, that the comfort and fecundity of family life thwarts man's impulses to create and to search for truth. In *To the Lighthouse,* family life and sexual completeness are antithetical to reaching the lighthouse, the symbolic representation of that possibility beyond ordinary humanity; *Mrs. Dalloway* goes further, for sexual completeness can even, for the sensitive, destroy the identity of the human personality, as Clarissa needs to remain virginal and Peter promiscuous in a kind of emotional virginity. Although the excessively remote and completely non-sexual is satirized in the characterization of Jacob Flanders, the novel in which he appears also indicates that interest in sexual relationships is, for man, an understandable distraction from the more significant human attempts to find the truth of experience. Even in the comic historic parable, *Orlando,* sex is regarded as a limitation under which the human being must suffer. Orlando changes from man to woman during the novel, but, whether man or woman, Orlando is presented as being able to communicate only with members of his or her own sex. In all these works, part of the control and dedication man needs in order to create is the ability not to be distracted by his own biology. *The Waves* reverses the terms in which Mrs. Woolf sees sexual experience, although the possibility latent in Elizabeth Dalloway suggested the theme earlier. In *The Waves,* the five characters who either cannot survive or survive only in a severely limited way either deny sex or subordinate it to their rigid definitions: Rhoda finds no meaning in sexual encounters, relationships with others only destroy her own identity; Louis uses sex as a way to climb into respectability, to impinge upon the class that denies him entrance; Neville is homosexual, feels that heterosexual relationships are sloppy and destructive; Jinny's social whirl prevents any lasting sexual commitment; Susan uses sex to create more children and build a securely pastoral world in which she suffocates. All of these characters evade sexual relationship, and this evasion is part of their circumscription, part of their failure. Only Bernard sees sexual relationship as an extension of the human personality, as a commitment that need not confine, as a partial definition that renders one still open and vulnerable to experience. In her granting Bernard a more comprehensive survival, Mrs. Woolf demonstrates her change in attitude, her recognition that sexual relationships, even if they do not discover truths beyond humanity, keep the human being more vital and resilient.

In terms of Virginia Woolf's career, *To the Lighthouse* alone is a moment, a point in time when experience gave the appearance of coherence and direction, whereas *The Waves* depicts the general condition, the flux in which moments dissolve. Through history, through psychology, through the process of life itself, all the moments eventually dissolve, sometimes to the extent that mere survival, the possibility of keeping alive at all, becomes as much as the battered human being can manage. Compassion is a constant attitude, a point of view the author holds toward all those seeking the permanence of the moment, attempting to give life a direction and a meaning that can never be sustained. Man, looking for truth, is regarded with compassion because the truth either cannot be found or dissolves as soon as it is discovered.

Mrs. Woolf's revolt against the Edwardians, sufficiently evident in technique, was considerably less thorough than she thought it was. Trying to assert man's permanent essence, his eternal character, Mrs. Woolf often saw her crystallizations dissolved by time, by history, by the complexity and flux of human experience, by the very sort of environment and material intractability she so sharply criticized the Edwardians for relying upon. In addition, her attempts at hard truth frequently ended in soft compassion for the human being who could neither find nor face the hardness of truth. She was closer to Arnold Bennett than either she or her contemporary reading public would ever have acknowledged. "Yes, there it is," is, in Mrs. Woolf's novels, a summary and descriptive statement of man's condition, a resigned and limited conclusion, far more frequently than it is a moment of apprehension of eternal meaning or truth.

IX

D. H. LAWRENCE

At first impression D. H. Lawrence's fiction seems to express little compassion. Lawrence always attempts to reveal hitherto unknown or neglected areas of experience, to challenge man to new insights and a deeper consciousness of himself. In badgering man to accept new dimensions of experience, he makes his characters often seem either projections of his own ideas, like Lilly in *Aaron's Rod* (1922), or, like Birkin in *Women in Love* (1920), models for a sensibility more highly developed than that of the average man. Were this first impression an adequate description of Lawrence's fiction, compassion would be irrelevant, for the characters would be judged, would either fail or succeed, as they conformed to the author's version of what was significant in human experience.

Lawrence would then be only a moralist, a sermonizer, one who praises the man who has found the truth, as the author sees it, and consigns the rest to the deserved hell of class-bound dullness and stupidity. This first impression is partially true, for Lawrence does badger and sermonize, does establish standards that attempt to force his readers to sense a deeper human experience than they may have acknowledged before. Yet Lawrence's judgments are not nearly so simple as this: the "truth" is blurred or revealed by the accidents of history and society, the message is visible only through all the ambivalence of the questing creature himself.

In the sense that they depict the influences of environment

on the human being, Lawrence's novels are richly social. His characters, in part products of a particular time and place, victims of historical process, are not always in a position to search for the "truth," to delve into new forms of human physical and psychological consciousness. Characters like Aaron in *Aaron's Rod* receive the author's compassion because, given the accidental world in which they find themselves, they dedicate themselves to the search for "truth." Aaron's failure is far less a judgment on Aaron than a statement about his world and a presentation of the dilemmas involved in any man's search. Similarly, Lawrence's novels do not simply compare a degenerate society to a healthy one, do not simply attack industrialism as evil and hold forth agricultural primitivism as an ideal. Societies, like individual men, are complicated and not easily categorized by a quick, evaluative judgment.

Two of Lawrence's early novels, *The White Peacock* (1911) and *Sons and Lovers* (1913), extensively depict agricultural society in a way that avoids both traditional pastoral stereotypes and the possible use of the society as a counter in an argument against the dominant industrial society. *The White Peacock,* in particular, conveys a hard, unsentimental impression of the problems, both societal and personal, facing the working farmer. At times, the description of farm life is richly comic, as in the scene of Will and Anna's wedding in *The Rainbow* (1915), a scene which combines a presentation of rural warmth and vitality with both satire directed against rustic simplicity and a sense of the changing times that make religion a less vital force than it was. In other instances, such as the haying scene between Will and Anna, the description is both a record of agricultural custom and a means of presenting the sexual attraction between the characters. Lawrence often avoids the allegorical tendency that would turn the description into the representation of one side of an abstract argument.

Much of Lawrence's use of social material takes the form of inserted vignettes or sharply satirical criticism, neither particularly conducive to the development of compassion. The vignettes, at which Lawrence is particularly adept, often stand only for themselves as bits and pieces of social commentary: the famous description of Morel's miners' breakfast in *Sons and*

Lovers; an account of the cheapness and the gaudiness of the early cinema in *The Lost Girl* (1920) ; a picture of discussions in the miners' pub in *Aaron's Rod;* a satiric description of the conventional outsider's veneration for the bullfight in *The Plumed Serpent* (1926). The social satire, frequent and biting, demonstrates a more consistent concern with the ways in which society infects potential value within it. The searchers in Lawrence are always confronted by characters who can be defined by their social designations, representatives of classes who are made ludicrous in the novel. The portraits of Hermione and her brother, Alexander (Alexander is introduced "striding romantically like a Meredith hero who remembers Disraeli"), in *Women in Love* satirize the popular conception of the intellectual Edwardian aristocrat. Fashionable Bohemians, of whatever period, are always ridiculed in Lawrence's novels. The world-weary aristocrats, the skeptical generation after World War I, are lampooned sharply in *Aaron's Rod:*

> "Here, let's write it down," said Lilly. He found a blue pencil and printed in large letters on the old creamy marble of the mantelpiece panel:—LOVE IS LIFE.
> Julia suddenly rose and flung her arms asunder wildly.
> "Oh, I hate love. I hate it," she protested.
> Jim watched her sardonically. . . .
> "Have another try," said Jim. "I know what love is. I've thought about it. Love is the soul's respiration."
> "Let's have that down," said Lilly.
> LOVE IS THE SOUL'S RESPIRATION. He printed it on the old mantelpiece.

More frequently and stridently, in Lawrence's later novels, satire is levelled against the upper classes, whereas, in the earlier novels, class snobbery is not always viewed as an unmixed evil. The narrator in *The White Peacock* is a sycophantic snob, and the author seems to endorse his attempts to rise above his background. The attitude toward Mrs. Morel in *Sons and Lovers* is more complex: on one hand, the author seems to sympathize with her efforts to propel her sons out of the miners' environment, and her aspirations toward a "finer" life; yet, on the other hand, her addiction to standard middle-class assumptions about what is "better" or "finer" provides one of the reasons for her son Paul's

revolt against her, one of the forces within society he must surmount in order to achieve his independence. Her social snobbery
is both a spur and a barrier to her son.

As Lawrence developed, however, his novels show a more
coherently satirical attitude directed against those who would
use a superficial social designation to enhance their estimate of
their own worth, an attitude that culminates in *Lady Chatterley's
Lover* (1928) in which Sir Clifford's impotence is always connected with his allegiance to his own class and his insistence on
the preservation of conventional social barriers. Sir Clifford uses
social designations only as a substitute for personal and human
adequacy. He becomes the stereotype, the comically handled
grotesque that embodies the false side in the weighted argument.

Lawrence's treatment of society is, however, not only of
the comic and grotesque. In *Sons and Lovers,* for example, Paul
must avoid various social as well as personal traps in a novel
which demonstrates his victory negatively, outlines only the
forces by which he is not defeated. He overcomes the simplified
personal statements each of his love affairs represents: the soul,
the body, possessive maternal love. But each of these affairs also
represents a simplified social perspective he must avoid: sentimental pastoralism in Miriam; Clara's progressive new world of
the shop, the strike, and votes for women; his mother's genteel
Rotarian climbing. This becomes, even negatively, a significant
perspective toward history and society.

Many critics, however, have felt that Lawrence spins too
far into the mystic realms of the blood or the cosmos to demonstrate anything central about society at all. One such critic,
Arnold Kettle, illustrates a fairly typical point of view in complaining that the pledge for a new society in *The Rainbow* is
shrouded in the "swamps of mysticism." Yet the pledge, the rainbow, is anchored securely in the earth, both literally and metaphorically. Ursula's dedication to the rainbow is her statement
that human capacity can surmount and transfigure the particular
society around her without ever leaving its earthbound and
earth-determined moorings. In fact, understanding of the rainbow requires a greater recognition of the earth (of sex, of the
body, of the feelings and perceptions fundamental to human
experience) than does the abstract, consciously elevated existence

lived by most people who never see the rainbow. The rainbow, tied to the earth, spans the heavens, but Lawrence's are anthropomorphic heavens, symbols of strictly human possibility that most of society either ignores or never sees. The rainbow is not a symbol of mystic transcendence; rather, it represents a unity of human experience (and human experience is always, in part, social experience) that includes more of human capacity than does the divisive and Puritanical society Lawrence examines in the novel. In fact, Lawrence's novels, like *The Rainbow,* show a constant concern with society, a concern never vitiated by his bitter attacks or by his apparent flights into other realms.

Specifically, *The Rainbow* outlines, through three generations in one family, the transformation of England from the predominantly agricultural society with its narrow focus and intense sense of individual presence to the industrial and suburban world of the early twentieth century. Love becomes more difficult for each successive generation of the Brangwens. The first, Tom and Lydia, had different cultures and memories to reconcile, but rural England left them the time and space to form the necessary arch of personalities. In the next generation, Will and Anna are less isolated. Issues from the social world around them, the church, art and status, intrude, helping to keep their relationship stormy and tenuous, alive only in momentary sexual encounters. They use the creation of a large family to cloak the central insufficiency they find in each other. Ursula, the third generation, is even more completely surrounded by the demands of society. She must find a socially approved means of earning a living; her first lover, Skrebensky, thinks of the world only in terms of all the slogans and capsulized headlines he reads in the newspapers; the world around her judges all her actions in terms of class and profit. She realizes that she must escape entirely from society's influence if she is not to destroy her own deepest responses to experience.

The growth of industrialism is a consistent element in Lawrence's awareness of society in all of his novels. His attack on it, however, developed slowly, for in his early novels, *The White Peacock* and *The Trespasser* (1912), he did not conceive of it as a major problem for man. The next novel, *Sons and Lovers,* recognizes the importance of industrialism for contemporary man but takes an ambivalent point of view toward its growth. Paul Morel is alternately attracted and repelled by the complex of machines and factories marking the countryside, and, significantly, he turns toward the lights of the city as the lights of life at the end of the novel. Subsequent novels, however, unequivocally establish industrialism as an enemy. In *The Rainbow,* even the building of the canal for transportation, early in the nineteenth century, cuts man off from the unity of his land, and from the view of the church spire that once gave his life meaning. Through the three generations (and the interest in generations and how a family alters is itself part of the interest in society, for exterior conditions invariably determine many of the changes in the human being) the problem of industrialism becomes increasingly acute. The most corrupt, in Lawrence's terms, of the characters, the second Tom Brangwen and Winifred Inger, finally prosperous in the colliery town and molding themselves to fit their society, are depicted in mechanical terms:

> His real mistress was the machine, and the mistress of Winifred was the machine. She too, Winifred, worshipped the impure abstraction, the mechanisms of matter. There, there, in the machine, in service of the machine, was she free from the clog and degradation of human feeling.

The terms, the tone and the point of view become characteristic of the later Lawrence. *Women in Love* develops the attack on industrialism further. With great clarity, Lawrence explains the changes in three generations of the mine-owning Crich family: the grandfather who, without conscience, took as much money from the earth as he possibly could, and assumed that what was good for him was good for his workmen as well; the father, schooled in mid-Victorian benevolence, who believed that the owner and the workmen were engaged in a corporate enterprise based on mutual love, and who was genuinely shocked when a business slump led to a strike in his mine; the son, Gerald, who, without sentimentality or justifications about benefitting his workmen, enjoys the struggle of running the mines and is captivated by his own efficiency. Geared to a mechanical system, glorying in his status and apparent victory within the system, Gerald ultimately partially destroys himself because, in Lawrence's terms, he has allowed the system to define him, measured all his triumphs and disasters within the confines of the industrial system. In the next novel, *Aaron's Rod*, the principal character, originally an able miner and secretary of the local union, must break away from both his job and his family before the issues of the novel can even begin. The rejection of industrialism becomes a prior condition even for the search for value, in Lawrence's later work.

In all of Lawrence's novels in which the action takes place before World War I, those through *Women in Love*, the capacity to escape from any kind of society, the ability to remain unshaped and undefined by one's immediate environment, is itself an indication of value. Because escape is still possible, compassion is unnecessary; the few worthwhile characters manage with great difficulty to escape, whereas most people are explained and bound by their environment. Ursula realizes at the end of *The Rainbow* that her rainbow, her allegiance to a unifying relationship, must completely transcend the bounds of her contemporary society. Skrebensky is inadequate for her precisely because there is nothing about him that cannot be defined in terms of custom or the jingoistic clichés of his time and place. Consequently, she begins to dominate him sexually, to use him like a drone for her own satisfaction, just as her mother has used her father sexually, watched him become less and less the artist, his work turning to empty imitation, and his church to arid symbol as he is conquered within his marriage. As always, in Lawrence's work, the quality of the sexual relationship indicates the quality of the man, and to dominate or to be dominated sexually is to destroy both the relationship and the worth of the individual personality.

The connection between the vital sexual relationship, the rainbow, and getting beyond the boundaries or limits of society is made even more articulate in *Women in Love*, Lawrence's most fully worked out positive statement. Here, the two principal couples illustrate different aspects of the connection between society and the individual relationship. Gerald and Gudrun are always attached to society and its values, either accepting them or intensely and bitterly rejecting them, but always defining themselves in reference to colliers or customs or conquests of society. They can never forget the German form of address which adds the occupation or the social role to the name, although they sometimes bitterly make fun of it. Gerald and Gudrun struggle to dominate each other, use each other in their fiercely competitive love scenes, and finally destroy each other. In contrast, Ursula and Birkin, who come to be genuinely indifferent to society, are able to establish a positive love that, transcending the limitations of the socially constituted relationship, has tenderness, mutual concern, intensity and direction. Conveniently, Lawrence gives Birkin almost no background in terms of parents or class, and Ursula's father (whom she revered earlier in *The Rainbow*) is made a ludicrous fool easy to ignore. We learn only that Birkin has a small income, that both can leave their sterile jobs with the state school system in order to concentrate almost entirely on cultivating a relationship in which neither dominates, in which both individuals can satisfy themselves and become, in combination, more than the sum of two individualities, can formulate a rainbow that arches over the triviality and emptiness of ordinary experience. Yet, Lawrence's point is not that the valuable relationship must transcend any society, that the ultimately destructive quality of the relationship based on society's values is universal or axiomatic. Rather, given the condition of society in the early twentieth century, given the inhumanities of industrialism and the inheritance of the long tradition consigning the body and the soul to separate and mutually exclusive divisions within human experience, worthwhile individuals must escape entirely.

The contrast between the two couples in *Women in Love* is also conveyed in discussions about art. Gudrun insists, quite belligerently, that the work of art shows nothing of the personality of its creator, represents nothing but itself. Ursula, on the other hand, clearly speaking for Lawrence, replies that no work of art can finally be separated from its creator, that the truly disembodied work only reveals the lifelessness that shaped it. For Lawrence, art, like religion, needs to be understood as a complex and interdependent whole, to be recognized and accepted with all its many subtle connections and relationships. Ideas in the world he depicts have been simplistically polarized, deprived of their humane wholeness by false abstractions such as the separation of the creator from his creation. Such divisions are the marks of Puritanism, the point of view that insists on dividing, isolating, simplifying things, that must damn the body to glorify the soul, a point of view that, for Lawrence, has crippled society's vitality.

Even as early as *The Trespasser,* Lawrence demonstrated his awareness that the divisions and the pressures of the society inhibit the individual's development of his own capacity. Siegmund, the hero of the novel, must get away from society to enjoy his five-day idyll with his mistress on the Isle of Wight. But Siegmund, unlike Birkin or Ursula, is unable to accept the consequences of his break from society and commits suicide after his return. In *Women in Love,* the Laurentian hero has developed far enough to ignore society, to escape the abstract and meaningless social divisions and accept the unity of his own being and his own relationships.

Escape is never, however, complete or permanent. Even *Women in Love* ends by qualifying the central human triumph. Despite the fact that he and Ursula have established a valuable relationship of intensity and direction, Birkin's last statement shows that he needs a close friendship with Gerald as well. And Ursula is unable to understand this need, to recognize that, in Lawrence's terms, the valuable man requires a secondary homosexual relationship which does not impinge on or contradict his primary heterosexual relationship. But Gerald is dead, victim of his own divided and destructive impulses. Birkin, despite his self-engendered sense of unity, and despite the fact that he comes closer to getting what he wants and deserves than does any other of Lawrence's heroes, is left without a close male friendship and with a wife, understanding in all other respects, who cannot understand his sense of loss. No hero ever achieves what he wants completely, no human relationship is ever perfect, yet, for Birkin, possible perfection is never completely destroyed by all the manifestations of human imperfection:

If humanity ran into a cul-de-sac, and expended itself, the timeless creative mystery would bring forth some other being, finer, more wonderful, some new, more lovely race, to carry on the embodiment of creation. The game was never up. The mystery of creation was fathomless, infallible, inexhaustible, for ever.

Despite the frequent use of the word "mystery," this is far more a romantic version of the doctrine of evolution than evidence of the "swamps of mysticism" of which Lawrence has been accused. Like all romantic doctrines, the aim invariably pulls away from the achievement, becomes more comprehensive, more complete, as the achievement approaches it. Lawrence's romanticism, like Keats's, can never be satisfied, for the desire pulls away from whatever man is, just as the romanticism can never finally be defeated as long as human possibility exists.

In this sense, the romantic doctrine injects a note of compassion even in Lawrence's most positive work, for the human being never gets all he wants, never develops into all he can apprehend and visualize. The romantic distance between aspiration and achievement, between possibilities man can envision and what man can actually become, necessarily involves compassion, conveys a sympathy for the human being who can never be complete.

In his later work, Lawrence's romanticism became less positive, generally less hopeful. The ability of the hero and heroine in *Women in Love* to create their own valuable synthesis, their full marriage, is never duplicated in those of Lawrence's novels that take place after World War I. In the novels set in the postwar world, escape is impossible. Partly because of the general catastrophe of 1914, partly, no doubt, because of Lawrence's personal experiences when he was hounded from Cornwall by militant patriots because he had a German wife, society becomes more monstrous and malevolent in the later novels, permitting no escape, allowing no one to ignore its maxims.

The first of the novels that uses the war as fictional material, *The Lost Girl,* provides a sense of the impact of 1914 on life in the provinces and life among the foreign members of carnival troupes that tour England. Although the isolation of the old provincial life was gradually breaking down before the war, gradually opening to commercial and international influences, the war hastens the process and leaves the characters in the chaos of not knowing what they are accepting and what they are rebelling against. Initially, the war seems insignificant and the more pompous characters keep saying that it will be over in six weeks. Yet the war gradually becomes the massive symbol of a more gen-

eral and vastly accelerated erosion, assuming more and more overwhelming importance, completely changing lives, perspectives,
relationships, and reactions to the society. The international
carnival troupe is sundered into its various national identities,
various simplifications in which the characters themselves only
half believe. Lawrence communicates the attitude that, however
the war might end, neither the society nor the individual will
ever be the same again.

Aaron's Rod, set just after the war is over, chronicles even
more sharply the differences the war has made. In the beginning
of the novel, Lawrence portrays these changes imagistically when
Aaron is walking to the pub late at night:

> Lights twinkled freely here and there, though forlornly, now
> that the war-time restrictions were removed. It was no glitter of
> pre-war nights, pit-heads glittering far off with electricity. Neither
> was it the black gulf of the war darkness: instead, this forlorn
> sporadic twinkling.

The postwar lights never become more than "this forlorn sporadic twinkling," for the prewar beacons cannot be re-established.
As light represents both illumination and security, postwar man
can find only transient glimpses or tantalizing hints of what, before the war, might have helped him on his journey. In the uncertain light, Aaron leaves his home, class-bound wife and children, wanders to London and then Italy trying to achieve the
kind of independence and meaning that would have been possible for the Laurentian hero before the war. He meets numerous veterans, all maimed in one way or another by their experience; he visits a wealthy expatriate family, isolated in its past by
money and fear of the modern world; his affairs with a spoiled
London Bohemian and a Florentine Marchesa, both of whom
would consume him, are unsatisfactory. Symbolically, his flute,
the rod which is his music and his maleness and his independence all at once, is smashed in an explosion that is part of an
Italian political uprising.

Aaron, unlike Ursula and Birkin in the earlier novels, cannot escape, cannot avoid the massive imposition of society on the
individual. The war has compressed Europe and manufactured
allegiances that cause society to impinge more and more on each

individual, for no one could really escape the war, the monster that society had set in motion. Aaron and all Lawrence's later heroes and heroines, less lucky than Ursula and Birkin, must face the public problems not amenable to private solutions and individual syntheses. Aaron, learning from the prophet, Lilly, recognizes that since the problem is public, since it necessarily involves society, the solution must be public as well. And *Aaron's Rod,* as well as most of Lawrence's later novels, cannot even suggest a solution as positive and as valuable as that of *Women in Love.*

The fact that the ills of society require public solution is complicated by Lawrence's aversion to the masses and mass action. In all the novels, the masses, composed of ordinary men, are dull, stupid, brutal, interested in only their own limited welfare, and unable to understand any ideas that have not been easily simplified and packaged for them. In *Aaron's Rod,* for example, the Italian masses who tear down flags and explode bombs resemble a beast let loose rather than the dedicated supporters of social reform they tell themselves they are; similarly, the English miners are sodden and brutal, anxious only for money.

Aaron leaves his post with the union initially because he sees his independence threatened by the mass. In another postwar novel, *Kangaroo* (1923), hatred of the masses is even more intense. Here Lawrence, speaking through his principal character, Somers, recalls the criminal mobs, equipped with mindless patriotic slogans and the force of a majority opinion, that ruled England during the war. The wartime mass reactions have permanently brutalized England:

> In the winter 1915–1916 the spirit of the old London collapsed; the city, in some way, perished, perished from being a heart of the world, and became a vortex of broken passions, lusts, hopes, fears, and horrors. The integrity of London collapsed, and the genuine debasement began, the unspeakable baseness of the press and the public voice, the reign of that bloated ignominy, JOHN BULL.
>
> No man who has really consciously lived through this can believe again absolutely in democracy.

Even in Australia, where Somers goes to escape European bullying and brutality, he encounters communists, militant nationalists, fascists, all people with public programs for restoring society. But he cannot embrace any of them, for the independent and worthwhile man is unable to submerge himself and his concerns in the leveling simplicities of mass action. Lawrence, by the time of *Aaron's Rod* and *Kangaroo,* had worked himself into a contradictory position. The world impinged sufficiently on the individual to demand that the individual's solution be public as well as private, that the individual recognize that he could not work out any valuable attitude toward experience on his own or with another single individual. At the same time, all possible public solutions, all forms of government, were dependent on mass support, on propaganda, on pandering to the criminal instincts of the mob.

Although Lawrence's frequent attacks on democracy and the doctrine of equality might suggest some form of fascism, his fierce objection to any form of social or political bullying as well as his specific derision of any notion of racial purity demonstrate clearly that no historically known form of fascism was acceptable to him. Both *Aaron's Rod* and *Kangaroo* illustrate his horror of the rampant criminal mobs attached to fascism. In addition, Lawrence's attraction to violence is to the intensity of the private violence of an emotional relationship, clearly not to the mindless violence of the public mob. As *The Plumed Serpent* makes clear, violence is sanctioned only when it is personally directed, personally meaningful and personally understood; the thugs who attack Don Ramon, the leader of the Mexican-Indian religion, like the cruel boys who stone the mud chick, like the fools at the bullfight whose sense of life is entirely vicarious, are all engaged in a meaningless and destructive form of violence. For Lawrence, despite the overwhelming need for some public solution, every known public solution, every doctrine, every posture, was ultimately unacceptable.

Caught by the dilemma in England, Lawrence moved his characters as he moved himself, out of England after the war. He had always viewed alien influences as vital and healthy, for, back in *The Rainbow,* the Brangwens are distinguished from other rural families by the acceptance of Lydia, the infusion of Polish blood into the English line. Directly after the war, Italy, the south, seems to represent something harder, firmer, nobler, more open and free to the gloomy northern Englishman. Ursula and

Birkin had, before the war, welcomed the journey from Alpine ice and Nordic character down into sunny Italy; after the war, Aaron tries to recover himself and find his direction by a journey southward, and Alvina Houghton, once the war has started in England, marries the Italian carnival actor and tries to escape English chaos by going to live with him in Italy. Yet Italy provides no solution. Aaron's rod, his independent power, is smashed in Italy and he realizes that he must develop something further, although he doesn't know what. The war catches up with Alvina again in Italy, as if the war were a massive cloud seeping down from the north and blotting out all of Europe. Even before war actually begins in Italy, Alvina recognizes that the hard and noble quality of Italy is primarily an intransigent malevolence, but the war itself finally demolishes the myth of a land of sunshine, flowers and peasant integrity. All Europe has become corrupt, all value has been swallowed by machines, money and masses.

Lawrence sends his heroes and heroines further away: Lou Witt in *St. Mawr* (1925) leaves her husband, a sterile and parasitic socialite, to seek space and pure being in the dry hills of the American southwest; Somers goes to Australia; Kate Leslie in *The Plumed Serpent,* finding no sense of value left anywhere in Europe, searches to renew vital energy among the Indians in the primitive regions of Mexico. In all these instances, the character looks not only for personal meaning and definition, but also for a society with direction and positive value. If the white man of Europe is dead or sterile, perhaps the red Indian or the new Australian can provide some sense of vitality. Kate Leslie, in particular, recognizes the need for breaking down purity in an attempt at emotional and physical assimilation with the dark races, for she tries to immerse herself fully in the primitive life of Mexico, to commit herself to both a man and a role in the Mexican-Indian society. She also realizes that, in social terms, the day of supremacy of the white race is over and the white man can save himself only by union with the Indian.

The necessary union of individuals and cultures never occurs. The white man may recognize that he needs to combine with the dark races, but this long inheritance of supremacy, his vestigial Puritanism and sense of purity, prevent his full acceptance of any world other than white, desiccated Europe.

The later novels, despite all the characters' fierce strivings and all the author's rhetoric, show even less positive possibility for man than did the earlier ones. Somers, somewhat regretfully, must leave Australia, for he has been unable to participate in its new amalgamation and he recognizes that his own dry inhibitions forbid immersing himself in a new world. Lou Witt stays in New Mexico, but she has only the hills, not even the horse, St. Mawr, who represented her search for pure being. Kate Leslie remains in Mexico primarily out of desperation. She cannot finally, physically or intellectually, accept all the ritual that accompanies her new life and she cannot worship Cipriano, Don Ramon's lieutenant, as she feels she ought. But she is forty years old, Europe is completely dead for her, the man she worshipped who fought for Irish freedom on the fringes of the old Europe is also dead, and he represented the furthest point from her standard upper-middle-class upbringing that she could unreservedly accept. In remaining in Mexico and staying with Cipriano, himself only the second-best man in his own world, Kate is choosing a flawed and alien version of vitality rather than surrounding herself with an imaginatively perfect version of death. Mexico, for her, will always be flawed: its cruelty and malevolence appall her, for she is very much like the mud chick she sympathizes with when it is stoned by the Mexican boys.

Lawrence's second resolution, the resolution that insisted that the public side of man, the social side, be satisfied as fully as the private or sexual side, was far less clear and resounding than was his first. Kate Leslie is Ursula Brangwen fifteen years and a disastrous war later; as the problems have become wider and far more difficult, the solution is far more tentative, qualified, and judgment on the worth of the character more difficult to render. We understand Kate Leslie and her world, but we cannot apply the kind of endorsement or condemnation, from the author's point of view, easily applicable to the characters in *The Rainbow* and *Women in Love*.

Lawrence never proposes any satisfactory solution to the extended problems and dilemmas he examines in the later novels. The impulse is still to escape from society, no matter how impossible the world's malignant forces and the characters' own inhibitions have made escape. An exception to the pattern of the later novels is *Lady Chatterley's Lover.* Although published in 1928, Lawrence's most widely read novel provides a highly simplified escape from the social and sexual issues it poses into the floral idyll with the gamekeeper. Whether *Lady Chatterley's Lover* is a demonstration of Lawrence's waning ability to come to terms with the complexities of the postwar world in his fiction or, rather, a deliberately simplified gesture intended to shock an imperceptive public by concentrating so forcefully and repetitiously on a single aspect of the problem, is a matter that only biographical evidence can determine. The novel itself, despite all its virtues, is an oversimplified treatment of the need to escape from the sterile and mechanized society, a neat and easily understood parody of some of Lawrence's other novels. It reveals no compassion, only defines truth and falsity, blatantly and single-mindedly. In contrast, Lawrence's other later novels, those in which the characters extend themselves in order to merge with other individuals and cultures, in which man tries to solve all the multiple dilemmas of his own nature and relationships, in which the romantic aspiration for completeness is both valuable and futile, are full of compassion for the searching human being. Aaron, Somers, Kate Leslie, even Lou Witt, are in their futile searches made richer and fuller human beings than is Constance Chatterley, who is understandably wrong when she marries, and then in escaping to her idyllic forest is right.

In addition to compassion for man as the romantic searcher who can never complete himself and never finally escape from a society that presses in upon him, Lawrence's fiction consistently demonstrates another kind of compassion. He attacks Puritanism, the tradition that divides, simplifies and harshly judges human experience. Lawrence's sense of humanity is always full, total, comprehensively accepting; consistently, he attacks the rigid cast of mind of men who establish neat little rules about punishing the body to save the soul, or whose primary allegiance is to the safe accumulation of money rather than to the more chaotic cultivation of men. The Puritan, the man who purifies by division, who judges himself and his fellows by narrow standards, who fabricates polarities in order to praise one side while damning the other, is always Lawrence's enemy.

Of course, Lawrence himself judges, in castigating those

who judge so narrowly, but the judgment against judgment, like the conformity of the nonconformists, is one step removed from the primitive simplicity of the original Puritanical judgment. Lawrence's social ethic, his rebellion against the narrowness of the Puritan tradition, is in itself a compassionate statement, a plea for greater width and understanding of human complexity. Then, in the later works, as the world impinges more forcibly and the characters are unable to escape at all, even the anti-judgmental judgment recedes as the novels focus on the futile struggles of romantic man locked in the all-pervasive mechanism of modern society. Accordingly, compassion becomes the humane means for understanding the romantic figure's situation, for appreciating Kate Leslie's ambivalent acceptance of an alien culture whose cruelty and hostility she can see as clearly as the author can. Her situation stands for that of modern man, one in which compassion provides an artistic resolution, the only kind of resolution possible in a world where no human effort finds satisfaction.

X

JAMES JOYCE

SINCE THE SUBJECT OF FICTION is man, attention to his particular environment generally connotes compassion because it details all man struggles against, all that forms or determines him, or all that he tries to overcome. One of the most comprehensive treatments of a social environment in fiction is contained in James Joyce's *Ulysses* (1922), a description particular enough to stimulate "Bloomsday" tours and guidebooks of Dublin constructed from the pages of the novel. What was displayed in shop windows, what was eaten in restaurants or sold at street stalls, the way people reacted to public events like the sinking of the *General Slocum* or Throwaway's victory at Ascot, the pattern of streets and pubs and public buildings in Dublin on Thursday, June 16, 1904—all provide part of the social texture of *Ulysses*.

Dubliners (1914), Joyce's early collection of short stories, similarly uses the minute recreation of local facts and attitudes, like the duties of the tea-lady at the laundry or the despair of the defeated Parnellites in the committee room, to provide a texture that is more than an accidental setting for the stories. Even *A Portrait of the Artist as a Young Man* (1916), superficially more rigidly selective in concentrating on theme than are *Dubliners, Ulysses,* or *Finnegans Wake* (1939), contains referential social material: descriptions of school and university life that provide both a sense of Jesuit and Irish education and focus on the qualities and reactions of the developing artist; the Christmas dinner scene that both establishes the environment for growing artistic perceptions and illustrates the ferocious conflict between the Parnellites and the Church at the time of Parnell's death. Joyce's novelistic precision, his method of creating the exact emotion by reproducing the exact detail, demands a concentration on the material environment. In order to show the causes of the artist's indifference or a character's despair, Joyce develops, with painstaking care, the precise material and social conditions relevant to the emotion.

Joyce is also a social novelist in ways far more significant than in the duplication of an exact material environment for his fiction. His themes are often social. As has frequently been noted, the stories in *Dubliners* are united by a theme of the paralysis of life in Dublin, a sense that all Dubliners, in very different ways, are held static and impotent in a city that is only a shabby version of its own past. *Ulysses,* full of characters who repeat their endless tales recalling the past in a constant round of pubs, shows a similar paralysis.

The city is both the setting for the novel and one of the principal issues within it, as the eighteen vignettes in the Wandering Rocks section, in which most of the principal characters pass by, serve as a miniature structural analogue (although not entirely a microcosmic thematic analogue) for the eighteen sections of the novel. And these eighteen vignettes are quickly presented images dwelling on the essential indifference, selfishness, and isolation of Dublin life. Both the bland, affable priest whose wanderings open the section and the remote Lord Lieutenant whose wanderings close it represent institutions which conventionally should provide some meaning and coherence; yet, the agents of both church and government wander through the city without any perceptible effect on the life or concerns of the inhabitants: Bloom is still the object of derision in the Dublin pubs, Dilly Dedalus is still poignantly poor. The sense of decline, of maudlin allegiance to a past more glorious than the present, is not confined to Dublin alone, for Joyce extends the commentary on society to all of Ireland and, metaphorically, to all the modern world.

In the very first section, Stephen refers to Irish art as "the cracked lookingglass of a servant," and the old woman who delivers the milk, an image of an older Ireland, is a shrunken crone who cannot follow most of the conversation around her. At a later point, Bloom recalls all the Irishmen who, with loud slogans, verbally supported the Boers in the recent war. In the scene at Barney Kiernan's pub, Joyce supplies numerous parodies of Irish bluster, blarney, and patriotism. Stephen also refers to his father, that prototype Irishman, as "all too Irish." Ireland, controlled alternately by shabby politicians and rigid, self-seeking churchmen, mired in a hopelessly false and extravagantly painted picture of its own past, is constantly satirized in *Ulysses.*

Joyce's irony, however, is not simply a one-sided weapon to demolish a single idea or institution. Presenting both sides of an issue, irony often cuts both ways, introducing what it seems superficially to destroy, showing the value of what it apparently castigates. If Joyce makes fun of the church's insulated indifference to the rest of society, he also makes fun of the idle spongers in the pub who make fun of the church. Similarly, Stephen's blasphemy introduces his devotion; his puns and his prayers are combined. Although he cannot accept the church's teachings as his guide or his salvation, he recognizes the tremendous force of church learning and ritual within his own perception and imagination. In addition, Stephen is looking for religious meaning, for a moral and metaphysical truth more coherent and more humane than anything presented in the world around him. The satire on religion introduces, in the various reversals Joyce's irony takes, a positive and forceful, although never systematized, religious dimension. Using the same method concerning social and national issues, Joyce satirizes both the Irish superpatriots who spend their days cursing England and its influence (while their jobs, their tradition, almost their very existence, are all dependent on the English establishment), and the dense and complacent Englishmen who regard Ireland as their charming and backward protectorate. English types and qualities are lampooned throughout the novel. Haines is the stereotype of the well-intentioned, literal-minded Englishman who wants to simplify nations and Gods to fit his pre-established categories. Private Carr is the mindless soldier, brutal and fiercely loyal to a set of words he never understands. King Edward VII enters the Circe scene as the perfect parody image of royal pomp and peace-making, understanding none of the issues and blandly on both sides at once. The English are also connected with nineteenth-century smugness and indifference, with the assumption that material improvement automatically guarantees improvement of the species. Like Virginia Woolf, Joyce characterizes Victorian customs, attitudes, and symbols with particular scorn, including frequent references like that to "Lawn Tennyson, gentleman poet."

Despite all the satire on particular societies, the Irish and the English, the church and the anti-church, Joyce's principal social comment is microcosmic, is presented through the epic structure of *Ulysses* itself. *Ulysses* is a wandering, an epic search for value, through a city that represents all cities, all civilizations, just as the classical epics are wanderings, quests for social and metaphysical value, throughout the known world. The very meaning of the epic form is partially social, for the principal figure in classical epics is always a hero, a man larger than life-size, who represents other men, whose struggles embody the issues of the whole group or society he stands for. Lesser men are automatically and intrinsically involved in the fate of the hero, fall with him on the battlefield or join in celebrating his triumph. *The Iliad* and *The Aeneid* deal explicitly with journeys and battles designed to establish a new society, to propagate new social values and attitudes, as the energetic barbarism of the Greeks in *The Iliad* overcomes sophisticated Trojan decadence. *The Odyssey* is less explicitly concerned with one society conquering another, but the contrast between Odysseus' social and domestic code and the lack of one in Penelope's suitors is dramatically demonstrated in Odysseus' victory. Both in wandering through the world and in representing his particular version of or attitude toward the world, the epic hero stands for something about society, a positive system of values endorsed by the author. In the classical epic, the conclusions, the positive statements endorsed, are not just social values, for the social, in part, stands for and particularizes the author's version of metaphysical and universal value.

With characteristic irony, Joyce's *Ulysses* is both epic and mock-epic, both example and parody of the historical form. As in the classical works, Joyce's *Ulysses* develops a structure of wanderings, in this case through Dublin, which suggest some central commentary, some evaluation, of the society itself. Yet, because *Ulysses* is also a mock-epic, the heroes have no followers, no positive system of social value is represented and the corollation between structure and social meaning in the classical epic is lost.

In *Ulysses,* as in the classical epic, the wandering is a journey both through and beyond society, both a kind of social analysis and a representation of the human being's search for meaning beyond himself. After both Stephen and Bloom have spent the day circulating in Dublin, the twin wanderers meet and drink cocoa at Bloom's house in Eccles Street. Their wanderings are extended:

> At rest relatively to themselves and to each other. In motion being each and both carried westward, forward and rereward respectively, by the proper perpetual motion of the earth through everchanging tracks of neverchanging space.

The range of the wanderings is definitively marked out in the final line of the section when, in answer to the question of "Where?" (i.e., within what area have the wanderings and their attendant speculations taken place?) , Joyce simply prints a large black dot. The black dot is here, the single time and place of the novel, the single society, Dublin, June 16, 1904; the dot is also, macrocosmically extended, everywhere, the universe, all human experience.

Unlike the classical epic, in which a single hero represents the best of a particular society, Joyce's epic has two heroes who stand in a complex and ironic relationship to each other and to the particular society. Both Stephen and Bloom represent crystallizations of the desires, emotions, intellects of all men, and their wanderings represent those of the special human being. In discussing the qualities accompanying Bloom's prospective journey (a journey which, characteristically, is never taken because of Bloom's physical inertia and the "lateness of the hour"), Joyce ironically underlines the representative nature of one of his heroes:

> What universal binomial denominations would be his as entity and nonentity?
> Assumed by any or known to none. Everyman or Noman.

"Everyman or Noman" Bloom, like Stephen his symbolic counterpart in this respect, both represents and does not represent other men. Bloom stands for a kind of humanity and sensitivity, yet he is also a particular man often foolish, ludicrous, destructively self-immolating; Stephen stands for a kind of human intellect and understanding, yet he can be arrogant, cold, almost perversely inhuman. The hero, the representation, is genuine yet spurious—an adequate symbol for general humanity and another example of the flawed and ignoble creature. Joyce's constant questioning of the symbolic relationship, his realization that his fictional heroes are "everyman" and "noman" but still themselves, indicates his compassion for the contemporary human situation. Man, looking for heroes, for models, recognizes that the models he establishes never fulfill their function completely, always are both heroic representations and isolated atoms that represent nothing. Compassion exists because of the difference between what man expects the symbol, historically and traditionally, to suggest, and what the symbol is, the difference between historical illusion and contemporary reality.

In contrast with other characters in *Ulysses,* however, Bloom and Stephen, for all their flaws and inadequacies, are heroic. Both are sufficiently aware of the world around them, sufficiently unencumbered by the conventionally mindless and heartless attitudes of their environment, to provide direction and commentary in the midst of their journeys. Both speculate, in contrast to other wanderers who attain nothing of epic stature or significance whatsoever. For example, the sailor Bloom and Stephen meet in the cabman's shelter has wandered almost all his life, but his experiences recounted comprise a litany of brutal gossip rather than any meaningful statement about man and his society.

Despite all their symbolic and representative capacity, Joyce's two heroes are aliens from the point of view of the common judgments and axioms of their particular society. In the scene in Barney Kiernan's pub, the narrator provides a common, gross, man-on-the-footrail portrait of Bloom:

That's an almanac picture for you. Mark for a soft-nosed bullet. Old lardyface standing up to the business end of a gun. Gob, he'd adorn a sweepingbrush, so he would, if he only had a nurse's apron on him.

[227

The scene continues with Bloom somewhat pompously trying to preach universal love, and meeting only the scorn and taunts of his audience. Bloom is a Jew in the midst of a Dublin full of anti-Semitism, an alien and a wanderer by birth as well as by temperament. Even before Bloom is introduced into the novel, Joyce prepares both the prevailing aura of anti-Semitism in characters like Haines and Mr. Deasy and the unconventional opposition to it in Stephen. Anti-Semitism is also vicious and pervasive in Barney Kiernan's pub, where Bloom, so often timid, sycophantic, and self-immolating, finally makes his great defense of the Jew. Given the atmosphere of Dublin and the crude and brutal men in the pub, Bloom's defense indicates some amount of courage. Yet Joyce does not allow the alien, the Jew, to become entirely heroic in publicly recognizable terms. Bloom never fully articulates his defense until he is safely in the cab with Martin Cunningham; then he turns and yells it back at the bullying citizen. In addition, the scene ends with Joyce providing a parody of Bloom, now courageous and martyred, ascending to Heaven:

> When, lo, there came about them all a great brightness and they beheld the chariot wherein He stood ascend to heaven. And they beheld Him in the chariot, clothed upon in the glory of the brightness, having raiment as of the sun, fair as the moon and terrible that for awe they durst not look upon Him. And there came a voice out of heaven, calling: *Elijah! Elijah!* And he answered with a main cry: *Abba! Adonai!* And they beheld Him even Him, ben Bloom Elijah, amid clouds of angels ascend to the glory of the brightness at an angle of fortyfive degrees over Donohoe's in Little Green Street like a shot off a shovel.

Joyce's irony, as always, works both ways. If the symbolic ascension of Bloom is lampooned, for no contemporary wanderer can warrant a pure and undiluted ascension, still the very fact that the symbol of an ascension appears at all shows something significant about Bloom's finally realized capacity to take a stand and reply to his persecutors. The ascension and its ludicrousness qualify each other, as the biblical prose is both mocked as inappropriate and used to indicate ironically something of Bloom's genuine transcendence over the citizen.

Stephen, too, is apart from his particular society. Although born into a conventional and accepted Dublin household, Stephen, by his intellect, his remoteness, and his attempt to be an artist, has removed himself further and further from the ordinary Dublin world. His alienation, unlike Bloom's, is primarily self-imposed, but both heroes represent, simultaneously, a specific severing from most of society and an abstract signification of some qualities, different in each hero, which represent what is best and potentially most heroic in contemporary man. Stephen, the intellectual and the artist, will not serve, will not prejudge, will not give in to the inanities around him. Although this intransigence is often made silly and adolescent, often restricts Stephen's perception of his world, it still insures something of a negatively heroic stature for the character. Both Stephen and Bloom are carefully balanced, the heroic placed against the childishly truculent or the foolishly sycophantic—epic figure against flawed human creature. Joyce's very balance, his tremendous care in allowing neither of his heroes to stand as exclusive symbols, or to be buried in the isolated trivia of human characterization, suggests his compassion for the human being. Man, looking for "truth," for the supreme and accurate representation, is sharply checked by the author's insistence on the other side, on the ludicrous fact of human experience that represents nothing at all.

Not only does Joyce balance our attitudes toward his two heroes, but he also balances the heroes against each other. Stephen and Bloom are related in the epic pattern as symbolic father and son. The characters, however, are generally unconscious of their connection to each other. Stephen, refusing to serve a God the Father in whom he cannot believe, and denying his real father, an aimless and alcoholically loquacious wanderer, constantly searches for a symbolic father; Bloom, whose only son Rudy died when eleven days old, constantly searches for a symbolic son. Several times during the day of the novel, Stephen and Bloom pass each other, come under the same cloud or enter the same newspaper office and library, before they meet. Joyce carefully prepares for the relationship before it is actually established. Both Stephen and Bloom, for example, play with words: Stephen with his sharp mind constantly makes knife-like puns and satirizes others; Bloom, in his rambling way, constantly speculates about the signs on shopwindows, economic facts, food, and the process of digestion. Both are frequently mentioned and mocked as progenitors, givers of life: Stephen in an Hellenic sense, as creating a tradition of reason and light; Bloom in an Hebraic sense, as generating an interest in conduct, sympathy, and honor. Yet, as life-givers, both are actually sterile, for, in the Dublin of the novel, neither Hellenic light nor Hebraic sympathy and honor has any actual impact. Some readers see Joyce's sense of compassion linked with the Hebraic life-force, with Bloom the victim and the sympathetic wanderer. But to place compassion solely on that side of the balanced equation is to sentimentalize Joyce's treatment of character, giving Bloom the role of the single dominant hero. Joyce sharply avoids such sentimentality in the novel. His compassion, never equated with that of a single hero or a single victim, inheres in the balance and the reconciliation of dual forces.

Bloom and Stephen are also linked unconsciously by numbers, each thinking of the sixteen-year difference between them and playing, cabalistically, with the numbers involved. Both use mathematics, abstract form, to try to control the mysteries of experience; both are Thursday's children, having "far to go." When they finally do meet, in the hospital where Mrs. Purefoy's baby is born, they, alone, refuse to laugh at the medical students' crude jokes. The apparently sterile life-givers meet at a birth, and they had earlier passed each other without meeting while Bloom was on his way to the funeral. Joyce finally presents the relationship in a more directly human way at the end of the brothel scene. Bloom, the father, protects Stephen after the latter has smashed the chandelier, and takes the symbolic son, now deserted by his other comrades, away from the brothel. Left alone with each other, Bloom and Stephen both try to convert the symbolic relationship into a literal friendship, but neither knows quite how or where to begin. In the style of the cabman's shelter section, Joyce parodies the circumlocutive fencing that goes on in the embarrassment at beginning the consciously special relationship.

They try to talk about music and the soul, to find subjects and attitudes in common. But their musical tastes differ, and each uses the word "soul" for a different set of concepts. Always too eager to be helpful and sympathetic, Bloom at one point tries to solidify the relationship by putting himself in Stephen's position and giving words to Stephen's ideas about Ireland and the artist. His words, as always, are slightly wrong, and Stephen sharply punctures the conversation by saying, "We can't change the country, Let us change the subject." A symbolic relationship is a great deal less difficult to sustain than a real one, and, as they leave the cabman's shelter, they have reverted to the symbolic.

The next section, the one that takes place at Bloom's house in Eccles Street, is written in a series of questions and answers, often dealing with precise information such as heights, weights, ages, dates, and distances. This precision, pedantic as it may sound, is a style appropriate to each hero's tangible quest and provides a necessary structure, a sense of established form, through which Bloom and Stephen can actually meet and talk. Bloom, Joyce relates, has not had a similarly honest and comprehensive conversation in eleven years, not since before his son's birth and death. Despite the structure, the mapping out of previous dates of encounter, and the listing of a great variety of subjects and correspondences, the relationship between Bloom and Stephen is still largely symbolic. Both are depicted as essential elements, abstractions from universal experience: Bloom is the universal solvent, the flowing sympathy, water; Stephen is the quick blaze, the aspiring, fire. At one point, when Stephen declines Bloom's suggestion that he have a bath, Joyce provides the reason: "The incompatibility of aquacity with the erratic originality of genius." Both elements may be equally essential, but they are, when placed alone together, incompatible. Only symbolically or negatively in defiance of or objection to the rest of society can the relationship between Stephen and Bloom be maintained. Or in silence:

> Silent, each contemplating the other in both mirrors of the reciprocal flesh of theirhisnothis fellowfaces.

And the minute that even this symbolic identity is formulated, Joyce, as always, provides the ironic counterpart by insisting upon both grossness and dissimilarity:

> Were they indefinitely inactive?
> At Stephen's suggestion, at Bloom's instigation both, first

Stephen, then Bloom, in penumbra urinated, their sides contiguous, their organs of micturition reciprocally rendered invisible by manual circumposition. . . .

Similarly?

The trajectories of their first sequent, then simultaneous, urinations were dissimilar. . . .

The trajectories may be dissimilar, but both Bloom and Stephen do traject, do, in their various ways, provide commentary that is both crudely direct and parabolically elevated on the paralysis of Dublin society.

Much of Bloom's and Stephen's heroism is negative. In addition, both are frequently satirized; more important, both are rendered partially impotent by the fact that their quasi-heroic positions, even at best, have no impact on the mass of men in the novel's world. They are far from epic heroes in the classical sense of the term. Yet, their heroic quality is evident in their standing for certain values, for sympathy and intellect, for curiosity and art, for humanity and will, for a consciousness that carries man beyond simply reflecting the stupidities of his environment. Their heroism is, ironically, most powerfully expressed in the final episode of the novel through the soliloquy of Molly Bloom, the figure of the earth. Despite all Molly's infidelities, and all her laughing at her husband's inadequacies, she retains a sense of pride about him. She is annoyed when others laugh behind his back, and she plans, toward the end of her soliloquy, to push her husband into being the man she'd always hoped he would be. She thinks of confronting him with her infidelities and forcing him to make love to her, to assert himself, to stop the self-immolation that has been crippling him for years. She recognizes that he has always been humane, always unlike the callous Blazes Boylan.

Although Molly takes advantage of Bloom's humanity, she respects it. Her final affirmation is the earth's multiple endorsement of Bloom, who ironically has been impotent for the last eleven years. Molly is saying "yes" to Bloom's request that she bring him his breakfast in bed the next morning, to his rare attempt to assert himself domestically; she is saying "yes" to the past with Bloom, to their courtship and romance sixteen years earlier; "yes" to the present and future with Bloom; finally, "yes" to life, to experience, best represented by Bloom's humanity, curiosity, and concern.

In a lesser way, Molly is also saying "yes" to Stephen, for she would like to take care of him, to bring him his breakfast in bed. When Bloom tells her that Stephen may come to teach her Italian, she is delighted and imagines the possibility of Stephen becoming another of her lovers. She also connects Stephen with her dead son, Rudy. In other words, for Molly, Stephen is projected into both lover and son. She, as symbol of the earth or generative force, can easily maintain the apparent contradiction, for, to her, Bloom is both lover and charge, both husband and wayward, sometimes incompetent child. Fathers and sons are, for Molly, mixed and identified with each other, achieving, in the symbol of her revery, an identity that is not possible in logic or in mundane fact. Molly, the earth, is also the embodiment of the author's compassion, the non-logical reconciliation of all the tortured and abstract masculine dilemmas. Although she is aware of the divisions, the differences, the fact that man cannot work out his salvation, cannot reconcile himself with modern society or with his Gods, Molly doesn't care. Rather, she embraces, incorporates beyond logic or rationality, emanates compassion for the two heroes and all they represent. It is, finally, through Molly's soliloquy, that the reader becomes convinced both of Stephen's and Bloom's special stature or heroic quality and of the symbolic father/son relationship between the two. Molly, the spirit of the earth, symbolically reconciles the father and the son, completes the Trinity which is never absent and is never literally achieved on earth.

Ulysses is also a comedy. Parodies are frequent, particularly in the last half of the novel where almost every passage is a stylistic parody. A great many of the parodies carry social implications. For example, the style of the Gerty MacDowell section echoes bad late-Victorian women's magazine fiction. Through this stylistic device, Joyce makes fun of both the taste and the illusory, romantic axioms of young, lower-middle-class Dublin girls. The style, played off against squalling infants, masturbation, and Leopold Bloom, is totally irrelevant to any of the real issues these girls encounter. The sinister and malicious patriots in Barney Kiernan's pub are parodied through long lists of names of Irish heroes, of international cosmopolites, of priests, of ancient tribes, of fashionable ladies whose names are all the names of trees. These parodies mock the idiocy and the pretense of the claims the citizens make for their past, their acquaintances, and their knowledge. In the hospital scene, Joyce uses many different styles from English literature, ranging chronologically from Anglo-Saxon kennings through the complexities of Sir Thomas Browne to contemporary slang, in order to lampoon the coarse and derivative quality of the medical students' jokes. Each parody is, in itself, funny and appropriate. But each is also directed against a specific aspect of Dublin life or society, the ineffectual boasting, the impotent reliance on a chaotic understanding of history, the inability to recognize other people's motives or impulses.

The parodies sympathize as well as satirize, construct as well as destroy. Joyce shows the Dubliners' pitiable limitations through their ignorant self-assertions. What Dublin is can be seen through all the particular examples of what it thinks it is but is not. All Joyce's intricate balance, what is and is not, what is simultaneously valuable and ludicrous, which of man's dreams are real and what of his reality is dream, gives *Ulysses* a multiple perspective toward human experience. This multiple perspective, this possibility within the comic method for the author's holding divergent points of view simultaneously, allows the novel to be both epic and mock-epic. The same comic multiplicity allows for two simultaneous heroic non-heroes, two impotent blunderers whom most of the world ignores, who nonetheless represent a kind of heroic value. This kind of multiple comic epic is not an entirely new form, although Joyce vastly extended its range and the amount of discordant material that could be packed into it. The form, however, is at least as old as Cervantes' *Don Quixote,* that tale of the man who begins as a foolish knight-errant tilting at wind-mills, the object of every sane man's scorn and derision, but who emerges as a crusader, ironically upholding genuine value in a society too depraved to see the point. *Ulysses* is a similar comic epic, but the world has, in Joyce's terms, become even more fragmented and decadent in the generations since Cervantes. Stephen and Bloom (the device of the divided hero demonstrates that no single man can any longer represent all heroic values by himself) need not even represent any positive moral virtue, any crusade to reform society, as Don Quixote does, in order to stand apart, with epic stature, from the rest of their society. They need only represent the combination of intellect and sympathy or art and humanity in order to stand distinguished from the rest of a vain, mindless, and paralyzed society. If Stephen/Bloom has come a long way from Achilles or Aeneas, so has modern Dublin fallen far from the way history and legend depict the strong and purposeful Greeks or the revived Trojans dedicated to founding the new city of Rome. But the hero still stands, in the comic epic, in the same kind of relationship to his society; he is still both the best representative of the possibilities within the society and a man superior to his fellows in energy, skill, and insight. The comedy is in the fact that both the hero and the society are so much less than they used to be in the literary representations of the classical societies.

Joyce's comedy thus has an historical dimension, a distance between imagined past and realized present, a location in contemporary time and space. In this way, as well as in its presentation of historical detail, the novel includes historical compassion, the sympathy for man inevitably influenced by the conditions of his particular time and place. Stephen and Bloom, with all their inadequacies, are the best that Dublin of 1904 can produce, and even they cannot be resolved, cannot be unified except through the symbols of the father/son relationship and the earth mother, the eternal feminine. Man is historically reduced, restricted. But the historical point is not the center of the novel, not the generalization in to which all the elements in the novel coalesce and thereby substantiate. *Ulysses* includes forms of compassion other than the historical: compassion for the difference between man's images, man's projections, and himself, compassion for what cannot be reconciled logically but must be unified only through the earth, the feminine embrace. Man's desire for completeness is always partially and tantalizingly satisfied, partially withheld. A kind of compassion other than that connected with historical determinism is also evident in Joyce's working his account of a specific day in a specific city into a statement on all human experience, in his mode of making connections to and associations with the specific situation, his exploitation of all the historical, religious, and psychological references. Joyce carefully charts the black dot, the dot that is both a tiny point in the history of the human being and the whole universe simultaneously. And compassion, the sympathy for what man is and where he is, the recognition that man can never get outside of or get some other perspective on that black dot, grows along with the metaphorical dimensions of the novel. An attitude that accompanies man's awareness of his humanity, his inevitable immersion within the black dot, compassion is a means for discovering the range, the shape, and the conformation of the dot itself. Joyce explores the totality of the dot in all possible dimensions; his compassion, never becoming soft or sentimental, acknowledges all the many bruises man gets bumping against the dot's periphery.

XI

FITZGERALD

FITZGERALD'S FICTION always reveals a strong element of moral judgment against which his heroes can be visualized. The Fitzgerald hero is charming, sensitive, intelligent, impressed by the glitter of a sparkling new world, a special person as the romantic hero always is—particularly sensitive, intelligent, and vulnerable. But Fitzgerald, measuring his heroes against the stern rebuke of his moral judgments, limits them in romantic stature and possibilities.

The hero is also the archetypal contemporary American, the confident and eager representative of his country trying his talents against an older and more universal moral order.

In Fitzgerald's earliest novel, *This Side of Paradise* (1920), the moral framework is not fully developed and the romantic hero's sin never reaches proportions sufficient to earn inevitable damnation. The next novel, *The Beautiful and Damned* (1922), however, articulates the doom of the special creature, and *The Great Gatsby* (1925) echoes the paradox implicit in the doctrine of Original Sin, the concept of man inevitably trapped by the difference between what he would desperately like to be and what he is. In subsequent novels, *Tender is the Night* (1934) and the unfinished *The Last Tycoon* (1941), the romantic hero is also doomed, but the moral framework, the judgment that makes the usurping hero's damnation inevitable, is more equivocal, more questionable, less confidently a statement about man's destiny. God weakens in Fitzgerald's last two novels and, although the hero never achieves his vision of experience, the forces that prevent him are more accidental and capricious, less articulately a moral order. The hero sometimes seems doomed by the lingering residue of firm moral commitment.

Most of *This Side of Paradise* depicts the trivial glitter of Amory Blaine's social conquests, and, through his student-like notebook, his philosophical and literary observations. Yet Amory Blaine is one of Fitzgerald's special creatures, established less by anything he does than by the quality of his introspection and by the assurances the author gives of Amory's special talents and sensitivity. Like many Romantic heroes, Fitzgerald's are distinguished *within* themselves, and, until the later novels, need not *do* anything to prove their special capacity. Although Amory spends most of his time at parties and in random intellectual speculation, he is conscious of the morality of his thought and actions. At times, he is fiercely Puritanical, disdaining the juvenile countryclub vamps at the very moment he is attracted to them. As he goes through Princeton and the army in World War I, he continues to lament the moral vacuum of his wild weekends and to question the unapologetic materialism of the society he sees around him.

Amory is also a patriot, looking for an American literature, an American destiny, a unique and valuable national synthesis of experience. Apart from the moralism and nationalism, however, he is explained most frequently as the Keatsian romantic hero strung between inevitably abstract polarities. Not as profound as the polarity involved in the doctrine of Original Sin, his polarity is that of the "cynical idealist," a paradox that both the author and Amory himself use frequently to explain the man always aware of two different sides of his own nature. Amory's ideal of nobility and magnanimity is undercut by shallow social snobbery; his interest in rising materially in the world bests his honest sympathy and concern for others; his pride in his exterior charm fights his intellectual self-examination. His language often expresses his doubleness: his charm at parties is "a spiritual tax levied"; he fears his need for money may cause him to "commit moral suicide"; he tells one of his girlfriends that "selfish people are in a way terribly capable of great loves."

Fitzgerald's point of view parallels Amory's two-sidedness, for the author often switches scenes and interjects comments to inflate then explode the romantic bubble. One chapter ends with Amory and a young girl moving together toward a cinematic kiss; the next chapter begins with her "Ouch!" and her continued petulance because his shirt stud had touched her neck. The paradoxes from the nineties, including the epigraph from Oscar Wilde are Fitzgerald's as well as Amory's, the language and structure that give the novel its dated smartness.

Although the doubleness of the "cynical idealist," the paradoxical characterization of the romantic hero, provides the novel with whatever unity it possesses, other elements important for Fitzgerald's later fiction appear. The novel contains many sharp observations on how social barriers operate between people, as well as a careful development of the complexities of combined close friendship and competition in the relationship between Amory and Alec. In addition, Amory acknowledges his sense of morality and connects it to established religion. Although he sometimes doubts and blasphemes, he sharply rebukes an unconventional girlfriend who is completely atheistic, invariably centers his self-examination on religious principles, and makes his intellectual confessions to Monsignor Darcy. The latter, wise and sophisticated, serves as Amory's surrogate father, guiding his reading, debating his ideas, maintaining frequent connection with him through letters and visits. He regards Amory as his spiritual descendant, part of his "family."

Since Amory's real father is shadowy and irrelevant, having abrogated all except financial responsibilities toward him, and Amory has been brought up by his eccentric, cosmopolitan, hypochondriacal mother, who keeps losing and regaining her faith in the Roman Catholic Church because she enjoys being converted, the surrogate is necessary for the transmission of any moral and spiritual ideas. Amory never loses his respect and affection for the older man; when he learns of Monsignor Darcy's death, he recognizes that he must become a man, must perpetuate, in his own terms, the humanity, spirituality, and wisdom of the Monsignor. The transmitted value has some effect. At the end of the novel, when Amory feels that he has finally found himself, Fitzgerald explains:

His mind turned a corner suddenly and he found himself thinking of the Catholic Church. The idea was strong in him that there was a certain intrinsic lack in those to whom orthodox religion was necessary, and religion to Amory meant the Church of Rome. Quite conceivably it was an empty ritual but it was seemingly the only assimilative, traditional bulwark against the decay of morals.

Fitzgerald, like Amory, is keeping his moralism in reserve, just barely below the surface.

The moralism as a central force in Fitzgerald's fiction emerges soon thereafter in one of the most brilliant early stories, "May Day" (published in *Tales of the Jazz Age,* 1922), which chronicles the waste and emptiness of selfish party-going and dissipation, contrasting this with the humane concern for all the inequities and injustices in American society. Early in *The Beautiful and Damned,* also, in many ways, a moral parable, the author places a Faustian dialogue between "Beauty" and "The Voice," in which "The Voice" promises "Beauty" fifteen years of triumph as "a ragtime kid, a flapper, a jazz-baby, and a baby vamp" in the new and opulent America, in return for which "Beauty" will inevitably be spoiled and tarnished by vulgarity. The dialogue serves as the model for the novel: Anthony and Gloria Patch, the special people, the beautiful couple of the new and exciting America, spoil and squander themselves, are damned as finally as if they had sold their souls to the devil. In part, they tarnish their own beauty. Gloria is selfish and extravagant, afraid for too long to spoil her figure by having a child, reckless, imperious, and narcissistic. Anthony, externally gracious and intelligent, superficially the perfect product of upper-class America, is centrally weak. He drifts, never works despite his many resolutions, and can only exert his will when he is drunk, making petulant scenes in public.

Fitzgerald's judgment of Anthony and Gloria springs from a puritanical perspective: indolence breeds decay, and hard work would save a man; behaving badly in public, the loss of public composure no matter what the circumstances, is the surest sign of hollowness and dissolution. In addition, Fitzgerald views his characters as originally "clean," spiritually antiseptic, not the "clean like polished pans," but the "blowy clean" connected with "streams and wind." As the novel progresses, as indolence, parties, and selfishness take their inevitable toll, the characters, particularly Gloria, become sullied and unclean, the beauty is tarnished. This is not caused by any particular act— Gloria is never unfaithful to Anthony—but remains an aura, a judgment that indicates both the decay of Gloria's freshness and beauty and the puritanical severity of Fitzgerald's perspective. The antiseptic sense of virtue seems to require a spiritual virginity. Once the woman is no longer the idol, remote and virginal, she introduces sin into the world. Anthony might have been able to save himself had he remained single, to redeem his transgressions by hard work and abstinence. But married, he has no chance for salvation; he is tied to the devil's agent.

Anthony's moral hollowness is also caused by the fact that he has no father, no law-giver, no agent to transmit a usable moral framework. His father, an ineffectual dandy of the nineties, had died when Anthony was very young, and the boy had been raised by his grandfather. In *The Beautiful and Damned,* unlike *This Side of Paradise,* a father-surrogate is too distant and too unconcerned to provide an acceptable substitute. Adam Patch, Anthony's grandfather, is a rigorous and strong old puritan who amasses a fortune and then decides to "consecrate the remainder of his life to the moral regeneration of the world." Adam educates Anthony carefully and expensively, but then expects him to engage in useful and ennobling work as well as to support puritanical causes like Prohibition. In the climactic scene of the novel, the staged drama which marks the inevitability of Anthony's doom, his grandfather visits him unannounced, to discover a particularly wild and dissolute party in progress. The judgment against Anthony, like his grandfather's withdrawal of financial support, is final and unyielding. Although severe and bitter from Anthony's point of view, his grandfather is highly respected by others, especially by those who see him only from a remote and public distance, like Bloeckman, who calls old Adam Patch "a fine example of an American." The example, removed and hardened by an extra generation, cannot help Anthony.

Other father-surrogates in the novel are no more successful. Like Amory Blaine, Anthony is both the cynic and the idealist. But, in this novel, the possibilities are extrapolated into polar characters, Anthony's friends, the idealist Dick Caramel and the cynic Maury Noble (the names themselves are ironic tags), who function as surrogates, constantly providing instructions and propounding their solutions to the dilemmas that face Anthony. They provide no help, for the cynic and the idealist cannot be reconciled. Each polar extreme goes in its own direction: Dick Caramel becomes foolish, soft-headed, unconsciously corrupt; Maury Noble becomes embittered and completely materialistic. Anthony, when he tries to combine the two qualities, is unable to act at all; finally, cut off from any father figure, any morality, he lapses into madness.

As they live out their doom, without morality, Anthony and Gloria are forced to feed more completely on one another, to exist only in terms of the relationship that is an inadequate substitute for a sense of human purpose. Their concentration on their relationship is the initial symptom of their decline, but Fitzgerald also probes the relationship itself with insight: the strong sexual attraction, the disastrous mixture of her nervous recklessness and his cowardice, the complete lack of self-knowledge at the beginning, the spoiled childishness of both, yet the moments of fierce loyalty to the marriage. The relationship develops with an ironic reversal of the initial balance, for, when first married, Gloria is willing to abandon people or relationships the moment she no longer feels attracted to them, and has no interest in antiques or traditions. Anthony says he is more committed to his choice and marriage, also more sentimental about history and its associations. Yet, finally, Anthony is unfaithful and petulant, while Gloria tries to keep the marriage together just because it is a marriage.

Gloria, the spoiled beauty who had married for "safety," needs to assume the dominant role and is capable of staking everything on their staying together. Anthony, having always evaded the hollowness at his center, increasingly lacks the capacity to deal with any relationship and is driven to literal madness when his wartime mistress later demands that her love be returned. A woman, if not governed by the dictates of a moral framework, is invariably the agent of destruction. Fitzgerald's interest in character itself, however, keeps obtruding into the structure of character used to illustrate the parable of doom.

Another example is Bloeckman, the Jew, who represents what in America is alien to the central moral tradition. Originally uncouth, naive, commercial, and too desperate in his attempt to get every social custom right, Bloeckman develops dignity as the novel progresses; he is also the only person willing to help Anthony when all his supposed friends have turned against him. Although, in view of Anthony's anti-Semitism, this reliance on Bloeckman demonstrates the hollowness in Anthony, who would hold superficial social standards rigidly at the same time he ignores moral standards completely, the rise of Bloeckman is also, in part, for Fitzgerald, a story of character, of humanity, apart from any moral framework. Yet Bloeckman is not at the center of the novel, nor, despite all its fascination, is the alternating humanity in the relationship between Anthony and Gloria; rather, the center is the moral parable, the dissolution of the potentially special couple.

Unable or unwilling to adopt but one pose, to live by a single attitude like that of the "idealist" or the "cynic," Anthony is damned. His choice of Gloria, of marriage, is sinful, but it is also more complex, more fully human, than the choices of his simplified celibate friends. Anthony and Gloria are the only fully human characters in the novel, the only people who don't hypocritically limit themselves to the singularity that survives. Contemporary America, as Fitzgerald depicts it, rewards hypocrisy, over-simplification, the person who restricts his humanity to the salvable single pose and rules out any humanely contradictory impulses. Anthony and Gloria are "beautiful" because they don't simplify, and they are spoiled because they are exceptional among the people around them; but their inability or unwillingness to simplify, to restrict themselves, insures their damnation in contemporary America. The novel's flaw is in never convincingly working out the balance between their inability and their unwillingness, never developing any coherent relationship between Anthony's and Gloria's responsibility for their doom, and an indictment of the American society that damns its "beautiful." Responsive, directionless, impulsive, capable at times of love for one another, as no other characters in the novel are capable of love, Anthony and Gloria try hopelessly to sustain their status as special people. They gain sympathy well beyond that usually accorded to illustrations in a moral parable because of the depiction of America, the relentless environment that promises so much and punishes so fiercely. Hollow as they finally are, and harshly as Fitzgerald judges them, Anthony and Gloria are still preferable to all the self-seeking simplifications around them. Fitzgerald never makes the relevance of the moral judgment clear, never allows the judgment to stand as a final statement about the principal characters but also never modifies the stringency of the judgment itself.

The moral structure of *The Great Gatsby* is far more coherent. The narrator of the novel, Nick Carraway, more honest than anyone else, serves as "a guide, a pathfinder, an original settler." Nick, frequently inserting judgments on characters and general observations on society, provides the perspective through which the issues of the novel are apparent. Nick speaks for the author when he cries across the lawn to the defeated, deluded, hopelessly naive Gatsby, "You're worth the whole damn bunch put together." Appropriately, Nick is close to his real father whom he quotes at the very beginning of the novel and returns to at the end. A solid, sane, highly moral Midwesterner, Nick's father provides the secure basis from which his son can see and judge the chaotic modern world morally and effectively.

Jay Gatsby is the embodiment of the American Dream: the mystery of its origins, its impossible romanticism, its belief in its capacity to recapture a past that may never have existed (as Gatsby believes he can recreate his past with Daisy), its faith in an unknown future, its ultimate futility. He attempts to create a new Eden, derived from the past, through money, silk shirts, and an Oxford accent. Gatsby is also the Horatio Alger hero in his dedication to "dumbbell exercise," the study of "needed inventions," and the pure vision of the future that involves making a lot of money. Like the Horatio Alger hero, Gatsby abandons his own ineffectual and undistinguished father, a man only too willing to relinquish his son to the demands of commercial manifest destiny, and attaches himself to a surrogate, the millionaire miner, Dan Cody. The romantic American myth, predicated on the democratic unpredictability of the origins of the specially virtuous and sensitive man, requires a surrogate father, a willful and deliberate attachment. But, in Fitzgerald's terms, the failure of Gatsby is further demonstration that the myth is false, for the moral guide can only be transmitted by a real father, a true God. The vertical line of virtue must be direct and close, from father to son, and only the vertical line can preserve the sensitive son from the chaos of the modern world.

In one sense, since America has become increasingly materialistic and increasingly distant from the morality of true fathers, Gatsby's vision might have been a more plausible version of experience in an earlier, simpler America. His aspirations, then, might not necessarily have involved him, as they do now, with the criminal, the callous, and the corrupt:

> He had come a long way to this blue lawn, and his dream must have seemed so close that he could hardly fail to grasp it. He did not know that it was already behind him, somewhere back in that vast obscurity beyond the city, where the dark fields of the republic rolled on under the night.

Yet, in another sense, as Nick so clearly sees at the end of the novel, the dream Gatsby represents was always flawed, always impossible to achieve, the promise of the glittering new land which could never be fulfilled no matter how dedicated the aspirant. The difference between promise and achievement, between vision and reality, is the story of America, but it also suggests, in Fitzgerald's terms, the story of man, the aspiring creature limited by himself and the world around him, the worthwhile human creature who invariably wants to have more than he has, to be more than he is. The two-sidedness of man, the difference between his vision and his inevitable destiny, has developed in range and meaning, far from Amory Blaine's superficial "cynical idealism." In *The Great Gatsby*, Fitzgerald's tightest novel both artistically and theologically, both sides of man are locked in, the romantic hero's aspiration and defeat are equally necessary. In Fitzgerald's moral and religious perspective, man's destiny, the sin of the attractive romantic hero, is immutable.

The continuity of the human paradox is also applied specifically to America, for all the characters are products of history, are intrinsically related to the past. Tom Buchanan, the stupid and corrupt aspect of the American past, triumphs over Gatsby, the idealized and romanticized version of the past, to win Daisy, the prize in the present which has been spoiled, corrupted, and victimized by the past. What Gatsby's vision represents has, in America, both past and present, never been articulated or imagined in concrete terms, has always been attenuated by Tom's kind of callous, brutal, stupid materialism.

Another paradox implicit in Fitzgerald's version of American history is apparent in the incompatibility of two American myths: the democratic myth of the importance of the common man and the myth of the opportunity for the special creature, the exceptionally visionary, resolute, and dedicated. The common man, Wilson, in revenge for the death of his common wife, kills the specially visionary and idealistic Gatsby rather than the specially corrupt and culpable Tom and Daisy. The common man can't tell one special man from another and finally destroys the American Dream that theoretically provides the symbol for his own aspiration. All these paradoxes, all these, for Fitzgerald, necessary destructions of the ideal or of the transcendence of human possibility, make the novel a moral fable. Fitzgerald's morality in *The Great Gatsby* is not, however, the simple morality of single-minded judgment, of excoriating the unrighteous. Rather, the morality, articulated through the wise and temperate Nick, is the inflexible necessity of the harsh dilemma of human experience, the invariable human defeat involved in the difference between vision and reality. Nick, who understands and accepts this, is able to survive and look back on the events of the novel through distance and time.

Dick Diver, the hero of *Tender Is the Night,* is characterized as an American moral agent in the amoral world of Europe after World War I. Initially puritanical in respect to both women and his work, Dick is depicted as a superior representative of America, powerful, intelligent, charming and not aware of his own charm, full of fresh ideas and naive illusions:

. . . the illusions of eternal strength and health, and of the essential goodness of people; illusions of a nation, the lies of generations of frontier mothers who had to croon falsely, that there were no wolves outside the cabin door.

Dick recognizes that the American is not perfect, that he needs to be less strident, to cultivate a "repose" that traditional culture brings easily to the European. At the same time, he attempts to exert an American moral force within European society, a force expressed in terms of personal relationships, of consideration for others, of humanity. And he does, at least early in his career, genuinely build a version of a humane, moral society around the small enclave of a Riviera beach he discovers, then molds and carefully rakes. Fitzgerald consistently points out the moral center of Dick's charm, the exquisite consideration, the recognition of the value of everything around him, the capacity to extract the full humanity from his associates in the same way that the priest, ideally, both guides and understands his parishioners. Dick's psychiatry, too, is moral, attempting to "cure" homosexuality and to "save" his patients from themselves. Even Abe North, the most self-destructive of the American characters, acknowledges that everyone must have a moral code; ironically and bitterly, he claims that his is an opposition to burning witches. For Fitzgerald, such a flippantly limited morality implies certain destruction.

Dick fails, like Jay Gatsby, partially because his innocent and moral ideals no longer apply to contemporary experience. Increasingly throughout the novel Dick's public moralism is inappropriate in a new, more private world that he cannot understand. He never appreciates Tommy Barban's private justifications for wandering service as a mercenary soldier, never understands the world of Mary North's Levantine second husband, nor the cosmopolitan skepticism of the newer rebels like Lady Caroline Sibly-Biers, nor, finally, the female nature of his wife, the new and revitalized Nicole, who successfully poses her "unscrupulousness against his moralities." Despite all his external charm, Dick is too committed to the past, to an old American morality, ever to recognize fully the private, separate particles of contemporary European life. At one point, when Dick is at a restaurant, he sees a party of middle-aged American women who impress him as forming a cohesive unit, and he discovers that they are a group of gold-star mothers who have come to Europe to visit their sons' graves:

For a while the sobered women who had come to mourn for their dead, for something they could not repair, made the room beautiful. Momentarily, he sat again on his father's knee, riding with Moseby while the old loyalties and devotions fought on around him. Almost with an effort he turned back to his two women at the table and faced the whole new world in which he believed.

Dick may believe in two worlds, the moral one of the old America and the new one of his women, but he cannot live in both. And increasingly, as he fails, his own morality, his own center, begins to dissolve. He works less and less, becomes more dependent on Nicole's money, and is increasingly drunk, careless, and inconsiderate. When told by Rosemary Hoyt, who had once idolized him, that he still seems the man he was, he replies that "The manner remains intact for some time after the morale cracks," almost as if he is Dorian Gray with a deeply embedded sense of sin just under the easy facade. Dick's "manner" eventually cracks, too, for he becomes violent and petulant, picks fights, indulges in self-pity, and is pointlessly vulgar in talking with Nicole. All these are symptoms of an advanced stage of dissolution, for, to Fitzgerald, not behaving well, not observing superficial amenities and conventions always indicated the hero's irreversible defeat.

The doom is not, however, as elemental and universal as that of *The Great Gatsby,* for *Tender Is the Night* is a more complicated novel. The father figures, for example, proliferate, suggesting a more equivocal morality than that of *The Great Gatsby.* Dick Diver's real father is an American clergyman who had taught Dick all he knew of "manners" and "matters of behavior," a man halfway between Nick Carraway's wise and sophisticated father and Gatsby's humble simpleton. Dick's father is honest and direct, but he lacks the intellect, the range, and the insight to be transportable to the new and more complicated world of postwar Europe. Despite the distance in space and time between Dick and his father, Fitzgerald explains that Dick often "referred judgments to what his father would probably have thought or done." Yet, he recognizes that, in choosing Europe, he has abandoned his father. Dick, too, attaches himself to a surrogate father, Dr. Dohmler, the psychiatrist in charge of the clinic where he initially works. Dr. Dohmler is fiercely moral, an instructor, a guide, and the younger man is strongly influenced by his precepts and judgments. Yet, Dick, in marrying Nicole, in confusing the separate relationships between husband

and wife and between doctor and patient, disobeys one of Dr. Dohmler's strongest injunctions. In this novel, the real father is not necessarily preferable to the surrogate, for either might have served to transmit his morality to Dick. But the latter abandons one and disobeys the other, and, left alone, is unable to sustain himself. In *Tender Is the Night,* the father also has responsibilities toward his child. Nicole's father, for example, in forcing incest upon her, in converting his daughter into his mistress, violates the relationship between father and child in the most disastrous way possible.

Dick Diver is a multiple father as well as a multiply errant son. In rejecting the Gods offered him, Dick establishes himself as a series of Gods, playing a different kind of father in each of his varying relationships. The world of *Tender Is the Night* is not monotheistic and, although certain moral judgments still obtain (like the prescription against incest), the plurality of Gods makes the moral issues more equivocal and perplexing than those of *The Great Gatsby.* As a real father to his two children, Dick finds his only lasting success. To Lanier and Topsy, he is warm and firm, able to mean something even after he has ceased to mean anything to anyone else. Dick is less successful as a surrogate father to Rosemary, the starlet who gains her first recognition as "Daddy's Girl." For her, Dick is the cosmopolitan father, introducing her to Europe, to history, to the world of sensitivity. When first attracted to her, he regards her as too much the child to make love to her; but eventually Rosemary, always having sensed the ambivalence between the father and the lover, grows beyond the need of a surrogate and recognizes the hollowness within Dick. Even so, in the scene in which they recognize that they have only been playing parts like the actors they are, that neither is really capable of loving the other, Rosemary says, "I feel as if I'd quarrelled with Mother."

More importantly, Dick is a surrogate father for Nicole, replacing the father that had violated her. First as psychiatrist and then as husband, Dick still plays the father, sheltering Nicole from the world, guiding her, and giving her the time and understanding necessary for her restoration to psychic health. But the roles of father and of husband are incompatible: once restored, Nicole must reject Dick because, as a grown-up woman, she no longer needs a father; Dick, in marrying the woman he needed to guide, had really committed a kind of symbolic incest. In the multiplicity of his fatherhood, Dick tries to be a universal father, the controller and guide for all the relationships around him, the lord and creator of the beach. Images like the "deposed ruler," or the "spoiled priest," applied to Dick after his decline is evident, underline the universal nature of his fatherhood. In general terms, Dick's doom is unambiguous, the folly and presumption of playing God, of attempting, while still a human being, to control all the lives around him. Yet the specific moral framework of the novel is far more ambiguous. The reader wonders which God, if any, might have been the true one: Dr. Dohmler? Dick's father? Dick as psychiatrist? Dick as charming and responsive master of the civilized world? The novel charts Dick's doom, but part of his doom is the confusion and ambiguity of whatever moral order specifically destroys him. When, in his final defeat, Dick makes the sign of the cross over the populous beach he had once created from the debris between shore and sea, his action is neither an ironically unrecognized truth nor a presumptuous falsehood, but, rather, a pathetic and irrelevant gesture of his failure. Man, in *Tender Is the Night*, cannot play God, but, then, who or what can?

In the moral ambiguity of *Tender Is the Night*, much of Fitzgerald's attention shifts from the vertical relationship, the transmission of truth or moral values from parent to child, to the lateral relationship, the equivalent relationship between man and woman, the mutual recognition of humanity. The focus often changes from fathers to women, to the representatives of an amoral principle of accepting what is and holding "things together." The father, for Fitzgerald, is more characteristically, although not entirely, connected with America, a continent that is a "nursery." In contrast, the new world of postwar Europe neglects the transmission of moral values, the father, and concentrates on the woman. Fairly early in the novel, after Dick has been presented at the apex of his talent and control, there is a shooting at the railway station, an unforeseen and unexpected event. Both Rosemary and Nicole wait in vain for "Dick to make a moral comment on the matter and not leave it to them." From that moment on, as a kind of counterpoint to the theme of Dick's dissolution, Fitzgerald develops an interest in the two women's attempts to discover themselves. Both Rosemary and Nicole begin to understand the world around them without Dick's guiding judgment.

Because she has had more to overcome and has been more completely involved with Dick, Nicole's is the more interesting consciousness, and, appropriately, Fitzgerald devotes more time to her gradual breaking away from dependence on Dick and developing an independent self-awareness. Like Gloria in *The Beautiful and Damned,* Nicole has a kind of reckless courage. Originally dependent, she is able to become wiser, more competent, more self-assured as the man she regarded as her master dissolves. Both novels show, to some extent, the roles of the partners reversing within the marriage. But Fitzgerald's attitude changed: in *The Beautiful and Damned,* as the wife became more human and competent, less the porcelain trophy, she was inevitably soiled, unclean; in *Tender Is the Night,* in contrast, the loss of spiritual virginity indicates the capacity for human relationship, and no moral judgment, no antisepsis, is involved. When Nicole realizes that Dick, the father, cannot also be a husband, she turns, in her new self-confidence, toward Tommy Barban.

After she and Tommy make love, Nicole almost expects an explanation or interpretation of the experience, such as Dick would have given. But Tommy provides none; Nicole is content, and a "child" no longer. Fitzgerald indicates his final approval of Nicole, or at least his refusal to pass judgment against her, by the fact that, when she decides to leave Dick, she is neither petulant nor bitter and can recognize that she, in her need, had contributed to his indolence and unwittingly encouraged his decline. She can be gracious, always the sign of a kind of virtue in Fitzgerald's terms. Most of the events in the last third of the novel are seen from Nicole's point of view. And, using her point of view, Fitzgerald is as interested in an incompatible relationship, the strain between a woman who needed a surrogate father before she was ready for a husband, and a man who was too much a father to change himself into a husband, as he is in chronicling the destruction of the romantic ego.

Despite the use of Nicole's point of view, the structure of the novel does not justify reading the emphasis on Nicole as equal to the emphasis on Dick's decline. A consideration of the structure, of the movement from one episode to another, focuses attention on Dick and his failure. Yet Fitzgerald himself was uneasy and unsatisfied with the shape of the novel. As originally published and as usually read today, it begins with Rosemary's point of view toward Dick on the beach, Rosemary naively worshipping the Dick who is then at the height of his power and charm. Then, following Dick, with flashbacks into the past and the meeting between Dick and Nicole, the novel traces Dick's decline. Fitzgerald later advocated, and some editions have followed this practice, placing the first ten chapters of Book II before Book I, a change that would make the story read chronologically. Like the original version, however, the chronological version emphasizes the rise and fall of the hero. The only real difference is that the chronological version places greater emphasis on psychological causes, on Nicole's illness, Dick's work, and Dick's disobedience of Dr. Dohmler's injunction. Since Fitzgerald's explicit treatment of psychological issues (in contrast with his implicit treatment of character in a way that could be explained in psychological terms) is so heavily moralistic and simplistically unconvincing to contemporary readers, the chronological organization seems even less satisfactory than does the original. The counterpoint to the theme of Dick's dissolution, the growth of Nicole's capacity to understand experience, and the partial shift to the amoral female perspective, is not represented in either structure, for the novel is not given coherently meaningful shape. A conversation about Abe North between Nicole and Dick illustrates something of the problem:

> Nicole shook her head right and left, disclaiming responsibility for the matter: "So many smart men go to pieces nowadays."
> "And when haven't they?" Dick asked. "Smart men play close to the line because they have to—some of them can't stand it, so they quit."
> "It must lie deeper than that." Nicole clung to her conversation; also she was irritated that Dick should contradict her before Rosemary. "Artists like—well, like Fernand don't seem to have to wallow in alcohol. Why is it just Americans who dissipate?"

Nicole is right, for the novel shows that it does "lie deeper than that." But whatever is "deeper," like whatever version of God dooms Dick, is never made fully coherent, never brought finally into focus. The structural reliance on only the theme of Dick's decline almost seems a substitute for the failure to control fully the ultimate skepticism about God and the issues of lateral relationship in the novel. Yet, despite this failure and the lack of a universal order as tight as that of *The Great Gatsby,* a sense of richness, density, and disordered humanity emerges from *Tender Is the Night.*

No fathers exist in *The Last Tycoon.* The protagonist, Monroe Stahr, is the man of enormous talent who has achieved his dominance over others, his special stature, by his own brilliance, energy, and hard work. No moral code or dedication to manners or principle infuses his background. In a scene with Kathleen, he explains:

> When I was young I wanted to be a chief clerk—the one who knew where everything was . . . I'm still a chief clerk. . . . That's my gift, if I have one. Only when I got to be it, I found out that no one knew where anything was. And I found out that you had to know why it was where it was, and whether it should be left there.

Stahr has sympathy as well as talent, the capacity to understand people around him, the willingness to soothe the narcissistic actor and to help the cameraman ruined by rumor. Yet all his talents and humanity are solely individual, not part of any country or code of truth. A humane employer, he is still not quite willing to side with Labor in a struggle against Capital over the principal issues of his time (this aspect was never fully worked out in the portion of the novel finished; Fitzgerald's notes indicate that he planned to develop the Labor agitation further, but arguing more fully from notes and guesses would be neither accurate nor rewarding) ; a capitalistic moviemaker, he is far from being a defender or a representative of the system. When in power, Stahr relies only on himself, even if he isn't always sure just what that self is. While flying in a plane, Stahr goes up to the cockpit to talk with the pilot:

> He was looking down at the mountains.
> "Suppose you were a railroad man," he said. "You have to send a train through there somewhere. Well, you get your surveyors' reports, and you find that there's three or four or half a dozen gaps,

and not one is better than the other. You've got to decide—on what basis? You can't test the best way—except by doing it. So you just do it."

The pilot thought he had just missed something.

"How do you mean?"

"You choose some one way for no reason at all—because the mountain's pink or the blueprint is a better blue. You see?"

In addition, Stahr is a Jew, an alien in America, a force without locus and a talent without background. The novel revolves around a man and his relationships rather than around an inherited principle and its application to the modern world.

In *The Last Tycoon,* the American past is false or irrelevant in the Hollywood that manufactures dreams for contemporary society. Abraham Lincoln eats the forty-cent dinner, including dessert, in the studio cafeteria and the Danish visitor who notices him feels that Lincoln now makes more sense than he ever had before; a telephone call to Stahr, supposedly from the President, turns out to be a joke to get Stahr to talk with an ape; a trip to the Hermitage, Andrew Jackson's home, taken because the plane is delayed by bad weather, holds no message for the characters and provides only the setting for a suicide. Comically, absurdly, the men of Hollywood make their myths, legends just as true and just as false as the ones enshrined by history. Stahr's dream woman, Kathleen, attractive to him because she resembles his dead wife, is also not American. An English girl who has been to "all the places that Stahr made movies of," Kathleen is first seen riding on the head of a Hindu Goddess, a stage prop for a movie, through a flood in the studio. Throughout the novel, fortunes change rapidly, people appear and disappear unexpectedly, and those concerned with the movies are likely to be powerful and arrogant one minute and jobless and desolate the next.

No one is secure and no one is even sure of himself. Kathleen tells Stahr that he is three or four people, a comment echoed by Cecilia Brady, the narrator of part of the novel, who claims that writers are all several people; a genuine Russian Prince refuses to play the part of a Russian Prince because he has turned Communist; in looking for Kathleen, after he has seen her only once, Stahr at first gets the wrong woman. In fact, the wrong woman is named Smith, a name Stahr also uses for anonymity when he flies across the country. And the man Kathleen marries is also named Smith. As the multiple Smiths, some true and some false, indicate, the principal concern of the novel is identity, discovering who or what one is, rather than any form of moral judgment or evaluation. At the same time, Stahr is another of Fitzgerald's doomed romantic heroes whose attempt to play God must inevitably be defeated. His role as the "last" tycoon amidst the changes of social history, the verdict from the doctor that gives him only a few months to live, as well as prophetic observations by other characters, all demonstrate, even in the uncompleted novel, that Stahr's dissolution and defeat were to be inescapable. Yet, as in *Tender Is the Night,* the cause of the doom, the triumphant morality or the true God, is never manifest. Playing God, to Fitzgerald, is a sin no matter how attractive, and it is a sin even in a chaotic universe with no moral framework or principle that can define or label what sin is. The guilt, the sense of sin, lingers even after the intellect and understanding can no longer accept the system that defined the sin.

Like all Fitzgerald's romantic heroes, Stahr tries to relieve the barren dedication of his quest with an interest in women. But, unlike the earlier heroes, Stahr changes, learns from his relationship with a woman. Kathleen, Stahr's mistress, is formless, can play mother, trollop, temporary wife, anything Stahr might momentarily need. Kathleen's previous relationship with a man had also been defined by the man, and in the course of the novel she marries Smith because he happens, decisively, to arrive unexpectedly at a moment when she and Stahr are between definitions. The other woman who loves Stahr, Cecilia Brady, also makes the point that women exist to understand men, to be defined by them and attach themselves to them. Significantly, Cecilia is "in" but not "of" the movies and Kathleen refuses to let Stahr show her around the studio; both are less interested in the product, which is the film that the man creates, than they are in the man himself. This, to Fitzgerald, makes them genuine women in contrast to the starlets who gain their only identity through being "of" the movies, created by the glittering and fabricated dreams. That Kathleen can marry Mr. Smith because of her uncertainty about Stahr indicates that

Stahr himself is, despite his success as a talented producer, far from certain about his own identity or about the definitions he wants to impose upon experience. Until too late, he doesn't know what he feels about Kathleen, what his personal identity is:

> Like many brilliant men, he had grown up dead cold. . . . And so he had learned tolerance, kindness, forbearance, and even affection like lessons.

Stahr's belated growth relates to public issues as well as to personal ones. Only during the course of the novel does he, the capitalistic entrepreneur of dreams, begin to realize how unfairly he has always used labor. Although he is still fascinated by the power one man can hold, by playing God, he begins to question himself more closely. He becomes more concerned with others, with politics, with art, as well as with women. Yet, for all his richer sense of humanity, Stahr is still doomed, and, if Fitzgerald's notes for the rest of the novel can be credited, the author might have finished him off melodramatically, because the sense of doom has no logical correlation with the terms of the novel.

The point of view of *The Last Tycoon,* like that of *Tender Is the Night,* is never developed sufficiently to order all the elements. Much of the novel's action is ostensibly seen through Cecilia Brady, the daughter of Stahr's partner. Cecilia is a Bennington girl, a "new" woman, honest, flippant, and direct. She is not even disillusioned when she accidentally surprises her father making love to his secretary in his office, for she has seen that before, and she has already shifted from a childish reliance on fathers and moralities to an interest in the humane development of the self. In this sense, she is a satisfactory narrator for the novel. But since the subject of the novel is Stahr, Cecilia tells more than she could possibly know. Fitzgerald has her collecting information from others, piecing together from several sources stories of Stahr's life in the studio, and acting like a Zoomar-lens consciousness when she enters Stahr's mind as he approaches Kathleen. The device of Cecilia's narration breaks down entirely in its remoteness from the central and private love scenes between Stahr and Kathleen.

As they mirror Hollywood, its gossip, the quick cutting from one scene to another, the disruptions in Cecilia's narrative are justified, even effective. She can also see the ironic pathos in Stahr's decline. But as a device to record Stahr himself and what defeats him, to present his growing humanity and to suggest the order in terms of which he sins, this point of view of the novel is inadequate. Cecilia is even further from the God who may not exist than is Stahr himself. And, in secular as well as religious terms, no structurally coherent device, at least none apparent in the unfinished novel, manages to articulate all that is there.

In his last two novels, Fitzgerald's compassion grew. His concern for his characters increased, as did his sympathy for their human struggles and relationships, for all the questions they could never answer. Correspondingly, the element of morality or judgment diminished, and God or truth disappeared; the romantic hero, although still doomed, seemed doomed less by a moral order or Original Sin than by accident. Still unable to control his own destiny as he so powerfully wanted to, the romantic hero turned his attention to the very human relationships that contributed to his doom, sometimes even, as is true of Monroe Stahr, ironically learning from them. Yet despite the interest in the strictly secular relationship and the lack of an implicit moral order, Fitzgerald's form was always that of the parable, no less in *Tender Is the Night* than in *The Beautiful and Damned*. In the last two novels, the parable form was less appropriate, less able to summarize and direct the issues of the novel, and Fitzgerald never found a form to express coherently the greater human dimensions and complexity of his later fiction. The form broke, particularly in *Tender Is the Night,* in which the energy and perception of the novel leap out from the inadequate structure and the ultimately superficial point of view. Yet in the breaking of the form, the collapse of the parable as an explanation of contemporary experience, the sense of Fitzgerald's achieved compassion inheres. Compassion seldom is tidy, or neatly measurable in a formal equation, and Fitzgerald's last two novels explode from the tidiness of judgment and evaluation of the "American experience" into deeper questions as well as richer and less systematic understandings about the perplexities of man.

XII

JOYCE CARY

L IKE MANY NOVELISTS working within the tradition of compassion, Joyce Cary frequently uses history to give his novels texture and density. To a certain extent, Cary's novels focus on a chronological account of the social and political history of England from the 1870's through the 1940's. *To Be a Pilgrim* (1942), the middle novel in the first or Gulley Jimson trilogy, spans about sixty years from the point of view of Tom Wilcher, the lawyer and care-taker. Tom's description of those sixty years is social as well as personal, recording public attitudes like the upper-class Victorian fear of proletarian revolution, the violent divisions of opinion between imperialists and liberals at the time of the Boer War, and the faith in the "cloth cap" victory in the 1906 election.

Much in the manner of the television documentary, Cary uses Tom's brothers and sister to represent the options for the late Victorian upper classes: one brother is the skeptical dandy, the talented golden boy flawed by his dilettantism; another brother is the square, staunch, stalwart Army officer; his sister is the Victorian rebel, abandoning security and wealth to follow the purpose and poverty of a fundamentalist preacher. Similarly, Tom's nephews and niece represent conventional possibilities for a later generation: the cynical survivor of World War I who deliberately dissipates his life and talents; the progressive doctor, a young lady tortured by intellect and self-doubt; the hard-working young man who wants to return to and reconstruct the earth of the family estate.

Tom, the sole survivor of his own generation, holds these two generations, the family, and the house together. In terms of both property and sensibility, in his jealous defense of historical continuity, he is the history of England. The sense of English history also helps to define, although less centrally and less seriously, the other two novels of the trilogy. Tom, the caretaker of house and family, reveres Sara Monday, his housekeeper and cook, even though she steals from him. He calls her "the key of my own soul. A key forged in English metal for an English lock." Treated comically as an historical commentator, Sara, the narrator of *Herself Surprised* (1941), often resorts to nostalgic stereotypes, recalling, for example, how the gasworks and the sewers began to cluster in the idyllic countryside of her childhood. Gulley Jimson, the narrator of *The Horse's Mouth* (1944), is the universal artist as conscious antidote to history. In 1939, Gulley claims to know of Hitler only as someone who hates modern art, and he mockingly praises the zeal of the workmen and students who help him erect one of his walls as "British to the core." References to time and place are peripheral. They provide material to satirize the anti-artistic and anti-intellectual English, as comic background for Gulley's artistic vision.

The second or Chester Nimmo trilogy, consisting of *Prisoner of Grace* (1952), *Except the Lord* (1953), and *Not Honour More* (1955), is more overtly concerned with the political history of England. As in the first trilogy, the middle novel reaches back furthest into time, for, in *Except the Lord,* Chester Nimmo, later to become a member of Parliament and part of the World War I cabinet, explains the forces of family and environment that led to his political career. From Chester's point of view, the reader sees not only the principled Victorian farmer/preacher, Chester's father, defeated by his own unswerving dedication to principle, but also the hard and violent world of the rural West Country in the 1860's and '70's, full of poverty, beatings, class prejudice, and fundamentalist religious fervor. As a result of and in reaction against these forces, Chester develops the combination of religious dedication, populist rhetoric, concern for poor workers, and hypocrisy, which marks his later political career. Since the events of *Except the Lord* end in 1880, the other novels in the trilogy advance the chronicle of social history far more explicitly than do the novels similarly flanking the center one in the first trilogy.

Nina Latter, Chester's wife for more than thirty years until she divorces him to marry Jim Latter, narrates *Prisoner of Grace* and recounts the history of riots, strikes, pacifism during the Boer War, and the strains of official life during World War I. Nina focuses on all Chester's ambivalences: both the genuine dedication and the shrill sloganeering of his religious and social principles; both the shrewd, sophisticated ability to manipulate the political world, and a class-consciousness so intense that Chester must interrupt even his love-making with a mock humility about his origins. *Prisoner of Grace,* spanning events of more than thirty years, depicts political and social definitions as constantly changing. What was once Chester's most stirringly effective political manner, winning elections and swaying crowds to his will, becomes, in the 1920's, as imitated by Tom, Nina's son who has been fondly brought up by Chester, a bitingly successful mockery in a seedy night-club act. *Not Honour More,* related from the point of view of Jim Latter, Nina's cousin, early lover, and second husband, focuses overtly on the events of the 1926 General Strike. Jim, in his hatred for Chester and his military veneration for earth-bound order and precise definition, provides another perspective on the political and social conflicts of the time, regarding bargaining and compromise as evidence of the degeneracy of the twentieth century.

In addition to the trilogies, other novels indicate Cary's emphasis on social history. *A Fearful Joy* (1949), for example, relies on the fascination of social history for its principal focus of interest. Written in the present tense, the novel follows Tabitha Baskett's career after she runs away from her doctor brother's suburban home. As mistress, wife, mother, and grandmother, Tabitha is successively involved with a literary and artistic group prominent in the decadent 1890's, the technological pioneers in motors and airplanes just before World War I, the psychologically educated in the 1920's who with severity refuse to permit their babies to be touched or cuddled, the disillusioned promoters of fascistic and anti-liberal opinion in England during the thirties, and the hardened, unsentimental survivors of World War II who believe in nothing but themselves.

A sample of the prose indicates the pace and the constant sociological references characteristic of the novel. At this point, Tabitha, still a member of the artistic coterie of the nineties, is on trial in a divorce suit brought by her lover's wife:

A sonnet of Boole's, read by her counsel, has a great effect on the jury, and does Tabitha immense damage. Sturge's counsel of course fights against this irrelevance, but it happens that the liberals have just won the great election of '05 [the election to which Cary refers actually took place in January, 1906—both the precision of the example and the slight mistake are characteristic of Cary's use of dates], there is a feeling of revolution in the air, and as in all revolutions, a sudden intensification of moral violence. The neurotics, the cranks of every shade of opinion, believing that the millennium has come, when their special whim will be achieved, are shouting at the tops of their voices that the Empire is Chinese slavery and also a divine trust; the British worker is a serf, and the fountain of wisdom; vaccination is a crime, but science is the hope of the world; marriage is bondage, but divorce is the cancer of the state—notions which renew themselves in a certain kind of brain for ever and ever.

Tabitha records and reflects the social history, although she remains curiously unaffected by most of her crowded historical experiences. Never really a person in her own right, Tabitha is a useful device for Cary in several ways. She sometimes serves as a spokesman for Cary's point of view on social change, for she objects to the silliness of cold and rigid child-rearing in the 1920's, and she is steadfastly "liberal," humanitarian, and antifascist in the midst of the polar political discussions of the thirties.

Tabitha is also useful in illustrating the ironies of historical and chronological change. As a young woman, she had fought fiercely to keep and bring up her illegitimate child; when her granddaughter is pregnant and unmarried during World War II, Tabitha argues just as fiercely that she give the child up for adoption and accuses the girl of having no "moral sense at all." When Tabitha is old, the artistic group of which she had been a part becomes famous as a group of legendary iconoclasts, important defenders of freedom and culture against a dull and conventional society. Tabitha, now conventional herself, has no interest in the arts or decadence and never even reads the books that praise her as an inspiration to long-dead poets and painters. In a general way, Tabitha embodies Cary's theme of the continuity of life, the change in which the vital human being constantly creates himself. Yet this is apart from the voluminous chronicle of social history within the novel, a chronicle that carries interest in and of itself. Tabitha is almost like the uninvolved narrator of a television spectacular composed of newsreel clippings of wars and meetings and fashions from the past sixty years.

Cary sometimes seems to share the metaphysical uncertainty characteristic of the tradition of compassion, for his irony, frequently planking the strongly asserted position against the changing historical fact that makes that position ridiculous, demonstrates the fallacy of most human judgments. At one point in *To Be a Pilgrim,* Tom Wilcher is tempted to judge a young nephew harshly for his apparent indifference to World War I until he realizes that most of the boys who were just a year older at his nephew's school have already been killed and that the nephew's "indifference" cloaks feeling far more intense and involved than that paraded in Wilcher's rather shallow patriotism.

Between 1951 and 1954, most of Cary's novels were reissued in the Carfax edition. For each of these novels, he wrote a brief preface explaining the issues he had in mind in creating the novel. In the preface to an earlier one, *Mister Johnson* (1939), Cary defends his use of the present tense, claiming that it both makes issues and characters more immediate and inhibits the reader from formulating hasty judgments. And in the preface to *A House of Children* (1941), Cary argues that it is the writer's job to "explore and describe," leaving judgment or evaluation to the "philosopher." Cary's novelistic practice is, in fact, less rigorously non-judgmental than these prefaces would suggest, but the prefaces indicate the intention to avoid judgment and the novels generally support at least a skepticism about the value of conventional judgments.

In *Art and Reality,* a series of lectures given at Cambridge in 1956, Cary objects to allegory as a form. Although allegory gives clear meanings, for Cary these meanings, given "to the conceptual judgment" as "dry precept," are false to the flux of experience, to the "world of free souls." For Cary, the easy categorical judgment both restricted and falsified human experience. In his fictional world, human beings seldom know one another well enough to make any sort of accurate judgment. The world is often like the pub scene at the beginning of *The Horse's Mouth:* a group of characters each talking along his individual line, one about the tugs and barges on the river, another about her religion, a third of the hereditary deafness in his family. Although the conversations never coalesce, the group does, foolishly enough, contribute to Gulley Jimson's collection for a nonexistent William Blake Memorial Association.

More primitive societies are no more unified or communicative. Even among the Africans themselves in *Mister Johnson,* the storekeepers and the farmers neither know nor care about each other and the only thing to do with a stranger is to "fleece him." The principal character of the novel, Mister Johnson, the African clerk who tries to live by what he thinks are the codes of the governing English, really understands neither the English nor his fellow Africans.

Cary's world, changing, multiple, difficult to understand and even more difficult to judge, is one that could appropriately be presented and made coherent through an attitude of compassion. But the possible artistic pitfall of compassion is sentimentality. If man, thrust into a changing world without knowledge or adequate guides for judgment, is portrayed as merely a victim, merely a repository for the author's generalized sympathy, the fiction becomes sentimental and loses force. To the extent that compassion is undifferentiated, unmitigated by comedy or irony or some other fictional tension, sentimentality can convert the compassionate depiction of man into feeble and meaningless heart-throbs, as if the author is requesting an emotional reaction he has done little to generate fictionally.

In *Mister Johnson,* the African clerk, a high-spirited, engaging, and willing young man, is the victim of a clash of cultures that he cannot begin to understand. Trying to please one master, he offends another and loses his job; later rehired, he works on one scheme successfully and tries to carry over the methods of that scheme to another with disastrous results. Taught to fudge accounts, he steals; in stealing further, he kills a white store owner. Mr. Johnson has been so thoroughly victimized that, at his trial for murder, he is willing to accept any version someone else will define, feeling that his white hero's interpretation must necessarily be true. The incident demonstrates the fact that Mr. Johnson is, finally, nothing other than victim, is only the hollowness left by the differences between English colonials and Africa. And the novel becomes sentimental. Cary does give the novel some amount of unsentimental force in the character of Rudbeck, the colonial administrator Mr. Johnson most admires. Rudbeck, for most of the novel indifferent to his hero-worshipping clerk, recognizes, at the end, some of his responsibility for what Mr. Johnson has become, and is therefore at the clerk's request willing to disobey orders and shoot the clerk directly instead of having him hanged. Yet this acknowledgment and change in Rudbeck is too slight a portion of the novel, too much a postscript to the story of Mr. Johnson, to alter the sentimental emphasis on the victim of cultural clash.

Another of Cary's early novels, *Charley Is My Darling* (1940), is similarly sentimental. The central character, Charley Brown, is one of a group of evacuees from the London slums in the first days of World War II who is sent to a country village. Although high-spirited and artistically talented, Charley, like Mr. Johnson, is forced to operate in a culture he cannot understand, and turns increasingly to crime and destruction. The villagers are not cruel or oppressive, but they cannot understand Charley and, certain that they know how to judge whatever they face, never listen to his explanations. In this novel, the sentimentality is compounded by Cary's treatment of the character of Liz, the village girl who becomes pregnant by Charley and tries to run away with him. Although supposedly deaf and feeble-minded, Liz is presented as the only character within the village able and willing to understand the complexity of Charley's reactions. This extreme wisdom of the dumb becomes less a device to attack the smugness of the village than an extreme and unconvincingly sentimental reversal of the expected. Cary also inserts essays concerning the sensitivity and vulnerability of children, expected, without ever being taught, to respond conventionally to the complex hypocrisies of the adult world. Charley and Mr. Johnson are both children, adolescent and almost-adult literally, but completely innocent and child-like culturally.

The focus on the child is apparent also in *A House of Children*, a novel, with many autobiographical points of reference, concerning a large family of children and cousins during holidays on the Irish coast. The narrator of the novel, Evelyn Corner, is looking back on his childhood, combining the child's view of older cousins and children's expeditions with inserted essays on the conservatism or sensitivity or natural goodness of children. The focus on the child, on the creature who experiences all the conflicts of adults without the adult's presumed capacity to understand and control these conflicts, invariably becomes sentimental in Cary's fiction. Cary's children are always judged by adult standards, yet are never given the adult's means of fighting and questioning those standards. The child, in Cary's fiction, is the archetypal victim. He is not even, as he often is in Dickens, the symbolic victim of his parents' inadequacies and mistakes, as if, in instances like that of the child of Caddie Jellyby and Mr. Turveydrop in *Bleak House*, the "sins of the fathers are visited upon the children," even through several generations. In Cary's early fiction the child as victim is never connected with anything else, never stands as anything other than a repository for fictionally undifferentiated emotion. Cary's focus on these children implies a sentimental view of the world.

However, the two trilogies, each with three different narrators exploring the same characters and some of the same events, avoid sentimentality. Each of the narrators is both victim and victimizer, both the sufferer and the agent of others' suffering, depending on the point of view. The idea of the trilogy itself, the three different points of view interlocking on characters and events, becomes a metaphor for human skepticism and complexity, an artistic means of avoiding the simplicity of unadulterated sympathy for the victim. The trilogies are metaphorical in subject matter as well as in structure, for both art—the ostensible subject of the first trilogy—and politics—the ostensible subject of the second—become metaphors for a much wider version of human activity. Art is the attempt to create the meaningful mirror of human experience, the shape given to experience by Sara Monday, Tom Wilcher, and Gulley Jimson alike. And politics, as Nina Latter keeps proclaiming in *Prisoner of Grace*, is a metaphor for all human relationships, a means of managing all the problems any man encounters.

Tom Wilcher's oldest brother, Edward, a charming and intelligent politician, ruins his career through his lack of faith, his unwillingness to sacrifice his graciousness to his political cause. The same final lack of faith in himself, the final unwillingness to take irrevocable stands, also, in Cary's terms, defeats him as a man. Even Gulley Jimson, the dedicated artist, sometimes connects art to religion and politics. Recalling the shock of seeing his first painting by Manet, after having been brought up on conventional nineteenth-century pictures at the Royal Academy, Gulley claims, "It was the Church against Darwin, the old Lords against the Radicals." The prefaces to the novels in the Carfax edition emphasize the metaphorical nature of the subject matter of each novel. The preface to *Prisoner of Grace* begins:

> The difficulty of a book about a politician is that people will tend to read it as a book about government. But politics is the art of human relations, an aspect of all life.

The preface to *A Fearful Joy* indicates a reversal of this use of politics as a metaphor for personal relations, explaining the intention to make the personal career of Tabitha a metaphor for the historical changes through which England passed during her lifetime. All the contrasts and ironic similarities between Tabitha and her granddaughter were meant to demonstrate the element of "return," the permanence within change, the constancy of a human and responsive spirit within the movement of history. Both Tabitha and her granddaughter become symbols for responsive humanity who survive through change. Yet, whichever is the metaphor for which, Cary consistently connects the personal with the social or historical.

Cary's novels are more effective insofar as they work more completely in terms of a dominant metaphor. The trilogies, in their interlocking points of view, are more forceful and coherent than the single novels. The view of the world through the conscious and iconoclastic artist in *The Horse's Mouth* is both sharper and deeper than the portrait of England through the more vague and diffuse metaphor of *A Fearful Joy*. From Gulley Jimson's opening simile, "Sun in a mist. Like an orange in a

fried fish shop," to his sharp insults to the people around him—
as when he upbraids his faithful follower Nosy Barbon, "You
ought to be a bath bun sitting on the road and waiting for the
steam roller to expand your soul"—to his graphic description of
the geography of Sara's breasts, the perspective and the language
of the artist give the novel both coherence and vitality. The mode
of the metaphor provides a persona Cary needs.

Similarly, in *Herself Surprised,* Sara Monday constantly
describes scenery and events with images from the kitchen she
knows so well. Skies are like "kitchen fires" or "new-cleaned
window glass," and Cary often gives Sara's descriptive passages a
domestic and an artistic perspective in a vast elaboration that
parodies them both:

> The sun was as bright as a new gas mantle—you couldn't look at it
> even through your eyelashes, and the sand as bright gold as deep-
> fried potatoes.

Part of the comedy is in the adoption of a unique perspective, a
particular point of view.

Sometimes, Cary uses the same metaphor in different
novels. For example, in *Mister Johnson,* Rudbeck regards building roads as the most important thing the British can do for the
Africans to bring them in contact with civilization. He uses any
means possible to get his road built, unintentionally first suggesting to Mr. Johnson the moral laxness and fiddling with accounts that, far too generally and vaguely interpreted, lead Johnson astray. Yet the road building, the opening of Africa to the
outside world, is, in Cary's terms, both inevitable and corrupting.
Later, in the Chester Nimmo trilogy, the same metaphor appears
again. Jim Latter, self-appointed guardian of traditional English
values, ruins his own career in Africa because of his violent opposition to road building, his defeated campaign to prevent
commerce and modern civilization from destroying the ancient
culture of his favorite tribe. This defines Jim as the hopeless
defender of an impossible past.

The structural metaphors of the two trilogies are, in some
ways, much like each other. In each trilogy, the first novel is
from the point of view of a woman, wife or mistress to both of
the two men who later give their versions of events. In each, the

woman is amoral, comfortable, seeking to avoid conflict and to succor whichever man she is with at the moment. The middle novel in each trilogy delves deeply into the past, follows the man, Tom Wilcher or Chester Nimmo, who has been formed by the past. In *Except the Lord,* Cary depicts the fundamentalist religion that influences Chester, a religion he rejects but then returns to as the source of his political principle and power. In *To Be a Pilgrim,* the account of the past chronicles Tom Wilcher's desire to be a "pilgrim," to wander, to discover, to be an adventurer. Early in his life, Tom and his sister had vowed to be pilgrims, and she had run off to her fundamentalist preacher. But Tom never becomes the missionary he had wanted to be; too tied to his family, his responsibilities, his ancestral house, he remains in the fixed point of his history and never wanders, never creates. Chester and Tom are also alike in that both are hypocrites, both constantly mediating between the claims of their pasts and the force of their own rebellions. The final novel in each trilogy deals with a man more dedicated to a principle or a code than formed by an historical background. Gulley Jimson has his art and Jim Latter his concept of honor. Neither ever violates his code and each murders the woman who relates the first novel of his trilogy. The man of principle, rather than the hypocrite, needs to destroy the amoral female.

As the critic Charles G. Hoffman said, in a recent book on Joyce Cary, the forms of the trilogies resemble a triptych, a three-panelled painting in which the middle panel is the largest. And, as Hoffman shows, Cary originally conceived both trilogies as triptychs, intending to concentrate on the central figures and regarding the figures of the smaller side panels as outside history and society. In the sense that the central figure in each trilogy is historical, the analogy of the triptych works well. But, despite Cary's original intention, the Gulley Jimson side panel apparently grew until it overwhelmed the trilogy.

In fact, particularly in the first trilogy, the triptych form finally does not explain the novels, and the two trilogies do not really fit into the same structural pattern. In terms of Cary's values, Gulley Jimson is the hero of the first trilogy and Chester Nimmo of the second, representatives of different panels, different functions, in the analogy of the triptych. In both trilogies, Cary ultimately sides with the man who creates his own reality out of experience and imposes it on the exterior world, the artist or the politician who is able to give his own shape to human events. Against the creative hero, Cary poses the man who would preserve, the guardian of an inherited or pre-existent principle, the Tom Wilcher or Jim Latter who sometimes resents and sometimes half admires the creativity he must stand against in order to remain in secure control of his world.

In the first trilogy, the creative force of Gulley Jimson works against the sense of history and of England represented by Tom Wilcher. Tom Wilcher is never his own man. Early in his career, he tried to ape his brother Edward, latching on to Edward's politics, his discarded mistress, and his tricks of speech and gesture. But Tom cannot endorse the depths of Edward's skepticism, conveyed in sardonic couplets which appear throughout the novel, about the folly of men and governments, and Tom is left simply preserving, simply reacting against and drawing away from definitions with no positive point of view of his own. Always sexually repressed, Tom is finally arrested for molesting young girls in the park. His purpose and, to some extent, his sanity have been lost in his futile attempt to apply his intelligence to preserving a past order. In contrast, Gulley Jimson, who paints "pictures for fun," uses all his intelligence and all his feeling to create. Through art, he gives his life individual form, a form that is always changing, for Gulley destroys as well as creates, tears down the walls he has built when they no longer represent the activity of creation itself. His art is closer to that of a happening than to the static picture immortalized on the museum wall. Throughout the novel, Gulley quotes William Blake, the poet-prophet-artist-philosopher who enjoined man to create out of the antithetical opposites of his own being, to achieve the synthesis of all the diverse human elements through artistic form. Against Blake, in whom he believes completely, he often poses Spinoza, the philosopher most highly regarded by Gulley's friends in the flophouses along the Thames. Spinoza appeals to the skeptical rationalism, the ultimate faith, and the masochism common to the intellectuals among the working classes; as Gulley explains, "Anarchists who love God always fall for Spinoza because he tells them that God doesn't love them." Gulley, in contrast, like Blake, glories in the joy of creativity.

In the second trilogy, the man of history, Chester Nimmo,

is also the man who creates his own value. In his early revolt against his father's religion, Chester had turned to the emerging trade union movement and worked for a strike among the dockers in southwest England. Yet, despite his belief in the cause, Chester cannot fully countenance the union leaders' complete indifference to the men and he hesitates at a crucial moment. The strike loses and Chester is hated by both sides. At the end of *Except the Lord,* Chester returns to his father's rural cottage and develops the combination of religious faith, humane feeling, and shrewdly practical hypocrisy which characterizes his subsequent political career. The combination is uniquely his own, a personal, political, and religious synthesis (even, in his oratory, an art as well) that can be creatively imposed upon the world. In contrast, Jim Latter, regarding all politicians as low crooks, is certain of his moral standards, of where to assign the blame and the praise. Militantly anti-intellectual and anti-creative, Jim stands squarely on his honor and demands that everyone else acknowledge the "truth." In Cary's terms, however, Jim's "truth" is only a set of facts, a chronicle of who was where at what time, a precise accounting that misses all the genuine truth of human motives and aspirations. Finally recognizing that his wife has doubly betrayed him—sexually with Chester (as, when married to Chester earlier, she had betrayed him with Jim), and politically in refusing to take an uncompromising stand with traditional law and order in the General Strike—Jim shoots her. His sterile lack of creativity can end only in a destructive explosion. Despite the fact that, in the trilogies, each character's point of view is given a complete novel, Cary's endorsement of the creative man comes through strongly.

The separation between the man of value and the man of history gives the first trilogy a greater balance, a greater tension between its various parts. As a trilogy it more successfully divides interest and sympathy between the various points of view. The second trilogy, however, is more like the triptych, focusing almost entirely on the middle panel, the middle character. This makes the second trilogy more unified, although the unity is achieved at the expense of interest in the final novel. Jim Latter does fill in a few details of plot, but the simplicity of his truculent and limited sense of honor cannot really sustain an entire novel. As the apotheosis of the uncreative, he is, in Cary's terms, an entirely negative character.

Cary's theme of the importance of the creative consciousness, his identification of a hero with creative capacity, is also apparent in the fiction other than the trilogies. Frequently, in the early fiction, the creative hero is doomed. Mr. Johnson can create himself, the model of the white man that he thinks he can become. The fact that his creation is not the synthesis he imagines it to be, that being neither African nor European white man he is doomed, does not diminish the creative impulse itself. And our sympathy for Mr. Johnson derives from the impulse. Similarly, in *Charley Is My Darling*, Charley represents the impulse to create, producing both art and an illegitimate child, in an environment that does not understand him. When told that he should be ashamed because he has impregnated Liz, Charley cries in silent hopeless protest against society's demand that he lie, for he cannot feel ashamed of what he has created any more than he can feel the force of social prohibitions he has never heard or understood. A creative vitality also characterizes Tabitha Baskett in *A Fearful Joy*. This quality keeps her responsive to all the changes in history she lives through, establishes her connection with her granddaughter, and generates her attraction to the lively but irresponsible Bonser, the crude charlatan who had originally seduced her and marries her some thirty years later. Bonser is another of Cary's creative characters. Loud, immoral, a war profiteer, full of expansive schemes and promises that rarely work out, likely to chase every available woman he sees, Bonser is, in Cary's terms, partially redeemed by the single fact that he is always recreating himself in new circumstances. And Tabitha, too, even as an old woman about to die, still feels "some mysterious warmth," that rises "to meet the warmth of the sun."

Cary's final novel, *The Captive and the Free* (1959), demonstrates the same veneration for the creative human force. Originally planned as a trilogy on religion, to match the other trilogies on art and politics, but compressed into a single novel because Cary knew his death was imminent, *The Captive and the Free* focuses on the career of Walter Preedy, a faith-healer. Preedy believes that people can be cured if they truly have faith in God's omnipotence. Against Preedy's belief, Cary poses and satirizes other contemporary and more sanctimonious forms of religion: belief in the sanely rational conventional religion of the Establishment, no different from the society itself, but emphasizing the spiritual side of man's nature; belief in Christianity as a social and political bulwark against "communist materialism" in post World War II Britain; belief in religion as a sophisticated counter-force to the empty atheism of all the bright young rationalists before World War II. All of these beliefs, including Preedy's faith-healing, are, for Cary, permeated with hypocrisy and contradiction. But, for Cary, the faith-healing is at least the product of a unique individuality, the creative force of a man making and asserting his belief out of his own experience. As such, the faith-healing deserves respect, and the Reverend Mr. Syson, an honest clergyman who begins by trying to have Preedy's doctrines banned, eventually changes his own views on religion and comes to recognize Preedy's force and spiritual power. The final "truth," a final statement about whether or not faith-healing really works, is absent from Cary's novel, but, in a world without "truth," the creative force of belief is a superior human accomplishment. In this novel, more frequently than in the trilogies, Cary inserts essays to establish his point of view more firmly, to underline the irony that what might seem to be the most spurious of religions from a rational point of view, in fact reveals the greatest quantity of genuinely spiritual human force.

The consistent emphasis on the creative in art, politics, and religion indicates that Cary's fictional world is not, as a recent critic has stated, morally "indeterminate" or relativistic. Quite the opposite, for Cary's endorsement of the creative consciousness is, if anything, too pervasively thematic and heavy-handed, particularly in some of the single works like *The Captive and the Free*. The structure of the trilogies, the narrations from three different points of view, might seem to make Cary's world relativistic, but the novels themselves, clustering around the theme of the importance of the creative, work against the implied indeterminism of the structure. In fact, the structure of the trilogies supplies a false lead. Although the tripartite structure gives the novels a superficial range throughout recent English history, a superficial multiplicity of character, and a coherence, the matter of the novels is much more narrow and restricted, more confined by the limitation of Cary's thematic emphasis. All the complexity suggested by the structure is finally a comic persiflage decorating Cary's insistence on the creative intelligence.

Cary uses specific chronology in much the same way. In the first trilogy, the reader notices that Sara Monday is seldom credible about dates. Talk of what age she was at given times, early in the novel, indicates that she was born in 1877, but, when her first husband dies in 1919, she speaks of herself as thirty-nine. Sara is, of course, just the woman to shade her age to the younger side of forty, and she is equally unreliable in repeating the minor facts of Wilcher's family and biography. Similar discrepancies appear in Tom Wilcher's account of his life in *To Be a Pilgrim*. Having begun the novel by saying he is seventy-one, as he looks back over his life in 1936 or early 1937, Tom later reports that he was thirty-eight during the revolutionary year of 1906. He is similarly inconsistent about his brothers' ages. There is less reason for these discrepancies in the character of Tom Wilcher than in that of Sara. In the third novel of the trilogy, Gulley Jimson only mentions his age once, so that from no other point of reference can one question him, and the reader may conclude that Gulley's apparent reliability about dates indicates his more general reliability from Cary's point of view. But similar inconsistencies mark both Nina's and Chester's accounts in the second trilogy, and Jim Latter's military precision about dates and times is certainly no indication of any other or more important reliability. In addition, chronology is similarly askew in *A Fearful Joy*, in which, following references from different points in the novel, one concludes that Tabitha was variously born in 1879, 1881, and 1884. The obvious conclusion is that the inconsistency is Cary's rather than any of his characters', a conclusion that fits with his general point of view that the person, like Jim Latter, too closely concerned with dates and matters of minute fact misses the central truths of experience. Yet, at the same time, Cary fills the novels with specific dates and events. The chronology, like the structure of the trilogies, is ultimately a kind of persiflage, a fabric that suggests a consistency and an interest that is not, in fact, supported by the novels. In one way, the conflict in Cary's work between structure and fiction, between container and material contained, is the reverse of the conflict between structure and fiction in Thomas Hardy's. Hardy sets rather narrow formulae, severely circumscribed containers, and the force and complexity of his characterizations, his material, constantly bursts their limits; Cary, on the other hand, at his most skillful, creates complex and intricate containers, but the material within is narrowed and shrivelled by the single theme. Hardy's fiction, despite all its lack of consistency, has in it great power and vitality as it explodes from its form; Cary's fiction, although suggestive on first reading, shrinks in its narrow "truth" behind the superficial intricacy of its form.

Like his chronology, Cary's narrators are generally unreliable. As the characters who narrate the trilogies explain and justify themselves, the reader becomes less convinced, sees more clearly all the contradictions, rationalizations, and spurious self-justifications. Sometimes, the other, more creditable or praiseworthy, side of a character is evident only in the narration of another. The female narrators are particularly unreliable, manifestations of Cary's consistent viewpoint that the female is soft, responsive, and gracious, yet ultimately untrustworthy, and loyal only to the emotion or situation of the moment. Sara Monday, the archetypal feminine, lies and steals, uses her religion as a convenience to bolster whatever she happens to feel at the moment, and parades a false innocence to cover her shrewdness. Although admirably resilient and genuinely devoted to Gulley, Sara is portrayed as essentially amoral, as indifferent to both society's standard moralities and the special creative morality of the artist. Gulley, the most direct and reliable of Cary's narrators, sees Sara clearly as an encumbrance to the artist. Although always strongly attracted to her, Gulley resents his own attraction and recognizes both Sara's hypocrisy and her possessiveness. Like his hero, William Blake, whose poetry he quotes concerning the woman who binds and parasitically feeds upon the man, Gulley sees the female as coddling and ultimately destroying the male creative purpose. And most of Cary's other women in the later novels are only more sophisticated versions of Sara Monday.

In *A Fearful Joy,* Tabitha lies and steals, follows her impulses, and always scraps her rational formulations or principles to respond sympathetically to Bonser or other men around her.

Nina Latter, far more complicated than either Sara or Tabitha, is the "prisoner of grace" the title of her novel suggests, imprisoned by the grace, the devotion, she invariably feels when confronted by Chester, no matter what her promises to Jim. Although Nina always claims that she loves Jim and is divided from Chester by issues of class, religion, and politics, she can never resist the lure or the appeal of the creative man. He requires her sympathy, and, in the face of his requirements, her resolutions and convictions dissolve. She can understand him, can recognize his curious balance of hypocrisy and sincerity, and she can, from the public point of view, corrupt him by making him devoted to luxury in order to indulge her, but she cannot really participate in his power or his creativity. She is a tractable, amoral, highly sympathetic leech. That she recognizes her own conflicts, both the conflict between her feelings for Chester and her love for Jim, is evident in the fact that she twice attempts suicide. But this recognition does not alter her role as the necessary encumbrance on the creative man. In *Except the Lord,* his own account of the origin of his power and creativity, Chester only mentions Nina briefly twice, conventional and fulsome declarations of the importance of her sympathy and devotion. Cary makes clear the fact that Chester's force originates in his rural and religious past, requires a strength of spirit and purpose that has little to do with Nina. Jim Latter, although he learns that she has been unfaithful to him and finally shoots her, always talks of her devotion and loyalty. He misreads her suicide attempt as evidence of her inability to lie to him, valuing her for a morality she does not possess. Each husband sees her only in his own terms, as part of his own delusion, ironically praising her for qualities she only partially possesses. Behind the narrators, Cary judges her more harshly, concentrating on the way in which female emotion and ambivalence impede the creative man and erode the man of stalwart principle. Ironically, too, and this for Cary is her saving grace, Nina recognizes enough of the necessary vice of the feminine to share her creator's judgment.

Cary's judgment of Nina, like his judgment of his other women, carries a note of condescension. The woman, ultimately, is not capable of deriving a genuine moral principle or of creating herself from the flux of experience. The woman is parasitic, unable to shape herself into a creative force, to impose herself on the world. This kind of stereotyping, this division of humanity into a masculine possibility and a feminine necessity, finally prevents Cary from writing the novel of compassion, for the attitude of compassion depends upon a recognition of the mystery, unpredictability, and complexity of human possibility. An attitude of compassion questions human values and examines the multiplicity of human character; Cary stereotypes human character, although he decorates his stereotypes with vivid charm and sometimes spectacular skill, and consistently asserts the value of one type over another.

Superficially, Cary's novels often resemble those within the tradition of compassion, sometimes relying on a structure that presents a multiple point of view and revealing a profound concern with historical change. Yet the underlying idea is too firm, too judgmental, too rigid a restriction of human possibility to the masculine creative consciousness. Cary's heroes are too heroic to belong with those in the tradition of compassion. His ironies, even those applied to Chester Nimmo, his most complex hero, are too much on the surface, too much the dramatic means of revealing the character rather than a central part of the character himself. When Cary's heroes are defeated, victimized, rendered impotent by an indifferent society, the fiction is sentimental. When, as in the later novels, the heroes achieve their own kind of triumph, creating themselves in a world that neither totally accepts nor totally defeats them, the response elicited is more comic and complicated and the fiction itself is more forceful and convincing. But the definition of the hero in Cary's work requires stereotyping, requires a violation of the very multiplicity the novels superficially present. And in this difference between the apparent range of multiple human possibility, comically treated, and the restriction of the hero to his appropriate thematic quality, Cary's novels, even at their most effective, leave an impression of shrinking, of emotional shallowness, of an ultimate lack of sympathy directly antithetical to the impression generated by the best novels of compassion.

XIII

ANGUS WILSON

URING THE LATE 1940's and early 1950's, Angus Wilson acquired a reputation as a writer of sharp, astringent short stories in which the pretense or hollowness of characters' poses were torn apart by people or events. Carefully analytic, the early short stories, collected in *The Wrong Set* (1949) and *Such Darling Dodos* (1950), give some support to Wilson's reputation as a satirist, but even in those, and more certainly in the novels that follow, the reputation is both oversimplified and inaccurate. In an interview published in *The Paris Review* (Autumn/Winter 1957), Wilson said that he did not regard himself as primarily a satirist, using Orwell's *Animal Farm* and Butler's *Erewhon* as examples of satire, but that he thought of himself as writing more traditional and less "abstract" fiction, with irony as a principal approach. In classifying satire as "abstract," Wilson was probably referring to the need for an assured standard, an aloof stance from which the actions and characters satirized can be seen as ridiculous, a point of view that in itself expresses an all-inclusive theme. More appropriately for Wilson's amorphous fictional world which is not amenable to a single, all-inclusive theme, irony, far from depending on a fixed standpoint, reverses or undercuts the expectations without making a judgment between the value of the expectation and the value of the reversal. Irony emphasizes man's lack of knowledge and assurance, his need to live and act in a world where he never fully knows the causes or consequences of his actions; satire, on the other hand,

[277

emphasizes man's foolishness, as if he could and should know better. In all his novels, Wilson never judges his estranged central characters from any single or assured point of view, never establishes an imperative that would have made life more rewarding or satisfactory for the central character.

In Wilson's first novel, *Hemlock and After* (1952), a consistent ironic mode, a questioning of motives and a skepticism about perceptions, protects the story, to some extent, from the potential sentimentality of the account of a central character discovering himself. Novelist, humanist, public figure, successful originator of a government scheme to provide a country house, Vardon Hall, for talented young writers, Bernard Sands is superficially at the apex of a distinguished career that is neither fraudulent nor hypocritical. He has always recognized and contended with a certain amount of ambivalence in himself: an individualist who generally ignores authority and governments, he has nevertheless been able to put through successfully his scheme to aid writers; since his wife, some years earlier, lapsed into a psychotic withdrawal, he has had two homosexual affairs. But, now, during the months in which the novel takes place, Bernard is troubled by a sense of "evil," a force in human affairs more nakedly malign than any he has noticed before. With his kind of conventional middle-class decency, he cannot handle the cruel plots of the sickly sweet procuress, Mrs. Curry, or the malice of some of the camp followers. In an episode central to the novel, Bernard also recognizes in himself an "evil" he had not hitherto known. While waiting for a friend in Leicester Square, Bernard is asked for a match by an importuning young man. He offers matches but does not respond to the advance. Then a police detective approaches, arrests the young man, and asks Bernard if he will offer evidence. Although Bernard refuses to join the aggressive belligerence of the police, he recognizes, within himself, connected with his own homosexuality, something of cruel pleasure in the harrassment of another:

But it was neither compassion nor fear that had frozen Bernard. He could only remember the intense, the violent excitement that he had felt when he saw the hopeless terror in the young man's face, the tension with which he had watched for the disintegration of a

once confident human being. He had been ready to join the hounds
in the kill then.

The insight into himself, even in these rather melodramatic
terms, influences Bernard throughout the rest of the novel,
causes him, for example, to make the darkly elliptical speech at
the opening ceremony for Vardon Hall, a speech which helps
turn the ceremony into a chaos of insults and polite destruction.
Bernard can neither extenuate nor move away from the glimpse
of his own basic nature, a glimpse that he connects with his failure as a husband, a friend, a father to his two children and to
the younger writers dependent upon him. He dies from a heart
attack, feeling that he has failed even to come close to the humane, intelligent man he tried to be.

Were this the whole novel, *Hemlock and After* would be
only a sentimental and melodramatic self-discovery suffused in
pity for the self-delusion of the humanist. But, ironically, Bernard's final judgment of himself turns out to be almost as inaccurate, and certainly as overstated, as his original complacent
decency had been. Just before his death, his wife, Ella, emerges
from the misery and isolation of her long illness, an illness in
which she learned to recognize and handle "evil." She is almost
miraculously restored to psychic health, a detail convincing
enough in ironically reversing Bernard's expectations even if it is
not clinically convincing, and she can deal with experience even
after Bernard's death. His death also has a salutary effect on some
of his other associates: his sister, with whom he quarreled at their
last meeting, resigns from teaching, finally able to recognize that
Bernard had been accurate and compassionate; the young homosexual with whom he had his more recent affair is able to leave
his suffocating mother and take a flat in London on his own. Yet
Wilson's sense of irony causes him also to qualify these triumphs
at the very end. In the final scene, taking place months later, one
of Bernard's most cherished principles about the writer's home
has been overthrown. He had insisted that the writers administer
it themselves, but they choose to hire a professional political
administrator to save time and trouble. Bernard, Wilson makes
clear at the end, never did know himself or his world very well.
His triumphs and defeats qualify each other through irony, an

irony which both defines precisely Bernard's limited degree of survival beyond death (a survival more dependent on personal influence than on public pose), and saves the novel from the sentimentality involved in excessively fondling his discovery of "evil."

The resolution of Wilson's next novel, *Anglo-Saxon Attitudes* (1956), is also presented through a series of ironies. The central figure, Gerald Middleton, recognizes, in his early retirement and his comfortable insulation from the banalities of his profession and family, that he has always avoided responsibility. In a large, extended world that contains many versions of "truth," the narrow scholar's petty documentation, the paranoid scholar's obsession with a fixed idea, one of Gerald's son's conventional codes of society and religion, another son's oversimplified and melodramatic public exposures of flaws in the social structure, Gerald's wife's indiscriminate and suffocating nourishment of everyone, his young grandson's assurance that patterns always fit together, Gerald manages to work out, with great difficulty, the "truth" of the past he has evaded for so long. But discovering the "truth" and acting on it in an attempt to redeem the past do not necessarily lead to triumph.

Irony qualifies and defines the motives and the impact of all Gerald's attempts to act on the basis of his newly discovered "truth." He does find out and publish the truth about an archeological fraud, which involves a number of reputations and careers he cares about, and his account of the fraud is generally heralded by the scholarly world as both an accurate solution of a discrepancy and an announcement of his return to active scholarship. But one important and pedantic new scholar accepts Gerald's new stature only because he sympathizes so strongly with the fact that one of Gerald's sons, the shabby pseudo-radical commentator, has been permanently injured in an auto accident. The narrow pedant regards the young man who invents wide and unsubstantiated public causes as a popular hero. Irony limits the utility of Gerald's actions even more strongly in his private life, for, although private and public concerns, domestic lives and careers, impinge on each other strongly, they are not necessarily resolved in the same way. Gerald acknowledges to his former mistress, whom he loved but abandoned in order to stay with his wife all the years the children were growing up, that he ought to have married her, but a realization and an acknowledgment cannot make up for thirty lost years. He also confronts his wife and daughter, in a dramatic scene, with the "truth" that the wife had, in a moment of hysteria and cruelty, deliberately pushed the daughter, when an infant, into the fire which maimed the infant's hand. But he learns that his daughter had suspected this all along and still, like her brothers, reveres her soft, wheedling, emotionally fraudulent mother more than her humane, truthful, but hitherto remote and indifferent father. These ironies suggest a constant lack of connection between cause and effect, between motive and consequence, in human behavior. The irony demonstrates how little man ever knows of what propels him to act or of what the consequences of his action will be. The final scene of *Anglo-Saxon Attitudes* adds another dimension to the irony by quickly presenting an exterior view of Gerald. After all his efforts to discover, acknowledge, and publicly affirm the "truth" of his experience, after fully abandoning his isolation, Gerald is about to leave to deliver two lectures in Mexico, a flight signifying the active resumption of his career. At the airport, he meets a prying and aggressive female novelist who, after he leaves, pronounces on the shame of men with brains, money, and good looks wasting their talents in easy, conscienceless inactivity. The irony of human misjudgment comes full circle.

Wilson's next novel, *The Middle Age of Mrs. Eliot* (1958), also depicts a character's efforts to come to terms with experience after a period of comfortable isolation. In this instance, however, the end of isolation is forced, for Meg Eliot's pleasant wrapping of social and charitable activity is ended when her husband is killed in Srem Panh by some students who intended to shoot a local government official. Left without sufficient money to continue living as she had been, finding relationships altered because her position in society is altered, Meg must emerge from isolation in order to establish a life for herself. The irony in this novel is frequently dramatic, the author's foreshadowing of events to come. Talking with her husband, the night before they are to leave on the fatal trip, Meg speaks of the horror of her mother's life with "the person you loved simply not there";

when she first sees Srem Panh, she thinks of it as only rather re-
motely exotic, a place where "nothing that happened . . . could
ever concern her." Dramatic irony, as in classical Greek drama,
informs the audience how blind man is. Blindly, Meg goes
through a series of episodes with old friends in which she either
manipulates or is manipulated, in which she finds no way of
working out her future, until, breaking down, she retreats to her
brother's large commercial nursery in the Sussex Downs. The
nursery restores her to health, but, after a year or so, she must
leave, for she cannot accept another form of isolation, another
protective wrapping that covers her in comfortable evasions.
Her brother, David, a pacifist, a quietist, a homosexual content
to live for years with a faithless lover, has been and is content to
swaddle himself in trivial tasks, but Meg cannot permanently
accept such passivity for herself. In addition, she fears changing
the direction of David's activity, pushing him to resume the
scholarly career he had abandoned at least fifteen years earlier.
And for Meg, dominating, always too easy, is another form of
evasion, another way of avoiding meeting experience. Ironically,
the environment that restored her to health must be abandoned,
at the end, for the amorphous world of contemporary London
that helped precipitate her collapse. Her decision marks her re-
discovered capacity to meet experience, a life of "sane" involvement within the contemporary world.

Wilson has himself commented in *The Wild Garden*
(1963), the published version of three lectures he gave at the
University of California in Los Angeles on his own life and
work, on the similar central figure apparent in each of his first
three novels. He views all three as estranged, as caught between
the hells of the contemporary failure to communicate despite
the cocktail parties and jobs and government connections, and
of the long and lonely reveries attempting to examine experience,
"the opposed hell of the maze of self-pity and neurosis." Bernard,
Gerald, and Meg are, at different times, caught in each hell. In
The Middle Age of Mrs. Eliot, the progression from one hell to
the other is most direct, Meg moving from the social hell of
superficial activity and meaningless communication to the hell
of neurotic loneliness after her husband's death. All three of the
central figures, fundamentally, in Wilson's terms, decent, sensi-

tive, and responsible, recognize their alternate hells, and Gerald and Meg go further than Bernard does in attempting to break down the estrangements, to live on the complicated earth instead of making themselves as comfortable as possible in one hell or another. And a frequent use of irony prevents these novels, particularly the latter two, from being read as the desperate struggles of noble put-upon heroes to emerge from loneliness. All the central figures are made too aware of themselves and their ambivalence, are too qualified by their own responsibility for their estrangements, to endorse such a sentimental reading.

Less fundamentally ironic than the earlier novels, *The Old Men at the Zoo* (1961), although in part a parable or fable applied to human government, also deals centrally with human isolation. The narrator of the novel, Simon Carter, the secretary of the London zoo during successive and very different administrations, is another of Wilson's detached, isolated, self-protective figures. Wilson uses some irony in having Simon discover himself through the fact that, in the midst of a war, fleeing the zoo on a mission alien to his principles, he is forced to kill and eat badgers, the animals he once protected as his primary zoological interest, in order to survive. The irony forces Simon to recognize the necessary atavism within the human creature, within himself, and this recognition chastens him, makes him less arrogant, priggish, detached, and inhumane. Yet the sense of irony that propels the change in Simon, that allows him to take principled stands in the necessarily political conflicts of a society instead of preserving his detached accommodation to whatever political or governmental mode temporarily reigns, is not made central to the novel or sufficiently complex to qualify human triumphs and defeats.

The focus on breaking down a central figure's protective evasion in order to admit a wider sense of life and the development of attitudes through irony are both dominant in Wilson's next novel, *Late Call* (1964). The central figure is Sylvia Calvert, the retired manageress of a seaside hotel who, with her husband, comes to live with her son, the headmaster of the secondary modern school in Carshall New Town. Early scenes at the seaside hotel before leaving and on the train to Carshall establish Sylvia as one who needs to minister to others, to help smooth things, to find herself through relationships with others. Accustomed to a lifetime of caring for the guests and burying herself completely in their needs and their concerns, she now, without occupation, needs to discover something more central about herself. In contrast, her husband, Arthur, is blustering, irresponsible, the old sport who uses any new acquaintance as audience for his tall stories and his aggressive geniality. As Sylvia, with genteel embarrassment, listens to Arthur rewrite the past or change his view of any friend or member of the family to suit his momentary convenience, she recognizes that relationships exist for great lengths of time which benefit neither party, and that communication is not always desirable or meaningful. After something like forty-five years of marriage, she summarizes:

> Stale rows leading nowhere; intimacy that did not signify. Yet in novels you read of family feuds that went deep enough to kill young love for ever, and that the brush of a hand roused tenderness enough to mend the fiercest quarrel. But books and life were not the same; there was no sense in expecting such a thing.

Sylvia of course reads only bad books. She is sound enough about her own life. Even when Arthur dies, having for months in Carshall New Town continued his career of story-telling, gambling, borrowing money from whomever he could with no intention of returning it, Sylvia's reaction is far from sentimental.

The avoidance of sentimentality in *Late Call* is important, for the story of Sylvia, the woman who develops a deep sense of the darkness at the center of human experience, who can pierce through the healthy busy-ness of New Town life to see the various darknesses that trouble each of her three grandchildren even though she misunderstands the smart, contemporary terms and references they use, is potentially sentimental. Yet Wilson's irony displays her inadequacies, her occasional denseness, her frequent self-abasement originating in misunderstanding. And Sylvia herself is not sentimental, for she clearly sees the rural slum, the poverty, the drunkenness, the parental brutality, and the rigid class system that helped to form her and prepare her for a life of service. Although she recognizes some of the pompous hollowness of the New Town, she also knows that it is generally less restrictive and less inhumane than her own background. Irony qualifies, prevents either the sentimentality of an overwhelming nostalgia for a dimly remembered past or the sentimentality of overwhelming faith in the progressive, problem-solving present.

Sylvia's own tendencies toward sentimentality are also depicted as her greatest inadequacy. In trying to discover relationships to replace those of her former occupation, Sylvia shows tremendous sympathy for victims: for benighted women in television soap operas and bad historical novels, for the lonely and helpless victims of famous murder cases, for a woman she once knew at the hotel whose niece was murdered, for her grandson's homosexual friend who gassed himself rather than face disclosure. Yet her recognition of human darkness and her sympathy for the victims are not enough to give Sylvia any sense of meaning. She identifies with her victims too closely, immersing herself in a subtle form of self-pity, falling into one of the lonely hells Wilson described for the central characters in his first three novels. To avoid isolation, Sylvia must do more than recognize and sympathize.

At first, in Carshall New Town, her efforts to help her family (her son's wife has recently died) seem futile. The organized and mechanized household runs without her; her son and her grandchildren patronize her into a remoteness from their concerns; the various trivial jobs thrust upon her, she can easily see, are meaningless and mechanical. Her only reaction is to immerse herself even further in the useless and banal sympathy for soap opera heroines and victimized old women. She needs, instead, to discover herself, the entity of individual reactions and attitudes behind the lifetime of service and sympathy, the self that can make demands on others as well as be imposed upon.

Her discovery of her past and herself emerges in ironically unlikely places. She first begins her awareness of self through the sermon of an old Scots preacher who comes to Carshall as a last-minute replacement on Easter Sunday. His homey and anachronistic sermon, asking for "God's Grace" and imploring man to face the hollowness and darkness of his own being, shocks the consciously contemporary and progressive local citizens, but reaches Sylvia. Later, on one of her walks outside Carshall, she saves a precocious American child from a bolt of lightning in a sudden storm, takes the child home, and collapses in the strange family's house. Recovering, she begins to talk to the child's parents, discusses her own childhood on the farm, her own opinions and perspectives, establishes a relationship that is not dependent on charity, condescension or service. Ironically, it is significant that the child's family is American, alien (like the Scots preacher), outside the normal range of Carshall life or of Sylvia's hotels, even includes customs and informalities hitherto strange to Sylvia. The "late call" of the title has changed from the instruction left at the hotel front desk to the self-recognition of one person's own value late in life.

Wilson himself has said that grace is the theme of the novel. But to talk of grace, or to say (as one critic has) that the novel advocates salvation by grace as opposed to salvation by works, is to falsify Wilson's position and oversimplify the novel. Wilson does not oppose the alternatives of grace and works as if he were a party in a seventeenth century theological controversy. Rather, he demonstrates that only by acquiring a personality, a force, a kind of non-theological grace, can Sylvia liberate herself sufficiently to establish any kind of constructive relationship, to have any impact on others. Good works, relationships, exterior activities, can be meaningless if they simply serve others or if a sentimental sympathy is the only motive; but good works can also be genuine and important if they originate in the response of a vital human being, if they emerge from a kind of human grace. In Wilson's agnostic theology, salvation by grace and salvation by good works are far from incompatible.

Once liberated from her own image of service, Sylvia can help her family more directly. When her son Harold suffers a minor mental collapse, breaks down in wailing that his children really hate him and that he is helpless without his wife, Sylvia, now a person instead of an object for charity, is able to understand and bury the darkness for him, return him to his safety of town planning and sociological questionnaires. The treatment of Harold introduces another kind of Wilsonian irony. Immersed in his ponderous principles, his schemes for organization, and his fascination with contemporary domestic gadgetry, Harold had, early in the novel, seemed simply an object of satire, a modern version of Dickens' Gradgrind. Yet, ironically, through the very satire, as Harold increasingly is isolated in his principles, fails to organize his family in his own terms, and fumbles ineptly with his gadgetry, the reader feels more and more sympathy for him as another human being whose schematic efforts to understand life are futile. Harold hasn't the capacity for Sylvia's grace, but he is, almost ironically, human as she is. Harold can never face the darkness as fully as Sylvia can, just as he cannot accept the fact that one of his sons is homosexual, for not all people in Wilson's fiction are equally sensitive and responsive, equally able to face the world without a protective fabrication like service or the progressive principles of New Town life. Only those of special sensitivity, like Sylvia, or Gerald Middleton or Meg Eliot, are able to accept and thrive on the breaking down of barriers, the abandonment of protective remoteness.

The preface to *Late Call* is a long chapter about a poor farm child, never named, in 1911, whose sense of joy and independence, of "beauty" and "wonder," is crushed by a combination of the exigencies of farm life, the ignorance and brutality of parents, and the ineffectuality and class snobbery of the rich family boarding with them for the summer. This preface hangs over the novel as contemporary events begin through the focus of Sylvia's consciousness. As Sylvia releases and discovers herself toward the end of the novel through talking of her background, references clearly indicate the farm girl as Sylvia, the story as the crystallization of events and attitudes that formed her. The preface is always there, although not understood, for the cause of the phenomenon is irrelevant until the phenomenon itself is recognized. The past is simply a story, a meaningless and unconnected lump, until its force and relevance are realized in the present, as the revelation of what happened to her two dead children and the real story of her marriage are carefully controlled by the utility of the past event for the present circumstance. The development of Sylvia's consciousness—the unravelling of the protective withdrawal into service that characterized the life-long hotel manageress, and the gradual emergence of the human being—is never violated.

Wilson's most recent fiction, *No Laughing Matter*

(1967), continues the emphasis on psychological causation begun in *Late Call*. In a vast novel that follows the lives of the six Matthews children and their separate careers for more than fifty years, a kind of history of middle-class England from 1914 to 1967, Wilson carefully demonstrates what has made each of the children what he is. In an early episode, just after World War I, when their parents cruelly drown a litter of motherless kittens belonging to the children, the children formalize "the Game," a ritual and ironic family drama in which each of the six enacts the role most relevant to him.

The oldest, Quentin, raised by his paternal grandmother because his financially feckless parents, constantly living beyond their inherited incomes, cannot take care of such a large family, plays Mr. Justice Scales, "the dispassionate, objective outsider," who governs the trial and arbitrates the issues and arguments that come up during "The Game." The second child, Gladys, the victim, imposed upon sexually by her father and then almost continually by a boorish lover for whom she goes to prison, fulfils a psychological role in the family in terms of class by playing Regan, the earthy Cockney cook who remains loyal in spite of not receiving her wages and not often being permitted to demonstrate her skill at French cooking. Rupert, the handsome young actor, his mother's favorite, plays his father, "Billy Pop," a dreaming writer full of financial and literary schemes that he never completes, a spineless and adoring husband who evades his wife's demanding scenes and her infidelities by spending most of his evenings with cronies at his club. Margaret, the analyst, the novelist even at an early age, portrays her great aunt, Miss Rickard, the sharp-tongued spinster who had brought up her mother, the intelligent and caustic wit who continually travels without ever finding a home of her own. Margaret's twin, Sukey, the girl who dreams of peace, order, and domesticity in an old-fashioned country house, plays her soft and conventional paternal grandmother, a survivor from an earlier age who believes in all the homilies she has never examined. The youngest child, Marcus, grandiosely effeminate, plays their mother, "the Countess," who has always hated and rejected him, who imposes on all her family to support a graciousness she has never earned and an aristocratic indolence she cannot afford, but who reserves her most bitter reproaches and denials for her youngest child.

"The Game" establishes the conditions for the novel, the deterministic framework in which each of the six develops. Products of inadequate parents and surrogates, each child mirrors the problems that ironically thwart his efforts to incorporate a wider and fuller life. Yet each child does, in his own terms, make efforts, does attempt to become something more than he is, an extensively demonstrated complexity that saves the novel from the mechanism of simplistic psychological determinism. Despite these efforts, however, all the children really work out magnifications of their childhood roles. Rupert, for example, the mimic of his father, becomes an actor regarded as brilliant in Chekhov's "Three Sisters," in which he plays Andrey, the parasite on his sisters, and makes "that fat white slug" seem "pathetic and loveable." The "fat white slug" is a repeated image for "Billy Pop." In later roles, however, in attempting more contemporary characterizations that do not mirror his father, Rupert is inadequate, shallow and imperceptive. And, like his father, Rupert is always dependent on his wife for any insight or personal definition.

The problems of remoteness and estrangement are still important to Wilson in *No Laughing Matter.* The three most intelligent and sensitive children, Quentin, Margaret, and Marcus, are frequently locked in isolation, desperately trying to establish contacts that their very intelligence inhibits. Quentin cannot trim his shrewd political judgment, although he loses jobs and is once beaten up for it, just as he cannot alter the sense of sharp pragmatic appraisal that makes him use women as only temporary bed partners. And Margaret cannot turn off the astringent perception that makes her a good novelist, cannot make her wit seem other than indifferent even though strong feelings shelter just behind the sharp tongue. Like her great aunt, she is an inconsolable traveler.

At the same time, in *No Laughing Matter,* even those with less intelligence and sensitivity are treated with compassion, for Wilson is here less limited to sympathy for a type with whom he feels some identity than he was in some of the earlier novels like *Hemlock and After* and *The Middle Age of Mrs. Eliot.*

Gladys, the victim, is given an emotional honesty and a concern for others which make her entirely sympathetic. Even Sukey, despite the demonstrated falseness and insularity of her country house dream and the appalling garbage of her heartening war-time broadcast talks, is, at the end of the novel, ironically made somewhat sympathetic as an aging woman, passed by time, who has lost her favorite son in one of Britain's futile imperial gestures, and who makes pathetic attempts to extend her own sympathies beyond the limited dream she has tried to live.

Wilson's attitude, in his novels, has always been one of compassion for the estranged, particularly for the estranged trying desperately to re-establish significant communication with others and himself. In *No Laughing Matter,* with its emphasis on all the complex forces that determine the shape of human beings, that compassion is extended, given wider meaning and reference, for the determined conditions of experience make many more of us isolated or alien, divide us from our dreams and our attempts. The focus on psychological causation widens the definition of the estranged or the remote, multiplies Wilson's central character by six, even beyond six in that "Billy Pop" and the "Countess" can also not be entirely condemned, and increases the compassion for the many who find human experience and communication so difficult. The greater the understanding of human hang-ups and their origin, the more dense and complex the explanation of human attempts to break through the protective prison of self, the greater the respect and compassion for the human being.

This focus on the individual is not, however, the only focus in Wilson's fiction. The novels also describe, characterize, and rely on a great many sociological and historical phenomena of the last fifty years. From the characterization of Bernard Sands's son as a specimen of the new post-war Tory with a taste for Anouilh's nostalgic plays, and the earnest young garage mechanics of the fifties who, in *Anglo-Saxon Attitudes,* listen to *Salome* on the gramaphone in suburban semi-detached houses, to the early sixties' progressive rhetoric of the New Town in *Late Call* and the evocations of night life with the military in the West End during World War I, clammy public meetings on worthwhile causes during the thirties, and the Bermondsey riots in *No Laughing Matter,* all of Wilson's novels provide extensive chronicles of the years they describe. On the level of social chronicle, the novels describe overall attitudes as well as evocative details, carefully delineate perspectives changing through time instead of merely ticketing by the year in the fashion of the television documentary. In addition to providing the chronicle, Wilson's novels also demonstrate how constantly public, social or historical issues impinge on the private existence of the individual. The public and private are always intertwined, as in Gerald Middleton's self-protective remoteness or in the fact that Sylvia Calvert's lifetime of service is both an echo of an older England and the account of a single individual. Nevertheless, as with Gerald Middleton or Bernard Sands, the public and private are not necessarily resolved identically. Rather, in Wilson's world, the individual is always connected with, although never completely defined by, public identities like society, class and history. The public and private can, at times, be separated, but the individual who separates them as completely as possible, who lives either in a world he has made for himself, or solely in terms of a public slogan, is either disastrously isolated or stupidly self-denying. The healthy self requires connections to entities outside himself, yet also requires some independence and some capacity to impose the self on the world outside.

Wilson's constant interest in public questions is most directly manifest in his fable, *The Old Men at the Zoo.* Constantly linking man and animal imagistically, the novel describes the assumptions involved in various ways of administering the zoo as analogues for more general human questions of both public management and private morality. Wilson examines the different forms of government: the rational and liberal government, giving the creature the greatest liberty commensurate with general security, which Wilson calls "limited liberty"; a rigid kind of Victorian conservatism that tries to balance its strict confinement of the animals with brass bands, colored lights, and patriotic slogans; the totally irrational neo-Fascistic government of the Uni-Europeans. The more liberal governments are unable to handle the human creature.

After the inevitable war, the Uni-Europeans gain control and establish a zoo in which the conventional difference between man and animal is diabolically reversed. In the early 1970's, the director sets up an exhibit with a chained, shoddy Russian bear and a caged, mangy, miserable American eagle, and then invites a mob of presumed people to tear the animals apart. Up to this point in the novel, the fable works well and the parallel between the terms of the novel and their application to human government is made convincing. But Wilson was apparently unwilling to leave his futuristic society to the Uni-Europeans, just as he was unwilling to leave his statement about the nature of man inextricably locked in the center of brutal depravity. Just at the point when the Uni-Europeans seem in complete control, when even the cautious, ironic Simon Carter, who retains some amount of outmoded sensibility, has been exiled to a concentration camp, the Uni-Europeans are inexplicably overthrown and human sanity is restored to the world. Wilson gives no indication of how, in terms of either plot or concept, the bestiality is removed from control of human government; he just refers, in a single sentence, to "Liberation Day." The defeat of the Uni-Europeans is only a gesture, a cry of faith, that does not mesh with the structure of the fable. The fable traces, in careful stages, the developments that lead to the primacy of the Uni-Europeans, the gradual steps that mark the increasing central darkness of the human being. But the steps back to the light are omitted, and, since the allegory of government consists in the examination of steps and causes and processes, the omission seems a serious one.

A novel can, of course, end in a gesture of faith, but, in this instance, the terms of the novel, the fable, work against the credibility of such a gesture, and it is difficult to accept a conclusion, however heartening, plastered on without reference to the demands of the form. The statement that I assume Wilson intended, in order to provide coherence for the novel, pertained to a bestiality at the center of man that is nevertheless palliated, civilized, controlled, by a sense of human sanity and rationality, a bestiality that exists but is seldom visible at its naked worst and is, fortunately, partially squelched by its very invisibility. Yet the complexity of this possible statement is made less articulate than it might be by the rigid demands of the fabulistic form. According to the expectation of the fable, Wilson's theme should "work out" in terms not only relevant for Simon Carter as an individual (which it does) but also relevant for the general political implications of the subject. Yet the political theme is too tenuous, too complex, too much a part of its shadings and emphases, to work within the confined abstractions of the fable.

The public and political dimensions of *No Laughing Matter* are handled more successfully because less rigidly than those of *The Old Men at the Zoo*. In *No Laughing Matter,* each of the characters' private concerns invariably leads him into public attitudes. The attitudes may be convictions or poses or merely by-products of personal relationships, but they become part of the person himself, part of the human being divided between an individuality and an extension into the public domain. Political attitudes also have their personal counterparts, working through each individual in different ways. Quentin, for example, becomes an able socialist journalist, gaining a reputation in the radical press of the thirties as an authority on housing. On a visit to Russia, he is disillusioned about Communism, noticing the strange absence of various distinguished friends from previous visits. When he returns to England, none of his radical associates can credit his disillusion with the Soviet's noble experiment and he is regarded as an outcast. After speaking at a political debate, he picks up a young girl art student and takes her back to his flat for the night:

And when she said, in a naive, schoolgirl's downright way, that, for her part, she couldn't see how it was possible to be anything but a party member, to be anything else was a failure to comprehend the logic of history, he forced her into bed again almost brutally. He thought with excitement of her reaction when she read his article the following Friday in The New Statesman, giving his analysis and his prophecies concerning hidden events in Russia.

For Quentin, politics and sex are completely mixed, even though, for Wilson, at this point in Quentin's career, his politics are admirable and his attitudes toward sex brutal and indiscriminate. Yet in both are evident the man who, thirty years later, will enthrall a wide television audience with supercilious comments like, "I have no concern for the common man except that he should not be so common."

[293

In both *The Old Men at the Zoo* and *No Laughing Matter,* political or public evil is associated with the Nazis. Although the Uni-Europeans in the former are, in part, a brutalized version of the idea of the Third Force so popular in the early and middle fifties, they are much more significantly and consistently an echo of the Nazis with their codified bestiality, their irrational intensity, and their insistence on purity in the human product. The leader of the Uni-Europeans is named Blanchard-White. In *No Laughing Matter,* all six of the Matthews children work themselves, in one way or another, into anti-Nazi positions during the thirties. Quentin and Margaret, always consciously political, are strongly anti-Nazi throughout the decade, but their brother Rupert joins them on the platform in a meeting at Kingsway Hall to protest the German treatment of the Jews. Gladys, usually so passive, rebels at her lover's statements praising the efficiency of the Nazis and affirming the importance of preserving good business contacts no matter what the political issues. Marcus, at a snobbish party, quite heroically asserts his philo-Semitism and, when accidentally involved in the Bermondsey riots, acts with energy and force against the British Nazis. Even Sukey, insulated in her narrow public school, belatedly summons sufficient conscience to take in a German Jewish refugee. In fact the Matthews family, including "Billy Pop," although excluding the snobbish and self-indulgent "Countess," consciously defends Jews in the midst of considerable British anti-Semitism. Although "Billy Pop" writes that anti-Semitism is not a problem unique in the thirties having existed in Britain throughout his lifetime, it does become a touchstone, a measure of the individual's humanity in both personal and political terms, during the decade of the Nazi threat. All the Matthews children, whatever their other deficiencies, pass this test; they are anti-Nazi, they can laugh at the idea of racial purity and oppose inhumane dogma and brutality. In the sense that the six children represent alternatives for the reasonably responsible, humane, and literate British middle classes, their actions during the thirties reveal them at their most cohesive and admirable point. Wilson wisely never grants the British middle classes the sentimental triumph of Mrs. Miniver or "their finest hour," but he does demonstrate something of political value in a class that refuses to abandon its humanity to what seems the inevitable direction of European civilization.

But, in this novel, full of examples of both dramatic irony and the irony of self-discovery, Wilson does not allow the triumph of the middle classes to stand without qualifying it through a final comprehensive irony. Nineteen-forty inevitably shades into 1967. By 1967, when the final scenes of the novel take place, Marcus, the youngest, is over sixty. Only Rupert and Sukey, always the least humane and the most self-involved, have themselves had children, and their grandchildren, who appear in the final scene, represent something different, something graciously alien to the Matthews generation. Margaret and Quentin, caught in all their remoteness and defenses against their feelings, have never been able to love, have symbolically never earned the continuity represented by children. Gladys, willing victim until too late, never married before she was almost fifty. Marcus is homosexual, yet his final achievement, the establishment of a cooperative factory in Morocco, seems momentarily to have the best chance of preserving through time whatever worth or value the Matthews family represents. Marcus plans to leave his factory to Hassan, a young Moroccan who had, as a pretty boy, been his lover about ten years earlier. Yet Hassan, never sufficiently sensitive to learn through art as Marcus had when an older lover had first given him paintings to begin his career as an art dealer, is callow and represents no continuing tradition of knowledge, insight, or humanity. The final passage in *No Laughing Matter* is from Hassan's point of view:

And perhaps Marcus—his good, noble, kind friend—might now see how absurd were these cooperative ideas at the factory. . . . It was not as if, when he was owner, he would pay low wages or any foolish old-fashioned thing like that, if Marcus feared it; on the contrary Miracle Germany—Stuttgart, Dusseldorf, Frankfort—all that he admired most in the modern world, even his favorite journal Time Magazine urged high wages, but also seemly ambition, high profits, and determined management.

Whatever virtue and humanity, individually and politically, the Matthews family represented is more inimical to "Miracle Germany" and to Time Magazine than to almost any other forces in the world of 1967. The more than fifty years of the Matthews family, the relatively sane, responsible, and self-aware British middle classes, are over. The family, despite all its flawed achievements and tenuous survival, has been dissolved by time.

Irony, however, qualifies; it doesn't destroy. The political stand of the Matthews family is part of experience, crucial at certain moments in time, like the thirties, less central and less visible at others. The incipient anti-Nazi is a starting point, a beginning for humanity. Beyond that, difficulties, complexities, ambivalences appear, but sufficient humanity to avoid belief in the purity and brutality of Nazism is necessary for Wilson's interest. To complain, as one critic has, that Wilson never analyzes or deeply examines the fascists he depicts is to miss the point: for him, the inhumane, the man who never doubts himself, the purist, or the ideologue is a political evil, and Wilson is far more interested in how the sane man, with all his doubts and ambivalences, combats evil than in the nature of rampant political evil itself. *No Laughing Matter* is far more effective than *The Old Men at the Zoo* in conveying the human being's struggle against evil, against the hardening of social generalization into dogma, brutality, or inhumane abstraction. *The Old Men at the Zoo,* the fable, is itself too abstract, too simplistic to present convincingly all the dilemmas and humane doubts that bother the sane and sensitive. In contrast, *No Laughing Matter* moves historically and chronologically rather than fabulistically. Issues change and dissolve as time moves, characters both change and remain the same, humanity coheres at specific points only to dissolve again, politics are and then again are not central to the human being. Through the framework of history, Wilson can achieve a complexity of individual and social characterization that the philosophical simplicity and single-mindedness of the fable restricts. History, in Wilson's non-teleological world, is the final irony for man.

In addition to social and political questions, art, in Wilson's novels, provides another possible extension beyond the isolated self. Art establishes a structure, a framework, through which the individual can understand and respond to experience. For Meg Eliot, art is a principal mode of perception. At the beginning of the novel, while her husband, good fortune, and assurance are still alive, she compares herself as hostess to Glencora Palliser, Oriane de Guermantes, and Clarissa Dalloway, sees herself in literary terms. On the flight to the Orient, full of the sense of confronting a new world before she passes over the empty desert that in an accurately premonitory way frightens her, Meg thinks of herself as Isabel Archer or Maggie Tulliver, girls with "high" and adventurous hopes, although Meg smugly feels that she has the advantage of a later century's cumulative experience. That her husband dismisses Isabel Archer as uninteresting and irrelevant causes Meg to focus on the desert, the blankness, that frightens her.

Throughout the novel Meg dramatizes her struggles to recover herself in literary terms. She even, during her convalescence at the nursery, attempts to resurrect David's interest in literature, to share with him a means of looking at the world. But David narrowly views the novel as an art form unconnected with "real people" and his notion of literary scholarship is minute and trivial. One of the reasons Meg must leave the nursery is implicit in the artistic and human narrowness David's construction comes to represent. This emphasis on art as a mode of human perception, in addition to the slow, careful development of Meg's point of view and the interest in the developing independence of the human personality, has caused critics to call attention frequently to the Jamesian aspect of *The Middle Age of Mrs. Eliot*. Although Wilson does not share the fundamentally moral and judgmental concerns implicit in much of James's fiction (Wilson is almost always more interested in the origins and effects, rather than the metaphysical meaning, of a human problem), the use of art and literature to give continuity to sensibility is common to both novelists.

Later Wilson novels use art in a more complicated way which also has its Jamesian counterparts. In *Late Call*, Sylvia Calvert immerses herself in the art of television soap operas and bad historical novels, recognizing easily enough that the art does not significantly correspond to the reality she faces either in the hotel or in Carshall New Town. Like the editing of her husband who changes his stories of the past to fit any present mood or circumstance, the art that engages Sylvia distorts, simplifies, and perpetuates only its own stereotyped tradition. At one point, when the guests present her with a final gift before she retires from the hotel, she recalls an old movie in which Marie Dressler was given a warm and dignified farewell presentation. Sylvia notices acutely that the crabbed, embarrassed ceremony with which she is honored has nothing in common with Marie Dressler's, yet adds, "But there you are, they've time and money enough on the films to make things real." Wilson's irony impugns Sylvia's definition of reality, not her perception. In fact, her very interest in bad art and her awareness that it does not, in any significant way, duplicate the conditions of real experience is, early in the novel, the principal indication of Sylvia's capacity to learn. A work of art itself may be fraudulent or superficial; the impulse to respond to art, to test the connections between art and life, no matter what the quality of the art work itself, is a sign of vitality and worth in the human being.

Three of the six Matthews children in *No Laughing Matter* are, unlike most of Wilson's earlier central characters, professionally involved in art. Margaret, the novelist, consciously connects herself with Jane Austen, writing her first ironic stories about a fictional Carmichael family in which she is the intelligent, direct, acidulous Elizabeth who is jealous of and condescending to her superficially sweeter and prettier sister, Jane. The Carmichaels are a combination of Margaret's own Matthews family and the Bennet family of *Pride and Prejudice*. Her art, for Margaret, is both a mode of perception and a protective device, both a means for understanding and a means of making her loneliness and her hostility acceptable. Rupert, the mimic, the actor, after his initial successes in brittle twenties comedies and in Chekhov, parts in which he is able to act out the familial relationships that formed him, is unable fully to understand and create characters in Shakespeare or in the contemporary realistic drama after World War II. At one point, in talking with his wife, he recognizes that he cannot give enough "love" to Malvolio to play him as well as one should. For Rupert, all love, all human impulse, has been channeled into himself and his early relationship with his family, and he is unable, in terms of either emotion or intelligence, to break through the narcisscism of his early role. His art is, first, his means of expression and connection, but later his limitation, as his mimicry becomes only the circular and hollow echo of himself. Marcus deals in paintings, amassing a sizable income through the soundness and acuity of his taste, escaping from the pressures and prejudices of his—particularly for him—loveless family into the world of art where his effeminacy is acceptable and charming. Art, for Marcus, provides both his escape and his means for exercising talent and judgment. For all three of these children, art is a form, a man-made structure through which the human being can crystallize, can define himself as an entity in relation to other entities. The definition is not always satisfactory, for Margaret feels that her art often shuts off her most human and emotional impulses and Rupert recognizes the profundities of character beyond his artistic comprehension, but art is, for all these characters, a necessary mode for any means whatsoever of engagement with the outside world.

Wilson himself, as novelist, has discussed the function of art as a form of definition and crystallization for the artist. In *The Wild Garden,* he extensively details various symbols of gardens, the enclosures of nonhuman growth and vitality that are yet amenable to human purpose, which appear in all his novels. The garden, like the zoo, gives man a sense of the copiousness of life and yet requires "administration, the exercise of power, discrimination" if it is not to overwhelm human life. It is difficult always to know, as Ella Sands in *Hemlock and After* thinks she knows, the distinction between weeds and flowers, yet man needs to eliminate the weeds and encourage the flowers. For Wilson, in the early 1960's, looking back on his first four novels, the symbols of garden and zoo became the definition of a conflict that had always been, and still remains, central to his writing: the need for man to be responsive to all forms of existence outside himself and yet retain the capacity to choose, to exercise intelligent discrimination.

Art enables his characters to define something of themselves and their relationships; similarly, for Wilson, his own art, his own constructions, have enabled him to define something of his sense of human experience. The danger of art is that it can, like Rupert's, become simply a protective device, a hollow and narcissistic pose to enable the artist to escape from all connection with reality outside himself. Many of Wilson's characters, however, like Sylvia Calvert or Marcus Matthews avoid the danger, employ all their perceptions of art as a means of keeping themselves in some kind of contact, no matter how ambivalent, with the outside world. Wilson as novelist has also avoided the danger, for his own novels—structures, forms, fabrications themselves —constantly reach toward individual and social connection with human experience.

Another way of stating the conflict symbolized by the garden and the zoo in Wilson's work is to describe the conflict between form or artifice and reality. In one sense, all Wilson's novels are heavily and consciously structured, vastly artificial. *Anglo-Saxon Attitudes,* which Wilson calls "the most 'thought' of my novels and the least 'felt,'" begins with a series of tableaux, static yet interconnected scenes in which each of a number of characters is introduced through his attitudes and statements concerning a lecture on medieval history. Wilson moves from one character to the next by playing key phrases or symbols ironically against each other, an artifice he still uses occasionally to get from one character to another in *No Laughing Matter.* Since the first section of *Anglo-Saxon Attitudes* is concerned with Gerald's public career as an historian, the second, in equally static scenes, is a series of flashbacks in Gerald's mind about his personal life, each scene initiated by the chance remark of someone else in the conversation after his wife's heavy Christmas dinner. At this point, Gerald decides he must investigate the "truth." His subsequent investigations are tied together by an elaborate series of coincidental relationships, for, in a Dickensian manner, almost all Gerald's professional contacts are connected with his personal ones. For example, the attractive young girl who is the granddaughter of the old actress Gerald stayed with when the archeological specimen was discovered is also one son's mistress and the other's secretary. Although the novel develops more slowly, seems less a prismatic series of interconnecting mirrors, *The Middle Age of Mrs. Eliot* is structured almost as carefully and consciously as is *Anglo-Saxon Attitudes.* After her husband has been killed and she rebels against being patronized by people in their former social set, Meg Eliot turns to the three lonely old friends, widowed or divorced, whom she had formerly patronized. In three parellel sections, Wilson demonstrates different versions of the follies of manipulation and dominance before leaving Meg to return to health at the nursery that cannot be her permanent home.

The Old Men at the Zoo is a fable, most of *Late Call* a chronological account distorted and dictated by Sylvia's expanding consciousness, and *No Laughing Matter* over fifty years of British middle-class history narrated from six alternating points of view interspersed with episodes of "The Game" and domestic dramas in play form. The episodes of "the Game" and the inserted playlets are structural devices to provide an exterior view of the Matthews family, underline the already determined role that each of the characters works out, which no one of the characters can really see himself. Yet all the heaviness of structure does not, except perhaps in *The Old Men at the Zoo,* block off the sense of life and reality in Wilson's novels. The structures provide coherence and order, but they also, when combined with all the details of characterization, history and analysis, become a device against which the complex and amorphous verisimilitude of experience can be seen. The structures illuminate the life they play against. Sometimes, Wilson even plays with the structures explicitly to demonstrate directly that the structure is not intended to channelize all experience or subsume it to an abstraction. In a playlet that takes place in 1925 in *No Laughing Matter,* Regan, the Cockney cook, supports her ideas by flourishing a copy of Bernard Shaw's *The Intelligent Woman's Guide to Socialism.* Quentin grabs the book, looks up the title page, and points out that Shaw's book was not published until 1928, adding "that's not for three years yet," to which his brother Marcus replies, "it's just one of those tedious Shavian jokes." Such mockery of the structure further demonstrates that structure alone cannot support fully the range and density of the novel itself.

In *The Wild Garden,* Wilson claims that both "fantasy" and "realism" are important for his novels, and that without a "fusion" of these two elements he could not produce a novel. The "fantasy," the artist's arrangement, the design visible in the conscious structuring of experience and symbolizing of issues, is necessary in order to convey the "realism," the sense of life, to the reader. Wilson makes the constant assumption (and it is only an assumption, for he does not demonstrate its metaphysical truth) that there is a "real" world outside the self, a tangible, although perhaps not completely definable, reality which man can know and about which he can say something. And, given the methods of fiction, that "real" world can be best conveyed in an imaginative reconstruction that is not concerned with the minute duplication of probability at every given point. "Realism" and "fantasy" thus fuse, the latter, the artifice, granting a greater measure of imaginative and emotional credibility to the former. Wilson has also written that he frequently multiplies plots and subplots, adds characters and connects them with his major ones, in order to convey a greater sense of expanding life. He feels that the thematic novel, "even at its most excellent, say in *Silas Marner* or *L'Étranger*," lacks sufficient life, the capability to disseminate "the moral proposition so completely in a mass of living experience that it is never directly sensed as you read but only apprehended at the end as a result of the life you have shared in the book." In his early novels, in order to create in the reader this sense of diverse and expanding life, Wilson typically added bizarre characters from the various London underworlds, spivs, procurers, psychotic criminals, and tied them to his major characters through the plot. In more recent novels, like *Late Call* and *No Laughing Matter,* the density of plot and subplot is less bizarre and contrived, the sense created of middle-class life is copious and all the more convincing because it is achieved less melodramatically.

Wilson's structural forms, like his use of politics and art, never completely express the novel, never solidify or become sufficiently a symbol for the universal, never permit categorization of the novel as thematic. Rather, the structure is exploratory, codifies some things within the novel and omits others, presents a form of partial definition through which and against which man, in all his complexity, can be seen. The form works both with and against reality, never (except in *The Old Men at the Zoo*) hardens in the set of its own premises. Literary form invariably establishes implications about an author's attitude toward his fictional world: a novel studded with flashbacks assumes the importance of the past for present circumstances and a fable implies the cohesive and applicable truth of the morality that directs it. Wilson's structural forms, however, clearly discernible as they are, work for only part of a novel, double back on themselves, or are mixed with and against other forms and techniques.

Wilson's forms are incomplete, as if no structural device, no analogue, can convey all that needs to be said about contemporary man. The incomplete form, the open form, the device that cannot serve as a full analogue for all the experience presented within the novel, leaves the reader with an increased compassion for all man's partial efforts, with partial knowledge in a "real" world that can, as the incomplete structures suggest, be only partially assimilated or understood. The incomplete or the undercut structure leaves the reader room for compassion for man who is himself less complete, less defined, less the triumphantly understanding sensibility, than he would wish and try to be. In the novels of both Hardy and Forster, the apparent forms and structures were destroyed to reveal a sense of compassion and an expanding sense of life that could not be delineated fully in terms of the form. Form and the life in the novel in a sense worked against each other. Wilson, however, plays form or structure against reality far more consciously and ironically than did either Hardy or Forster. Hardy, for example, may have intended to write the complete and thematic novel, but accidentally revealed a far wider and less easily defined conception of man; Wilson purposely undercuts or leaves incomplete the forms he establishes to reveal his sympathy for human energy and multiplicity. Structural form, for Wilson, is the starting point, the set of coherent terms in which the exploration of human behavior begins; form is not, for Wilson, the analogue that summarizes, wraps up neatly, assumes the entire meaning of the fiction. Form suggests rather than encloses the experience Wilson presents.

Wilson's use of the incomplete form, like the constant mode of irony, like the formulations through art or the generalizations about political man, helps to keep the novels open, engaged with and exploring a sense of reality. In focusing on characters who attempt to know themselves, Wilson's interest is constantly psychological and historical, constantly involved with the explorations going on in the open novel. Yet the process of self-knowledge is never complete, never reaches the definitive form in which it can enclose the novel. In this sense, Wilson's later novels, like *Late Call* and especially *No Laughing Matter,* are more effective than his earlier ones, for, in the later novels, examination of self is more a process and an activity, a form that suggests and engages human experience, than an end that reaches firm and desirable conclusions. Bernard Sands's discovery of "evil" within himself is psychologically too pat and simplified, requires the posthumous irony that protects against simplicity to avoid a sentimental conclusion. In contrast, the irony of the last two novels is richer and more complicated. The human search for self-knowledge engages the characters in the midst of the recognition that one can never completely know himself. This more fundamental, more completely determined, irony increases both the psychological sophistication and the comprehensive compassion in Wilson's later novels, makes them more searching and more humane. Then, too, the early novels, like *Hemlock and After* and *Anglo-Saxon Attitudes,* needed to depict a large range of characters outside the middle classes in order to support their vast social inclusiveness, yet in depicting spivs and criminals relegated them to the bizarre and over-simplified. Wilson's more recent novels, less melodramatically, stay within the realm of the reasonably humane and self-conscious British middle classes, not because the middle classes are the whole world or the only classes of value, but, rather, because through history and tradition, they are people who engage in and abide by the kind of self-examination Wilson depicts. As Wilson has sounded the middle classes more profoundly and more psychologically, the need to obtain inclusiveness through bizarre outsiders, the need to add unconvincing melodrama, has vanished. The open novel has less need for universality than does the enclosed fable. Rather, the open novel gains its force and credibility through a presentation of some part of human experience with intensity, depth, and credibility, recognizing in its very openness the difficulties involved in trying to present human experience as if it were complete or completely knowable.

XIV

SAUL BELLOW

TYPICALLY, the protagonist in American fiction has been, at least potentially, the representative American hero, the man who could symbolize the strength and insight of the New World. He might, in the course of the novel, be defeated by his world or by himself or by a combination of the two, but he began, in youth, strength, and freshness, with heroic capacity, with extraordinary possibilities. Even Theodore Dreiser's doomed protagonists began as potential heroes and were corrupted and defeated by American life; and most of the heroes of the proletarian novels of the 1930's, the central characters of writers like Steinbeck and Farrell, were similarly incipiently special people limited and contorted by circumstance. But during the 1940's the concept began to change: the representative American's capacity for heroism, even his capacity for being representative began to diminish. In an increasingly fragmented world, in a society without a central tradition or a central meaning, no one could convincingly represent special heroism in the American experience. One of the first non-special protagonists, the first a-hero (anti-hero is a term too deliberately diabolic for Bellow's characters) alienated from the society around him in a form that has come to characterize so much fiction of the past two decades, was the principal character of Saul Bellow's first novel, *Dangling Man* (1944).

Joseph, never given a last name in the novel, is the estranged or alienated man, writing his thoughts, feelings, opinions, and experiences in his journal over a four month period before entering the Army during World War II. Joseph has wife, father, brother, niece, but, although he sees them occasionally, he has little connection with his family and ignores the advice they constantly offer him. At one point, he even spanks his fifteen-year-old niece when she is bratty and arrogant, openly violating the family's ethos of close feeling and indulgence. Joseph and his wife barely talk, and she berates him for his indifference. He has, in the months just past, had a mistress, but he has abandoned her because "the strain of living in both camps was too much." He seldom sees his old friends, frequently quotes injunctions from his schooldays that he finds no longer applicable, and reports on acquaintances whose families break up completely because of the war, as if he is just setting down facts. He never praises or blames, never judges. When he did work he was a clerk in a travel agency, estranged from the productive American economy, and existing on the desire to get away from it all; but, even here, his occupation lacked decision and purpose, for Joseph had no particular interest in travel and only used his time at the agency to acquire the mistress he soon abandoned.

As a Jew, Joseph is apart from the central emotional and theological Christianity implicit in the American tradition. At the same time, he is also apart from his Jewishness, accepting it without believing in it, finding no particular value or identity in terms of his accidentally Jewish tradition. He is, unlike many of Bellow's later protagonists, more the man estranged from all religious or sociological traditions than an alien from a tradition specifically labelled as central. Most of the world around him, from Joseph's point of view, seems to express a kind of assurance that Joseph cannot share. Like the poor tailor who is convinced that Hoover's plan for the war-economy in 1942 must be brilliant because the latter had once been elected President, most people live by beliefs and convictions that Joseph finds ridiculous and irrelevant.

His behavior, too, departs from the commonly accepted model of the rational, self-contained, and dignified young man. He directly asks his father-in-law how the latter had been able to stand a nagging, self-pitying wife for so many years. Originally calm and even-tempered, Joseph, increasingly through the novel, becomes angry over trivial issues. His conscious rejection of the conventional American standards for masculine behavior is apparent in the very first entry in his journal:

But to keep a journal nowadays is considered a kind of self-indulgence, a weakness, and in poor taste. For this is an era of hardboiled-dom. Today, the code of the athlete, of the tough boy—an American inheritance, I believe, from the English gentleman—that curious mixture of striving, asceticism, and rigor, the origins of which some trace back to Alexander the Great—is stronger than ever. Do you have feelings? There are correct and incorrect ways of indicating them. Do you have an inner life? It is nobody's business but your own. Do you have emotions? Strangle them. To a degree, everyone obeys this code. And it does admit of a limited kind of candor, a closemouthed straightforwardness. But on the truest candor, it has an inhibitory effect. Most serious matters are closed to the hardboiled.

Bellow, thus, at the beginning of the novel, specifically attacks the Hemingway code, rejects the American cliché of the tough hero standing up to destiny. Knowing what he rejects without having worked out any coherent alternative, Joseph dangles, just as he dangles between the job he quit seven months earlier when he thought induction was imminent and the Army which will not take him for another four months.

In his reaction against the sordid and self-assured urban world around him, against the thief in the room next door who won't close the bathroom door, and against the faith in money and position expressed by his brother, Joseph becomes increasingly confined within himself. But he is not at all sure what that self is. At times, in narrating his own experience, Joseph slips into referring to himself in the third person, catching himself just when it seems as if the subject is someone completely different. He wonders whether he has a devil inside him, a parasitic visitant. Toward the end of the novel, he engages in dialogues with himself about human nature, conscience, and the role of reason; the dialogues are between Joseph and the "spirit of Alternatives" or between Joseph and "You who are also right." Joseph never resolves, never even fully defines, his dualism. Rather, he accepts his limitations, recognizes that there is little he can do and that "Personal choice does not count for much

these days." Although the greatest "freedom" for the human personality is the ostensible object for all his introspection, he happily accepts his draft call and the diminution of freedom that it
entails:

I am no longer to be held accountable for myself; I am grateful for
that. I am in other hands, relieved of self-determination, freedom
canceled.
>   Hurray for regular hours!
>   And for the supervision of the spirit!
>   Long live regimentation!

The environment, the war, and Joseph's own dilemmas cause
him to welcome a function, an activity, that he has not made
himself. He will, in the Army in World War II, presumably be
able to relate to others because they will be given meaning and
definition by a corporate force stronger than their own identities.

The idea that war, apart from the presumed justice of
either side, provides the only function available for the individual man, the only discipline that can give form to the perplex-
ingly amorphous human identity, was not represented in American fiction in World War II before *Dangling Man*. Yet the idea
was current in Western Europe, apparent in the memoirs and
essays of both the Oxford flier Richard Hilary and the heroic
pilot of the French resistance forces, Antoine de Saint-Exupéry.
Bellow's intellectual connections, as always, are more European
than specifically American. Yet the sense, in *Dangling Man,* that
war provides a desirable or a meaningful function for rootless
man does not mean that a choice between two sides cannot be
made. In several long passages, Joseph realizes that if "full choice
were possible," he would take our side, the side of the Allies,
rather than that of the Nazis. Yet "full choice" is never possible,
for the accidents of birth, nationality, and origin determine a
large proportion of human possibility and, in Bellow's terms,
generally "Alternatives, and particularly desirable alternatives,
grow only on imaginary trees." This recognition insures the
realization that Joseph's willingness to join the Army cannot be
interpreted as narrow patriotism or enlistment in the service of
some brave new cause or ideal. The war provides a temporary

and limited definition for the chaotic and uncertain man lucky enough to be placed on the side that is less brutal and less inhumane. Joseph knows that this definition, this function, can be permanent only if he is killed in the war; otherwise, the same problems of individual identity and corporate choice will emerge again, in new forms dictated by forces stronger than the individual, after the war is over. Joseph both accepts his role in the war and knows that "in no *essential* way is it crucial." He thus becomes, in American terms, the first genuinely existential a-hero in fiction.

Bellow's existentialism in *Dangling Man,* like that of many of the members of the French resistance (that represented in Camus' *La Peste,* for example), was first defined through terms particularly relevant to World War II. The definition revolved around the balance between essential chaos or nothingness and existentially limited choice for limited aims. In Bellow's next novel, *The Victim* (1947), contemporary existential man is given a more extensive and more psychological definition. The principal character, Asa Leventhal, an editor on a trade paper in New York, is a sensitive and responsive man, sincerely concerned with others and able to sympathize with them. Like Joseph in *Dangling Man,* Leventhal does not always control his emotions: he once was sufficiently angry at his wife to knock her down; he frequently blew up at interviewers when he was unsuccessfully trying to get a job; during the course of the novel, both his anger and a sense of suffering that verges on self-pity are frequently manifest. Unlike Joseph, however, Leventhal cannot be described as simply alienated or estranged. A Jew who sometimes suffers from anti-Semitic remarks and prejudice, Leventhal feels close ties to his family, his friends, and his work. He remembers his harsh and bitter father fondly, sometimes quoting the old man's satirical maxims, but he recoils from his father's scorn of non-Jews and people who work with their hands as well as from the old storekeeper's crude philosophy that it doesn't matter what people call him as long as he gets the money. Asa Leventhal is both entangled with others and separate from them, a kind of Leopold Bloom who sympathizes, speculates, can easily seem a fool, and is frequently intensely involved in his own emotions.

[309

During the few weeks in which the events of the novel take place, Leventhal is at his most lonely, emotional, vulnerable point, for his wife, whom he loves, who is his single permanent and significant connection to another, is away helping her recently widowed mother move from Baltimore to Charleston. Left to himself, Leventhal often misjudges people and situations. He assumes that his sister-in-law, Elena, and her mother, an old Italian woman who had originally opposed her daughter's marriage to a Jew, blame him for his young nephew's death. Yet, after his absent brother returns for the funeral, Leventhal discovers that his perceptions had been entirely wrong. Both Elena and her mother were more frightened than hostile, more concerned with their own grief than with representing sociologically definable attitudes. In reference to the central issue of the novel—his relationship with Kirby Allbee, the New England Protestant down on his luck who, at this time of lonely intensity, attaches himself parasitically to Leventhal—Leventhal runs around seeking advice from his friends. He, however, misinterprets his friend Harkavy's advice and later talks as if Harkavy could automatically follow all the changes in knowledge and emotion that have taken place in Leventhal himself.

Often incoherent in his continual efforts to explain himself, Leventhal misperceives how others regard him and assumes that his honesty and his depth of feeling will be understood and applauded by anyone who is not a bigot. Excessively conscious of his Jewishness, Leventhal sometimes exhibits a mild form of paranoia: he interprets a quick anti-Semitic sneer from his boss as proof that his boss has no regard for him at all, yet, at the end of the novel, Leventhal realizes that his boss has valued his work highly and would have offered a substantial raise to keep him; even Harkavy accuses him of "ghetto psychology" after a discussion of Disraeli, Bismarck, and nineteenth-century politics. Allbee is often consciously and viciously anti-Semitic. Leventhal realizes, resents, and reacts to this. At the same time, in Bellow's terms, Leventhal often judges Allbee too harshly, is militantly puritanical about Allbee's love for drink and smugly assured about the reasons for Allbee's lack of success. One of Allbee's tirades against Leventhal carries something of the author's point of view:

It doesn't enter your mind, does it,—that a man might not be able
to help being hammered down? . . . . No, if a man is down, a man
like me, it's his fault. If he suffers, he's being punished. There's no
evil in life itself. . . . It's a Jewish point of view. You'll find it all
over the Bible. God doesn't make mistakes. He's the department of
weights and measures. . . . But I'll tell you something. We do get
it in the neck for nothing and suffer for nothing, and there's no
denying that evil is as real as sunshine.

Leventhal sometimes acts as if he is a "department of weights
and measures," but his instruments are seldom accurate or relevant. Having scored this point, Allbee goes on to make his tirade
more bitter, personally recriminatory, and crudely anti-Semitic.
Leventhal, ignoring the viciousness, answers only generally:

I don't see how you can talk that way. That's just talk. Millions of
us have been killed. What about that?

This time, Allbee has no reply, as if each is speaking primarily
out of himself with no central connection to what the other has
said.

Yet Bellow does not make this episode a model for contemporary failure to communicate, for, at other times, Allbee and
Leventhal understand one another extremely well, feel an
extraordinary closeness and, from Leventhal's point of view, an
irrational and distressing sympathy. *The Victim* depicts a wide
range in the amount of communication possible between two
human beings. At one extreme, Leventhal and his wife understand each other fully and have unqualified confidence in one
another. At the other extreme, a dignified old man, aptly named
Schlossberg, gives a long speech on the importance of human
dignity to six or seven others sitting around a table. Leventhal is
impressed, yet the faith in human dignity runs counter to his
experience and his concerns. He never refutes the speech, either
to himself or to others, and Schlossberg doesn't remember him
the next time they meet. The testimony to human dignity, like
Schlossberg himself, is just there, an attitude, a point of view, a
part of life extrinsic to the central concerns of the novel. Most of
the time, however, communication is partial, half-understood
and half-misinterpreted. In an intense form, this partial understanding characterizes the relationship between Allbee and

Leventhal. In a less intense form, Leventhal and his brother illustrate the same kind of partial understanding, an ambivalence and lack of assurance about each other apparent in the various drafts of a letter Leventhal thinks of sending his brother when the child is ill—a use of letters as a means of examining characters and relationships that anticipates something of the letters in *Herzog*. Generalizations about vast abstractions like "alienation" or the "lack of communication" cannot explain the density of Leventhal's experience or the intensity of his suffering.

The center of the novel is in the attachment between Allbee and Leventhal. Years before when Leventhal had been jobless, Allbee, whom Leventhal had known slightly, had arranged an interview for Leventhal with his boss. Leventhal had blown up at the boss, a teasing and tyrannical man, botching the interview completely; shortly after, Allbee had been fired. At the beginning of the novel, Allbee, now jobless, almost destitute, often drunk, his wife dead, comes to Leventhal charging him with the responsibility for his, Allbee's, currently pitiable state. At first, Leventhal refuses to acknowledge any responsibility whatever, but he then begins to feel something of himself in Allbee: he has, in the past, known poverty and near hopelessness; he also recognizes that Allbee is one of those who "can see to the bottom of your soul" and he feels, at times, an almost physical intimacy with him "seeing with microscopic fineness the lines in his skin, and the smallest of his hairs, and breathing in his odor." Allbee is Leventhal's double, his *alter ego*, the former's destitution balancing the latter's economic good fortune, the dead wife balancing the living one, the drunken rebellion from a puritan tradition balancing the puritanical need to rise in class by keeping one's wits, aggressive selfishness balancing the emotional and self-pitying concern, the decadent New Englander, descendant of ministers, and conscious anti-Semite balancing the son of immigrant Eastern European Jews as the doubleness extends to sociological commentary about contemporary America. The theme of the double gives the novel a Kafkaesque quality, as Joseph in *Dangling Man*, in his cryptic response to the sordid and meaningless life around him, often sounds something like a Kafka hero. Yet, in *The Victim*, the theme of the double is less complete, less inexorable, than it is in Kafka's fiction, for Leventhal and Allbee eventually separate and resume separate identities; the doubleness, the existence of its antithesis in the midst of the personality, is a momentary intensity, a psychological revelation rather than the expression of man's permanent condition.

Once Leventhal realizes that Allbee's charge may not be as ridiculous as it at first appears, once he recognizes his own psychological connection with his antithesis, Leventhal runs around trying to discover the truth. He asks the opinion of Williston, a kind of Anglo-Saxon God-figure, a man who was both close to Allbee and had helped Leventhal get his present job. Williston feels that Leventhal was partly responsible and needs to make amends. This only increases Leventhal's anxiety and guilt, for he knows no way in which he can help Allbee without endangering his own carefully nurtured security; despite his recognition of his double, he fights hard to preserve his separateness. Williston, the God, the "benefactor," does not, however, offer any specific advice; he offers only a cryptic concern that works on Leventhal's guilt. Only when Leventhal is able to achieve independence from Williston, by returning the ten dollars Williston had given him to relay to Allbee, is he psychologically able to sever himself from his persecuting double. Only when belief in God disappears or no longer causes guilt can man be free from himself—or, on another level in the novel, only when the immigrant no longer sees the American Establishment as God-like can he stop feeling guilty for his own hard-earned success.

Throughout the major portion of the novel, Leventhal and Allbee persecute and victimize each other and themselves. Allbee persecutes Leventhal by attaching himself to him, moving in with him, even, finally, trying to kill him in, as Leventhal says, "a kind of suicide pact without getting my permission first." Yet part of what persecutes Leventhal is his own vulnerability, his sensitivity and guilt. As he explains when Harkavy claims he has been sold "a bill of goods" in allowing Allbee to live with him, "I must have wanted to buy." Allbee is also a victim of society, of the change that no longer brings security to the sons of New England ministers, of a harshly commercial world, initially of Leventhal's energy and temper. But Allbee, by excessive drinking and vicious recrimination, has helped to cause his own decline.

In Bellow's view, we all, both personally and sociologically, victimize each other, prey on each other as well as on ourselves. But the victimization, the psychological dependence on our own antitheses or doubles, on our compulsive opposites, is never total or complete. We can live in terms of our simple separateness, our trivial illusions, once we abandon a compulsive dedication to the profoundly true but self-defeating antitheses within us. We need to abandon God, both the God of the exterior Establishment and the God of the psyche, in order to live in terms of the limited and partial identities which allow us a limited freedom and choice.

At the very end of the novel, after several years have passed, Allbee and Leventhal meet again at a theater, but without mutual identity or searing intensity. Both have survived. Allbee is reasonably successful in a "middle-sized job," content to be a "passenger" on the train instead of the "conductor" he had always expected to be, but decidedly on the train, on the continuum of life. Leventhal, too, is more comfortable, with his wife back and a better job. His wife is pregnant, and Leventhal will soon become the specific father he has always wanted to be instead of the universally anxious and generalized substitute father he had formerly played at being. Both Leventhal and Allbee accept their limitations, having escaped the destructive intensity of the duality at the center of personality and at the center of society, having surfaced to the more circumscribed realm in which individual choice and freedom, although partial, have meaning. Both have accepted what existence is.

The definition of existential man, primarily and intensely psychological in *The Victim,* is given a more sociological meaning and density in Bellow's next novel, *The Adventures of Augie March* (1953). In wandering over America, in addition to making excursions to Mexico and to Europe for about twenty years, and in happily accepting whatever experience offers, Augie March, the protagonist, is contrasted with his brother Simon. Simon, who begins with "schoolboy notions of honor" derived from *Tom Brown's Schooldays,* invariably makes rules for his own conduct and prescriptions for his own success. He excels at school, marries money, and works hard in the standard

American pattern, but his efforts to rise in the jungle of American economic life dehumanize him: he is sometimes callous to Augie and brutal to the poor men he works among; he superficially accepts his loveless bargain of a marriage, while underneath he berates and punishes himself bitterly. Unlike Augie, Simon cannot lie directly. Even when they are children, the younger Augie is given the job of getting free glasses for their mother from the state dispensary, for he is more skillful at lying about their income. As in *The Victim,* the "truth" is often intense, bitter, self-defeating, a pair of insoluble alternatives that grind man between them; the lie, a more exterior simplification, a pose, allows man to survive. In addition, in his success, his intensity, and his ruling out of his own human impulses, Simon represents something of the "truth" of man in the standard American social perspective. Augie, in contrast, is generous, and forgiving, always able to sympathize with people, unconcerned with material success, and full of love for Simon no matter what the latter has done. Easily dominated by momentary emotions, Augie retains his humanity because he never defines it consistently or attempts to extract and live by its essence.

In the long, comic, episodic novel, Augie is a picaresque figure who observes and reports, registers and reacts, but does not impose himself upon the world. Although responsive and sympathetic, with a kind of natural goodness like that of Tom Jones, Augie is far from heroic, for he steals books and money, abandons any intense relationship, and evades any possible crucial struggle. Like the conventional picaresque protagonist, Augie is often treated comically, made to look ridiculous. He is frequently dressed by someone else, outfitted for the particular purpose or definition that someone else is making for him: Simon dresses him in natty double-breasted suits and silver-gray ties when attempting to make him a Chicago junkyard tycoon, and Thea outfits him as an Abercrombie and Fitch sportsman when she takes him to Mexico to hunt iguana with an eagle. Augie, temporarily dominated by Thea during their affair, has no desire to hunt iguana, but when the eagle, like Augie, proves a coward and is ignored by Thea, the man is able to turn around and manifest genuine sympathy for the bird. At times like this, his sentimentality is made ridiculous, but it is also, ironically, an indication of his value, of the diffuse and unsystematized feeling that allows him to be responsive to everything he sees.

Augie is constantly susceptible to flattery and carried by events and mechanisms already in motion. When he is leaving Thea to drive off with another woman, he says that he cannot stop, although he thinks he might like to, because the car he is driving has already started. Always in motion and dragged off by others to transport fugitives or agitate for strikes or escort an older woman at a Michigan lake resort, Augie evades the problem of coming to terms with himself or what he wants. He happily cultivates the pose of his own innocence. Yet, Augie never allows his gentle willingness to become subservience, never fully succumbs to any of the people who are anxious to adopt him and make him a duplicate of themselves. Whenever a strong force threatens to absorb him completely, Augie runs off, preserving his own sentimental and undifferentiated human sympathy. As Einhorn, a crippled entrepreneur in the Chicago slums who both employs and helps Augie, tells him, "You've got *opposition* in you. You don't slide through everything. You just make it look so."

Although he recognizes himself only in negative terms, only in terms of the definitions others impose, Augie realizes the value, almost the inverse triumph, of his refusal to embrace for any length of time any of the commitments offered. He knows that his resilience enables him to survive, that his flexibility prevents his being consumed by the limitation of the single idea in a world of many ideas. At the very end of the novel, Augie can recognize, even extend beyond himself, something of his own value.

The most intensely positive person, the one most sure of himself and his panacea, is, in Bellow's terms, the most evil. Augie encounters this fact in the form of Basteshaw, the man with whom he shares a raft when the ship on which both have been crew members is torpedoed during World War II. Basteshaw, originally a biochemist who had been kicked out of six universities, experiments with cells, with the origins of life, and he wants Augie to help him change human chemistry and create "a new brotherhood of man." When Augie, who has already

seen that Basteshaw's motives are pure hate, refuses to help and
sanely tries to get them rescued, Basteshaw attempts to kill him.
Yet Augie never entirely retreats, is always willing to listen to the
next single-minded fanatic, or to become attracted to someone
else who has plans for him:

> To tell the truth, I'm good and tired of all these big personalities,
> destiny molders, and heavy-water brains, Machiavellis and wizard
> evildoers, big-wheels and imposers-upon, absolutists. After Baste-
> shaw clobbered me I took an oath of unsusceptibility. But this oath
> is probably a mice-and-man matter, for here the specter of one of
> this breed was over me. Brother! You never are through, you just
> think you are!

Experience, in the picaresque, is repetitive, without a significant
or necessary pattern, and Augie learns what is substantially the
same lesson numerous times. Similarly, characters from his past
keep turning up in unlikely places: Jimmy Klein; Johnny
Gorman, a thief; Thea, whom he had known at the Michigan
resort, who tracks him to Chicago years later and carries him off
to Mexico. A purely comic character, never important in any
single episode, who surfaces periodically throughout the novel, is
the dedicated Sylvester. Son of the owner of a slum Chicago
movie house which later becomes a wallpaper and paint shop,
Sylvester appears successively as aspiring scientist, flunked-out
engineer, New York subway worker, and one of Trotsky's body-
guards in Mexico. Always an intense believer in what he is doing
at the moment, Sylvester spots the novel with instances of imperceptive and ludicrous certainty.

Because the novel is so long, so episodic, so repetitious, so
deliberately not profound about human psychology, a number
of recent critics have found *The Adventures of Augie March*
Bellow's least satisfactory novel. But the novel fits Bellow's concept of wandering, existential man finding no purpose or specific
direction in life but managing to survive through his very resilience. The life of this novel is not in any coherent message or in
any obscurely brilliant analysis, but rather in the elaborate details of Augie's adventures themselves. As he finds no specific
direction and embraces the variety of human experience, so the
novel itself extends to depict all aspects (or at least the fictional
simulacrum of all aspects) of that experience. The elaborate de-

tail, the density of social and historical description, both presents the plethora of issues and choices confronting existential
man, and provides the principal interest in the novel.

Bellow, here, is writing history, the record of what man
has done and thought, rather than philosophy, the meaning or
direction or purpose of human activity. And history, which
chronicles or records but does not guide or judge, is the appropriate mode for the happy or surviving side of the existential
creature, the side not suffused with anguish for the certainty it
does not have. Bellow fills the novel with accurate social description, a sharp sense of many times and places over a period of
twenty years, documentary-like lists of books, radio programs,
and ideas, and literary, historical, and classical allusions. The
copious detail of the book conveys a sense of the excitement and
interest possible for the man who cannot believe in direction or
purpose, for whom specific purpose is restrictive and destructive.

The density of social and historical description is matched
by the density and humanity of the relationships in which Augie
is involved. Bellow entangles Augie with a wide variety of
women. With some, like the matronly Mrs. Renling, who tells
the young Augie so many tales concerning the horrors of lust
that she arouses an excitement of which neither is conscious, and
the girl Mimi, almost a parody of the Hemingway ideal of the
compliant mistress, whom Augie helps when her affair with
someone else requires that she get an abortion, Augie seems very
much the good-natured innocent. As the novel moves, Augie becomes wiser. He recognizes how Lucy Magnus uses sex as a tease
in order to strike a marriage bargain. He understands Thea's
fierce idealism and capacity for intense emotion, but he cannot
sustain his casual existence alongside her compelling fascination
with eagles and snakes. He values the uncomplicated affair with
Sophia, the chambermaid who intends to have her fling with
Augie before settling down to marriage with "a calm, responsible-
looking gink." He finally marries Stella, a girl very much like
himself, who lies and who notices that they both "are the kind
of people other people are always trying to fit into their schemes."
They are able to love because they do not try to make love into
something else, into "truth," or God, or business success. And
the love, the relationship, the continuing existence of a connec-

tion between two people, is about as far from the chaos of the self as the human being can get in the world of this novel. Augie remains vital because he is always in love, always responsive to human relationship.

The Adventures of Augie March, despite the density of its description, presents only one side of existential man, the accidentally adaptable, amorphous, "larky" quality of Augie. Its complement, the other and less palatable side of the existential protagonist, is apparent in Tommy Wilhelm, the central character in Bellow's next novel, *Seize the Day* (1956). Like Augie, Tommy has no sense of purpose or direction, is vulnerable to any influence that comes along, and is honest enough with himself to recognize what lies he has told to others. Tommy, in his midforties, has been an unsuccessful actor, salesman, and manipulator, and, during the novel, is an unsuccessful speculator trying to earn on the market in lard and grain a little of the money he desperately needs. He has never been rationally decisive; having wisely chosen not to go to Hollywood, not to marry, not to speculate, has then impulsively done all of these. Tommy, again like Augie, uses clothes to act a part, but his never fit very well: the pants are baggy or the coat collar turns up. Tommy is also less lucky than Augie, more trapped and perplexed by all the dilemmas of contemporary urban living he cannot solve. Unfortunately, and for Bellow this is a matter of chance or fortune, Tommy is not very bright. He doesn't know the difference between "moral" and "morale"; he has complete faith that anyone written about in *Fortune Magazine* must be genuine, and that every good American worships the skill required for scientific invention; frequently duped, he finally acknowledges that he is "a sucker for people who talk about the deeper things of life." Much less happy than Augie, he endlessly recounts his own sufferings to himself and to others, frequently lapses into selfpity. His tremendous self-pity, his concentration on his own sufferings, cuts him off from relationships with any of the people around him. He is separated from his wife, sees his two sons only to take them to occasional baseball games, has been abandoned by his mistress ostensibly because his wife would not divorce him so that he could marry the mistress, and is condescended to and toyed with by his father.

The latter relationship is the most thoroughly depicted and the most important in the novel. Dr. Adler (Tommy had changed his name in his search for an identity in Hollywood) is a hard and respectable old man, appalled by Tommy's self-pity, disappointed that his son has no college education, and full of rules for conduct that Tommy cannot follow. In public the father sometimes brags falsely about his son's earning power as a salesman, but in private he rejects all Tommy's pitiable claims on his sympathy or his pocket. Both physically and metaphorically, Dr. Adler is "clean," an old man who has a steam bath daily and rigorously follows the rules by means of which he worked himself up from the Brooklyn slums to a prosperous medical career. Tommy, who has internalized his father's values and scorns people who don't take baths, can never forgive himself, as his father can never forgive him, for being a "slob," for living in messy clothes in a messy room and stubbing out his cigaret butts in his pockets, for failing to find or follow a set of rules that would carry him successfully through life. Tommy is certainly unattractive and unpleasant, but, in Bellow's terms, the old man, the rigid dogmatist who rejects his own son, is even more culpable. When he finally refuses to do anything to help his son, whom he always calls by his boyhood name of Wilky, Dr. Adler cries out:

"You want to make yourself into my cross. But I am not going to pick up a cross. I'll see you dead, Wilky, by Christ, before I let you do that to me."

Dr. Adler, despite all his education and all his formulae, does not recognize his own false dramatization, his own phoniness, has less self-awareness than does his son.

Tommy is also involved with Dr. Tamkin, the restless charlatan who claims to be a psychologist and who persuades Tommy to invest his last seven hundred dollars in the commodities market. Tamkin, a parasite on others, is full of definitions, of certainties, always spuriously diagnosing the psychological ailments of everyone around. False, invulnerable, and successful, Tamkin tries to teach his own route through the modern morass to Tommy:

"The spiritual compensation is what I look for. Bringing people into the here-and-now. The real universe. That's the present moment. The past is no good to us. The future is full of anxiety. Only the present is real—the here-and-now. Seize the day."

Tommy is not, however, an apt pupil, for he is too committed to his own past, to the memory of his long-dead mother and to half-forgotten poems from his courtship, as well as too anxious about the future of his sons ever to "seize the day." History and human possibility are too much a part of some men ever to permit them to operate parasitically upon the given moment, and history is a part of human vulnerability, human sensitivity. Unable to stand independently, and equally unable to stand on "Tamkin's back," for the "Dr." cheats him financially and then disappears, Tommy frenetically hunts for Tamkin along crowded upper Broadway. Caught in a human mass outside a funeral home, Tommy is pushed into the line to see the body of the recently dead. In a catharsis of self-pity, in this very last scene in the novel, he weeps for the corpse he never knew, weeps so heavily and deeply that others assume he must be the dead man's "cousin from New Orleans," or even his brother, which, of course, symbolically, he is.

The form of the single, crystallized day on which all the events of the novel take place, the day that incorporates all the past behind it, is appropriate to Tommy's intense anguish, just as the wandering aimless years of the picaresque were appropriate to Augie's adventures. Although *Seize the Day* is given coherence by the day's unity, the day is not the only or even the necessarily final summation of Tommy's experience. As in *The Victim,* the period of the novel is the period of the most intense and revealing anguish, but not necessarily of the whole of life. Tommy blandly expresses this near the end in a phone conversation with his wife: "This has been one of those days." The setting, too, the intense glare and bright confusion of New York on a warm June day, contributes to Tommy's anguish. All the elements of the novel focus primarily on the theme of the protagonist's suffering, its origins and its intensity; outside of a few highly effective descriptive passages concerning New York the book has little of the sociological density of *The Adventures of Augie March.* The two works, with all their differences, complement each other, present both sides of existential and purposeless man, both victim and victimizer. Bellow's point of view is consistently one of compassion, of pleasure at watching the happy Augies who roll through life without restricting definitions, and of sympathy for the anguished Tommies who never find the definitions they seek with such intensity. Both men, all the existential protagonists, are forced into limitations, forced to do without a sense of meaning or purpose, denied the comfort or the delusion of a God. The very definition of existential man implies compassion, for the very concept of man presented assumes the impossibility of essential truths, of guidelines or formulae, assumes the difficulties and perplexities in just managing survival.

Both Bellow's next two novels, *Henderson the Rain King* (1959) and *Herzog* (1964), attempt to go beyond a definition of existential man, attempt to work out what choices within a framework of limited choice might be meaningful, to examine whether man can consciously load his luck a little bit. In these novels, with their reliance on the choices man does make and the triumphs, no matter how limited, man can achieve, an attitude of compassion is in danger of sliding into sentimentality. Self-pity can, in fiction, be convincing when it is, as in *Seize the Day*, part of a definition; when it becomes tangled with a solution, no matter how tentative, self-pity like sentimentality can seriously damage a novel. These next two novels confront directly the twin problems of what existential man is to do, to choose, and how compassion for the plight of man can be kept from sentimentality or self-pity in a world in which rational guides, truths, and formulae do not exist.

The solution in *Henderson the Rain King* is comic and fabulistic. Like Bellow's other protagonists, Eugene Henderson is vulnerable and responsive, a man with great vitality and an equally great sense of suffering. His past, as millionaire bum, multiple husband, war hero, and pig farmer, has been aimless and he is still trying to discover who he is. He is also still trying to define himself against his father and earlier ancestors, who included a Secretary of State and ambassadors to England and France, and he attempts to reach his long dead father by playing on the old man's violin. Henderson is the Bellow protagonist comically magnified, abstracted into an exaggeration. Physically huge and almost unbelievably strong, he exaggerates everything; he claims "I am to suffering what Gary is to smoke. One of the world's biggest operations." Alone among Bellow's protagonists he is not a Jew but an Anglo-Saxon Protestant who, in his revolt against his forebears, talks with Jewish locutions and often acts in terms of a comic magnification of Jewish perspectives. In addition to wanting his oldest son to become a doctor, he also thinks, long after he has sons, that he might want to become a doctor himself.

His journey to Africa is magnified, becomes a wandering into the unknown, the center, the crucible of burning heat in the darkest heart of man. Many of the images, the jungle, the incessant heat, the sense of primeval life, the correspondence between the center of Africa and the center of human nature, echo the novels of Conrad. But the echo is comic and the Conradian symbol is satirized:

I thought his wrinkled stare, the stern vein of his forehead, and those complex fields of skin about his eyes must signify (even here, where all Africa was burning like oceans of green oil under the absolute and extended sky) what they would have signified back in New York, namely, deep thought.

Crying, "I want. I want," although he doesn't know what he wants, Henderson goes off to Africa in a comic version of the search for the Holy Grail. As he explains to one of the tribal African kings he encounters, "Your Highness, I am really kind of on a quest."

Africa itself, in *Henderson the Rain King*, is a grandiose comic invention, a satirical compilation of anthropological lore. One tribe is without water because frogs have gotten into their supply and they are convinced they will be cursed if they kill the frogs; another tribe forces each new King to prove himself by killing a lion which has been specially bred because as a cub it consumed the maggot that contained the soul of the dead previous King. Both tribes are led by young men who have studied at American mission schools in the Middle East, speaking English with perfect formality and venerating Henderson's talents and enthusiasm. At a feast in his honor, Henderson is served "mouse paws eaten with a kind of syrup," and engagement customs include a serenade on a "rhinoceros-foot xylophone." At another point, the King of one of the tribes, Itelo, introduces his two aunts to Henderson as women of "Bittahness":

> "Bitter? I don't set up to be a judge of bitter and sweet," I said, "but if this isn't a pair of happy sisters, my mind is completely out of order. Why, they're having one hell of a time."
> "Oh, happy! Yes, happy—bittah. Most bittah," said Itelo. And he began to explain. A Bittah was a person of real substance. You couldn't be any higher or better. A Bittah was not only a woman but a man at the same time. As the elder Willatale had seniority in Bittahness, too. Some of these people in the courtyard were her husbands and others her wives. She had plenty of both.

Henderson himself, in Africa, is also highly comic. Generally wearing just his helmet and his dirty jockey shorts, he wins wrestling matches, moves immovable statues, establishes a ritual to bring needed rain in a dry season, performs all the feats of strength and ingenuity requisite for the knight in quest of the Holy Grail. Not all Henderson's activities, however, are successful, for, in trying to get the frogs out of the water supply, he blasts the cistern apart and loses all the water.

Yet, within all the anthropological comedy, Henderson's quest has a serious side as well. He recognizes that African tribes, like all other people, have silly and life-denying rules, that humanity and creatureness are to be valued above any of the rules established to judge them. He learns to value creatureness more than he did, for he had once refused to let his teen-age daughter keep a baby she had found abandoned in a parked car, and now is able to acknowledge his mistake when he returns from Africa with a foundling lion cub. In addition, through his talks with the Kings, Itelo and Dahfu, he learns to make distinctions within creatureness, sensible choices within the realm of existential humanity. He learns that lions are better than pigs, the creatures he had always been fond of, with cattle somewhere in between. Lions have dignity, posture, and the capacity to love; cows, dignified but aloof, can inspire love but cannot show it, although one of the tribes esteems cows sufficiently to have developed a vocabulary of hundreds of words just to express the ranges of facial expression and behavior among cattle; pigs, lowest on the scale, are "basically career animals," responsive to human control, but without any force of their own beyond perversity. Metaphorically, Henderson has grown from the pig through the cow to the lion, all within the realm of creatureness. He has lost his own perversity, the motive for his establishment of the pig farm in the first place, and has developed, lionlike, the capacity to absorb the blows of experience without having to hit back, the ability to avoid revenge. When Dahfu, his friend, is killed because he cannot kill the lion cub that carries the soul of his predecessor, Henderson takes the lion cub and leaves. Henderson stops the continuum of killing and revenge, the brutal tribal custom, by absorbing the grief for Dahfu within himself. His new, leonine dignity also permits him to feel greater warmth for his current wife, allows him to replace the insistent "I want" with some sense of "she wants," despite the fact that she never cleans the house and often tells lies. In one sense, Henderson's size and emotional capacity had always given him something of a leonine quality. Yet, in Africa, he found the dignity and posture within himself even more surely, found something of the interior grail, the only kind of grail available for contemporary man.

The use of the grail and the consistent animal metaphor designate *Henderson the Rain King* as a fable. The fable is a more stringent form than that in Bellow's other novels, a form that inevitably suggests a direction, a lesson, an intellectual coherence about human experience. Although Henderson does learn something, what he learns seems too small, too trivial, for all the paraphernalia of the form. The grail, in fabulistic form, would seem more convincing were it something more positive, more definite, a touchstone for human experience, more universally relevant and of greater human dimension than the superiority of lions to pigs.

For me, *Henderson the Rain King* is Bellow's least satisfactory novel because the fabulistic form suggests an intellectual and thematic tightness, a coherent structure for human experience, that the novel itself does not fully develop. To develop the implications of the form fully, to give human experience the kind of directed shape that the fable suggests, would be to violate the definition of existential man in the first place, would be to postulate more possible choice for man than the limitations of the existential condition ever warrant. The form itself, used either comically or seriously, and Bellow uses it in both ways, suggests a more grandiose and certain version of experience than he ever offers. In terms of the fable, Africa should represent something unique about the heart or the center of man, should be, as it was for Conrad, an unknown primeval jungle. Bellow's Africa, however, is a joke, highly amusing, but essentially extrinsic to the issues within the novel, representing nothing necessary for Henderson's quest. Henderson might just as easily have discovered Dahfu or Itelo in Danbury, Connecticut.

A fable can be comic, but, if so, the rigor of the form requires that the comedy be carefully shaped, that the satire castigate human foolishness from a clear and positive perspective. A novel might also mock the fable form itself, but Bellow both mocks and uses his form directly. His comedy is different: it mediates and moderates, shows human folly and sympathy for human folly, but offers no clear and unequivocal perspective from which the folly can be judged and labeled. Bellow's comedy is too thick, too human, too resistant to abstractions about its guiding principle or its point of view, to fit the directed and purposeful structure of the fable. This first attempt to go further than a copious definition of existential man, to show and judge the kind of choice possible for contemporary man, is strung between a carefully comically qualified, almost trivial, choice and a fabulistic form that promises something more positive and important than the novel provides. Fables, with their intellectual and metaphysical rigor, do not fit Bellow's version of experience.

Herzog, Bellow's second attempt to go beyond definition, returns to the familiar Bellow framework of dense, confused, contemporary, urban America. The protagonist, Moses Elkanah Herzog (the name itself is that of one of the minor characters in *Ulysses*), is another Bloom-like wanderer, interested in people, emotions, ideas, bank robbers, Houdini, minerals, atoms, refurbishing old houses, and history. Like Bellow's other heroes, in a combination of Augie March and Tommy Wilhelm, Herzog is vital, responsive, a victim, a sufferer, often full of self-pity, and frequently lucky. As victim, he has chosen his own torturer—Madeleine, his second wife, who was unfaithful to him and enjoyed her triumph over him and whose shadow causes the depression that follows Herzog through most of the novel. Madeleine, the cold, hard beauty, the antithesis of Herzog, represents the specter of the demolished possibility of his own completeness, his own universality, which Herzog must conquer in order to survive. In a conversation with his understanding brother, Will, Herzog explains that initially he needed Madeleine to bring ideology into his life.

Existential man, attracted to his ideological opposite, tries to assimilate it and fails, but, even this far, the presentation of Herzog carries the depiction of the protagonist a dimension further than did the treatment of Augie March. The portrait of the parasite, Valentine Gersbach, the supposed close friend who sleeps with and later lives with Madeleine, is also carried further than was the theme of the parasite in *Seize the Day*. The treatment of Gersbach is complicated when, late in the novel, in a switch to the perspective of Gersbach's loyal and abandoned wife, Herzog realizes that Valentine, false and calculating as he seems, had genuinely adored Herzog, tried to provide comfort, conversation, and flattery for him, emulated him as much as he could. Even the motives of the parasite are strangely mixed.

The most important and distinctive extension of Bellow's themes in *Herzog*, however, is in the development of history, the recognition that man is public as well as private, has a job as well as a love life, ideas as well as experience. Herzog's attempt to get over Madeleine is also his attempt to get back to work, to finish the second book defining Romanticism on which he has been stalled for so long. He views the desire to work itself in historical terms, "The liberal-bourgeois revision, the illusion of improvement, the poison of hope," terms that refer both to his own attempts to construct his work and to the last few hundred years in the history of Western man. In thinking of his dilemmas historically, Herzog tries to avoid conventional cant about "the cheap mental stimulants of Alienation" and "the commonplaces of the Wasteland outlook," having nothing but scorn for characters like the preying and hypocritical lawyer Himmelstein who "had never even read a book of metaphysics" and was "touting the Void as if it were so much salable real estate." He also ridicules those who see in history nothing but "decline and fall."

Herzog focuses on the changes in man's sensibility we have retrospectively termed Romanticism, the greater reliance on the individual's emotions and the decrease in the tendency to apply human problems to an external, immutable, universal scale. He attempts to define and use the historical generalization.

Bellow's novels have always demonstrated his interest in various aspects of Romanticism: Joseph in *Dangling Man,* for example, speculates about how the romantic freedoms of the Werthers and the Don Juans might have helped to create the individual brutality of the Napoleons. In *Herzog,* however, the interest in Romanticism becomes part of Herzog's central problem, part of the question concerning how much control man can achieve over his emotion, how much choice responsible and existential man can manage. Herzog challenges the "Romantic errors about the uniqueness of the Self" and the excessively sentimental "swarmings" of Rousseau; at the same time, he feels, with the Romantics, that the heart is the most important element of human experience, and he deplores the "bottled religion" and "sterility" of the anti-Romantics like T. E. Hulme. Both for history and for himself, both for Herzog the representative contemporary man and for Herzog the individual, the attempt to work out a rational Romanticism, a reliance on feeling that can also survive in the world of hard facts, becomes the central problem of the novel. The responsive man can be neither squelched nor dissolved, like Nachman in the novel, in the chaos of his own throbbing responsiveness.

The interest in history, both general and personal, leads to depicting the past with a density of detail. Each of the principal characters has a mother, father, aunts, a stepmother, all carefully delineated because the past as it affects each character is part of the present. In addition, Herzog, always one to extend himself and his problems, has numerous friends, fellow scholars, lawyers, doctors, a psychiatrist. The density of human relationship is part of the barrier man builds against death:

But what is the philosophy of this generation? Not God is dead, that point was passed long ago. Perhaps it should be stated Death is God. This generation thinks—and this is its thought of thoughts —that nothing faithful, vulnerable, fragile can be durable or have any true power. Death waits for these things as a cement floor waits for a dropping light bulb.

Man evades thinking of the certainty of death by concern with his relationships to others in a world where God or human truth outside of death does not exist.

Herzog also needs to see himself not only as an individual against other individuals, but as a member of a group or class against other groups or classes. The meaning of Herzog's Judaism, for example, becomes clear only through extensive contrast with both non-Jews and other Jews. In one sense, Herzog rebels against his Jewishness, for he is not religious, clannish, ideological, or willing to confine his relationships to the safety of other Jews; but, in another sense, Herzog recognizes his own Jewishness because he feels strong ties with his family, both in the present and in the past, and he knows that the "Faustian" bargain, an idea of sin and retribution planted in every Christian, is a concept totally irrelevant and meaningless to him. Herzog can see the comic ambivalence of his position as squire of Ludeyville, owner of the large house in rural Western Massachusetts, one of the last remaining preserves of the White Anglo-Saxon, but he rather enjoys the ambivalence and is not about to relinquish his role and willingly retreat to an urban ghetto just because others think that Ludeyville is no place for a Jew. Herzog's Jewishness is complex, partially symbolic, and very different from Joseph's in *Dangling Man*. Joseph's Jewishness was isolated from Christianity, and the modern, young alien rejected both traditions; Herzog's Jewishness is both like and unlike Christianity, a special form of the social and theoretical estrangement that he shares with many rebellious contemporaries. He needs others, other people and other traditions, in order to define himself.

Herzog's principal means of self-definition, however, emerges through his relationships with women, his loves, for, as he says in talking about another man's willingness to risk everything on a single issue or person, "Now that it can't be political, it's sexual." Throughout the novel, Herzog, always highly vulnerable and responsive, tries to distinguish genuine love for a particular person from the fallacy of the excessively romantic which he calls "potato love—amorphous, swelling, hungry, indiscriminate, cowardly potato love." In this attempt, his sexual relationships become central to the novel, the sexual the closest and most intensely revealing relationship possible. His first wife, Daisy, had been cold, formal, full of domestic rules, and addicted to listing all duties and engagements on a large bulletin board. She evaded Herzog's feelings and his warmth, and he felt that no full relationship was possible with this sensible and limited woman. Madeleine, in contrast, invited his warmth only to freeze it, welcomed his confidences only to use them against him. Intense, dedicated to what she thought of as "truth" and despising all lies, Madeleine had never forgiven Herzog for making love to her at a time, before they were married, when she, as a convert to the Roman Catholic Church, had wanted to be able to go to Confession in a morally pure state. Yet she had wanted to make love just as much as Herzog had. Madeline, in her intensity, is deeply divided, loving Herzog at night and hating him in the morning as she puts on make-up in a conscious effort to obliterate the night before. Life for Madeleine is a series of alternatives, each violently struggling against the other. Marriage to Herzog replaces the Roman Catholic Church, but graduate study in Slavic Languages and Valentine Gersbach soon replace Herzog. And, as Herzog realizes, the intensity with which each of the alternatives is embraced is closer to irate fury than to any sort of warmth. Madeleine is always depicted in terms that suggest the cold: her cold blue eyes, her "Byzantine" face, "the terrifying menstrual ice of her rages."

Some of Herzog's other women, his mistresses, like Sono Oguki, have expressed only warmth and emotion, have represented something too close to "potato love" to hold his interest for very long. Ramona, Herzog's current mistress, an attractive and experienced woman who owns a flower shop in New York, is warm and vital, although she has a tendency to lecture Herzog in rather platitudinous terms about the need for humility or self-confidence. Still, Herzog recognizes the genuine substance buried beneath the chicken-soup and, at the end of the novel, is waiting to entertain her at dinner in Ludeyville. Through his affair with Ramona and his realization that it includes but also goes beyond sexual need, Herzog comes to accept a relationship with someone who is not an intellectual, who values materialistic comfort, whose insights are never in the bookish or academic terms to which Herzog is accustomed. This acceptance allows him to write more sanely to the psychiatrist:

You gave me good value for my money when you explained that neuroses might be graded by the inability to tolerate ambiguous situations. I have just read a certain verdict in Madeleine's eyes, "For cowards, Not-being!" Her disorder is super-clarity. Allow me modestly to claim that I am much better now at ambiguities. I think I can say, however, that I have been spared the chief ambiguity that afflicts intellectuals, and this is that civilized individuals hate and resent the civilization that makes their lives possible. What they love is an imaginary human situation invented by their own genius and which they believe is the only true and the only human reality.

Historically, as Bellow indicates at several other points in the novel, intellectuals have been, despite all their genuine examination of experience, more fatally attracted to absolutes than have many less learned and intelligent people. Ramona and his brother Will, neither an intellectual, come to mean more to Herzog at the end of the novel than do his learned friends or brilliant women.

Herzog, in his acceptance of ambiguity, is, however, far from anti-intellectual. He still reasons, studies, relates himself to history and ideas. But he does know that the kind of control he needs to govern his vulnerable heart cannot be formulated in intellectual terms or established in a series of rules. Nor is the control, on the other hand, the automatic "gyroscope" he thought he had within him before the disaster of his marriage to Madeleine. The control he finally gains is symbolized in the episode in which, returning to Chicago and getting his father's ludicrous old pistol, Herzog sees but does not shoot Gersbach.

Rationally and intellectually, he can formulate no reason not to destroy Gersbach, Madeleine, and himself; emotionally, he is sufficiently worked up to shoot the pistol. What prevents him is the recognition that shooting would be theatrical, part of a literary and historical tradition that is not necessarily Herzog himself. Herzog looks through the window, watching Gersbach give little June (Herzog and Madeleine's daughter) a bath. After the bath, as Gersbach stoops to clean the tub, Herzog "might have killed him now," but refrains in a scene ironically suggestive of Hamlet's refusal to kill Claudius at prayer. Herzog acknowledges the origin of his perception:

To shoot him—an absurd thought. As soon as Herzog saw the actual person giving an actual bath, the reality of it, the tenderness of such a buffoon to a little child, his intended violence turned into *theater,* into something ludicrous.

Reality works against part of Herzog's social and religious tradition as well as against the literary one. After this, Herzog recalls that his Aunt Zipporah, the wealthy dictator in the family, had scorned his father because he could not use his gun, although he dealt daily with thieves, swindlers, and gangsters. In not shooting the gun, in a negative action that denies part of both his literary and his personal tradition, Herzog understands himself more fully, recognizes that he is not only a composite of forces, asserts an element of Moses Herzog that achieves genuine independence. Yet the achievement is not solely individual, for Herzog's father, unlike him in so many ways, also never fired the antiquated pistol he kept for fifty years. When, later, Herzog is arrested because, while out with June, he has a minor automobile accident and the loaded gun is found in his pocket, the scene at the police station—an embarrassed Herzog and a coldly furious Madeleine—returns the novel to the ludicrous comedy of the external Herzog, squire of Ludeyville, in the real urban world. The change in Herzog has already taken place, but the change isn't visible to Chicago—or even to Madeleine.

Neither picaresque nor fabulistic in form, *Herzog* is unified by the numerous letters Herzog writes and never sends during the crucial weeks in which the action of the novel takes place. In this novel, Bellow's form works brilliantly, for the letters function in a number of ways relevant to the novel. On the simplest level a safety-valve for Herzog, the letters take the reader into his mind. The letters also fit the point of view of the intellectual, the man who can articulate his experience, can fabricate ways of explaining and dealing with what he encounters. The letters are Herzog's art, his means of discovering his intellectual range, of providing commentary on politics, power, history, and theology. In the letters to public figures, Herzog demonstrates a skepticism about public man, about power ("Invariably the most dangerous people seek the power"), that helps reinforce the idea that he must work out his solution for himself, must rely on the Romantic agent of discovery, the individual. This, in turn, helps to justify the structural role of the letters, the creations of one individual man trying to survive in a society in which institutions, corporate powers, severely limit the area of individual control. The letters, like a journal, are one of the only weapons the individual has. Many of the letters, however, are personal, written to friends or associates, and become a means of formulating both the actual past experience between the two and the communication theoretically possible. These letters mediate between the ambiguities of human communication.

Herzog is always concerned with communication, with reaching other people, and the novel illustrates a wide variety of the kinds of communication possible. Sometimes people can understand, like Libbie and her husband whom Herzog briefly visits on Martha's Vineyard, but the understanding doesn't help. At other times, people like Ramona and Will can unexpectedly reach and be reached by Herzog. Other forms of communication are chaotic or parasitic, like the relationship between Herzog and Gersbach. Herzog, always paternal, sometimes sentimentalizes his relationship with children, and his hearing about a child violated in a New York courtroom sends him rushing to Chicago to see June. But, at other times, Herzog is more carefully balanced and he sometimes connects love of children with the sentimentality of "potato love." These other forms of communication are ambivalent, perplexing, difficult. Therefore, Herzog, through most of the novel, retreats into himself to work out the kind of communication he wants and needs. But, as he realizes clearly, the letter, the product of a single man, is always artificial, always an easy fabrication. When, at the very end of the novel, Herzog has enough control temporarily to feel at ease about his relationships, his position, he need no longer write letters. The condition may not last—he could start writing letters again the next day—but he can momentarily suspend construction for reality, can exercise that limited degree of freedom within the existential world.

For a number of critics, Herzog is most vulnerable in ex-

pressing a kind of self-pity that comes dangerously close to sentimentality. Because Herzog has a kind of triumph, an acceptance,
a solution although a severely limited one, the self-pity that is
part of his character might come closer to being a recommenda-
tion, might leak into the perspective of the author. Bellow
guards against this by frequently satirizing Herzog, by making
his emotions excessive, and by numerous stories that make the
character's alienation comic. He also employs psychological
speculation to present the idea that the manifestation of self-pity
has something of its opposite, rational judgment, just as the
reluctance to cause pain can be a "delicious form of sensuality."
In addition, in a letter to the historian who has scooped his projected new work on Romanticism, itself an ironic undercutting
of Herzog's uniqueness that still does not completely destroy
that uniqueness, Herzog deplores "the advocacy and praise of
suffering," pointing out that this can be as florid and apocalyptic
as any absolute, can turn man away from the discovery and the
acceptance of himself as a human being. The self-pity, a recognizable part of man, is held in check by Bellow's intelligent
presentation of many other parts of man, of human complexity.
Herzog's suffering and responsiveness are balanced both by his
own serious, intelligent judgment and by Bellow's multiple
comic perspective on him.

Bellow's attitude toward his central character is equally
multiple although less comic in his most recent novel, *Mr.
Sammler's Planet* (1970). Mr. Sammler, a seventy-four-year-old,
half-blind survivor of a Nazi concentration camp, looking at
criminal and festering decay in contemporary New York, rejecting his own past allegiance to the scientific optimism of H. G.
Wells, provides the central perspective for Bellow's treatment
of the planet, the lifeless stones that fall apart, "dilapidate."
Sammler, regarded as wise, understanding, and compassionate
by the selfish younger relatives clustered around him, listening
to his niece assert that no one could ever refer to him as a "poor
creature," has, in his intelligence and his central aloofness, almost come to believe in his own image until he experiences the
crowded events, the threats, violence, insults and death, in the
few days during which the novel takes place.

As in *Herzog,* the incident crucial for self-discovery in-

volves violence, but, whereas Herzog learned that he was happily
incapable of using the pistol no matter how depressed or temporarily deranged, Sammler learns the much less flattering truth
that he is partly responsible for the violence he abhors. Sammler
has lived knowing that during the war he had killed a man he
might have allowed to live, had, under extremely difficult circumstances, let a desire for understandable revenge overcome
his sense of humanity. But he has tried to bury that knowledge
in his survival. During the course of the novel, in his obsession
with the Negro pickpocket, his telling the story to the irrational
Feffer, and his demands, at a crucial moment, that his son-in-law,
who knows no English, stop the pickpocket from grabbing Feffer's camera, Sammler becomes a central cause for the brutal
assault he would never sanction. He even hurriedly leaves the
scene, allowing others to explain and clarify. He then rushes to
the hospital, where in a cathartic prayer over his dead nephew's
body, reminiscent of Tommy Wilhelm's weeping at the funeral
at the end of *Seize the Day,* Sammler recognizes his own "terms,"
his own necessary nature, the aloofness and lack of involvement
embedded in his own "soul." And, in coming to accept what he
is, Sammler can also accept the necessary limitations in all the
others around him, can tell his thieving and feckless daughter
that he loves her, can feel genuine guilt for trying to control his
spoiled and promiscuous niece. He exchanges a rather self-
consciously martyred acceptance of his own image for a genuine
compassion, a capacity to accept the limitations of others and
of self, an understanding of guilt, a willingness to abandon the
attempt to control all experience through distance and intellect.

In *Mr. Sammler's Planet,* Bellow has moved away from
the definition of man as existential, as creating his own values
in the manner of Augie March. Rather, man is seen like Sammler
and like the others in the novel as possessing a definition, almost
an essence that has long since been determined. In this novel,
which, like *Seize the Day,* contains far less of the density of contemporary experience than Bellow's novels usually do, and focuses on all the characters other than Sammler as types of different crumbling stones in the younger generation, Bellow
characterizes man's nature as inevitable and necessarily limited,
almost suggests a version of the doctrine of Original Sin. Man's

only choice is whether or not to accept his inevitable nature, confirm his knowledge. The concept of man's nature in *Mr. Sammler's Planet* is more certain, more inflexibly deterministic, than that usual in the fiction of compassion or in Bellow's other novels; yet the insistence on not judging, the sympathy, the sense of suspending salient moralities in order to understand the vast confusions of contemporary life, remain the same.

Generally, in depicting man as a creature who can never or only rarely know his essence, God, or ultimate truth, whose only choices are severely limited, to prefer lions to pigs or to stop writing letters, Bellow's attitude is strongly compassionate. Man, often estranged, misunderstood, victimized by others and by himself, has a rough time. The novel of compassion in contemporary terms, terms which frequently deny the possibility of a reigning truth by which man can be judged, plays close to sentimentality, close to the dissolution of all perspective in a wash of indiscriminate sympathy. In the same way, the drama of domestic problems, no matter how serious, can begin to sound like soap opera. Bellow is often close to sentimentality, generally insistent enough on man's comic combination of heart and folly to seem trivial, but the density of his depiction of experience, the comic multiplicity of his perspective, the richness of his historical understanding, and his usual abolishment of heroic pretense avoids both sentimentality and triviality. In fact, some of his work, like *Herzog,* gains particular force from its flirtation with sentimentality, for he manages to incorporate a responsiveness to all experience, a refusal to inhibit tightly or exclude, that makes the fiction seem particularly rich and compassionate. In addition, the fiction defends the idea that history, the story of what has been and is, is a more rewarding study than philosophy, the account of what man means. And Bellow, even in *Mr. Sammler's Planet,* is pre-eminently a novelist of human history, of the origin, the development, and the consequences of the Romantic sensibility in terms of contemporary urban man. At his best, Bellow avoids the fable, the metaphysically directed form, or the metaphysically essential statement about man, and shapes his material from the dense and complex historical flux that is also a central part of his subject.

XV

Compassion in Contemporary Fiction

CERTAIN ELEMENTS IN CONTEMPORARY CULTURE would seem likely to reinforce the attitudes implicit in the fiction of compassion, to propel authorial attitudes of skepticism and sympathy into a dominant role. For many contemporaries, God does not exist. The genuine achievements of science, in addition to the hangover of nineteenth-century faith in the scientific progress theoretically attainable, give little support to fixed and immutable definitions of man. At the same time, the last sixty or seventy years of public chaos, accompanied by an increasing general awareness of all the millions of individual chaoses, allow for little belief in human behavior as part of some universal meaning or purpose. The combination of scientific attitudes with a recognition of the chaos in terms of which we live, destroys, for many of us, the doctrine that human nature can be understood or judged in terms of universal principles. All this contemporary distrust of abstractions or of theories of "truth" about man, would seem, on the face of it, to indicate that there would now be a marked increase in the range and quantity of fiction belonging to the tradition of compassion. Yet, in fact, such a logical expectation has not been realized, and there is, despite the frequency with which the term "compassion" is discussed and is bandied in advertising blurbs, no appreciable trend toward the dominance of a searching and thorough-going attitude of compassion in contemporary fiction.

A number of forces in literary culture and practice during the last forty or fifty years have worked against the possible dominance of such a tradition. The increasing recognition of the sprawling chaos of the world and ourselves has often led to a reaction of excessive reliance in fiction on artistic neatness and comprehensibility. The writer, fearing the dark incomprehensibility around him, carefully confines his fiction to artifice, simplifies his construction to an order which he defines and poses against the indefinable. To an extent, any author does this. But contemporary authors often make their structures relatively more complete and limited, erect highly conscious and artificial bulwarks against the dark unknown. Both formally and conceptually, this neatness, this concentration on comprehensible artifice, excludes compassion.

Contemporary criticism, too, insofar as criticism influences the general ideas about literature which, in turn, influence the writers, has often worked against the fiction of compassion. The symbolic and textual criticism of recent years dominating the universities, although a welcome antidote to both the vaguely bland wine-sampling of literature, and the arid, over-generalized historicism which preceded it, has tended to concentrate on those novels which could best be explained through critical formulations of symbolic and textual consistency. The novel has been viewed as a consistent structure, examined as artifice, and this critical tendency has helped to create more novels amenable to its pattern.

The concerns implicit within the tradition of compassion, the sense it gives of never fully formulated experience, its breaking of the forms it establishes, have often been regarded as creating inept or inferior art. In this regard, the literary critical attitudes prevalent in recent years have tended to reduce and devalue the fiction of compassion, elevating rather a more succinct, neater, more consciously directed fiction—or emphasizing the consciously artistic elements in the work of those writers, like Lawrence and Joyce, whose art is copious enough to be fully amenable to either critical point of view. In addition, simplified and banal examples of the fiction of compassion are abundantly visible in the endlessly unstructured television soap opera, long serials in which the one virtue, momentarily and sporadically acute characterization, is subsumed in the general and incessant sentimentality. The serious writer often over-protects against the possibility of banality or sentimentality, rules out any manifestation of the loose or open form, any of the attitudes connected with compassion.

Within this literary and cultural context of shoring form against any hint of possible mawkishness, many writers have turned to closely directive and heavily thematic forms. They shape consistently in order to moralize, rely on structure or a consistent pattern of imagery in order to control experience. Consequently, the fable, either as a contemporary reconstruction of some classical or Christian myth or as the author's directed fabrication of experience, has become quantitatively significant in contemporary fiction. The non-fable gains its coherence from a loose kind of verisimilitude. The plot, the characterizations, the images—all the elements of the novel—are held together by a fairly flexible concept of probability, by the reader's sense that the novel, to some extent, reflects and comments on human experience. The fable, however, gains its relevance by more abstract means, by its message or its universal meaning, and is more likely to depend upon itself and its own machinery for fictional coherence.

Many young contemporary writers seem to have moved from the risky vagaries of the novel of verisimilitude to the safety and self-sufficiency of the fable. Andrew Sinclair, for example, after several novels concerning rootless young men in contemporary Britain struggling within established institutions like the Guards and the University, and after having published excellent historical studies on American Prohibition and the career of Warren G. Harding, wrote *Gog* (1967). Dependent on the ancient legend of the twin giants, Gog and Magog, good and evil, the novel depicts the good giant, Gog, rediscovering himself and England after World War II. In a series of fantastic incidents, the Gog principle, a large, earthy, free sense of life, is contrasted with the Magog principle, dramatized as Gog's crabbed, snobbish brother, a conventional civil servant. The legend magnifies and gives meaning to a simple and stereotyped contrast, decorates with a pretense of universal meaning an otherwise undistinguished novel.

Another talented young English novelist, David Storey,

followed two sharply perceptive novels about class and love in northern England with a fantastic parable in *Radcliffe* (1963) . *Radcliffe* has two heroes who alternately attract and repel each other in a series of violently improbable actions. On one level, the heroes represent the two social classes in a northern town, and their attractions and repulsions are given a social dimension. But the upper-class character is also made the "soul" and the lower-class the "body," their friendship representing an uneasy, frequently violent, and finally destructive alliance. Storey has claimed that all his novels fit a pattern, that the first, the novel of the professional rugby player, *This Sporting Life* (1960) was the novel of "body," that the second, *Flight into Camden* (1960) was the novel of "soul," and that the third, *Radcliffe,* is the impossible combination of the two. Yet, despite Storey's intention, the first two novels did not depend on their symbolic function; they conveyed a kind of complex verisimilitude that overwhelmed and enlivened the symbols. Only in *Radcliffe* is the symbolic machinery obtrusive, solemnly necessary to provide both coherence and relevance.

The interest in the fable is not only a contemporary British phenomenon, for skillful American writers have also relied on it extensively. John Barth, for example, cloaks all his perceptions in terms of fable, like his man/beast, Pan/Christian hero in *Giles Goat-boy* (1966) or his bumbling picaresque poet in *The Sot-weed Factor* (1960) who voyages from England to Maryland in the late seventeenth century. Through the picaresque journey, Barth provides parodies of history, literature, politics, military affairs, sex, and religion. The whole fable mocks the absurdity of any human activity, including all its own literary and historical sources.

The comic grotesque fables of Nathanael West, another perspective that underlines and bitterly castigates human absurdity, have been widely popular and seem to be echoed again and again. However, not all contemporary comic versions of the absurd are fables with a directed and moral perspective. For example, Thomas Pynchon's *V.* (1963) , a surrealistic and deliberately fragmentary treatment of rootlessness and failure in any kind of personal or political connection over the past seventy-five years, avoids easy moral judgment, and establishes as the point of reference an assumption that it describes and duplicates the conditions of ordinary experience. Such fabulistic and extravagantly iconoclastic forms come closer to the fiction of compassion.

Generally, however, the fable—amusing, inventive and well-written as it may be—restricts and channelizes the conditions of contemporary experience to a degree that poses serious questions of relevance. The fable most often depends upon its message or its "truth" for its relevance. For many contemporaries, whose sense of truth is muddled, distorted, partial, complicated, and concrete, the point of reference for the kind of systematic, abstract, and generalized truth which the form of the fable demands is difficult to find. The fable is a kind of locked metaphysic, the credibility of which requires the acceptance of some truth outside and beyond the terms of the fable itself, the truth of some nation, or organization, or concept of man or God. The fable is often a lighter, swifter version of allegory. As allegory frequently marshals details in a pattern of Christian or theological argument, so the fable, if the implications of the form are to be followed, arranges experience within a pattern governed by some version of the truth beyond human experience, some version or representation of a metaphysical entity. The fable demands belief—not literal belief in the verisimilitude of its characters or incidents, but abstract belief in the message toward which it is directed.

For example, the work of one of the most able contemporary fabulists, William Golding, contains a rigid schematization that tends to force response on the basis of agreement or disagreement with the validity of the author's controlling abstraction. *Lord of the Flies* (1954), by its very form, insists on the recognition of the truth of the orthodox Christian version of essential human depravity: the concept and meaning of the novel rely on the validity of its Christian parallels. Similarly, the whole organization and direction of *Free Fall* (1959) depends on accepting the relevance of the Faustian bargain, the anguish of selling one's soul to Satan, just as *The Spire* (1964) is dependent on realizing the combination of pain and glory in building the monument that aspires to touch the heavens. To question whether the bargain for the soul is applicable to contemporary experience, or to ask if aspiration is really crucially important for man, to wonder about what Satan or the heavens are or even what they might stand for as metaphors, is to destroy the impact of either novel. Golding's novels are so tightly shaped, so intricately structured, that they rest almost entirely on the acceptance of the authenticity of their Christian parallels. Yet when, as in *The Pyramid* (1967), Golding abandons the fable for three tenuously related episodes in the development of a young man, he frequently lapses into sentimentality. Golding seems to require the rigidity of the fable, the strength of fictional commitment to Christian belief to give shape to his own perceptions about experience. The rigidity of his own shapes, his fables, demands an equal rigidity from the reader.

In addition to the rigidity and to the metaphysical implications the form imposes, the fable establishes another barrier against contemporary relevance. The most frequent problem treated in contemporary fiction, treated so frequently that its terms have become a cliché, is that of estrangement, the individual's remoteness from his society, his supposedly close relationships, and himself. The fable, often reflecting this condition, is itself remote, abstract, removed into the realm of a protective self-sufficiency. As such, in its very abstractness, the fable intensifies the alienation, becomes the writer's device for removing himself from his characters and human concerns, just as the characters themselves are removed from the human concerns around them. The fable may reflect our world, but it does so abstractly, sometimes too easily, cheaply, catching the attitudes without the experience or texture that has given those attitudes force or meaning. Certainly, given the social and psychological chaos of the contemporary world as well as the fear of seeming banal or sentimental or stupidly involved, the attraction of the fable for the author is clearly understandable and justifiable. Most of us abstract and intellectualize, remove ourselves in order to survive more comfortably. But the fable sometimes seems, particularly in the work of writers like Donald Barthelme and John Hawkes, or in a novel like John Cheever's recent and disappointing *Bullet Park* (1969), the kind of intellectualized evasion in fiction that it so often is in life, a comfortable abstraction that need not be questioned further.

The categories of fable, novel of verisimilitude, and novel cohering through a moral message are not, of course, mutually exclusive. One able contemporary who has worked in all these forms and sometimes combined them is John Updike. In *Rabbit, Run* (1960), the novel of verisimilitude, conveyed with a rich texture of sociological and psychological density, shaded into the novel-with-a-message since Rabbit could finally be viewed as a "picaresque saint" representing the value of the searching man running away from a society that increasingly excludes him; in *The Centaur* (1963), the novel of verisimilitude was combined with the Greek fable of Chiron and Prometheus, alternating chapters establishing connections between the ancient fable and the elements treated in contemporary experience. In neither of these novels, however, did the metaphysical or fabulistic suggestions restrict the sense of contemporary experience. Rabbit's "sainthood" was vague, negatively and existentially expressed, primarily depicted in terms of all the narrow rules of the society he could not follow. His search for a God, for some directed principle of experience, had a positive quality, but that quality was less the author's insistence on a message than Rabbit's refusal to accept his in-laws' superficial and contradictory rule of responsibility or his boredom with the conflict between the stern old minister and the silly young parson addicted to teen-age discussions of petting held in soda fountains. Finding no value within his world, refusing to abandon his search, Rabbit could only run.

In *The Centaur*, the fable never became restrictive because Updike never applied it universally to contemporary experience. The story of Chiron and Prometheus was made relevant to one father's sacrifice for his son, one man's cheerful self-immolation to insure the survival of full human possibility for his offspring. In both these novels, Updike seemed to be moving toward the attitudes implicit in novels of compassion: Rabbit was viewed with a rich and complex ambivalence, understood, sympathized with, but not entirely identified with, sometimes satirized and not finally judged; *The Centaur* left the universal implications of the myth to the shadowy possibilities of a future outside the boundaries of the novel. Updike's more recent fiction, however, has moved sharply away from compassionate attitudes. Judgment is more severe and more conventional. *Of the Farm* (1965), the tale of a young advertising man's weekend visit, with his second wife, to his mother on the farm where he grew up, coheres around the recognition that the simple, old-fashioned way of life is, after all, the best. The young man's liberation from the farm has resulted only in directionless searching, guilt and wasteful ambivalence. Finally, in an ending that seems to cultivate a quality of unsubstantiated misery and loss, he returns to his job in the city, regretting his inability to recapture a past grace, as if a crabbed Pennsylvania farm where even chickens are no longer kept is a prelapsarian paradise. His sense of the farm, connected with his enduring and church-going mother, compounds nostalgia with a moral and religious dimension never fully specified in the novel. In *Couples* (1968), Updike's moral and religious framework is clearer and more certain. Strongly slanting a great amount of sociological observation, he skewers his characters firmly on the point of a rigorous judgment.

In this novel, Updike dissects the hypocrisies, the postures, and the sexual relationships of the ten couples who comprise a social group in a contemporary New England town. The dissections, however, are not equally severe on all the corpses, for, throughout the novel, those few characters with some sense of religion (particularly some form of the Protestant religion, for the Roman Catholics and the Jews are either less perceptive or more hypocritical) are also those with a richer, more understanding sense of human responsibility. The hero, Piet, a searcher, is decorated with Christ-like imagery, and, although he is also the principal satyr of the novel (sleeping with five of the ten women), he is made the most responsive and most fully human man. With thematic consistency, he eventually marries the other religious Protestant among the characters, the two of them able to maintain a form of communication not available to those who have not been enriched by belief in God. Updike even saddles Piet and his second wife with the responsibility for an abortion to make the surmountable trials of the believers even more dramatically remarkable. When, toward the end of the novel, the local church burns, its symbol, a weathercock that had been on top of the steeple, is brought to Piet, the rightful in-

344]

heritor of the traditions of belief, no matter how irreverent or unorthodox his superficial behavior may have seemed.

Although the characters all sound alike, all talk exactly like the different positions in a debate taking place in the author's mind, they are carefully distinguished as representations. Each man's occupation is a symbol: the two stockbrokers, accustomed to swapping and adjusting on the exchange, trade wives back and forth in a setting of adjustable accommodation; the dentist is obsessed by decay, both in his patients' mouths and in the human relationships around him—sexually, he is impotent; one scientist is pettishly legalistic, applying trivial logical forms to all human affairs; the airline pilot is irresponsible and rootless, enjoying whatever temporary mistress he can pick up in any part of the world; only Piet, the hero, like Christ a carpenter, can build and create, can construct buildings and relationships, can salvage houses and souls. Piet, as searcher, has certain resemblances to Rabbit. But, whereas Rabbit could only search and run, could never find the truth or God he faithfully sought, Piet can settle into the discipline of church attendance. He "likes the official order and the regular hours." All the complexity of social observation in *Couples* is finally reduced to a contemporary statement of the value of orthodox religion. The novel is a jazzy reassertion of the importance of the *Wasp* New England past.

Couples maintains this *Wasp* point of view in sociological as well as in metaphysical terms. The novel has a patina of anti-Negro, anti-Semitic, and anti-Catholic feeling that is not only a part of the characterizations. Most of the remarks stereotyping Negroes, Jews, or Catholics are observations by characters, useful in delineating sociological attitudes. Yet the author lingers on such remarks, dwells on Negritude or Jewishness to the extent that the prejudices of characters slide over into the stance of the whole novel. One minor character, a scientist, is described for over a page, yet tucked in the middle is the single phrase "Jewish only in the sleepy lids of his eyes." The only Negro in the novel is comically superstitious, like a Step'n Fetchit character; the principal Jews, one of the ten couples, are pretentiously intellectual and always aware of how hard they must strive for ac-

ceptance in *Wasp* society, unable to keep their Jewishness out of
any conversation; the principal Catholic couple are dry, tight,
and hypocritical, the man the only character who openly and
stupidly denigrates Negroes and who bitterly mocks Piet's preference for restoring genuine old New England houses rather
than making fortunes with jerry-built subdivisions; the only
Oriental, supposedly a brilliant scientist, is characterized almost
entirely by condescending jokes about his inability to communicate in English. Updike's ethnic depictions are often copious elaborations of vulgar stereotypes, and the novel, despite all
the fascinating contemporary description, witty observation, and
interesting variety of detailed sexual experience, sometimes reads
like a morality play, sure of its God and its judgments, consigning all heretics to deserved hells. Much of *Couples* is alien to the
assumptions about man and his world implicit in the fiction of
compassion.

Sometimes the fable or the morality play is more complicated, as, for example, in the fiction of Iris Murdoch, in which
the fable, handled ironically, often destroys those who believe
in it, and the apparatus of the novel turns around on itself. In
Iris Murdoch's first four novels, *Under the Net* (1954), *The
Flight from the Enchanter* (1955), *The Sandcastle* (1956), and
The Bell (1958), the author deals with symbolic structures of
human experience, designs elaborate patterns that presumably
explain and articulate life. But, in each of these novels, the pattern breaks down, the abstract structure is shown to be foolish
or irrelevant, and man is left in his formless chaos. Miss Murdoch's next novel, *A Severed Head* (1961), a highly patterned
dance of sexual relationships among a group of people, full of
bizarre incidents and unlikely relationships, carries the philosophical skepticism further. The characters are shown as creating their own patterns, their own forms, manufacturing the
false Gods that eventually destroy them. In the intricate series
of switches in the novel, they constantly fabricate a God out of
another character and what he represents, fashion the metaphors
and truths they try and are unable to live by. In some of her
subsequent novels, *An Unofficial Rose* (1962), *The Unicorn*
(1963), and *The Time of the Angels* (1966), Miss Murdoch is
more Gothic and macabre, concentrating on the intrusion of

the strange and unknowable into human affairs. The chaos implicit within the world of all her fiction is magnified in these novels which depict isolated and mysteriously powerful women, men subject to bizarre and inexplicable passions, and preternaturally wise and sensitive children.

One of her recent books, *The Nice and the Good* (1968) returns to the intricate patterning and unlikely, mysterious couplings of *A Severed Head*. A principal character, himself an atheist, plays God, dispenses understanding and advice to a number of different women involved in a complicated series of sexual problems. Yet his advice, sound and sympathetic as it seems, is frequently wrong, the measured irrelevance of a fastidious bachelor who plays vicariously at passion and feeling. When he later rescues a boy caught in an underwater cave by the rising tide he realizes that advice involves judgment and that judgment, the secular substitute for God, both restricts others and devalues the self. Having learned not to judge, and recognizing that "Love is the only justice," he is himself able at the end of the novel to fall in love. His role as universal father-figure has diminished, he is, in terms of the novel, less "nice"; at the same time, he becomes more a man, more able to recognize what he can and cannot do in both his personal affairs and his job as trouble-shooter and special mystery-solver in a government office, considerably less God-like, and "good." Throughout the novel, characters motivated by what they regard as their altruism are merely "nice," whereas characters who recognize and act in self-interested awareness can be "good." God, no matter how anthropomorphic, never gets beyond the category of "nice." Yet, in an even more recent novel, *A Fairly Honourable Defeat* (1970), this idea of the human "good" is itself demolished. A couple, already atheistic, is established as "good," humane, compassionate, although they are also given a foolish sense of confidence in their priggish virtue. They are completely destroyed by an agent of "evil," a playfully sinister character whose designs finally cause a suicide, and who wants primarily to demonstrate that all human attachments are tenuous and faithless, all beliefs in virtue and consistency hollow and vain. More melodramatic and banally simplified than most of the other fiction, *A Fairly Honourable Defeat* does confirm that, for Miss Murdoch, no generalization about humanity, no abstraction, can remain unchallenged for very long.

The Nice and the Good, like *Bruno's Dream* (1969), the novel which immediately follows it chronologically, works through more highly conscious and sophisticated artifice, using frequent ironies that reverse expectation, parallel scenes that emphasize the pattern by playing one character ironically against another, and the construction and arrangement of houses to contrast and represent people. Yet, as an artifice, it destroys its own premises, attacks the conscious rationality and control from which it originates. *The Nice and the Good*, like *A Severed Head*, becomes a morality play on the human need for compassion, love, and freedom from structure instead of direction and morality. The form carries a message which itself would destroy the assumptions of the form. In philosophical terms, Iris Murdoch demonstrates the inadequacies and inhumanities of philosophy. In her best work, *The Flight from the Enchanter*, *A Severed Head*, and *The Nice and the Good*, the message fights the form and the mode is philosophical; the attitudes of compassion emerge negatively, through the destruction of the abstract pattern that set the novel in motion. Yet, in Miss Murdoch's less highly structured and philosophical novels, in *An Unofficial Rose* and *The Italian Girl* (1964), she frequently becomes exotically banal and sentimental. Her one attempt to use history instead of philosophy as a framework, *The Red and the Green* (1965), a novel set in Dublin during the Easter, 1916 rebellion, is similarly flawed by sentimentality and stereotyped characterization. She seems to need philosophical structures to undercut, artificial buildings to demolish, in order to give strength and excitement to her fiction.

Generally, as many of the novelists discussed in earlier chapters in this book illustrate, the framework of history, the recording of changes and inconsistencies in the human situation, helps give vitality to the fiction of compassion. And, similarly, an overwhelming interest in philosophy, in the formulation of a universally applicable message for man, indicates an authorial prescription that works against an attitude of compassion. Iris Murdoch's fiction is an exception, centrally presenting the philosopher's abstract cast of mind in which the novels have no faith, relying on the destruction of the philosophical message for the fictional and human energy.

In a similar way, for contemporary fictional practice is sufficiently complex to blur the lines of almost any categories established, a framework of history does not always lead to an attitude of compassion. In contemporary fiction, the interest in history often becomes material for the fable; the historical incident or continuity provides the documentation for the object lesson. For example, William Faulkner was, throughout his career, highly interested in history, telling and retelling the history of the South through his novels and stories of Yoknapatawpha County. In some of his greatest fiction, like *The Sound and the Fury* (1929) and *Absalom, Absalom!* (1936), the historical framework reinforced an attitude of compassion, a sympathy for the victims at the end of a predetermined segment of human history. Elements of Christian legend or Old Testament parable were subservient to a national, inherited, and historical force that restricted the choices and possibilities for the central characters, that rendered moral judgment irrelevant. Yet, in his later work, Faulkner frequently turned his historical incidents into more moralistic, universally applicable fables. In *A Fable* (1954), the history of a mutiny among French troops during World War I becomes the occasion for a prescriptive version of the legend of Christ, including conviction, execution, and a brilliantly ironic resurrection in the form of entombment as the unknown soldier. Although the early portions of the novel describe the accidental ineptitude and purposeless quality of war in passages reminiscent of the magnificent treatment of the battle of Waterloo in Stendhal's *The Charterhouse of Parma,* the novel centers more and more on its symbols, restricts human and historical experience more stringently to the Christian terms of the fable.

A more recent example of history serving as the occasion for an object lesson is implicit in William Styron's *The Confessions of Nat Turner* (1967). Using the historical story of Nat Turner, an educated slave who led a violent revolt against a white community in Virginia in 1831, Styron establishes the device of Nat's confessions while awaiting trial and execution. Through the confessions, the author convincingly analyzes some of the causes for Nat's revolt: his training as an "experiment," the conflict between his superior abilities and the inferior role his color often forces upon him, his love for the white girl who is the only one he personally kills during the revolt. In addition, Styron depicts the environment with complexity and skill: the decline in prosperity of Virginia's tobacco country and the resulting hard intransigence of poor white farmers; the horror of splitting black families in forced migrations south and west; the hypocrisy of the religion drilled into the blacks. Yet, increasingly throughout, the novel sounds like an essay diligently and fair-mindedly examining the causes of black unrest in America in 1967. Some of Nat's reflections on black attitudes sound like a sociological account of the ghetto, and Nat's account of his inept leadership as a revolutionary seems a course in the origin of mindless and uncontrollable riots. Rather like Arthur Miller's play "The Crucible," Styron's novel seems to have invented the historical incident in order to provide a respectable past for contemporary observations. In a short preface, Styron himself claims that he is less interested in the " 'historical novel' in conventional terms" than in "meditation on history." The "meditation" involves emphasizing the lessons of history at the expense of fully creating a credible version of the experience of history. Although, in the same preface, Styron hedges as to whether or not he intended his history to point a "moral," the moral lesson for America concerning the conditions and attitudes that cause racial revolt seems paramount in the novel. History as object lesson is implicitly prescriptive, leads away from history as a record of all the shifts, changes, differences, and lack of connection that characterizes it in the fiction of compassion. Styron's history warns us; history in the fiction of compassion describes.

Another use of history central in fiction is alien to the tradition of compassion. This is history as rambling chronicle, a loose form that serves as a framework for frequent digressions on topics of particular interest to the author. The history involved is seldom explained or made relevant to the narrative; rather, it comprises a convenient chronology to tie together superficially all the author's essays and observations. The recent work of Alan Sillitoe, *The Death of William Posters* (1965) and *A Tree on Fire* (1967), the first two novels in a projected trilogy, provides an example of this kind of rambling chronicle as a loose history of several characters in the late fifties and early sixties. One of the characters, like the working-class protagonist of D. H. Lawrence's *Aaron's Rod,* abandons his family to roam the country, and spends months running guns to the F.L.N. in Algeria; another is a proletarian artist who suddenly achieves success and affluence in the new swinging culture. Despite some excellent scenes of working-class domestic life and a few comically inventive details, the novels never cohere and the history is never really relevant to the characters. Lacking the cohesion provided by a complex articulation of a working-class perspective in *Saturday Night and Sunday Morning* (1958) or *The Loneliness of the Long-Distance Runner* (1959), without the abstract or fabulistic structure of *The General* (1960), without even the concentration on a single historical episode such as the colonial wars in Malaysia that provide focus for the rebellious attitude in *Key to the Door* (1961), Sillitoe's recent fiction sprawls episodically. And, within the sprawl, the author inserts essays that document his social preferences and animosities.

More closely allied to the fiction of compassion than Sillitoe's referentially episodic framework or the more conventional historical chronicle, a form still practiced ably by writers such as Pamela Hansford Johnson in *The Survival of the Fittest* (1968), is the historical novel through multiple perspectives in John Fowles's *The French Lieutenant's Woman* (1969). Fowles's Victorian story concerns Charles Smithson, who is safely engaged to Ernestina, and who, in spite of himself, pursues the shadowy and socially ostracized Sarah Woodruff. She becomes, in part, an image, a sense of experience Charles creates. The novel is highly literary, surrounded by relevant Victorian quotations on science, skepticism, sex, and politics, framed by stylistic and thematic spoofs of almost every Victorian novelist from Jane Austen through Thomas Hardy, and explored through a series of Victorian and contemporary points of view. The literary quality of the novel gives the appearance of an academic game, an exercise in puncturing various Victorian stereotypes to isolate the reality underneath. Yet the multiple endings to the novel, each itself a spoof of a novelistic convention, lead the reader to question what Fowles's version of Victorian reality is. And the questions, the

inability to isolate the Victorian story precisely and the awareness of the intervening one hundred years, reproduce for the contemporary the ambivalent emotions of abandoning the sheltered
sanctuary to chase the more exciting, victimized and unknowable
phantom. Yet, at the same time, certain problems concerning sex,
class, custom, and politics are given Victorian definition, are
clearly different from their modern equivalents as they are also
different from our easy stereotypes or our possibly single-minded
versions of what they once might have been. In its attempts to
show the past both similar to and different from the present, impossible to define precisely as an entity in itself, vulnerable to no
easy lesson or judgment, and itself open-ended and partially re-
created, *The French Lieutenant's Woman* illustrates how contemporary historical fiction can fit into the tradition of compassion. Complexity, lack of certainty, and emotional responsiveness
are achieved through the construction of a literary and historical
game, for literature and history themselves, vague and open-
ended as they are, are the only forms capable of carrying the existential density of perceptions, emotions, thoughts and abstractions simultaneously through time.

Contemporary interest in history has also developed the
shaded area between fiction and nonfiction. In explaining his intentions in writing *In Cold Blood* (1966), Truman Capote defended the idea that nonfiction, the kind of portrait often previously dismissed as mere journalism, could be as much the
appropriate concern of the serious and thoughtful novelist as
could fiction. This as an argument is convincing enough, although far from new, for the re-creation of an historical event
could, if done with sufficient skill and insight, always convey the
emotional and intellectual excitement of superior fiction. Yet
In Cold Blood itself seems a substitute for the novelist's concerns.
In attempting to stick so literally to the story and in placing his
authorial stance so completely within his characters, Capote
evades the responsibility of an author to understand and comment upon his characters through some kind of complex perspective that is not necessarily theirs. The apparent objectivity
is really an immersion in the characters, unalleviated and un-
transformed by any attributes of mind, which ultimately produces the effect of relishing the characters, revelling in all the

details of their inhumanity and perversion. History is an escape, an evasion for the author, a chance to write from a stance entirely severed from his conscious self. Capote's book is simplified and distorted by the elaborately careful removal of the author as conscious self, producing the feeling that he has not really dealt with the implications of his material and has used history or nonfiction as a convenient and comforting substitute. In contrast to this evasion, history or nonfiction can also be used with the author's conscious and intelligent involvement, as apparent most strikingly in Norman Mailer's *The Armies of the Night* (1968) .

In reporting the protest march on the Pentagon in October, 1967, Mailer is fully conscious of all the difficulties and complexities of working with an historical event. He introduces one section by showing that his is the point of view of a minor participant, of a person not likely to be aware of all the more general movements and reactions, but he acknowledges that the view is simultaneously egotistic, humble, self-assertive, active, detached, novelistically objective, sharply critical, and dispassionate about others and himself. Mailer uses the device of talking about himself in the third person; this enables him to shuttle gracefully from a close involvement with self to an examination of self critically from a distance. On one hand, he is able to see the march as what it represents in American history, as a protest not only against the war in Vietnam but also against the increasing inertia of the corporate, affluent, impersonal machinery that dominates American society. In these terms, he enriches the work with relevant digressions such as that on the connection between obscenity and the spirit of democracy, or the political naiveté of always assuming an inevitable "sound-as-brickwork-logic-of-the-next-step" in mass action, or the relationship of the American small-town mentality to the repression of dissent. On the other hand, his description of the central self in the third person enables him to convey all the ambiguities of the individual on the fringes of an historical event, involved deeply enough in a small part of something so enormous that he, despite his careful examination, cannot be blandly or condescendingly panoramic. All the concentration on his various roles, his veneration for the football player and the bullfighter, his complicated relationships with Robert Lowell and Dwight Macdonald, his account of previous marriages in his incessant reshaping of the past for contemporary relevance, his relationship with his fourth wife, his explanation of the genesis and meaning of his political definition as a "Left Conservative,"—all these develop the rich ambivalence of his point of view, a stance copious and complicated yet sufficiently involved in both the specific action and concern for its meaning to create a comprehensive and intelligent attitude toward history. In the very complexity of the point of view, in the recognition that man manufactures his attitudes out of the interplay of multiple personal, social, environmental, and historical forces, Mailer's contemporary history is close to the fiction of compassion. The complicated historical event becomes both the center of narrative focus and the author's portrait of all the vagaries and inconsistencies of the contemporary American.

Mailer's career, abrupt, uneven, inventive, and inconsistent as it is, has always manifested some similarity with the assumptions implicit in the fiction of compassion. *The Naked and the Dead* (1948) depicted the purposeless and accidental nature of war, presented man caught in a military mechanism he could not understand or control. Yet man, the victim, was never sentimentalized; his actions were far from noble or heroic, yet he gained sympathy from the reader because of his predicament. *Barbary Shore* (1951), a more philosophical and inventive novel, examined the myths of political commitment in the thirties, the meaningless political structures man evolves, the abstractions he creates and cannot live by. In its function of presenting abstractions in order to demolish them, its intellectual examination that produces no intellectual conclusion, and its incipient existentialism, *Barbary Shore* resembles a less comic and less tight version of Iris Murdoch's early novels. Mailer moved closer to the fable in *The Deer Park* (1955), developing a point of view that castigated the amoral and rootless careerism of contemporary Americans, of both those who consciously betrayed the dreams of the thirties and those who never knew what they betrayed. The most stridently moralistic, preaching a "connection of new circuits" that begins with the sexual, *The Deer Park* is the least compassionate of all Mailer's fiction, the most depersonalized, the most severe in judgment, the most formally self-enclosed.

In his more recent fiction, Mailer is compassionate by implication, devising fables to mock the form and the concerns of the fable itself. *An American Dream* (1964) is a Pop Art blow-up satirizing conventional fiction and popular myths, a parody. Carried to grandiose absurdity, the depiction of the hero mocks the conception of the political, athletic, and sexual superman in popular fiction. The black organizer of the night club and the local Mafia, for example, is a kind of composite parody pop-representation of Frank Sinatra and Sammy Davis, Jr., a fantastic blow-up of the man-in-the-street's myth, just as Cherry is the contemporary version of that timeless legend, the innocent whore with instincts both of and for gold. By mixing his myths with inconsistencies and removing them from a residual iconoclasm into the bright lights of blown-up parody, Mailer suggests a greater complexity and inconsistency in man than anything allowed for in the literary or the popular tradition surrounding the "American Dream." The "American Dream," as legend and as literary device, restricts the human possibilities open even to the American.

Similarly, *Why Are We in Vietnam?* (1967) mythologizes those aspects of American experience that have led to the national lunacy of recent years, the testing of the young man on a bear hunt, the violence, the chauvinism, the magnified and hypocritical claim to self-sufficiency, which have developed the ethos that could sustain an expedition like Vietnam. The most grossly American masculinity, self-righteousness, stupidity, and desire for power characterize the father, the instigator of the bear hunt to try his son's manhood in Alaska, the newest frontier. Yet the son, in passing the test, also rebels against his father, recognizes his bluster and hollowness. The development of the son, like the realization that the issue is the war in Vietnam which numerous Americans protest, conveys a hint that another kind of American may be reaching the political power represented in the novel by the boy's maturity.

We are not always what we were schooled or conditioned to be, and consequences, in this existential environment, are never wholly predictable. The new American may, by implication, represent a more complicated, intelligent, and compassionate man, one less involved in himself and his sense of grand national power, just as *The Armies of the Night,* by implication, suggests a megalotopian vision of a new urban and unselfconscious American force that might emerge from the current sociological underside. Both *An American Dream* and *Why Are We in Vietnam?* suggest an attitude of compassion negatively, a view of man and his world opposite to the one blown up and dissected mercilessly in the novel. The attitude of compassion is not, however, fully articulated until *The Armies of the Night,* as if Mailer required the historical incident to give structure to a direct and involved account of his version of human experience.

History is not, for all authors, the only means of obtaining the combination of involvement and critical detachment necessary for an unsentimental fiction of compassion. Philip Roth gains complexity in point of view through the brilliance and range of his mimicry. In his earlier fiction, *Goodbye, Columbus* (1959) and *Letting Go* (1962), Roth's talent for mimicry was superbly evident, but it tended to focus on a character or particular scene, to bring to life an interplay of personalities or a dramatic confrontation without providing any perspective or attitude. In his more recent work, however, Roth has developed the mimicry from an able parroting to a means of entering and revealing another consciousness. In *When She Was Good* (1967), for example, Roth uses the perspectives of Lucy Nelson's stalwart, old grandfather, her drunken, self-pitying father, and her indolent and dependent young husband to reveal the hard, destructive, truth-seeking character of the girl herself. Each of the males is seen partly in the rigid way Lucy defines him, partly through the more charitable perspective of his own defenses. Similarly, Lucy is seen through both the opaque geniality and frightened banality of the three men who think they care for her, and the literal and uncompromising logic with which she views her own experience. All these points of view flash against each other powerfully, are permitted full development without explicit authorial mediation or control.

The reader sympathizes with all the male resistance to Lucy's terrifying demands, her hard and tight-lipped insistence on "truth," "right," and consistency; at the same time, one feels compassion for Lucy, for the girl who plays it straight and believes the myths about "honor" and "truth," who takes promises literally and is betrayed by men who never mean what they say or know what they feel. One cannot really choose between the hypocrite and the self-righteously demanding. In addition, Lucy is not only a character, but the representative of the middle classes, the focal metaphor for the origin of American middle-class tightness and repression, just as Liberty Center itself is the metaphor for all the myths and self-deceptions of corporate American experience. Roth's compassion begins with his attitude toward the characters and is extended to treat his themes.

When She Was Good shows how the middle-class perspectives originate, how the insistence on guarding oneself, keeping oneself from any central kind of involvement, is necessary protection in the face of necessarily hostile experience; Roth's *Portnoy's Complaint* (1969) demonstrates the other side of the same tradition, the rebellion against middle-class perspectives. For Roth, White Anglo-Saxon Middle-Western Protestant and Eastern European migrant Jew are, in America, part of the same tradition: the mobile, rising, rootless middle class, the bourgeoisie, the class that must keep tight control over its instincts in order to avoid chaos. Far from being a local-colorist or, like Bernard Malamud, a believer in the aesthetic and ethical value of a presumably unique Jewish tradition, Roth provides an account of the axioms of the middle class apparent in the fifties and sixties in America. He has more in common with the Thomas Mann of *Buddenbrooks* or the Arnold Bennett of *The Old Wives' Tale* than he does with Malamud. In *Portnoy's Complaint,* the novel of rebellion, sex is the instrument for revolt from the middle class, for sex dissolves the tight uninvolvement, the rigid defense of the integrity of aloneness, necessary for the bourgeois figure to make his way in a hostile world. Pleasurable sex relaxes, resolves, dissipates the force intent on striving, becomes inimical to the sense of aspiration in the middle class. Yet Alexander Portnoy himself is less the rebel than he would like to think he is. Less liberated than The Monkey, whose rebellion is also manifest in sexual terms, Portnoy is still snob enough, still sufficiently wrapped in his verbal rationalizations, still enough part of and influenced by his mother, to be unable to love The Monkey. He has internalized his tradition and never realizes what he does; only at the very end of the novel, can he expiate the middle-class self-involvement of his past and "begin" to understand his experience. *Portnoy's Complaint* brilliantly chronicles the necessary steps to begin breaking away from the middle class, outlines the conditions of revolt. Yet, as in *When She Was Good,* Roth does not provide a one-dimensional defense for his central character. Rather, Portnoy, like Lucy Nelson, is seen from numerous perspectives, is made silly, strong, intelligent, dependent, cowardly, and knowledgeable all at once. Roth's compassion, an extension of his mimicry, of his ability to enter into the framework of other human beings, of his own creations, need not require the sentimentality and defensiveness of a single point of view.

The fiction of compassion requires this point of view of sliding detachment, the ability of an author both to approach closely and to view objectively his characters and his world. In recognizing and achieving such complexity, the author is perhaps best not restricted by primary allegiance to truths or guiding abstractions or moral lessons about human experience. The vitality of the fiction inheres in the complexity itself, seldom amenable to formulation in abstract or thematic terms and held together both by a fairly flexible sense of verisimilitude and by a point of view combining involvement and detachment. This is the kind of fiction written by Trollope, Hardy, Bennett, the later Fitzgerald and others, the kind best represented among contemporary novelists by Angus Wilson and Saul Bellow. But, certainly, the fiction of compassion is not the only kind of fiction, nor the only good fiction. It is not, for example, the fiction of Dickens, George Eliot, Melville, Evelyn Waugh, or Hemingway.

To belong to the tradition of compassion is not like membership in a club, not a writer's conscious direction of his fiction to adhere to certain specifications and definitions. Rather, the term, "the tradition of compassion," is a critical term imposed from the outside and designed to explain elements in the quality and texture of a particular kind of fiction. As a tradition, the tradition of compassion has no definable termination or dominance, cannot be enclosed by dates or labeled as the principal fictional style of a particular period. Rather, for the last hundred years in England and America, some fiction can be designated as belonging to this tradition and some cannot. Despite the many changes in contemporary fiction and the contemporary world, the term "the tradition of compassion" is still useful in designating a kind of fiction. The tradition is still vital, its history, like its characteristic form and its frequent use of historical change and continuity, still open, flexible, and unfinished. The open form, the suggestion of incompleteness, in the fiction of compassion often achieves its greatest appeal in allowing the characters, the problems, and the speculations conceived in fiction to live in the reader beyond the boundary of the novel, to live not as truths or as abstractions, but as concrete entities and possibilities. The art in the tradition of compassion is not self-enclosed, not transmitted in a single package; rather, the art radiates, sometimes partially or randomly, strikes response in isolated pockets or unpredictable perceptions, duplicates in literary terms the conditions of non-literary experience. The fiction of compassion is, for many people, more difficult to discuss abstractly or academically than is fiction which can be understood by its pattern of symbols or its fabulistic structure or its moral lesson. But it is not, therefore, more difficult to respond to and appreciate, and it is not the less profound just because ways of talking about it are less precise and less abstract. The fiction of compassion shares more fully the concreteness, the emotional depth, the uncertainty of articulation or definition, and the irresolution of most human experience.

Editions Used for Quotations

THE FOLLOWING LIST, arranged by chapters, gives the source of all quotations in the text. Within each chapter, sources are listed, regardless of dates of edition used or original publication, in the order in which quotations appear in the text.

CHAPTER I: Joseph Conrad, "Henry James: An Appreciation," in *Notes on Life and Letters*. New York: Doubleday, Page, 1921.
Edmond and Jules Goncourt, *Pages from the Goncourt Journal*, ed. and trans. by Robert Baldick. New York: Oxford University Press, 1962.

CHAPTER II: Anthony Trollope, *An Autobiography*. Berkeley and Los Angeles: University of California Press, 1947.
Anthony Trollope, *Ayala's Angel*. London: Oxford University Press, World's Classics Edition, 1960.

CHAPTER III: George Meredith, *Rhoda Fleming*. London: Constable, 1897.
George Meredith, *Diana of the Crossways*. London: Constable, 1897.
George Meredith, *The Egoist*. New York: Random House, Modern Library Edition, 1947.
George Meredith, *Beauchamp's Career*. London: Oxford University Press, World's Classics Edition, 1950.
George Meredith, *The Ordeal of Richard Feverel*. London: Constable, 1897.

CHAPTER IV: Florence Emily Hardy, *The Later Years of Thomas Hardy, 1892–1928*. New York: Macmillan, 1930.
Thomas Hardy, *The Return of the Native*. New York: Harper and Bros., 1920.

[3 6 1

Thomas Hardy, *The Woodlanders.* New York: Harper and Bros., 1920.

Thomas Hardy, *Far From the Madding Crowd.* New York: Harper and Bros., 1920.

Thomas Hardy, *Jude the Obscure.* New York: Harper and Bros., 1920.

CHAPTER V: Richard Chase, *The American Novel and its Tradition.* New York: Doubleday, 1957.

William Dean Howells, *The Landlord at Lion's Head.* New York: New American Library, Signet Edition, 1964.

CHAPTER VI: Arnold Bennett, *Hilda Lessways.* London: Methuen, 1961.

Arnold Bennett, *The Old Wives' Tale.* New York: Harper and Bros., 1950.

Arnold Bennett, *Journal of Arnold Bennett, 1896–1928.* New York: Viking, 1933.

Arnold Bennett, *These Twain.* London: Methuen, 1962.

Arnold Bennett, *The Pretty Lady.* New York: George H. Doran, 1918.

CHAPTER VII: Lionel Trilling, *E. M. Forster.* London: Hogarth Press, 1944.

E. M. Forster, *Aspects of the Novel.* New York: Harcourt, Brace, 1927.

E. M. Forster, *Where Angels Fear to Tread.* London: Edward Arnold, 1947.

E. M. Forster, *A Passage to India.* New York: Harcourt, Brace, 1924.

E. M. Forster, *Howards End.* New York: Vintage, 1954.

E. M. Forster, *Abinger Harvest.* New York: Harcourt, Brace, 1936.

CHAPTER VIII: Virginia Woolf, *Orlando.* New York: Penguin, 1946.

Virginia Woolf, *Mr. Bennett and Mrs. Brown.* London: Hogarth Press, 1924.

Virginia Woolf, *To the Lighthouse.* New York: Harcourt, Brace, 1927.

Virginia Woolf, *Jacob's Room.* New York: Harcourt, Brace, 1923.

Virginia Woolf, *Mrs. Dalloway.* New York: Harcourt, Brace, 1925.

Virginia Woolf, *The Waves.* New York: Harcourt, Brace, 1931.

EDITIONS USED FOR QUOTATIONS

Chapter IX: D. H. Lawrence, *Aaron's Rod*. New York: Viking, Compass Edition, 1961.
D. H. Lawrence, *The Rainbow*. New York: Viking, Compass Edition, 1961.
D. H. Lawrence, *Women in Love*. New York: Viking, Compass Edition, 1960.
D. H. Lawrence, *Kangaroo*. London: William Heinemann, 1950.

Chapter X: James Joyce, *Ulysses*. New York: Random House, Modern Library Edition, 1961.

Chapter XI: F. Scott Fitzgerald, *This Side of Paradise*. New York: Scribner's, 1960.
F. Scott Fitzgerald, *The Beautiful and Damned*. New York: Scribner's, 1922.
F. Scott Fitzgerald, *The Great Gatsby*. New York: Scribner's, 1925.
F. Scott Fitzgerald, *Tender is the Night*. New York: Scribner's, 1934.
F. Scott Fitzgerald, *The Last Tycoon*. London: Grey Walls Press, 1949.

Chapter XII: Joyce Cary, *A Fearful Joy*. London: Michael Joseph, Carfax Edition, 1952.
Joyce Cary, *Prisoner of Grace*. London: Michael Joseph, Carfax Edition, 1954.
Joyce Cary, *Herself Surprised*. London: Michael Joseph, Carfax Edition, 1951.

Chapter XIII: Angus Wilson, *Hemlock and After*. Harmondsworth, Middlesex: Penguin, 1956.
Angus Wilson, *Late Call*. London: Secker and Warburg, 1964.
Angus Wilson, *No Laughing Matter*. London: Secker and Warburg, 1967.
Angus Wilson, *The Wild Garden*. Berkeley and Los Angeles: University of California Press, 1963.

Chapter XIV: Saul Bellow, *Dangling Man*. New York: Meridian, 1960.
Saul Bellow, *The Victim*. New York: Viking, Compass Edition, 1956.

Saul Bellow, *The Adventures of Augie March*. New York: Viking, Compass Edition, 1960.

Saul Bellow, *Seize the Day*. New York: Viking, Compass Edition, 1961.

Saul Bellow, *Henderson the Rain King*. New York: Viking, Compass Edition, 1965.

Saul Bellow, *Herzog*. New York: Viking, 1964.

I N D E X

Adams, Robert M., *Strains of Discord: Studies in Literary Openness*, 8–9
Anouilh, Jean, 290
Aristotle, 1–2, 4, 101, 163
Austen, Jane, 50, 56, 351; *Emma*, 18–9. *Mansfield Park*, 19. *Pride and Prejudice*, 17, 298. *Sense and Stability*, 18

Barth, John, *Giles Goat-boy, The Sotweed Factor*, 340
Barthelme, Donald, 342
Bayley, John, "Against a Now Formalism," *Critical Quarterly* (Spring and Summer, 1968), 9–10
Bellow, Saul, 19–22, 25, *305–336*, 358; alienation in, 306–7; archetypal American hero, 305; comedy in, 323–4, 326, 334; compassion in, 322, 335–6; emotional vulnerability in, 307, 315, 321; existentialism in, 309, 314–5, 317, 319, 321–2, 324–5, 327, 333, 335; fable in, 325–6; form in, 321, 332–3; freedom in, 307–8; history in, 318, 327–8, 336; Jewishness, 306, 309–12, 323, 329; picaresque in, 315, 317; romanticism in, 328, 332, 334, 336; sentimentality in, 322, 333–4, 336; social and historical description in, 317–8; theme of communication in, 311–2, 333; theme of control in, 331–3; theme of the double in, 312–4; values in, 316, 320–1; violence in, 331–5; women in, 329–30
——Works: *Dangling Man*, 305–9, 312, 328–9, 363; *Henderson the Rain King*, 322–6, 364; *Herzog*, 312, 322, 326–36, 364; *Mr. Sammler's Planet*, 334–6; *Seize the Day*, 319–22, 327, 335, 364; *The Adventures of Augie March*, 23, 314–9, 321–2, 364; *The Victim*, 309–16, 321, 363
Bennett, Arnold, 20–2, 25, *129–155*, 204, 358; compassion in, 129, 146,

154–5; history in, 149–51; issues of class in, 132–3; judgment in, 137–9; justice in, 142–4; marriage and women in, 147–8; material environment in, 129–31; physicality in, 133–7; point of view in, 144–6; thematic interest in, 151–4; theme of power and control in, 141–2; theme of work in, 140
——Works: *A Great Man*, 131; *A Man from the North*, 131; *Anna of the Five Towns*, 131, 147; Clayhanger trilogy (*Clayhanger, Hilda Lessways, These Twain*), 129–31, 133–9, 142–8, 153–4, 362; "Elsie and the Child," 153–4; *Helen with the High Hand*, 131; *Hugo*, 142; *Imperial Palace*, 134, 139, 141, 146–7, 154; *Journal of Arnold Bennett, 1896–1928*, 129, 137, 143–4, 362; *Leonora*, 147; *Lillian*, 145; *Lord Raingo*, 139, 141, 147, 153–4; *Mr. Prohack*, 140; *Riceyman Steps*, 152–3; *Teresa of Watling Street*, 142; *The Card*, 131; *The Grand Babylon Hotel*, 142; *The Lion's Share*, 144; *The Old Wives' Tale*, 4, 130–6, 144–5, 147, 149–51, 153, 155, 357, 362; *The Pretty Lady*, 141, 147–9, 151–3, 362; *The Roll-Call*, 131, 140, 143, 148–9; *The Vanguard*, 142, 145; *Whom God Hath Joined*, 146
Blake, William, 269, 274
Booth, Wayne C., *The Rhetoric of Fiction*, 7
Browne, Sir Thomas, 234
Butler, Samuel, 187; *Erewhon*, 277

Camus, Albert, *La Peste*, 309; *L'Étranger*, 302
Capote, Truman, *In Cold Blood*, 352–3
Cary, Joyce, 5, 22, *258–276*; chronology in, 273–4; compassion in 258, 262–3, 276; history in, 258–62; judgment in,